TO THE Ends of Japan

To the Ends of Japan

Premodern Frontiers, Boundaries, and Interactions

Bruce L. Batten

University of Hawai'i Press
Honolulu

Printed in the United States of America
08 07 06 05 04 03 6 5 4 3 2 1

Library of Congress Cataloging-in-Publication Data

Batten, Bruce Loyd.
To the ends of Japan : premodern frontiers, boundaries, and interactions / Bruce L. Batten.
p. cm.
Includes bibliographical references and index.
ISBN 0-8248-2447-4 (alk. paper)
1. Japan—History. I. Title.
DS835 .H6316 2002
952—dc21 2002011946

University of Hawai'i Press books are printed on acid-free paper and meet the guidelines for permanence and durability of the Council on Library Resources.

Designed by Jeanne Calabrese

Printed by The Maple-Vail Book Manufacturing Group

To my mother and my father

Contents

List of Illustrations

Maps

Figures

Acknowledgments

I have been working on this book for a long time and in the process have incurred a number of debts, intellectual and otherwise. It is a pleasure, therefore, to take this opportunity to thank the many individuals who have helped me along the way.

I owe my interest in Japan to various people, but especially to my teachers at the University of Oregon, where I was an undergraduate in the late 1970s. I am particularly grateful to Yoko McClain, who introduced me to the Japanese language, and to Kate Nakai (now at Sophia University in Tokyo), who encouraged me to pursue further work in Japanese history. Thanks are also due to Bill Orr, of the Geology Department and the Condon Museum, for general intellectual stimulation over the years.

My graduate degrees in Japanese history are from Stanford University, where I studied in the early 1980s (finally receiving my Ph.D. in 1989). Although none of the work I did at Stanford appears directly in the present study, my interest in frontiers and boundaries dates from this period. I will always be grateful for the education I received from my dissertation adviser, the late Jeffrey Mass, and from other members of the Stanford faculty, particularly Peter Duus, Albert Dien, and Thomas Hare. My fellow graduate students, especially Karl Friday, Andrew Goble, and Joan Piggott, have also provided much camaraderie and advice over the years.

A number of the ideas in this book stem directly from conversations with my colleagues at Obirin University in Tokyo, where I have taught since 1989. Lee Kwangi-Il and Chūjō Ken, in particular, opened my eyes to recent developments in the humanities and social sciences, of which I would otherwise have remained blissfully unaware. Many of my ideas were later "field-tested" on the students at Obirin, particularly in my course entitled "Japan in World History." In many ways, I probably learned more from my students (and their responses to my lectures) than they did from me.

This book could never have been written without the benefit of the sabbatical year I enjoyed in 1999, and I am grateful to President Satow Toyoshi and to the rest of my colleagues at Obirin for giving me time off to pursue this project.

An earlier version of the book was published in Japanese (as *Nihon no "kyōkai": Zenkindai no kokka, minzoku, bunka*) by Aoki Press in April 2000. In preparing the Japanese text, I received substantial help from Murata Katszuyuki and also from my editor, Harashima Masashi. Just before the book came out, I was invited to present my research at a symposium held at the Historiographical Institute of the University of Tokyo. At this event, I received a number of helpful comments from Ishigami Eiichi, Kuroda Hideo, Murai Shōsuke, and other members of the audience. I regret only that it was too late to take these comments into account for the original version of the book.

Publication in Japanese resulted in additional feedback from historians and other readers. In this regard, I owe particular thanks to Mark Hudson, Katō Akira, Tessa Morris-Suzuki, Sakaue Yasutoshi, Tominomori Kenji, and the late Tsujiuchi Makoto. Most helpful of all, Hashimoto Yū wrote a review, later published in *Rekishigaku kenkyū* (March 2002), which pointed out a number of inconsistencies and factual errors.

In the course of preparing the present version, I profited from discussions with Robert Borgen, Ronald Toby, and Kenneth Robinson. The entire manuscript was read by Ethan Segal, Brett Walker, and two anonymous readers for the University of Hawai'i Press. In response to their detailed and constructive suggestions, I rewrote most of the chapters and also rearranged the basic structure of the book. The result is less an English "version" of the Japanese original than an entirely new (and, I hope, improved) work.

Academic Press, Inc., kindly granted me permission to use material from an earlier version of Chapter 1, which appeared as "Frontiers and Boundaries of Pre-modern Japan" in the *Journal of Historical Geography* 25.2 (1999).

Patricia Crosby at the University of Hawai'i Press deserves special mention for believing in this project and shepherding it through to completion. Pat was a pleasure to work with from start to finish. I would also like to extend heartfelt thanks to Ann Ludeman, also of the University of Hawai'i Press, and to copy editor Rosemary Wetherold.

All of these contributions notwithstanding, the book no doubt still contains various errors and omissions, for which I cheerfully accept full responsibility. No author could have asked for better help and support than I have received from my friends and colleagues in both Japan and the United States.

Finally, I want to express my gratitude to my parents for instilling in me a love of learning, and to my wife and children for putting up with this and other academic pursuits and projects over the years—and for teaching me that while work is important, there are other things that are more important.

Introduction

My first exposure to Japanese history came during the late 1970s, when I was an undergraduate at the University of Oregon. At that time, Japanese manufactured products were beginning to make rapid inroads into American markets, and the country's economic importance was widely acknowledged both by opinion leaders and by members of the general public. And yet few people, in America at least, had a good understanding of contemporary Japanese society, far less of Japanese history[1] (with the possible exception of the events immediately surrounding World War II, which remained fresh in the minds of some Americans).

This state of affairs was reflected in the popular and academic literature on Japan—that is to say, there were not a lot of books to read. Fortunately, the few textbooks by knowledgeable authors presented a view that was relatively consistent and easy to understand. To paraphrase their basic message, the Japanese people were homogeneous and group-oriented, and they had a unique language and culture. The emphasis on the group resulted from the historical importance of wet-rice cultivation, which was labor-intensive and demanded the cooperation of all village members. The other distinctive features of Japanese society, meanwhile, stemmed from the country's geographic isolation from the rest of the world—so the story went.[2]

These views are evident, for example, in the work of Edwin Reischauer, a "missionary kid" born and raised in prewar Tokyo, who after the war went on to become a leading American historian and also, during the early 1960s, U.S. ambassador to Japan.[3] Reischauer's first major scholarly work, a translation and study of the diary of a ninth-century Japanese pilgrim to China, emphasized the importance of foreign relations and intercultural contacts in early Japanese history.[4] Somewhat ironically, however, the many survey histories and popular works published by Reischauer in later years all stressed the overriding historical importance of geographic isolation.

In one of his last books, published originally in 1980, Reischauer wrote, "The Japanese, like all other peoples, have been shaped in large part by the land in which they live. Its location, climate, and natural endowments are unchangeable facts that have set limits to their development and helped give it specific direction."[5] The most important geographic fact about the country, he wrote, was that "[t]hroughout most of its history Japan has been perhaps the most isolated of all the major countries of the world."[6] This isolation had several important consequences, in Reischauer's opinion. For example, it "has made other people, even the nearby Koreans and Chinese, look on the Japanese as being somehow different and has produced in the Japanese a strong sense of self-identity and also an almost painful self-consciousness in the presence of others." Isolation had also resulted in "Japan's unusual degree of cultural homogeneity."[7] According to Reischauer, "the Japanese today are the most thoroughly unified and culturally homogeneous large bloc of people in the world, with the possible exception of the North Chinese."[8]

Many years have passed since those lines were written, and Japan if anything occupies an even more visible place in the world than it did in 1980. There has been a flood of writings on Japan and the Japanese in English and other languages, and many Americans, at least, have an easy familiarity with at least some aspects of Japanese culture—not only automobiles and electronic gadgets but now also karaoke and *anime.* It is striking, therefore, to note that Reischauer's historical vision of Japan remains largely intact, at least at the textbook level.

To take but one example, a well-received text published by W. G. Beasley in 1999 begins with the following statement:

> The history of Japan . . . has a high degree of continuity from ancient times to the twentieth century. The Japanese have always occupied part or all of the same territory, its borders defined by the sea. They have

> spoken and written a common language, once it had taken firm shape in about the tenth century. Their population has been largely homogenous, little touched by immigration except in very early periods. Awareness of this has given them a sense of being racially distinct. "We Japanese", *ware-ware Nihonjin*, is a phrase that constantly recurs.[9]

Beasley goes on to argue that the Japanese islands were far enough from the Asian mainland to prevent foreign invasions but close enough to allow much cultural borrowing: "The sea was less of a barrier to foreign culture than to foreign armies. From the seventh century onwards, if not earlier, the religion and philosophy, the art and literature, the economic skills and governmental institutions of China found their way to Japan, at first via Korea and the Tsushima Straits, then more directly across the East China Sea."[10] But while acknowledging the importance of cultural borrowing, Beasley is clear that Japan has a distinctive culture and society that developed as a result of the country's geographic isolation.

Why have these ideas enjoyed such tremendous staying power? One reason, of course, is that they contain important seeds of truth. However, another reason is that many English-language works on Japan are less "views from outside" than they are repackaged versions of Japanese views. Throughout the second half of the twentieth century, most Japanese people—scholars and members of the general public alike—saw their country as a kind of primeval nation-state whose natural borders had historically protected it from the outside world. This view of the past probably reflected a general need to retain national pride and cultural identity following the traumatic events of the midcentury, when Japanese military expansion in Asia was followed by defeat and occupation by the United States. In part, this view of the past was also actively promoted by the Japanese government through the school system for the purpose of creating a homogenous, unified labor force that could be mobilized in the name of economic growth.[11] Many foreign scholars seem to have absorbed this "worldview" from their Japanese colleagues and acquaintances, later disseminating it to the English-speaking world in the form of textbooks and other publications on Japan.

But times are changing, and a new view of history—and of geography—has begun to emerge among some Japanese scholars and even members of the public at large. The person most responsible for these changes is Amino Yoshihiko, a medievalist who has authored or edited more than one hundred books since the late 1970s. Amino's books are enormously popular in Japan, sometimes selling upwards of one hundred thousand copies.

Although it is difficult to summarize his work in a few sentences, Amino offers a view of a socially and regionally diverse Japan. In addition to farmers, nobles, warriors, and monks—the main actors in most traditional histories—he calls attention to the lives of fishermen, traders, entertainers, gamblers, prostitutes, pirates, and social outcasts. Amino's Japan consists of a dizzying variety of local traditions as well as a rich and vibrant tradition of movement and communication—not just within the Japanese archipelago but also between it and the outside world. The sea, to Amino, is not a barrier but a connecting force.[12]

Outside Japan, a small minority of scholars has always emphasized diversity and fragmentation, but this view now seems to be coming to the fore. Symbolic of this trend is the 1996 publication of *Multicultural Japan: Paleolithic to Postmodern*, a collection of essays by mostly Australian scholars. This book, according to one of the editors, "challenges the conventional approach by arguing that Japan has long been 'multicultural', and that what is distinctive is the success with which that diversity has been cloaked by the ideology of 'uniqueness' and 'monoculturalism.' "[13] Specifically, the editor writes, "[w]hile the monolithic and homogeneous myths of the past served the interest of elites intent on preserving order and control, helping to legitimize established authority, the common people preserved rich and diverse counter-traditions, which were open, bridged social and class distinctions, and had little time for the pretensions of their rulers."[14]

This view of premodern Japan is in many ways the complete opposite of the old "commonsense" picture still enshrined in many of our English-language textbooks. Instead of homogeneity, we have diversity; instead of isolation, we have open and wide-ranging communication and exchange. Although I would not pretend to speak for Amino himself, the eagerness with which his vision has been embraced by other scholars and members of the Japanese public suggests an important change in attitudes during the past several decades. Evidently, people in Japan want to believe in a golden, medieval age of freedom and diversity—either because they are frustrated with their own straitlaced lives, or just as likely, because their lives are changing as Japan, and the world, enters the "postmodern" age. Society, even in Japan, is more fragmented and diverse than before, while at the same time social boundaries are becoming more fluid, and the forces of globalization and the borderless world economy are becoming impossible to ignore.

The change in viewpoint from the orthodoxy represented by Reischauer to the postmodern vision offered by Amino might be seen as a classic "paradigm shift," in which a host of factors have converged to cause researchers (and members of the reading public) to abandon one worldview in favor of another more in line with their current values and assumptions.[15] But just because people are changing their minds does not mean that they are right.

Which, then, of these views is closer to the truth? Oddly, no systematic attempt has been made to address this question. One reason is that most practicing historians of Japan, unlike Reischauer and Amino, limit themselves to discussing a single period or, in some cases, just a single locality. And although they usually take care to draw appropriate comparisons across time and space and to place their work in proper historiographical context, the end result often remains fairly narrow.

A vast and growing literature in both Japanese and English, for example, is devoted to showing that Japan was not, in fact, a "closed country" in the early modern, or Edo, period (1600–1867).[16] This literature is a needed corrective to earlier views, but there has been a tendency to lose sight of the forest for the trees: a good case could be made, in my opinion, that Edo Japan *was* a relatively closed country by comparison with earlier or later periods of Japanese history.[17] What is lacking here is the "big picture"—early modern foreign relations is seen as a topic unto itself, not as part of the larger flow of Japanese—or of world—history.

Similarly, recent years have seen a vigorous debate about whether Edo Japan was politically or culturally unified, or whether it was fragmented along regional and/or class lines.[18] But the answers to these questions also depend fundamentally upon one's point of reference: Edo society *was* highly fragmented in comparison with any modern nation-state, but by comparison with other periods in Japanese history (or with premodern societies in many other parts of the world), it appears remarkably integrated and cohesive. A full view of the significance of this period becomes possible only if we are prepared to look backward (and sideways) as well as forward.

Another problem is that little effort has gone into defining the terms of the debate. As noted above, the tradition represented by Reischauer and Beasley simply assumes that "Japan" is and always has been a meaningful unit of analysis—a predefined social and political community occupying a fixed, geographically determined territory. Amino comes off somewhat better in this regard when he argues, for example, that the very name "Japan" (Nihon) dates from the late seventh century and that before this date there was no concept of a unified country or society.[19] And yet in all of his work, Amino plays fast and loose with other terms and concepts. To take but one example, his 1982 book, *Higashi to nishi ga kataru Nihon no rekishi* (Japan's history as told by east and west), argues that eastern Japan and western Japan were virtually separate "countries" *(kuni)* in premodern times, but what this term means is nowhere made clear.[20] Are we talking about different states? Cultures? Ethnic groups? These would seem to be important distinctions, and yet Amino glosses over them without comment. Other authors, of course, are more careful with terms, but because there is little standardization in usage scholars talk past each other, and it is difficult to get a sense of the big picture.

The present work is, I believe, the first real attempt to weigh the pros and cons of these two opposing visions of Japanese history. Like Reischauer and Amino, but unlike many other historians, I am interested in the "big questions," specifically: What is "Japan"? When did it come to be? How did it change over time? And how does it fit into the larger world? In trying to answer these questions, I have made an explicit attempt to avoid some of the pitfalls evident in previous work. The result, I believe, is a new synthesis on Japanese history, one that is at once broader, more theoretically rigorous, and more explicitly comparative than other available works on the subject.

Introducing a study of Japanese-Ainu relations, Tessa Morris-Suzuki once noted that "[t]he shape of things becomes clearer when one looks at the edge than when one looks at the center."[21] I likewise believe that we can best discover what "Japan" is by simultaneously asking what it is not and by examining the nature of the *border(s)* between the "Japan" and "not-Japan." Accordingly, the focus of this study is on Japan's historical *frontiers* and *boundaries*—not just the seas and coastlines emphasized by Reischauer and Amino but also the various land frontiers that formerly existed within the archipelago. (For definitions of these various terms, please turn to the end of this chapter.)

The academic and popular literature on frontiers and boundaries is vast, and it is proliferating daily.[22] Probably one reason for this, paradoxically, is the current trend toward globalization, which brings people of different backgrounds and cultures into closer contact than ever before, forcing them to confront their identities and to think more deeply about the significance of borders and border crossings. Based on my own reading,[23] most recent historical research on frontiers and boundaries exhibits one or more of the following interrelated characteristics:

1. There is a tendency to emphasize the complex or multifaceted nature of borders. Whereas researchers in the past were often content to focus on geopolitical aspects, and in some cases on cultural ones, they now increasingly recognize that these facets of border life cannot be divorced from other considerations, particularly what might be called the three Es: economy, ethnicity, and ecology.
2. Just as disciplinary boundaries have fallen, so have temporal ones—with the result that many recent studies today cover centuries, not decades, and emphasize continuities, not disjunctures.
3. There is a growing tendency to view the border from both sides. Whereas it was formerly commonplace to talk of the expansion of frontiers into "virgin territory," now the emphasis is on interaction, two-way influence, and accommodation between (or among) adjacent polities, cultures, and societies. Frontier history has become decentered, featuring multiple, subjective points of view.
4. There has been an increasing focus on ambiguity—both upon the fuzzy, ragged nature of the frontier itself and upon the multivalent, situational identities embraced by its inhabitants. Borders are not clear-cut lines between "us" and "them"; rather, they are zones where "we" are gradually transformed into "them," and vice versa, areas where assumed and ascribed identities depend upon circumstance and contingency, not upon blood or geography.

5. There is a tendency to portray frontiers as places rather than processes. While denizens of the frontier continue to occupy the historical foreground, researchers also take care to examine the land and the natural environment, which influence, and are influenced by, frontier society.
6. Borderlands are now frequently studied for their own sake, not for what they tell us about the nature of the larger polities or societies they circumscribe. The result has been a groundswell of "bottoms-up," "on-the-ground" frontier histories, offering a strong contrast to the "top-down," "statist" histories they replace.
7. There is now a distinct aversion toward "grand theorizing." Case studies abound, but little attempt is made to draw broad conclusions or posit hypotheses that can be tested against other situations.

These seven trends are evident in all subfields of frontier history—even the oldest and most conservative, Roman studies.[24] But they reach their greatest development in what has been called the New Western History, that corpus of research devoted to refuting old views of the American West—and most especially those articulated a century ago by the most famous of all frontier historians, Frederick Jackson Turner.[25]

Two of the most important New Western Historians are Patricia Nelson Limerick and Richard White.[26] Limerick is perhaps best known for her 1987 book, *The Legacy of Conquest*, which effectively stood Turner on his head.[27] Where Turner saw a predestined American expansion into virtually uninhabited territory, Nelson saw a multisided encounter involving, among others, white Americans, American Indians, blacks, Mexicans, and Chinese and Japanese immigrants. Where Turner saw a fixed process of development through discrete economic phases, Limerick saw a region unified by its geography. Where Turner saw an "end to the frontier" in the 1890s, Limerick saw continuities lasting until the present. And where Turner spoke in terms of generalities, Limerick recorded the voices of specific historical actors—without prejudice based on race, ethnicity, religion, cultural background, or gender. Limerick's critique of the "Turner thesis" is perhaps symbolized most clearly by her rejection of the very term "frontier," on grounds of its alleged ethnocentric, exclusivist connotations.[28]

A similar perspective is offered by Richard White, author of the acclaimed 1991 book *The Middle Ground*.[29] In this work, White describes how native Americans and Europeans created new systems of meaning and exchange in North America during the seventeenth through nineteenth centuries. The "middle ground" of the title refers to "the place in between: in between cultures, peoples, and in between empires and the non-state world of villages," White writes. "It is a place where many of the North American subjects and allies of empires lived. It is the area between the historical foreground of European invasion and occupation and the background of Indian defeat and retreat."[30] Ultimately, the "middle ground" was a place of accommodation, where different peoples had to adjust to each other because no one group was able to establish a monopoly on power.

These general trends have recently begun to make their mark in the field of Japanese history. Paradoxically, although the changing image of Japan's past as a whole seems to be largely internally generated (with, of course, a few important exceptions), the new view of Japanese frontiers emanates at least in part from abroad. One reason for the prominent role that foreign scholars play in this area is a difference in perspective—Japanese people looking around themselves see the internal workings of society, while foreigners looking in come face-to-face with borders before they see anything else. However, it is also true that frontier studies in Japan have been held back by the fact that many (probably most) Japanese historians do not read English or other foreign languages and are thus unfamiliar with the research trends described above.

There is, of course, a huge corpus of specialized Japanese works on borders, peripheries, and foreign relations. Much of it is written from the perspective of institutional history, but some authors do touch upon themes similar to those discussed above. One thinks, for instance, of Murai Shōsuke's many publications on trade, commerce, and piracy along Japan's western maritime frontier during the medieval period (roughly the twelfth through sixteenth centuries).[31] Another good example, though from a very different genre, is Oguma Eiji's massive *"Nihonjin" no kyōkai* (Boundaries of the "Japanese"), a study of changing Japanese perceptions of Self and Other as reflected in nineteenth- and twentieth-century colonial policy.[32] I will be referring to these and many other Japanese-language studies in later chapters, but for now let us turn to some of the recent contributions to this field by foreign scholars.

In English-language scholarship alone,[33] the past decade has seen exciting new publications by David Howell, Tessa Morris-Suzuki, Richard Siddle, Brett Walker, Ronald Toby, Gregory Smits, Mimi Yiengpruksawan, and Mark Hudson.[34] Of these authors, the first five have concentrated on historical developments of the sixteenth through nineteenth centuries; the last two are concerned with far earlier times.

Howell, Morris-Suzuki, Siddle, and Walker have all chosen to study the Ainu, the indigenous residents of Japan's northern island, Hokkaido. At the risk of brutal simplification, Howell's work focuses on Ainu ethnicity, on the one hand, and the spread of capitalist labor relations in Hokkaido, on the other.[35] Morris-Suzuki is concerned largely with the construction of Japanese and Ainu identities in the frontier zone.[36] Siddle's research is on the assimilation of the Ainu as an ethnic minority within the Japanese nation-state.[37] And Walker has studied Japan's "conquest" of Ainu lands from a cultural and ecological perspective.[38]

Toby and Smits, meanwhile, have produced important studies of another kind of boundary—that between Japan and overseas countries. Toby, the author of a pathbreaking 1984 study discrediting the *sakoku* ("closed country") thesis,[39] has since turned his attention to how Japanese notions of the world were irrevocably altered by the country's sixteenth-century encounter with the West.[40] Smits' research is not on Japan per se but on the Ryukyu kingdom, its neighbor to the south. Smits shows how Ryukyuan elites of the seventeenth and eighteenth centuries managed to construct a distinct cultural and political identity without being overwhelmed by Japan, on the one hand, or China, on the other.[41]

Art historian Mimi Yiengpruksawan and archaeologist Mark Hudson have gone much further back in time than any of the other authors. Yiengpruksawan has written a vivid portrait of the hybrid culture of Hiraizumi, a border town in northeastern Honshu (Japan's "main island") during the twelfth century.[42] Hudson, meanwhile, has produced a broad-ranging, theoretical study of ethnogenesis in the Japan islands. Among other things, this contains a detailed analysis of the origins of the Ainu people.[43]

Many of these studies fit squarely within the emerging mainstream of contemporary border studies as outlined above. This is most clearly seen, perhaps, in the work of Tessa Morris-Suzuki and Brett Walker. Morris-Suzuki's historical analysis of Japanese-Ainu relations, and more generally her work on identity, owes an obvious debt to postmodernism. Walker, meanwhile, explicitly (and successfully) models his approach on the New Western History of Limerick and White.[44]

The present study both builds upon the results of these earlier works and departs from them in significant ways. The main differences are of approach. First, unlike many of the authors mentioned above, I am interested in borders not so much for their own sake but for what they tell us about Japan. Borderlands and frontiers are fascinating in their own right, but readers interested in learning about the lives of individual frontier residents, for example, will be disappointed because that is not the subject of this book. This study is unapologetically centered in Japan, not in the frontier zone per se. My interest in the latter is a means to an end, not the end itself.

Second, I do not think of borders or frontiers as geographic *places* but as social *margins* or *interfaces.* To be sure, these may be located in particular places at particular times, but they are not necessarily tied to the land—or, in Japan's case, to the coastlines or the seas. To say otherwise is to accept that Japan's boundaries are geographically determined, a position that I reject entirely. The boundaries of Japan, like those of other societies, are social and political creations,[45] and they do not necessarily coincide with the coastlines of the main islands. At times in history "Japan" has been considerably smaller than the Japanese archipelago; and at other times (most notably in the mid-twentieth century) it has been substantially larger.

Third, this study does not eschew theory. As noted above, I want to ask big questions, and answering them sometimes requires heavy ammunition. For this reason the book is explicitly theoretical. A concept like the "middle ground" is evocative and useful in understanding the experience of borderland peoples and societies, but it does not go very far toward explaining larger social trends—unless, of course, one cares to argue with Frederick Jackson Turner that the frontier experience can be, and has been, paramount in shaping entire nations.

To answer questions such as "What is Japan?" and "How does it fit within the larger world?" we need more powerful theories—and I have made use of a number, drawn eclectically from fields such as geography, political science, anthropology, sociology, and linguistics. Some of these, such as world-systems theory, are on the cutting edge of social science research. Others, such as my references to "culture areas" and "stages" of ethnic development, may strike some readers as old-fashioned. This is not the place to debate the merits and demerits of each theory I invoke—these are discussed more fully in the text itself. Here I will merely note that I have read fairly widely in each of the fields mentioned, and I have made an effort to recruit those theories that seem best adapted to explaining the Japanese case—both separately and in tandem. There is no point, for example, in describing the development of the Japanese polity in terms that are contradicted by later explanations regarding cultural patterns or ethnogenesis. If the pieces don't fit, our puzzle of Japan is still on the floor in a mess.

Now for some similarities. As will already be clear, I view borders, and more generally human societies, as complex phenomena that cannot be understood without breaking down some traditional academic boundaries. So the study is interdisciplinary—although because of its emphasis on theory, it is certainly not "undisciplined." And like most other recent studies of borders, I make an effort to acknowledge and engage various points of view: not only those of contemporaries living on opposite sides of the border but also the differing ways in which contemporaries and modern observers have construed the same reality.

I am in philosophical agreement with most of the other trends as well—but at least some of them, I believe, involve empirical questions whose answers should be derived, not assumed. Regarding the question of temporal continuity, Patricia Nelson Limerick is certainly correct to argue that the history of the American West is one of enduring legacies. But we should not automatically assume that all historical processes are continuous. Nor should we assume the opposite. It is common in the social sciences, for example, to see a fundamental difference between the modern world and conditions in premodern times. The discourse of disjuncture is invoked every time we contrast the modern nation-state with more "primitive" forms of political organization, assert the qualitative difference between the capitalist world economy and earlier modes of production, or postulate an "epistemological break" signaling the emergence of modern modes of thought. Similar ideas have frequently carried over into the literature on frontiers and boundaries, with many writers asserting that early peoples had only vague ideas of territoriality and that political borders such as we understand them today did not exist before the modern nation-state. Perhaps this is correct, but we should not take it as a given—it is an empirical question that can, and should, be addressed by looking at actual case studies. What continuities, and what discontinuities, can we identify across time, and how can we explain them?

A similar point can be made with respect to the spatial or social characteristics of borders. Borders are places where things change, but how abrupt is the transition? As noted above, it is common today to emphasize social continuity within and across frontiers. No doubt such continuity exists, or has existed, in most cases, but again this should be treated as a hypothesis, not an assumed truth. It is at least possible that some social transitions are more abrupt than we give them credit for. Again, a look at the specifics will yield the correct answers.

Finally, there is the matter of cross-border interaction. While most authors today prefer to emphasize sustained, intense interaction and mutual, reciprocal exchange across borders, wishing for these things does not necessarily make them so (at least, when discussing past events). Is it not more likely that the volume and nature of interaction and the prevailing direction of influence should vary according to location and historical circumstance? If so, then this variation, and the reasons for it, become important subjects for investigation. One reader of an earlier version of this work took offense at my discussion of the reasons behind Japanese expansion into Hokkaido, which he read as an apology for Japanese-style "manifest destiny." Nothing could be further from my intentions: Japan's conquest of Ainu territory is just as reprehensible as, for example, U.S. expansion into native lands in the American West. To deny the reality of the conquest or to avoid seeking the reasons for it is to shirk our responsibility as historians.

These themes and others will be pursued in greater detail in the remainder of the book, which consists of ten chapters arranged in three parts. Part I, "Borders," attempts to define what "Japan" is, by examining and comparing different types of social borders: political (Chapter 1), biological and cultural (Chapter 2), and ethnic (Chapter 3). In Part II, "Interactions," I try to evaluate the significance of these boundaries by using a version of world-systems theory (described in Chapter 4). Specifically, I examine four different categories of cross-border traffic—political/military interactions (Chapter 5) and flows of bulk goods (Chapter 6), prestige goods (Chapter 7), and information (Chapter 8)—in order to establish whether Japan's borders have historically functioned as barriers or as conduits of exchange (Chapter 9). Finally, in Part III, "Dynamics," I attempt to provide a general explanation for shifts in the location and nature of Japanese borders on the basis of long-standing (but not predestined) imbalances in "social power," both within the archipelago, and between the archipelago and neighboring regions on the Asian continent (Chapter 10).

Style, Conventions, and Definitions

This book, then, represents an attempt to organize the facts of Japanese history within the framework of social theory. One reader of a draft version panned it on these grounds, arguing, in effect, that I had no new facts to interest historians of Japan and no new ideas to interest theoreticians. This may be true, but it misses the point. Historians of Japan don't just need new facts; they also need new ways to organize and think about them. And while theoreticians may need new ideas, they also need specific case studies to test their arguments against. The needs of both groups, I hope, are met by the present study.

Nor is the book intended only for specialists. Most important ideas in the humanities and social sciences, I believe, can be explained in ordinary English without resort to formulas or jargon. As Patricia Nelson Limerick has noted, however, much academic writing is willfully obfuscatory. Essentially, it says to the reader, "If you can't understand this, it's your fault for not being smart enough."[46] My opinion is that if something is not clear, it is probably the fault of the author. In this book, therefore, I make an effort to explain things in simple language—not just "wherever possible" but consistently, throughout the book. In many places I could have avoided taking sides on a particular issue by resorting to academic jargon. I have not done so, because I think it is intellectually dishonest. My frequent use of the first person also reflects the same policy; if something is my opinion, I think I owe it to the reader to say so, rather than trying to create a misleading impression of objectivity where none exists. All of this goes to say that I have tried to make the book accessible not just to fellow academics but also to other readers with a general interest in the subject matter.

For all of these reasons, no extensive knowledge of Japanese history or of social theory is assumed on the part of the reader; relevant facts and concepts are introduced as needed, generally when they first appear. Nor is the reader expected to be particularly familiar with the geography of Japan (or, more broadly, East Asia). On the theory that "a picture is worth a thousand words," I have attempted to include as many maps as possible, both to identify the places mentioned in the text and to convey my ideas in visual form.

Because this book is about Japan, it contains a large number of Japanese names and terms. All Japanese words in the text are romanized according to the standard, modified Hepburn system. (The few Korean and Chinese terms are given, respectively, in McCune-Reischauer and Pinying transcription.) Japanese, like all languages, has changed over time, but for purposes of simplicity I use the modern pronunciation or form of all words. Consonants in modern Japanese are generally pronounced as a native English speaker would guess, except for *g*, which is always hard, and *r*, which sounds like a cross between an English *r* and *l*. Vowels are pronounced as in Italian. Long or double vowels are indicated with a macron (e.g., Jōmon), except in the case of place-names that will already be familiar to most readers (e.g., Tokyo, Osaka). Personal names are given in the Japanese order, that is, with the surname preceding the given name.

Finally, let me briefly define three important terms that I have already used repeatedly: "border," "boundary," and "frontier." As noted, some practitioners of the New Western History have rejected use of the word "frontier" because of its supposedly statist connotations. David Howell and Brett Walker have also expressed similar reservations about use of the term with reference to the former Ainu territories in Hokkaido.[47] I respect the views of these authors, but I think it is a case of throwing out the baby with the bathwater. The concept of the frontier is a useful one that has a long and respected academic pedigree—not only in history but in other fields as well. In this study, building on the tradition in political geography, I use "frontier" to refer to a vague, spatially diffuse division between social groups. A "boundary," likewise, is also a social interface, but it is one that is relatively well defined—a line that can easily be drawn on a map, as opposed to a zone. Finally, "border" is used in this study as a generic term for social divisions regardless of degree of geographic clarity. I will be the first to admit that I have not been completely consistent in my use of these words (if only to preserve a modicum of variety and readability), but where I have deviated from them, the intended meaning should be clear from context.

PART ONE

Borders

1 State

Japan Today

I live today, and have lived for some years, in a suburb of Tokyo. This makes me one of some 1.7 million foreign residents of Japan, a country whose total population is about 127 million.[1] Foreign residents are not eligible to vote in national, or most local, elections, but other than that we have most of the same rights and obligations as Japanese citizens. I pay Japanese taxes on my income as a professor, I pay property taxes on my house, and I observe Japanese laws. I and my family are eligible for Japanese health insurance, and I expect to receive a pension from the Japanese government when I retire. My children attend local schools with their Japanese neighbors.

These personal observations illustrate the relationship of the individual to the modern nation-state; by extension, they also reveal the power of national boundaries. All of the above facts are contingent on the territorial sovereignty of the Japanese state: the more or less exclusive authority it exercises over Japanese territory and the people who live there, whether of Japanese or foreign nationality. If my family lived in the United States, we would have much the same relationship to the U.S. government as we now do its Japanese counterpart; we would pay taxes, obey local laws, and take advantage of available social welfare and educational opportunities. In fact, with some allowance for local variations, the same would be true almost anywhere we lived in the modern world. The only real difference would be which government had jurisdiction over our lives. This, of course, is a very important difference, and it is determined largely by location of residence, that is, whether one lives on this side of a national boundary, or on that. National boundaries affect our lives in the most fundamental ways.

What are the boundaries of Japan, my present home? First, some basic geographic facts (see Map 1). Japan is a volcanic arc of islands located on the eastern fringe of Asia, which stretches approximately 3,000 km from Hokkaido in the northeast to the Ryukyu Islands in the southwest. Its total land area is 377,837 km^2, about 1.5 times the area of the United Kingdom, or slightly less than 4% that of the United States. (Japan is often compared in size with California or Montana.) Altogether, Japan consists of some seven thousand islands, but the four biggest are, from north to south, Hokkaido (83,452 km^2, or 22.1% of the total land area), Honshu (231,058 km^2, or 61.2%), Shikoku (18,785 km^2, or 5.0%), and Kyushu (44,424 km^2, or 11.8%).[2] The figure for Hokkaido also includes the so-called Northern Territories, consisting of several small islands (Etorofu, Kunashiri, Shikotan, and the Habomai group) located immediately northeast of Hokkaido in the Kuril archipelago; these are currently the focus of a territorial dispute with Russia.[3]

As this last fact indicates, there is some ambiguity about the location of Japan's borders. In addition to the Northern Territories, disputes also exist with South Korea over Takeshima (K. Tok-to), a small, uninhabited island in the Sea of Japan, and with China and Taiwan over the Senkaku Islands (C. Diaoyutai), which are located in the East China Sea.[4] (We might also note that the Ryukyu Islands—now known as Okinawa Prefecture—themselves were administered by the United States from 1945 until 1972.) But these are relatively minor exceptions; for the most part, no one questions which islands do and which do not belong to Japan.

The casual reader might be forgiven for equating Japan's borders with the coastlines of the islands themselves; as a little thought will make clear, that is not the case. Governments throughout the world today lay claim not only to land but also to territorial waters and airspace. Under contemporary international law, coastal states may claim possession of "territorial seas" within 12 nautical miles of shore, as well as "adjacent seas" within 24 nautical miles and an "exclusive economic zone" of up to 200 nautical miles from shore. Regarding airspace, territorial claims are generally recognized up to the upper lim-

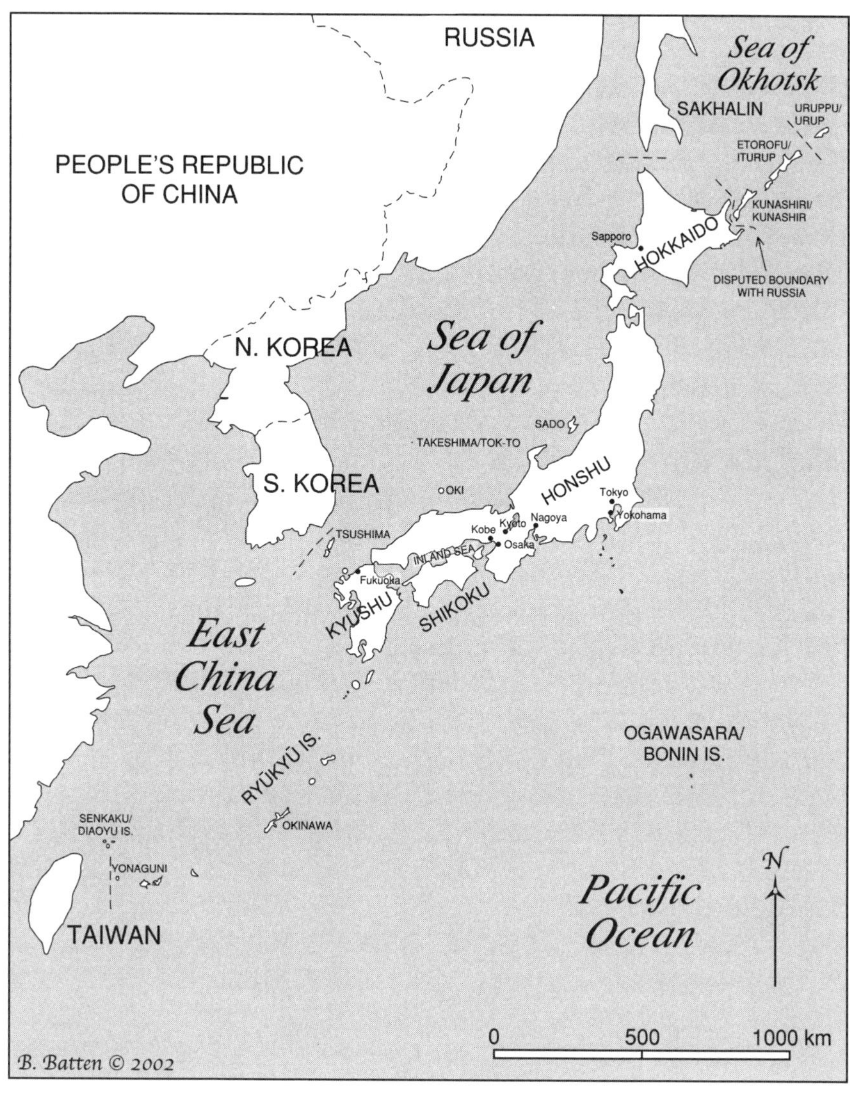

MAP 1. JAPAN TODAY.

its of the atmosphere, although no fixed altitude is usually specified.[5] What all of this means is that Japan's international boundaries are not identical to its coastlines per se; rather, they consist of two-dimensional planes extending perpendicularly above (and below) the surface of the ocean surrounding the archipelago. Still, this rather abstract image is of little practical significance to the lives of most Japanese people, who continue to think of their country's "boundaries" in terms of the outlines of the main islands.

In Japan, the first "modern" political boundary is said to date from 1855, when the Russo-Japanese Treaty of Shimoda set the mutual border of the two countries between Etorofu (Iturup) and Uruppu (Urup) Islands in the Kurils. The actual location of the border changed afterward as the result of further treaties (e.g., the 1875 Treaty of St. Petersburg) and hostilities (e.g., the 1904–1905 Russo-Japanese War).[6] As noted above, the status of several islands in the Kurils is still a matter of dispute. For our purposes, however, the precise location of the border is unimportant; what *is* important is its mutually recognized existence. Since 1855, Japan and Russia have viewed themselves as adjacent sovereign states divided by a shared international boundary—a line drawn in the ocean. Although these two countries may disagree about where to draw the line, they have no argument about the underlying principle that such a line should (and does) exist. This is an essentially modern worldview that did not exist in Japan prior to the nineteenth century.[7]

This is not to say, however, that no border existed before 1855. Quite to the contrary, Japan has had borders of one kind or another for as long as it has been a state. What is a "state"? Here I will use the definition by sociologist Anthony Giddens. According to Giddens, "A state exists where there is a political apparatus (governmental institutions, such as a court, parliament or congress, plus civil-service officials), ruling over a given territory, whose authority is backed by a legal system and by the capacity to use force to implement its policies."[8] If, as this and most other definitions imply, all states are territorial, then ipso facto they must also have borders, that is, geographic limits.[9]

When, then, did Japan become a state? We will be examining this issue in more detail later in the book; suffice it to say here that this is also an area of contention. Some authors place the origins of the Japanese state in the third century C.E., with the emergence of a "tumulus culture" centered in the Yamato area of west-central Honshu. Others look to the fifth century, when the Yamato polity began to display bureaucratic tendencies, or to the seventh century, when a succession of strong queens and kings finally established centralized rule over most of Honshu, Kyushu, and Shikoku.[10]

Actually, these different interpretations are by no means mutually exclusive. For one thing, whether we place the origins of the state in Japan in the third century or the seventh involves subjective judgment. It depends not only on how we define "state" but also on how we choose to apply that definition. For example, in Giddens' definition, what do we really mean by terms such as "political apparatus," "rule," "authority," "legal system," and so on? And even if all workers agreed on definitions and terms, it hardly seems likely that something as complex as a state could emerge overnight. For these reasons, I think it is best to view the origins of the state in Japan not as an *event* but as a *process*—one that began in the third century and was completed in the seventh.[11] But whether this "compromise" position is accepted or not, the fact remains that a state has existed in Japan for well over a thousand years; and so, by definition, have state borders.

It is the purpose of this chapter to explore what these premodern borders were like, where they were located, and how they changed over time. Perhaps surprisingly, these are questions that have never been systematically addressed in print. One reason, of course, is that the topic is so broad. Foreign historians writing about Japan generally limit themselves to one particular period or region. In Japan itself the situation is even worse. The sheer size of the historical literature is so overwhelming that scholars feel constrained to specialize (one might say, overspecialize) in order to make an original—if limited—contribution. As a result, almost no one attempts to pursue "big questions" of any kind, including those relating to frontiers and boundaries.

A second, more fundamental reason why no one has asked the "big questions" about Japan's historical borders is the widespread assumption that because Japan is an island-country, its boundaries are somehow "natural" and require no particular explanation. As I will argue, however, this assumption is completely false. Borders are sociopolitical entities, not geographical ones; there is no such thing as a "natural" boundary, either in Japan or elsewhere. Japan's borders were certainly influenced by geography, but they were hardly determined or preordained, and the assumption that they require no particular explanation or study is fundamentally wrong.

Frontiers and Boundaries in Theory and in World History

This is probably a good time to provide some general theoretical and comparative background, beginning with concepts and definitions of terms. Political geographers writing on this topic generally start off with the distinction between "frontiers" and "boundaries."[12] Both of these represent geographical limits to political authority and thus serve to distinguish states from their external environments (including other states). The difference is that a boundary takes the form of a *line* whereas a frontier takes that of a *zone*. In cases where the limits to state authority are clearly and precisely demarcated, we have a boundary. When those limits are poorly defined and state authority fades out gradually, as a function of distance, we have a frontier.[13]

Apart from the issue of dimensionality (line versus zone), frontiers and boundaries exhibit many other qualitative differences, which have been described in detail by the geographer Ladis Kristof. According to Kristof, frontiers are not just spatially diffuse boundaries; rather they reflect an entirely different way of thinking about the world. Frontiers did not originate as legal or political-intellectual concepts but emerged as manifestations of the "spontaneous tendency for growth of the ecumene." Kristof writes that "given the theory that there can (or should) be only one state—a universal state—the frontier meant quite literally 'the front': the *frons* of the *imperium mundi* which expands to the only limits it can acknowledge, namely, the limits of the world." Frontiers for this reason are "outer-oriented" and "centrifugal" in nature, according to Kristof, and tend to act as mediating forces or "integrating factors" between different "worlds" or ways of life. In all of these respects they differ from boundaries, which are "inner-oriented" and "centripetal" in nature and tend to act as "separating factors" between adjacent political units.[14]

Frontiers and boundaries, then, despite their superficial similarity, are qualitatively different entities that should not be confused.

With this idea firmly in hand, let us now turn to a brief survey of frontiers and boundaries in world history. The literature on this subject is a vast one that I have no hope of adequately summarizing here. However, it is possible to make a basic distinction between (1) works that touch upon the history of frontiers and boundaries as part of some broader theoretical or comparative study and (2) more empirical studies of individual states and/or borders.

Good examples of the first type are works by Anthony Giddens and Benedict Anderson. Giddens, in his influential textbook on sociology, writes, "The territories ruled by traditional states were always poorly defined, the level of control wielded by the central government being quite weak. The notion of sovereignty—that a government has authority over an area with clear-cut borders, within which it is the supreme power—had little relevance to traditional states."[15] A similar idea is conveyed in the study by Benedict Anderson of "imagined communities," his term for modern nation-states. According to Anderson, "In the modern conception, state sovereignty is fully, flatly, and evenly operative over each square centimetre of a legally demarcated territory. But in the older imagining, where states were defined by centres, borders were porous and indistinct, and sovereignties faded imperceptibly into one another."[16] In a word, modern political units have boundaries, whereas premodern ones had frontiers.

This idea finds support in many works of the second type, that is, case studies of specific premodern polities.[17] An excellent example is provided by Thongchai Winichakul's recent book on Siam (Thailand).[18] According to Thongchai, the borders of premodern Siam were determined not by any central authority but by local circumstances, specifically the area that could be protected by outlying towns. Beyond these limits were only vast stretches of virtually uninhabited territory, a no-man's-land that formed a "border without boundary line." Thongchai notes that this border "could be defined without the agreement or ratification of another country."[19] He goes on to show how the vaguely defined "geo-body" of premodern Siam was transformed into a precisely demarcated modern nation-state as the result of Western imperialism in the nineteenth and twentieth centuries.[20]

However, as the case literature also attests, not all premodern borders were necessarily vague. As noted long ago by geographer Stephen Jones, "It is easy to assume that primitive men have primitive ideas about boundaries, and that these are more or less alike around the world. A common assumption has been that primitive men have no linear boundaries but only zones. [Such cases] undoubtedly are common, but there certainly are exceptions."[21] The same point has also been recently made by S. L. Davis and J.R.V. Prescott in their wide-ranging comparative study of aboriginal boundaries in precontact Australia.[22]

Regarding state-based societies, with which we are principally concerned, the most interesting (albeit somewhat ambiguous) example is ancient Rome. For our purposes, Roman history can be divided into two phases: the Republican period, when the empire was expanding in all directions as the result of military conquests; and the period after Augustus, when expansion largely came to a halt and military actions began to assume a defensive, as opposed to offensive, posture.

According to one common view, Rome's borders took the form of "frontiers" in the first period but "boundaries" in the second. This idea is espoused by Edward Luttwak, who argues that during the first period Rome used a "hegemonic" strategy of rule. There were no formal limits of empire, and defense was accomplished through the skillful manipulation of client states and tribes. After Augustus, however, a new "territorial" model of rule was adopted. Under this, the limits of the empire came to be "demarcated very precisely, on the ground, so that all could tell exactly what was Roman and what was not." Luttwak continues, "The established client states had been absorbed, and . . . the land borders of the empire were guarded by defended perimeters that complemented the natural barriers of river and ocean. The invisible borders of imperial power had given way to physical frontier defenses.[23] Although Luttwak uses slightly different terms, the basic idea here would seem to be that after Augustus, Rome's "frontiers" were transformed into something rather like modern political "boundaries." Following the publication of Luttwak's book, this view came to be widely accepted in Roman frontier studies and is still seen in many popular and semipopular accounts.[24]

Contemporary scholarship, however, tends to be critical of this view. One good example is the recent study of Roman frontiers by

C. R. Whittaker.[25] Whittaker's views are highly nuanced and difficult to summarize in a few words. In short, however, he agrees that during the first period the dominant ideology was of universal empire. At the same time, he notes that within this larger system a distinction existed between an inner zone of direct administration (the Roman "state"?) and an outer zone of indirect control (the rest of the empire?), and that the border between the two could be quite precisely defined. Regarding the second period, Whittaker sees continuity where Luttwak saw change. According to Whittaker, the idea of universal empire was never abandoned, and frontier policies and strategic aims remained essentially unchanged until the end of the empire. Whittaker does not deny that a large number of defensive fortifications (such as Hadrian's Wall and the like) were constructed in the second period, but according to him, they were all located behind, rather than on, Rome's frontiers and functioned more as internal tactical controls than as external defenses. They were marks of Roman authority and presence designed to control, but not prevent, movements within and across imperial frontiers.

Debates among specialists notwithstanding, I think it is possible to draw several general conclusions about Roman borders from this brief discussion. First, there was not always an exact correspondence between border *concepts* and borders as they existed on the ground. Concepts of universal empire, for example, could coexist with actual physical borders. Second, Roman borders were highly complex, exhibiting some of the features of *both* boundaries and frontiers. Frontier zones could coexist with sharp administrative boundaries and linear fortifications; the fortifications served as focuses of "inner-oriented" state control and also had definite symbolic value. And third, the balance between "frontier-like" conditions and "boundary-like" ones could change dramatically over time.

I would argue that these same points could be made for many premodern polities, including Japan. In the remainder of this chapter, I will attempt to trace the history of Japan's political borders from the earliest times to the nineteenth century. For convenience, I shall follow the common practice of dividing this long span of time into three major blocs: the "ancient" era (through the twelfth century C.E.), the "medieval" era (twelfth–sixteenth centuries), and the "early modern" era (seventeenth–nineteenth centuries).

Ancient Japan

In the case of Japan, as in the case of Rome, it is important to distinguish between worldviews, on the one hand, and geopolitical realities, on the other. Regarding the former, the first point to make is that residents of the Japanese islands embraced a variety of worldviews in all historical periods; no "one-size-fits-all" set of beliefs can be identified. Some cosmographies were overtly religious, whereas others were more secular in orientation. Here, and in the remainder of this chapter, I will focus mostly on secular worldviews, which are more directly relevant to the topic of physical borders.[26]

Secular political ideology in ancient Japan was ultimately based upon Chinese models, specifically the so-called "middle kingdom ideology" *(kai shisō)*. In its original form, this ideology placed China at the center of the world, both politically and culturally. China was ruled by the "son of heaven" on the basis of "virtue" *(de)*, "ritual" *(li)*, and "law" *(fa)*. Outlying regions beyond the "son of heaven's" direct control were viewed as "uncivilized," inhabited by the "barbarians of the four directions." However, these regions were not seen as fully independent of China; although they had their own rulers, these rulers were thought to be politically subordinate to the "son of heaven." Moreover, there was a basic assumption that outlying regions could in principle be incorporated within the sphere of "civilization" through the geographical spread of "virtue," "ritual," and "law."[27] In short, the "middle kingdom ideology" was an ethnocentric vision of the universal state or universal empire, and in this sense it was fundamentally similar to the worldview of ancient Rome.

Over time, modified self-referential versions of this political ideology were adopted by various satellite states on the Chinese periphery, most notably in Southeast Asia, the Korean Peninsula, and Japan.[28] In the Japanese archipelago the concept makes its first appearance in a boastful "memorial" sent by "King Bu" to his Chinese counterpart in 478 C.E. Describing the achievements of his ancestors, Bu wrote: "In the east, they conquered fifty-five countries of hairy men; and in the west, they brought to their knees sixty-six countries of various barbarians. Crossing the sea to the north, they subjugated ninety-five countries."[29] However, it was not until the formation of a centralized state in the seventh and eighth centuries that a nativized "middle kingdom ideology" reached its full, mature expression.

Whereas the Chinese (like the Romans) could with some justification claim to rule a universal empire (or at least, an impressively large one), in the satellite states the fit between image and reality was very poor. During the Nara period (710–784), for example, Japan maintained loose tributary ties with the Tang empire in China through the periodic dispatch of *kentōshi*, or "missions to Tang."[30] In this sense, the country was more or less an equal of other Tang tributaries such as Silla (on the Korean Peninsula) and Parhae (in Manchuria). In the imperial ideology adopted by the Nara state, however, China was conceived as an equal "neighbor state" *(rinkoku)*, while Silla and Parhae were treated as "vassal states" *(bankoku)* tributary to Japan.[31] Finally, tribal societies within the Japanese archipelago (most notably the Emishi of northeastern Honshu) were viewed as subordinate (if obstreperous) "barbarian societies" *(iteki)*.[32]

Although the "middle kingdom ideology" would appear incompatible with any clear concept of territorial boundaries, in fact the situation is not so simple. Little credible historical evidence survives from pre-Nara times, but the presence of some primitive boundary concepts is suggested by archaeological finds from the island of Okinoshima in the Genkai Sea between Kyushu and the Korean Peninsula. These artifacts indicate that the Yamato court conducted religious ceremonies on Okinoshima to ensure safe passage on the sea routes to the continent.[33] If so, the island itself may have served as a sort of primitive "boundary marker" for the early Japanese state.

With the establishment of the Nara state, boundary concepts become somewhat clearer. Much as in Rome, a sharp distinction came to be drawn between the "inner lands" *(kenai)*, that is, areas under direct Japanese control, and the "outer lands" *(kegai)*, that is, areas outside the zone of administration but still located within the greater Japanese "world." The emergence of this distinction was linked to the state's role in creating internal administrative units, especially the first-order divisions known as "provinces" *(kuni)*. The act of creating the provinces forced the state to differentiate between areas included within, and areas excluded from, the new administrative system.[34]

Using the distinction between "inner lands" and "outer lands" as a rough guide, let us now discuss the location and nature of the Nara state's borders with Silla in the west, with the Emishi in the north, and with other peripheral tribesmen (the Hayato and the Nantōjin, or "Southern Islanders") in the south (see Map 2).

The western border cannot be identified with precision, in part because it was located at sea, not on land. For our purposes the most important section of the border was the Korea Strait, located between the island of Tsushima and the Korean Peninsula. Tsushima itself was included within the Japanese provincial system from the very beginning, but this is where territorial expansion stopped; indeed, the Korea Strait is the one clear example of a static political border in Japanese history. Aside from the late sixteenth century, during Hideyoshi's invasions, and the early twentieth century, during the colonial period, the strait has always defined the western limit of Japanese territory. (Formerly, many scholars believed that Yamato "ruled" part of the Korean Peninsula in the early centuries C.E., but this view is now largely discredited, even in Japan.[35]) However until modern times no clear line was ever drawn in the strait—the border consisted of a vague belt of ocean; it was a maritime frontier, as opposed to a boundary.

The northern border with the Emishi was also vaguely defined. Modern maps of Nara-period administrative divisions show the two provinces of Mutsu and Dewa extending all the way north to the tip of Honshu. However, it is doubtful that they were originally conceived in this way, given the government's general ignorance of geographic conditions.[36] A better sense of the northern border can be gained from looking at the second-tier administrative units known as "districts" *(kōri).* According to research by Kudō Masaki, there was a south-to-north progression from (1) districts identical to those in the interior, to (2) special "frontier districts" centered on stockades inhabited by Japanese colonist-soldiers, to (3) "Emishi districts" ruled by indigenous, pro-government chiefs, to (4) Emishi territory completely outside the government's authority .[37] The border, in other words, took the classic zonal form of a frontier. This frontier moved progressively northward during the Nara and early Heian (794–1185) periods as the result of military campaigns.[38] Overt warfare largely ceased after

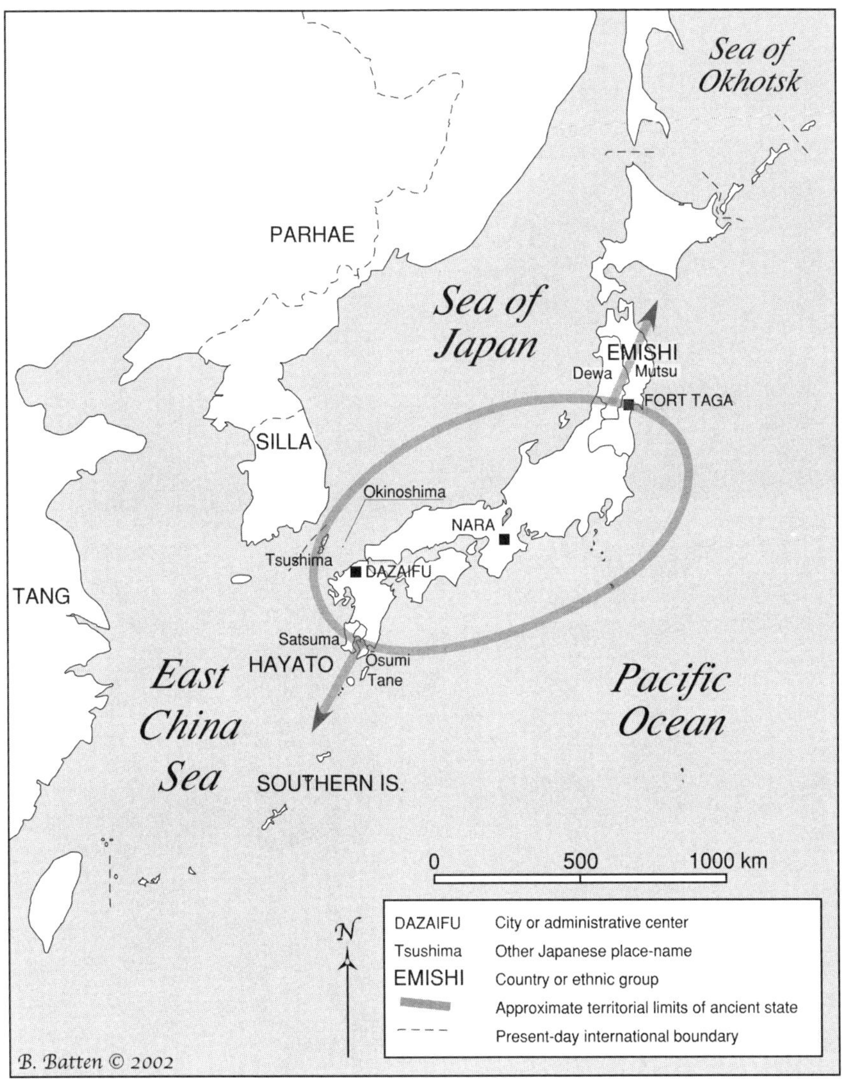

MAP 2. JAPAN IN THE EIGHTH CENTURY.

the ninth century, but the process of establishing new districts continued until all of northern Honshu had been incorporated by the end of the Heian period.[39]

A similar situation existed with regard to the third border, in the south. Again, modern maps show the provinces of Satsuma and Ōsumi extending all the way to the southern tip of Kyushu, but at the beginning of the eighth century some areas of southern Kyushu—mostly inhabited by tribes known collectively as Hayato—still lay outside the district system.[40] This land came under government control in the early eighth century, when the government crushed a series of Hayato "rebellions." The "Hayato districts" established in the former native territories, however, retained some "frontier" characteristics until the early ninth century; specifically they remained outside the system of public land allotment used in the interior, and their residents were required to pay "tribute" instead of "taxes."[41] Sources from this period also make reference to the inhabitants of various islands south of Kyushu. The state exacted tribute from these "Southern Islanders" during the eighth century, but most of the islands were never fully incorporated within state territory. One exception was Tane, located just off the coast of Ōsumi on the Kyushu mainland. Tane was administered as a separate province during the eighth and early ninth centuries, after which it was placed under the jurisdiction of the Ōsumi provincial office.[42]

How can we explain the locations and movements of these various borders? One suggestion is provided by political scientist Robert Gilpin's model of the growth dynamics of premodern empires. In premodern societies, according to Gilpin, territorial expansion was both the result and the cause of generalized growth in state power. In Gilpin's words, "when agriculture was the basis of wealth and power, growth in power and wealth was nearly synonymous with conquest of territory."[43] Powerful states tended to expand territorially, and in doing so, they gained access to additional agricultural resources and became still more powerful, leading to another round of expansion. Of course, as Gilpin also notes, "In the absence of countervailing forces, the logic of this situation would culminate in a universal political empire or global economic monopoly. . . . [H]owever, the growth and expansion of a state and economy at some point encounter and even generate countervailing forces."[44] Among the various countervailing forces noted by Gilpin are natural barriers; what he calls the "loss-of-strength gradient" (by which state power tends to diminishes in proportion to distance from its political center); and the presence of opposing power.[45]

All of these factors were clearly operative in the case of early Japan, although their importance varied from location to location. On the western maritime frontier, state expansion was presumably limited by a "natural barrier" (the ocean) and the presence of an "opposing power" (Silla). As I have argued in detail elsewhere, Japanese rulers essentially drew a line (actually, of course, a zone) in the ocean around northern Kyushu to protect themselves from Silla and Tang China after Japan's defeat in the so-called Battle of Paekchon River in 663 C.E.[46]

The presence of "opposing power" (although not geographic barriers) is also evident in the north and south in the form, respectively, of the Emishi and the Hayato. The balance of power between Japan and these peripheral societies clearly had an effect on the location of their mutual frontiers. A very clear example of this is given by Murai Shōsuke. Murai describes how the Emishi, operating from a (temporary) position of strength during the so-called Gangyō War, proposed in 878 that the lands north of the Akita (now Omono) River be recognized as theirs.[47]

Overall, however, the "loss-of-strength gradient" was probably the most important factor limiting state expansion along the northern and southern frontiers. In fact, the very presence of opposing powers such as the Emishi and the Hayato may have been at least partially a function of distance. Common sense suggests that "as distance from the center increases, there is a diminution of the effectiveness of integration of all types."[48] This situation would seem likely to encourage the growth of rival groups such as the Emishi and the Hayato.

The relationship between distance and territory in early Japan is best illustrated by considering some actual numbers. Here we are concerned less with the number of miles or kilometers separating two given points than with what might be called "administrative distance"—travel time, cost of communications, etc.[49] A tenth-century legal compendium, the *Engishiki*, preserves information about travel time from the capital to the various provinces along the network of official roads established in the late 600s and early 700s. These figures are based on the capital of Heian-kyō (modern Kyoto, founded in 794), rather than Heijō-kyō (modern Nara), but for our purposes the difference is negligible. For convenience I have used four-day increments to divide the islands of Honshu, Shikoku, and Kyushu into zones of increasing distance from the center (see Map 3). Note that

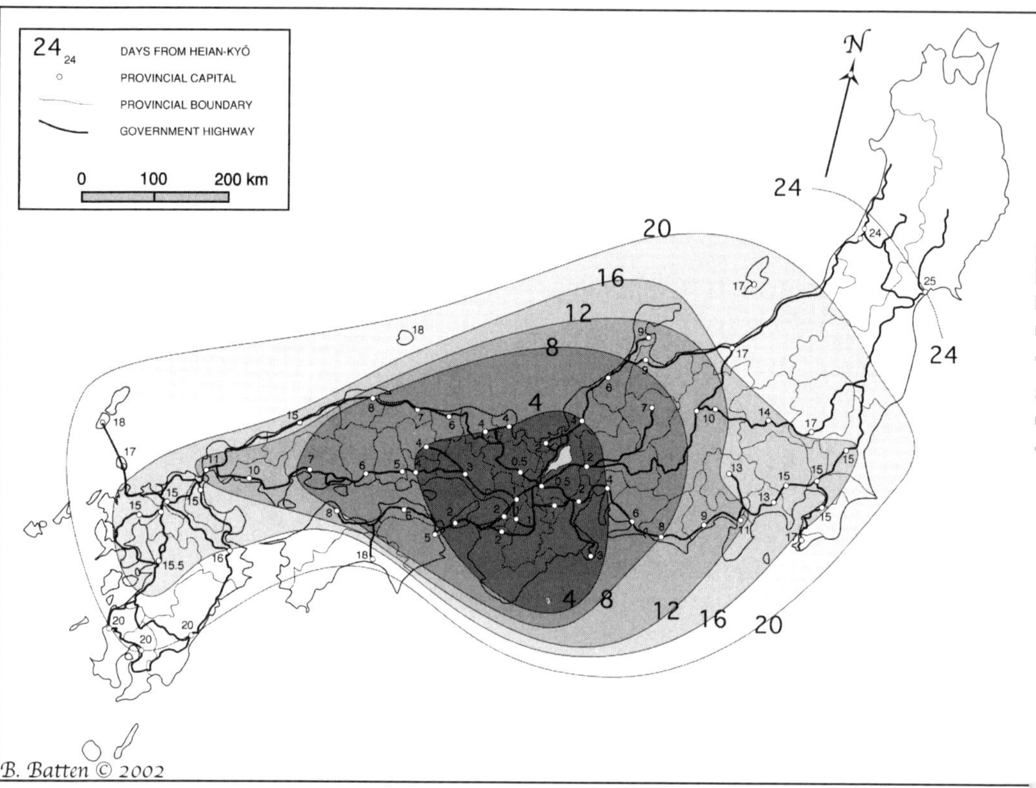

MAP 3. TRAVEL DISTANCE FROM HEIAN-KYŌ CIRCA 900 C.E. BASED ON DATA IN *ENGISHIKI* (SHUKEI JŌ), PP. 602–622.

the Nara-period frontier zones in both northeast Honshu and southern Kyushu were approximately equidistant from the center, at a distance of twenty to twenty-four days. This figure presumably represents the maximum distance over which the state could effectively exercise political control during the early eighth century.[50]

Medieval Japan

During the Nara period, as we have seen, the establishment of a strong, centralized state was associated with the emergence of an imperial ideology; the recognition of a clear distinction between incorporated "inner lands" and unincorporated "outer lands"; and an ongoing attempt to convert the latter into the former through a process of territorial expansion. Later, political authority became fragmented among multiple power-holders in Kyoto and in the provinces. This trend began during the Heian period and culminated during Japan's "middle ages," consisting of the Kamakura (1185–1333) and Muromachi (1336–1573) periods. As I will argue in this section, political decentralization had important implications for the nature of Japan's borders, both imagined and actual.

First, in the area of ideology, the medieval period saw a profound change in boundary concepts: specifically the emergence of a "closed," inward-looking worldview, on the one hand, and its association with strong ideas of "pollution," on the other. These characteristics emerged around the year 900 and remained dominant until the sixteenth century.

The shift to a closed worldview is testified by frequent references to Japan's "boundaries" *(sakai, shiishi)* in medieval literary sources. This contrasts strongly with works from the Nara and early Heian periods, which are almost devoid of references to "boundaries." Although there is some variation among sources, the most commonly cited medieval "boundaries" were Sotogahama and/or "Ezogashima" in the east, and the islands of Iki, Tsushima, and "Kikaigashima" in the west and south.[51] Sotogahama, or the "Exterior Beach," was located at the northern tip of Honshu, while "Ezogashima," or "Island of Ezo," refers vaguely to Hokkaido. ("Ezo" is the term used in medieval times for the native inhabitants of the far north.) "Kikaigashima" is an ambiguous term, but if it has any specific geographical referent, it is probably Iōjima ("Sulfur Island"), a small volcanic isle 50 km south of Satsuma Peninsula (see Map 4). Both Hokkaido and Iōjima, together with Sado Island off the northern Sea of Japan coast, were frequently used as places of exile during the medieval period.[52] The use of these areas to "cast out" vanquished political foes is perhaps also evidence of the "closed" nature of medieval boundary concepts.

It is important to note that the change from the open, expansive ideology of the Nara state to the static, closed ideas of the medieval period does *not* represent a shift from "frontiers" to modern political "boundaries." Although these medieval "boundaries" may have had

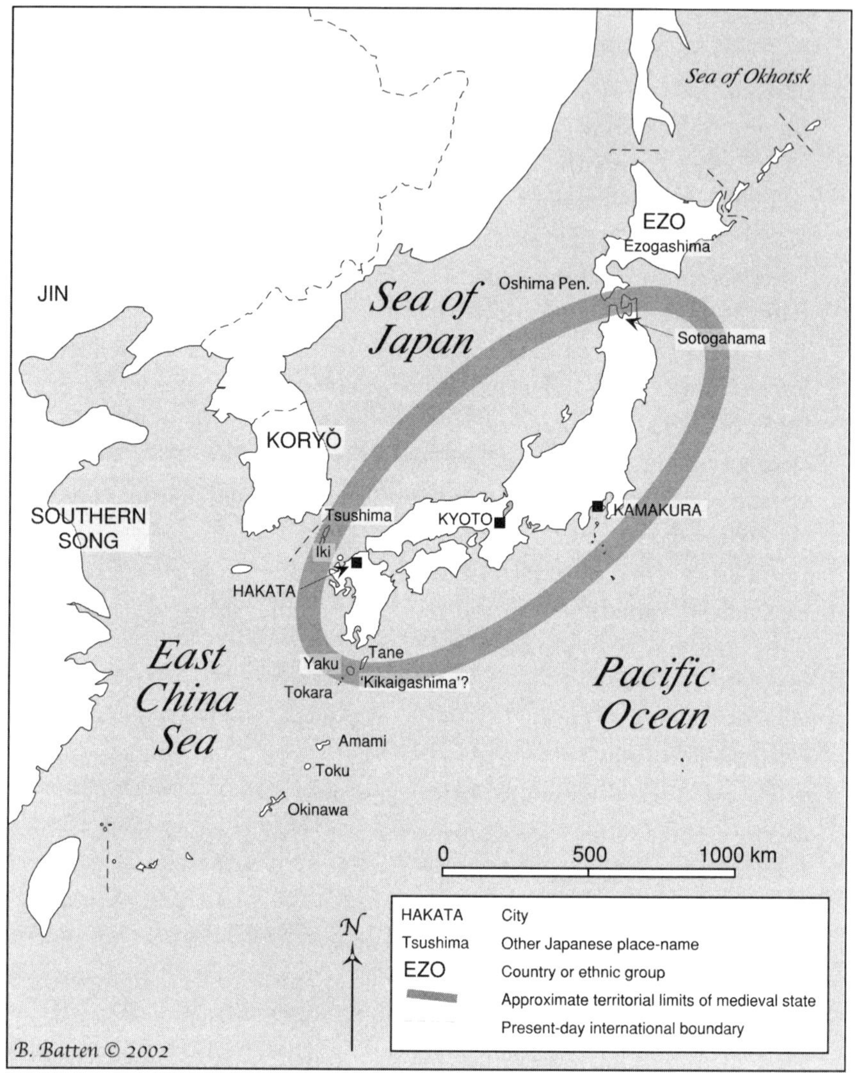

MAP 4. JAPAN IN THE THIRTEENTH CENTURY.

their origin in the Nara-period distinction between "inner lands" and "outer lands," they had lost their original administrative meaning. Medieval boundary concepts, in other words, were no longer linked to any specific institutions of control or territorial rule. This is not to say that they had no political significance—otherwise islands such as Hokkaido and Iōjima would not have been used as places of banishment. It is also true, nonetheless, that these "boundaries" began to take on a stereotyped life of their own in the imagination of the central elite.

Another way of putting this is to say that medieval elites had a weak sense of political territory. According to Amino Yoshihiko, this disinterest stemmed from changes in the nature of the Japanese state and particularly from changes in the communications system. Amino argues that the Nara-period imperial state "looked on the seas as boundaries and based its transport system on straight land highways of military significance." When this communication system broke down in the Heian period, it was replaced by one based on "river or marine transport," according to Amino. "After the tenth century this extended throughout the whole archipelago, became stabilised and supported the communication of peoples and the transport and distribution of goods. In this sense, from the tenth century at the latest, the society of the archipelago entered upon a 'river and sea period' in which the sense of national boundaries was very weak."[53] Amino's point is well taken, although his use of the term "national boundaries" is misplaced. (To speak of "national" borders presumes the existence of a "nation," but as I will argue in Chapter 3, no such entity is to be found in Japan before the nineteenth century.)

The second important characteristic of medieval boundary concepts was their association with the idea of "pollution." According to Murai Shōsuke, medieval elites conceived of their world as a series of "concentric circles of purity and pollution" extending outward from the capital of Kyoto to the "external regions" *(iiki)* beyond Japan's "boundaries." Each successive zone was more polluted than the last, and the "external regions" were the most polluted of all, being inhabited by "devils" rather than human beings. According to Murai, "[T]he calamities brought from abroad by these devils, whether military invasion or contagious disease, were beyond human control; therefore, the purity of the emperor and his realm could be protected only by the transcendent powers wielded by the gods and buddhas, not by practical political control or military power."[54] This worldview could hardly be further removed from the modern concept of political boundaries.

Literary references aside, where were the objective limits of state authority in medieval Japan? In general we see a pattern of limited expansion followed in some cases by retraction. In the north, Japanese warlords moved across the Tsugaru Strait to establish the "Twelve Forts of Southern Hokkaido" in the Oshima Peninsula.[55] In the west, the frontier was relatively static, with Tsushima continuing to define the limits of state authority (although it should be noted that political actors in the Korean Peninsula also sometimes claimed this island for themselves[56]). And in the seas south of Kyushu, we see another cycle of expansion followed by contraction. Murai Shōsuke argues that during the fourteenth century, Japanese territory extended all the way to Toku in the Amami Islands. During the fifteenth century, however, the frontier retracted to the vicinity of the Tokara Islands, located just south of Tane and Yaku near the Kyushu mainland. Murai attributes this retraction to the growth of the Ryukyu kingdom centered on the island of Okinawa.[57]

One problem with identifying the location of medieval frontiers is that during this period we lack any obvious criteria for assessing what did and what did not constitute Japanese "territory." The old provinces and districts continued to exist, at least in name, but the state ceased to play an active role in defining or maintaining territorial units of local administration. On a smaller scale, the government was involved in defining the boundaries of private landholdings, both by conducting land surveys (such as the *ōtabumi* of the Kamakura period) and by resolving land disputes through the judicial system. However, these activities had merely local significance and did not result in any clarification of Japan's borders as a whole. As a consequence, it is difficult to say where the frontiers of the medieval Japanese state lay; we know the locations of individual landholdings, and we know the general spheres of activity of the various public officials, but we do not know the outer limits of the system itself—precisely because little attempt was made to define these limits at the time.

The medieval state also gradually lost control over "boundary functions," that is, regulatory authority over cross-border flows of people, goods, and information.[58] During the ancient period, boundary functions were generally monopolized by the state. For example, traffic across the western maritime frontier was supervised by the Dazaifu ("Government-General Headquarters"), a branch office of the central government located near Hakata. The Dazaifu was intended to facilitate the state's monopoly over foreign contacts by functioning as a "barrier gate" between Japan and the outside world.[59] Likewise, military administration of the border with the Emishi in northeast Honshu was managed by another branch office known as the Chinjufu ("Pacification Headquarters").[60]

During the medieval period, however, control over boundary functions became more and more decentralized. In the north, for example, the frontier fell under the control of a succession of "boundary powers"—the Abe, Kiyohara, and Fujiwara families of the Heian period; the Andō family of the Kamakura period; and the (probably unrelated) Andō family of the Muromachi period.[61] Many, and perhaps most, of these were of mixed "Japanese" and Ezo blood ("Ezo" being the preferred medieval term for native inhabitants of the far north). Over the course of the medieval period, these "boundary powers" changed in character from local delegates of the central government (i.e., the imperial court and, later, the various shogunates) to autonomous warlords.[62]

In the west and south, as in the east, power often devolved from the court and the shogunates to their local representatives. One example, described below, is the Chikama family of southern Kyushu; another is the Sō family of Tsushima, who eventually came to dominate commercial and diplomatic relations with the Korean Peninsula.[63] One difference in this region, however, was a tendency toward total anarchy, manifested most clearly in the activities of the pirates collectively known as Wakō. The Wakō have been described by Murai Shōsuke as "marginal men"—individuals of no particular nationality or affiliation, who operated freely in what Murai calls the "Pan–East China Sea Region," which "straddled the borders" of Japan and Korea.[64] Murai's image of a maritime zone of activity located in the political vacuum between Japan and the continent is attractive and fundamentally correct. However, one note of caution is in order: the idea that the Pan–East China Sea Region "straddled the borders" makes sense only if "border" is understood in the narrow sense of a sharp political boundary. No such boundaries existed in the medieval period, though. The most important characteristic of medieval borders was their vagueness—they were *frontiers*, not boundaries. The "Pan–East China Sea Region" is a classic example of such a frontier. For this reason it did not "straddle the border"—it *was* the border.

The example of the "Pan–East China Sea Region" illustrates another important point, namely that cross-border traffic tends to increase in direct proportion to the breakdown of central controls over boundary functions. We will explore this topic in greater detail in subsequent chapters. Here, suffice it to say that both traditional historical sources and archaeological evidence point to a significant increase in cross-border traffic over the course of the medieval period. In earlier centuries, when the state retained a near-monopoly over boundary functions, the level of cross-border traffic was fairly low. In the medieval period, however, Japan's frontier zones came under the control of multiple, competing "boundary powers," each eager to exploit foreign contacts for parochial commercial and/or diplomatic purposes. The result was a dramatic increase in traffic of all kinds, a trend that peaked in the late sixteenth century.

The growth of cross-border trade has been invoked by Murai Shōsuke as a causative agent in the growth of Japanese territory during the medieval period. Murai analyzes Kamakura-period testamentary documents left by members of the Andō family, in Tsugaru (Sotogahama), and the Chikama family, in Satsuma. Some of the documents relate to territories in Hokkaido and the Ryukyus, respectively, which lay beyond the administrative jurisdictions of these families as recognized by the Kamakura shogunate, and thus arguably outside "Japan" itself as conceived by central authorities. Both the Andō and the Chikama were heavily involved in trade, a fact leading Murai to conclude: "By their very nature, trading activities tend to extend as far afield as possible, and the growth of trade can result in an outward shift of boundaries. Conversely, if trade should for some reason fall into decline, then the boundaries will similarly recede. At the same time, because trade represents a relationship with people beyond the boundaries, boundaries will be determined by the interrelationship between the two parties. Thus the variableness of boundaries was sometimes due to the vicissitudes of trade."[65]

Superficially, Murai's arguments would seem to contradict the geopolitical model I presented above, which attempts to explain the location of borders in terms of power relationships among states and/or societies. In fact, there is no real contradiction, but the cases of the Andō and the Chikama *do* provide a good opportunity to enhance our understanding of the nature of power, on the one hand, and that of the medieval Japanese state, on the other.

First, regarding power: Gilpin argues that growth of territory is linked to growth in state power, but there is no need to understand power in narrow political terms. I will save a full analysis of the nature of power for the final chapter of this book. Suffice it to say, however, that power can have many aspects, and all of them can affect state "strength" and thus the location of frontiers. In the case of trade, differential trends in the accumulation of wealth could easily tip the balance of power, resulting in a shift in the location of the physical border between two societies.

The second, more fundamental point relates to the nature of the Japanese state itself. What the points raised by Murai suggest is that borders could expand outward (although perhaps at a slower rate) even when Japan as a whole was becoming fragmented or decentered. In other words, the disappearance of a unitary state did not lead immediately to a retraction of Japan's borders. This territorial "resilience" again underlines the point that social power may have many manifestations and that a deficit in one area (centralized political authority) may be more than made up by surpluses in others (e.g., economic strength). But it also suggests that we may need to take multiple "centers" into account when using balance-of-power models; the location of Japan's medieval borders may have been determined as much by the role of "boundary powers" like the Andō and the Chikama as by the strength of the central government. A multicentered polity calls for a multicentered analysis.

The process of political decentralization that was medieval Japan reached a peak in the so-called Sengoku, or "warring states," period (1467–1568). During this century of near-anarchy, "Japan" as a country became so fragmented that its "external" borders lost most of their independent meaning, paling in importance beside a new set of "internal" borders.

Although the history of this period is too complex to describe in detail here, regional powers became more and more independent after the Ōnin War of the mid-fifteenth century.[66] During the late fifteenth and sixteenth centuries these warlords, known as *sengoku daimyō*, consolidated their rule over domains that were essentially sovereign "mini-states."[67] Admittedly, they were not necessarily *conceived* as such at the time: the idea of "Japan" as a single country remained fairly strong in the Sengoku period, as is clear from the writings of the various Europeans who visited Japan during the sixteenth century.[68] But in practical terms each *sengoku daimyō* was more or less independent of the others and of any higher authority. For that reason the boundaries between their domains can be thought of as emergent "state borders."

Unfortunately, there is little research on the nature of these borders. We know that they shifted frequently because of the fluid political situation. In some respects, however, they are likely to have been more like boundaries than frontiers. *Sengoku daimyō* were very active in surveying their territories in order to clarify land rights and tax obligations. This strong emphasis on control over territory, coupled with the high state of military tension between adjoining warlords, would seem likely to have encouraged the emergence of fairly well-defined borders. But on the other hand, it is possible to find cases of interleaving landholdings. Just to cite one example, a number of villages within the Later Hōjō domain in the Kantō were in fact owned by warriors subject to the Takeda family, which controlled the adjoining domain.[69] This interleaving of boundaries is reminiscent of that found between feudal regimes in medieval Europe.[70]

Early Modern Japan

The "warring states" period came to an end in the late sixteenth century as a result of the activities of the "three great unifiers," Oda Nobunaga, Toyotomi Hideyoshi, and Tokugawa Ieyasu.[71] During the ensuing Edo period (1600–1867), the shogunate established by Ieyasu served as Japan's central government, while most parts of the country were administered directly by daimyo chosen from among the ranks of Tokugawa vassals. This regime is known to Japanese historians as the *bakuhan taisei*, or "shogunate and domain system."[72] In the English literature, it was formerly described as "centralized feudalism."[73] Now, both in Japan and elsewhere, there is a tendency to downplay the centralized aspects of the system and emphasize the autonomy of the daimyo domains. Mark Ravina, writing from this perspective, has recently described Edo Japan as a "compound state."[74] This is a useful concept to the extent that it redresses the tendency of earlier research to overemphasize the importance of the shogunate. Edo Japan was certainly far more fragmented than most modern states. On the other hand, this should not be allowed to obscure the fact that it was also more centralized than anything seen in Japan since ancient times.[75] "Centralization," after all, is a relative term.

The events of the late sixteenth century had importance consequences for Japan's borders. First, as daimyo territories were incorporated within the reemergent Japanese state, their borders were "demoted" to the status of internal administrative boundaries. Second, the area under "unified" rule expanded rapidly in this period, even going beyond Japan's "traditional" boundaries for a brief period in the 1590s as a result of Hideyoshi's invasions of the Korean Peninsula.[76] However, upon Hideyoshi's death, all attempts to conquer Korea were abandoned, and Japan's territory reverted to more or less the same dimensions as in the medieval period—the three islands of Honshu, Shikoku, and Kyushu, plus the southern tip of Hokkaido. At least in a formal, political sense, Japan's borders remained more or less unchanged until the end of the eighteenth century.

The Edo period also saw important changes in the areas of political ideology and boundary concepts. The supernatural worldview of the medieval period, for example, was rapidly abandoned. No longer were inhabitants of outlying regions viewed as devils or carriers of pollution. Instead they were seen as human beings, interactions with whom could be regulated by practical political, economic, and military tools. This changed viewpoint undoubtedly emerged from accumulated experience in dealing with the outside world and from the renewed strength and institutional capabilities of the state.

What emerged in place of the medieval worldview? As in other periods of Japanese history, there is no single answer—early modern Japanese subscribed, sometimes simultaneously, to a number of competing cosmologies. Ronald Toby, for example, has shown on the basis of maps and pictorial representations how the "three realms" (Japan, China, and India, or "trans-China") of Buddhist thought gave way to a cosmopolitan vision of "myriad realms" *(bankoku)* following Japan's first encounter with Europe in the sixteenth century.[77]

More important in terms of political ideology, however, was the cosmology referred to by specialists as the "Japanese-style middle kingdom order" *(Nihon-gata kai chitsujo).* As the name implies, this represented another attempt to fit Chinese ideas to Japanese realities. Within the context of this hierarchical, ethnocentric worldview, the rulers of Edo-period Japan maintained ties with five separate states and/or ethnic groups: the Ryukyu kingdom (present-day Okinawa), Korea, China, Holland, and Ezochi ("Ezo-land," that is Hokkaido). Of these, Korea and Ryukyu were considered "diplomatic partner states" *(tsūshin no kuni),* while China and Holland were "trade partner states" *(tsūshō no kuni)* without formal diplomatic ties. The Ezo (or Ainu, as they were also sometimes known in this period), lacking a formal state structure, were classed in neither category.[78]

Rapid growth in state power was also reflected in a recentralization of authority over frontier regions and boundary functions. For example, the Edo shogunate permitted contact with the outside world at only a limited number of sites—the "four mouths" *(yottsu no kuchi).* Relations with Holland and China were conducted via the "Nagasaki mouth"; those with Korea via the "Tsushima mouth"; those with the Ryukyu kingdom via the "Satsuma mouth"; and those with the Ezo via the "Matsumae mouth"[79] (see Map 5).

It is true that the degree of central control varied from "mouth" to "mouth." Centralization was most advanced at Nagasaki, which was administered directly by the Edo shogunate through a special magistracy; the other three "mouths," by contrast, were administered indirectly, through the mediation of local daimyo.[80] These differing administrative arrangements presumably reflected differences in the shogunate's priorities—the West (represented by Holland) and China were seen as more important than Korea, Ryukyu, or Ezochi.

Still, it is important to note that while the three "mouths" of Tsushima, Satsuma, and Matsumae were managed indirectly through local daimyo, these daimyo ruled by permission of the shogunate, and the rules of their interaction with the outside world were also determined centrally. To give just one example, the rules governing Matsumae's relations with the Ezo were specified quite precisely in a series of documents issued by Tokugawa Ieyasu and his successors.[81] If daimyo failed to observe these rules, they stood the risk of forfeiting their domains. For example, Sō Yoshinari nearly lost his position as

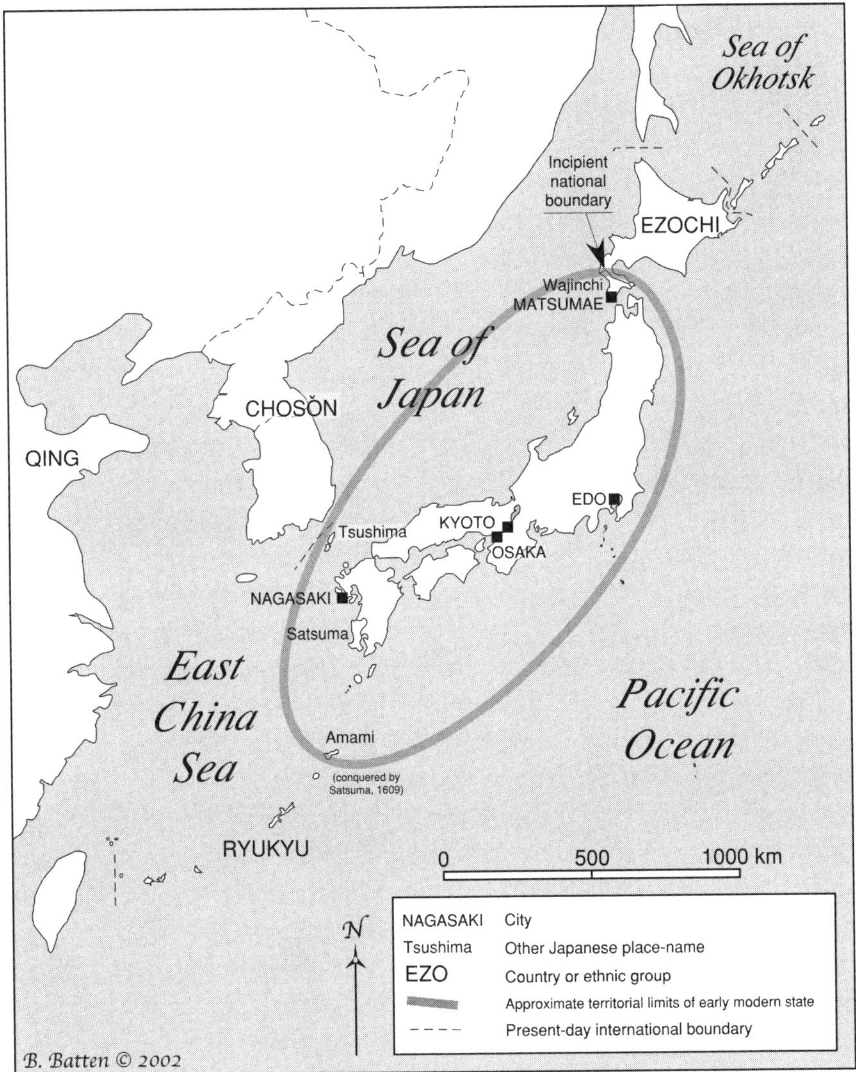

MAP 5. JAPAN IN THE EIGHTEENTH CENTURY.

daimyo of Tsushima in the 1630s when it was discovered that the domain had been involved in forging official letters of state.[82]

The reextension of central authority over frontier regions was also accompanied by a reduction in the volume of cross-border traffic. The term "closed country" *(sakoku)* has fallen out of favor among specialists, who rightly emphasize Japan's continued interaction with Asia during the early modern period.[83] Nonetheless, it is a fact that during of the Edo period the frequency and volume of foreign contacts declined from the levels of the late fifteenth and sixteenth centuries, when the vacuum of central authority had facilitated unimpeded traffic across the borders.[84]

Another related phenomenon was the emergence of fairly clear administrative boundaries, at least in southern Hokkaido, the site of Japan's only contiguous land border during this period. This trend can be identified as early as 1551, when a trade agreement between the Kakizaki (Matsumae) family, which ruled southern Hokkaido, and the Ezo chiefs to the north put an end to endemic warfare between the two and established a dividing line between their respective territories.[85] As in the case of *sengoku daimyō* domains in the interior, a state of continuous tension across a political (and in this case, also ethnic) border facilitated the formation of a relatively clear "boundary."

Later, the border between the Kakizaki family and the Ezo emerged as the "boundary" for Japan "proper" as part of the general process of political unification. The Kakizaki family were appointed lords of Matsumae, and the border between the "Japanese territory" (Wajinchi) under their rule and the Ezo lands to the north was defined quite precisely as the result of surveying activities during the 1630s. This boundary was clearly marked both on the ground, where barrier gates were established to control the flow of traffic, and on contemporary maps of Japan, such as the "Genroku Kuniezu" of 1702.[86]

The latter point is particularly important because this was the first time that mapmakers in Japan had given explicit attention to state boundaries. The Edo-period maps were *not* the first to depict Japan as a whole. Numerous so-called Gyōki-zu are known from the medieval period. The earliest surviving example dates from 1305, but the style of depiction is said (perhaps apocryphally) to derive from the mapmaking efforts of Gyōki, a peripatetic monk active in the early eighth century. All surviving "Gyōki-zu" follow roughly the same format; the various provinces of Japan are shown in outline, but no effort is made to depict a boundary for the polity as a whole. In these maps, "Japan" is no more, and no less, than a collection of bubblelike provinces, with no overall form or outline of its own (see Figure 1). In this sense, the Edo-period maps were truly revolutionary in concept.[87]

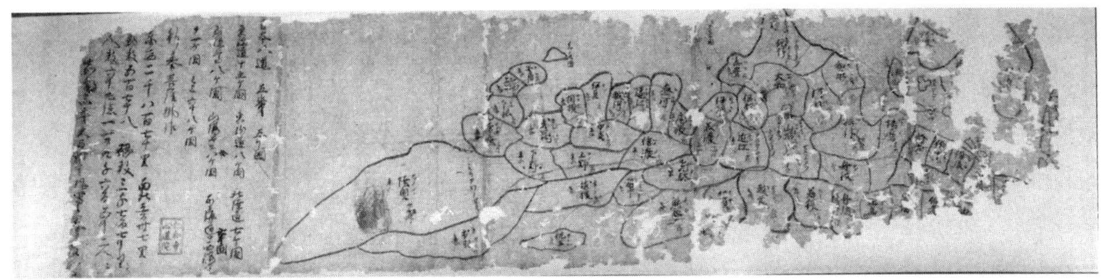

FIGURE 1. The earliest surviving "Gyōki-zu." Dated 1305; property of Ninnaji temple, Kyoto. Used by permission of Ninnaji temple.

In sum, the establishment of the unified Edo state was accompanied by a redefinition of Japan's place in the world on the basis of the "middle kingdom ideology"; a reassertion of central controls over Japan's frontier regions and boundary functions; a reduction in cross-border contacts of all kinds; and, in at least one case, the emergence of a well-defined political boundary separating "Japanese territory" from its external environment.

It is important to note, however, that the border in Hokkaido (and, of course, elsewhere) was not conceived as an absolute limit to Japanese authority, for the notion of territorial sovereignty remained unknown. The border merely represented the outside limits of the sphere of directly administered territory within the larger world order defined by the "middle kingdom ideology." Ezo territory was part of Japan's larger "world"—it just happened to be outside the borders of the domainal system of local government.[88]

Nor, on a more practical level, did the border act as a limit to the extension of Japanese influence and control into Hokkaido during the Edo period. As noted above, the shogunate specifically limited contacts with the Ezo to the single "mouth" of Matsumae. Matsumae's monopoly rights over trade with the Ezo led to egregious and pervasive exploitation; eventually, the whole of Hokkaido was turned into a virtual dependency of Matsumae.[89] (A similar phenomenon can be noted in the relationship of the Ryukyu kingdom to the lords of Satsuma, although there the dependency had been more explicit from the start as a result of Satsuma's military invasion of Ryukyu in 1609.[90])

At any rate, these developments paved the way for the next stage in the historical evolution of Japan's borders—the formal annexation of new territory and the establishment of a modern international boundary in the late Edo and Meiji (1868–1911) periods. In the last years of the eighteenth century, security concerns over Russian expansion, coupled with a desire for control over economic resources, prompted the shogunate to organize various exploratory missions to Hokkaido, the Kurils, and Sakhalin. Partly as a result, eastern Hokkaido was annexed by the shogunate in 1799, and the entire island was placed under direct central control between 1807 and 1821. Finally, in 1855, Japan's northern border was formally defined in the Russo-Japanese Treaty of Shimoda, which drew a line in the sea between the islands of Etorofu and Uruppu in the Kurils. This act of delineation, which created Japan's first modern political boundary, symbolizes the replacement of the old "middle kingdom ideology" by the new concepts of the nation-state and of geographically limited sovereignty.[91]

Frontiers and Boundaries of Premodern Japan

In discussing the territorial limits of premodern "Japan," it is necessary first of all to specify which "Japan" we are talking about. In this chapter I have focused on two different but related entities: Japan as a political or administrative entity, that is, a state; and Japan as an ideological construct, that is, a worldview.

Regarding the Japanese state, perhaps the most obvious conclusion to be drawn from this brief survey is that Japanese territory tended to expand over time. The first Japanese state, which emerged between the third and seventh centuries C.E., enclosed Honshu south of the Tōhoku region, Shikoku, and most of Kyushu. By the early nineteenth century, not only Tōhoku but also Hokkaido had come under Japanese control, as had the northern half of the Ryukyu chain. Okinawa remained under the control of the Ryukyu kingdom, but this was less an independent regime than a tributary of Japan. (In a fascinating example of dual political allegiance, the Ryukyu kingdom simultaneously maintained tributary relations with Qing-dynasty China.[92]) As I have argued, the expansion of Japanese political space reflects a generalized growth in social power—broadly defined to include organizational, technological, and economic/ecological factors—over the course of the premodern period.

Second, within this general trend, the rate of territorial expansion seems to have varied over time, with periods of rapid expansion followed by periods of slower growth (or even stagnation and/or fragmentation). In very broad terms, there seems to be an association between rapid outward movement of frontiers and periods of strong central government, for example, the Nara and early Heian periods. Periods of slower growth, by contrast, tend to be associated with weak or decentralized political regimes. It is important to note, however, that although the pace of expansion may have slowed, it never really came to a halt—with the possible exception of the "warring states" period, when "Japan" itself temporarily disappeared as a political entity. During times of political decentralization, the center, by definition, was weak, but the slack was often taken up by local rulers. Those near the border used their power to expand their own territories, which had the effect of increasing the size of "Japan" as a whole. As this example illustrates, what is important is not the power of the central government alone, but the sum total of power residing in the society, including both central and local components.

A third point regards the direction of expansion. Just as the rate of expansion varied over time, it also varied according to direction. In general, the Japanese polity tended to expand to the north and south; in the west, by contrast, little or no movement can be detected. The island of Tsushima, in the Korea Strait, represented Japan's western border in the eighteenth century, just as it had in the eighth. If territorial expansion reflects the general growth of Japanese power, then directional variation presumably reflects differences in physical or human geography. With regard to the former, it is probably true that expansion was easier along the north–south axis of the archipelago itself than across the ocean "barrier" between Kyushu and the Korean Peninsula. Nevertheless, the more important difference, I think, was in the nature of the societies Japan faced across these various borders. Indigenous societies in Hokkaido and the Ryukyus were relatively weak in comparison with Japan; those on the Korean Peninsula and other parts of the Asian mainland were not. (Again, for a more extensive analysis of the determinants of social power, see Chapter 10.)

Fourth and last, it is also necessary to consider the spatial characteristics of the borders themselves. Arguments by Giddens, Anderson, and others to the contrary, the borders of premodern polities were not uniformly vague. In the case of Japan, at least, they evidently ranged from classic "frontiers," at one end of the spectrum, to entities with many of the characteristics of "boundaries," at the other.

Frontiers could emerge under two different sets of conditions. First, in periods of weak government (i.e., the medieval period), the state lacked both the will and the ability to impose control over border regions, which thus frequently took the form of diffuse frontiers (e.g., Murai Shōsuke's "Pan–East China Sea Region"). However, frontiers could also emerge in periods of strong government when the state expanded into regions inhabited by less powerful neighbors. Good examples are northeastern Honshu and southern Kyushu during the ancient period. Such "frontiers of expansion" tended to be somewhat better defined and controlled than their counterparts in times of weak government, if only because the state acted as the driving force behind expansion and was actively involved in the creation of territorial administrative units.

At the other end of the spectrum were borders exhibiting some or all of the characteristics of "boundaries." They were more linear than zonal, were more "inner-oriented" than "outer-oriented," and acted more as "separating forces" than as "integrating forces." Good examples include the maritime border with Asia during the ancient period (which was not necessarily linear but *was* placed under strong centripetal controls through the Dazaifu) and the various borders of the early modern state, most especially the northern border with the Ezo.

Both the ancient state and the early modern state were characterized by relatively strong central government, but this was *not* a prerequisite for the emergence of political boundaries. The "Wajin-Ezo" boundary in southern Hokkaido, for example, first emerged in the mid-sixteenth century (a period of exceptionally weak government in Japan) as the result of local, as opposed to central, initiative.

But whether the impetus was central or local, boundaries (as opposed to frontiers) tended to emerge in times and places where (1) "Japanese" on one side of the border came into close contact with "foreigners" on the other; (2) competition between the two societies for territory or access to resources had reached a temporary (or permanent) stalemate; and (3) interest in regulating cross-border traffic was high. The establishment of the Dazaifu in the late seventh century as the direct result of a failed Japanese expedition to the Korean Peninsula is a perfect example of this;[93] the 1551 truce between the Matsumae and the Ainu chieftains in Hokkaido is another.

In sum, from a purely geopolitical point of view, the differences between premodern and modern national borders are not as absolute as is generally supposed. Although well-defined boundaries were uncommon in premodern times, they could still come into existence at certain times and places under the right set of circumstances. What changed with the emergence of the nation-state and the modern world-system was that these circumstances—a combination of state capabilities and perceived needs—became near-universal for the first time, with the result that boundaries, as opposed to frontiers, became the norm for interstate borders. However, this was a relative change, not an absolute one.

If there is an absolute difference between modern and premodern borders, it is not in the realm of geopolitical realities but in the realm of the imagination. Even in cases where premodern states (or local power-holders) formed relatively clear boundaries, they did so for practical reasons, and they did so in spite of, not because of, the prevailing political ideology.

As we have seen, a fully modern concept of territorial sovereignty was unknown in Japan prior to the end of the eighteenth century. Although geographic limits to state authority existed in an objective sense, subjectively such limits were seldom recognized. Japanese leaders did, of course, recognize the existence of other states and societies—they did not believe that Japan was in fact a universal empire. But—except perhaps in the medieval period, when a systemic breakdown of central institutions led to the emergence of an insular, circumscribed worldview—they did see Japan at the center of a "world" that included "subordinate" societies in Hokkaido, the Ryukyus, and (depending on the period) the Asian mainland.

Only in the nineteenth century, as the country was gradually incorporated within the modern world-system, was this graded, hierarchical notion of sovereignty finally abandoned. At that time, Japan's self-image was scaled down to match contemporary geopolitical realities, and the two "Japans"—the real and the ideal—were reconciled for the first time in the body of a modern, territorial nation-state.

2 "Race" and Culture

Japan as "Nation-State"

Political boundaries are important, but they are only one way of dividing up the world. People today are separated not only by circumstances of birth or citizenship but also by differences in culture, language, race, and ethnicity, to name but a few common categories. What relationship, if any, exists between political units and these other social categories? The answer is that although the territories claimed by states sometimes conform to the distribution of other social traits, the fit is rarely, if ever, perfect.

Take, for example, the "nation-state," said to be the fundamental unit in today's world. The nation-state represents a fusion between a political unit (the "state") and a social group (the "nation"). Is the fusion complete? Not according to political scientist G. P. Nielsson. In 1985, Nielsson compiled a "global taxonomy" of states and what he called "nation-groups," defined as "ethnic groups which have become politically mobilized on the basis of ethnic group values."[1] At the time of writing, Nielsson counted 164 political units and 589 nation-groups worldwide. No doubt these figures have changed since the 1980s, but not enough to affect the basic fact that there are many more ethnic groups than states in today's world. What this means is that most states contain more than one ethnic group. Among the 164 political units surveyed, Nielsson identified (1) 19 "multination-group states" (e.g., India, Malaysia, and Nigeria), with a high degree of ethnic fragmentation; (2) 21 "bination-group states" (e.g., Belgium,

Peru, and Fiji), where two major ethnic groups constitute more than two-thirds of the population; (3) 17 "one nation-group dominant states with fragmented minority groups" (e.g., the former USSR, the Philippines, and Sudan), where a single ethnic group makes up between 40% and 60% of the population; (4) 62 "one nation-group dominant states" (e.g., Britain, the United States, Nicaragua, Sri Lanka, and Zimbabwe), where a single ethnic majority makes up 60% to 95% of the population; and (5) 45 "single nation-group states" (e.g., Iceland, Japan, and Somalia), where the ethnic majority makes up more than 95% of the population.[2] As these figures clearly show, the fit between states and nations is a messy one at best. As Nielsson puts it, "the conventional concept of the nation-state fits only one-fourth of the members of the global state-system. For nearly one-half of the states in the world, 'nation-state' is a misnomer."[3]

Actually, Nielsson's findings probably overstate the degree of congruence between political units and underlying social realities. The reason is that, even in a "single nation-group state," ethnic boundaries are often highly ambiguous. This point is well illustrated by the case of Japan, often cited as a prime example of the modern nation-state.

Japan, while homogeneous by comparison with most countries, is still home to various minority groups.[4] The largest of these are the so-called Burakumin, an outcast group subject to hereditary discrimination. The total number of Burakumin is said to exceed 3 million out of the total Japanese population of 127 million.[5] The Burakumin are technically a caste, not an ethnic minority, but Japan also contains several of the latter. Numerically, the most important are the resident Koreans, referred to by scholars as "old-comers" because most are descended from forced laborers brought to Japan during World War II, when Korea was ruled by Japan. Some 635,000 Korean nationals, many of them second- or third-generation, live in Japan today. Japan is also home to about 1,051,000 other foreigners, most of them lured by the economic promise of the postwar years. Among these "newcomers," the largest contingents are from China, Brazil, and the Philippines.[6] These figures systematically understate Japan's ethnic diversity, given that some foreign residents, both Korean and otherwise, go on to take Japanese citizenship, thus disappearing from the official statistics on resident aliens. Also absent from official statistics are children of Japanese nationality born from the more than 20,000 international marriages that take place in Japan each year.[7] Finally, since the 1980s there has been a growing, although of necessity uncounted, underground population of illegal aliens.

In a sense most of these groups are irrelevant to a discussion of geographic boundaries per se, because they live dispersed within the Japanese islands. (Foreign nationals tend to settle in major urban areas and also in northeast Honshu; Burakumin communities tend to be located mainly in west-central Japan.) Of more interest for our purposes are the residents of areas now part of Japan that were formerly independent, and, conversely, areas now under foreign control but that formerly belonged to Japan.[8]

Good examples of both categories can be found in the north, that is, in Hokkaido, Sakhalin, and the Kurils. All of this land was foreign soil until the very end of the eighteenth century. Its native inhabitants, the Ainu, originally numbered perhaps 40,000, a figure that was reduced sharply by disease in the nineteenth century.[9] Approximately 24,000 people identify themselves as Ainu in Hokkaido today, although most are of mixed Ainu-Japanese descent and few, if any, speak Ainu as their native language.[10] But after a long period of near-obliteration at the hands of Japanese colonialism, Ainu ethnicity and nationalism are clearly on the rise again in Hokkaido today, giving the Ainu an importance beyond their mere numbers.[11] In 1997 the Japanese government enacted the "Ainu New Law" *(Ainu shinpō)*, recognizing the Ainu for the first time as a separate ethnic group and calling for the "promotion" and respect of their cultural traditions.[12]

Then there are the residents of Sakhalin and the so-called Northern Territories. Sakhalin was jointly occupied by Japan and Russia as a result of the 1855 Treaty of Shimoda, but Japan traded its rights there for the Kuril Islands in the 1875 Treaty of St. Petersburg. Japanese forces retook Sakhalin during the 1904–1905 Russo-Japanese War, and although northern Sakhalin was later restored to Russia, the southern part of the island remained a Japanese colony until it was retaken by the USSR after World War II. Japan's possessions in the Kurils—the "Northern Territories"—were also seized by the Soviets at this time.[13] The ethnic background of the inhabitants of all of these areas is quite complex; Ainu and other native indigenous groups are present, but so are the descendents of Russian colonial settlers. (Ethnic Japanese colonists and their descendents were all removed to Japan at the end of the war.[14])

To the south, the Ryukyu Islands present only a slightly less confusing picture. The Ryukyu kingdom emerged as a trade entrepôt in the fifteenth and sixteenth centuries, maintaining tributary relationships with China and, later, Japan, which came to exercise indirect control over the islands during the Edo period. Following the Meiji Restoration, the kingdom was forced to end its ties with China and then to relinquish its sovereignty in 1879. Under the name Okinawa Prefecture, the islands were administered as part of Japan until invaded by Allied forces at the end of World War II. In the postwar era, Okinawa was controlled by the U.S. military until 1972, when the islands were finally returned to Japan.[15]

Further examples could also be given. Aside from Sakhalin, Japan maintained many other colonies during the early twentieth century, including Korea, Taiwan, the Kwantung Territory, and the Pacific Islands. The total land area of these possessions was almost 300,000 km^2, corresponding to some three-quarters of the area of Japan itself. Japanese rule of these areas was, at least by historical standards, relatively brief (only a few decades) but has still left a complex ethnic and cultural heritage—children of mixed parentage, cultural and linguistic overlays, and confused identities—as well as a lasting aftertaste of mistrust.[16]

Finally, people of Japanese ancestry or citizenship have also settled overseas, both in the former colonial possessions and in other countries. During the late nineteenth and early twentieth centuries, many farmers in economically depressed areas of Kyushu and Okinawa emigrated to Hawaii to work in sugarcane plantations, and later, to Australia, Canada, Mexico, and Peru, among other destinations, to serve as laborers in agriculture and mining. During the 1930s, another wave of emigrants, both from the countryside and the urban elite, began to settle in Japan's colonial possessions in Asia.[17] In the postwar period, emigration has been more limited, but many Japanese nationals still reside overseas on a temporary or permanent basis. As of the year 2000, Japanese nationals living in other countries such as the United States, Brazil, and the United Kingdom numbered 812,000.[18]

Further examples could be given, but the point is clear: even in a "single nation-group state" such as Japan, social boundaries can be highly ambiguous. Are resident Koreans full members of the "Japanese" national community? Are the Ainu or the Okinawans? What about people of Japanese descent in the former colonial possessions or elsewhere? Obviously, it depends on whether "Japaneseness" is defined as a matter of citizenship or residence, or whether it is viewed as a matter of culture or language, blood or ethnic self-identification. In many cases, of course, there is no clear-cut answer, because people may have multiple identities: dual citizenship, mixed blood, the ability to speak two or more languages, bicultural family backgrounds, and complex, even self-contradictory self-images.[19] In sum, Japan may have relatively clear political boundaries—although even here, as I have argued, there are areas of contention—but as a social unit it is surprisingly hard to define. The harder one tries, the more difficult it is to draw a line around something called the "Japanese people."

If Japan's social boundaries are elusive today, what were they like in the past? I propose to examine premodern Japanese society from three separate but related perspectives: race, culture, and ethnicity. Of course, there are other important categories for understanding the nature of society, for example, gender. Of the various candidates, however, race, culture, and ethnicity seem particularly relevant to the topic of social boundaries, because of their strong territorial component.

All three of these concepts are notoriously hard to define. First appearing in the West, they were later imported to Japan, where during the nineteenth and twentieth centuries ideas of *jinshu* (race), *bunka* (culture), and *minzoku* (ethnic community or nation) fueled debates on Japanese national identity and Japan's role in the world.[20] In Japan, as well as in the West, the terms have meant different things to different people at different times, and even today no consensus exists as to their precise meaning or content. This is not to suggest that the concepts themselves are meaningless; quite the contrary. In what follows, I will define each term as it arises, in a way that best fits the overall flow of the argument.

Of course, it might be argued that applying essentially modern concepts to premodern conditions is meaningless, given that people at the time did not understand the world in these terms. Certainly, historians in Japan and elsewhere frequently do violence to the past by examining it through modern spectacles. To take just one example, the image of an ethnically homogeneous Japanese nation-state is frequently projected back into the distant past by scholars unable (or unwilling) to put aside their "commonsense," modern assumptions.[21] To avoid anachronisms like this, it is clearly important to rid ourselves of preconceptions and make an effort to understand our subjects on their own terms. And yet, I would argue, this is not enough, because the historian produces no "value added." To say something new about the past, we need to add new perspectives. Applying the concept (for example) of "ethnicity" to seventeenth-century Japanese society can provide such a perspective—even though the people living at the time would not necessarily have understood the terms of analysis. Of course, we should not imagine that our own analytical categories are necessarily "objective" or absolute. Far from it: they, too, are subjective, contingent products of the historical process.

With these caveats, I will attempt in this and the following chapter to draw some broad conclusions about the nature of social borders in premodern Japan. Instead of trying to present a comprehensive account with equal emphasis on all geographic areas, however, I have chosen to focus mainly on Tōhoku (northeast Honshu) and Hokkaido, drawing information from other regions only when necessary for comparison or discussion. The main reason for this choice is that the north has been much better studied than other frontier areas, primarily because of Japanese interest in the identity of its inhabitants, known variously as "Emishi," "Ezo," and "Ainu." (Another, intellectually less defensible reason is that I myself am better acquainted with the history of the north than with that, for example, of Okinawa.)

In terms of organization, the present chapter focuses on the topics of "racial" and "cultural" origins, and the following chapter focuses on "ethnicity." I have chosen this particular order for chronological reasons. In general terms, Japan's population achieved its present "racial" makeup prior to or concurrent with the emergence of recognizable "cultural" zones in the archipelago, which in turn predated the emergence of ethnic consciousness. The narrative of social boundaries in Japan is one of biological origins overlaid with cultural formations and capped with distinctive concepts of ethnicity.

"Race" and Biological Origins

Our first topic is race—a concept of tremendous importance for the history of the modern world, but also one that has been largely discredited by contemporary social science. As a concept, "race" refers to the idea that human beings can be readily divided into distinct groups or populations on the basis of physical (or genetic) characteristics. Various classifications were devised in the past, with the total number of human races being given as anywhere from four or five to several dozen. This very lack of agreement suggests that attempts to classify humans into racial categories are inherently subjective. Many scholars today would agree with Anthony Giddens that "human population groups are not distinct, but form a continuum."[22]

Nonetheless, the concept of race remains important because people continue to single out certain physical characteristics, such as skin color, as a basis for making value judgments about the supposed superiority or inferiority of one group of people as opposed to another. As Giddens puts it, "There are clear physical differences between human beings and some of these differences are inherited, but the question of why some physical differences, and not others, become matters for social discrimination and prejudice has nothing to do with biology. Racial differences, therefore, should be understood as *physical variations singled out by the members of a community or society as ethnically significant.*"[23]

Here, then, we are really dealing with two questions: First, what sort of physical or genetic differences exist between human populations? Second, how are such differences perceived by the groups involved or by others? For example, the racial identity of the Ainu has been the subject of much debate during the nineteenth and twentieth centuries, not only in Japan but also in the West. Although the debate is too complex to summarize here, one recurring theme has been the idea that the Ainu are racially distinct from the Japanese because they somehow "look different." In much of the older literature, the Ainu are described as being "hairy," or hirsute. This observation led many authors to conclude that the Ainu were not Japanese (or Mongoloid) at all, but rather "remnants of a proto-Caucasian people."[24] Whether the Ainu are or are not more hirsute than other residents of the Japanese islands is a biological question that can be answered empirically. By contrast, the question of why this particular characteristic has been viewed as significant, and more generally, why there is a tendency to view the Ainu as racially distinct from the Japanese, relates not to biology but to social definitions of Self and Other—that is, to ethnicity.

Of course, in practice, the biological and ethnic aspects are often hopelessly intertwined. Nonetheless, it makes sense to distinguish between them for analytical purposes. In the remainder of this section, I will touch briefly on the question of biological or genetic relationships, drawing on recent research in physical anthropology. Discussion of ethnicity will be postponed for the following chapter, after we have had a chance to review the topic of "culture."

The topic of biological variation within the Japanese archipelago has received much attention from physical anthropologists in Japan and elsewhere. Most of these studies involve comparisons of skeletal morphology among populations from different parts of Japan. Specifically, human bones from different regions are measured to obtain indices of cranial length and breadth, nasal height and breadth, facial height, body height, and so on. Studies based on modern skeletal material generally show gradations, or "clines," in measurable characteristics from west to northeast, with the residents of west-central Honshu representing one extreme and the Ainu of Hokkaido another. (A similar clinal variation is seen to the south, with the residents of Okinawa closely resembling the Ainu in physical type.) Similar clines have also been found in other characteristics, such as dental morphology, blood types, and the like. These variations presumably all have a genetic basis, and so it is gratifying to find that analyses of gene frequencies among Japanese populations also show a similar pattern of regional variation.[25]

Hanihara Kazurō, one of the principal investigators in this field, has compared this modern data with archaeological material from earlier periods. The result is what he calls the "dual structure model" of Japanese population history (see Figure 2). According to Hanihara,

Ainu (and Ryukyuan) skeletal morphology resembles that of Japan's earliest inhabitants, the "Paleomongoloids" who arrived mainly from Southeast Asia via the Ryukyu chain during the ice ages. (The earliest near-complete skeletons of this type belong to so-called Minatogawa Man, which was discovered in 1971 in Okinawa. "Minatogawa Man" has been dated to about 18,000 B.C.E.) These Paleomongoloids, who are associated with the Paleolithic (Pre-Ceramic) culture of circa 30,000–10,000 B.C.E. and the Jōmon culture of circa 10,000–400 B.C.E., were short in stature, with low, wide skulls and pronounced facial features.[26] A second wave of immigrants began arriving in northern Kyushu via the Korean Peninsula in perhaps the sixth century B.C.E. These northeast Asians, who introduced the Yayoi (400 B.C.E.–250 C.E.) culture of wet-rice farming to Japan, were relatively tall, with high, narrow skulls and flat faces. Over the course of a few centuries, their descendents spread throughout the archipelago, replacing the existing Jōmon population more or less completely in northern Kyushu, Shikoku, and western Honshu, but only partially in more distant areas. The result was the concentric distribution of physical (and genetic) types we see today, with northeast Asian (Yayoi) traits most common in west-central Japan and "archaic" (pre-Yayoi) traits most common in "peripheral" areas such as Hokkaido and the Ryukyus.[27]

If this finding is correct, we can conclude that there are, and have been since the Yayoi period, biological differences between the inhabitants of central Japan and the inhabitants of the far north (and south). However, this does *not* tell us anything about the presence (or absence) of genetic or anthropometrical *boundaries* in the Japanese islands. The simple fact, for example, that the average Ainu differs in appearance or genetic makeup from the average resident of Honshu is not sufficient justification for considering them to be of two separate biological groups. The real question is whether variation between the two extremes is continuous and smooth, or whether there is some sort of identifiable discontinuity or "boundary."

Interestingly, regarding this point, Hanihara argues that variation is more or less smooth, with one exception. Specifically, he finds discontinuities in stature, cephalic and facial morphology, and fingerprint and palm print patterns, as well as in blood types and genetic characteristics, between the residents of "western Japan" and those

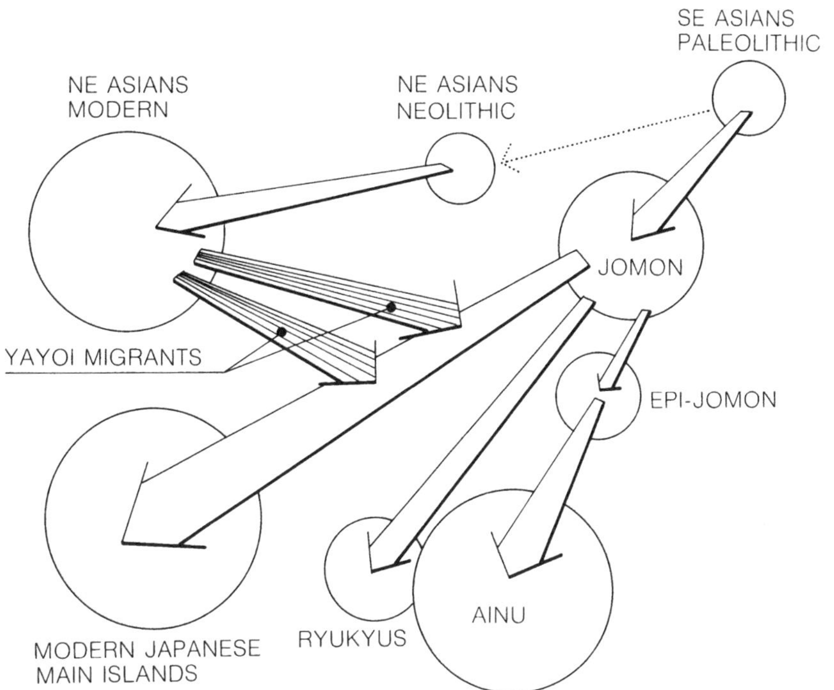

FIGURE 2. Schematic representation of Japan's population history. From Hanihara Kazuro, "Dual Structure Model for the Population History of the Japanese," copyright © 1991 by International Research Center for Japanese Studies. Used by permission of International Research Center for Japanese Studies.

of "eastern Japan." The boundary between these two groups (or regions) lies more or less at the Fossa Magna, a geological rift zone extending from Niigata Prefecture on the Sea of Japan coast to Shizuoka on the Pacific. Judging from Hanihara's explanation, the natural environment and ecological niches to the east of this line were more hospitable to Jōmon-style hunting and gathering than to Yayoi-style agriculture. The Fossa Magna thus served to temporarily slow the eastward spread of Yayoi culture (and the Yayoi people), leaving a permanent trace in the genetic map of Japan.[28]

According to Luigi Luca Cavalli-Sforza, "genetic distance between two populations generally increases in direct correlation with the geographic distance separating them."[29] However, the rate is not always constant; local discontinuities can be caused by obstacles to migration or marriage. These obstacles can be either geographic or cultural. Research in Europe, for example, has "found 33 genetic boundaries that corresponded in 22 cases to identifiable geographic features (mountains, rivers, seas) and almost always (in 31 cases) to linguistic or dialectic boundaries."[30]

Although Hanihara only discusses the Fossa Magna boundary, it is certainly possible that other, less pronounced genetic discontinuities exist or have existed within the archipelago—for example, between the Ainu (or the residents of southern Kyushu/Ryukyu) and "mainland" Japanese. Unfortunately, it is difficult to test this idea for the Ainu (or their ancestors), owing to the paucity of good skeletal material from Tōhoku/Hokkaido. The Goshōzan Cave site in Ishinomaki, Miyagi Prefecture, has yielded the remains of several individuals buried around 600 C.E. Interestingly, some of these have typical "Ainu" features, whereas others resemble skeletons of the Kofun period (c. 250–645 C.E.) from central and western Japan.[31] The significance of this finding is not totally clear, but at the very least it suggests people of different physical features and genetic background living in proximity to one another. Much better information is available from the other end of Japan, in southern Kyushu, where tombs of the Kofun period have yielded the remains of at least three hundred individuals. Interestingly, these remains seem to represent two distinct populations: a "Yayoi" type, who lived in floodplains and river valleys and are similar to modern Japanese, and a "Jōmon" type, who tended to live away from the coast, in the hills and mountains.[32] Whether the boundary between these two groups persisted or disappeared over time is unfortunately not clear.

In summary, although it is not meaningful to speak of a Japanese "race" or an Ainu "race," the population of the Japanese islands is (and has been) far from homogeneous in a genetic or biological sense. Body type and genetic makeup vary significantly by region, with archaic, "Paleomongoloid" features prevailing in the north and south, and newer, northeast Asian features prevailing throughout most of central Japan. In general, geographic variation is smooth, but there are also areas of discontinuity, notably in the Chūbu region of Honshu (the Fossa Magna) and, at least historically, in southern Kyushu and/or Tōhoku. In this limited sense it is meaningful to speak of distinct biological "populations" within the archipelago. The Ainu of Hokkaido may represent one such population.

"Culture"

Some of these points apply with equal force to our next topic, "culture." "Culture," like "race," is now a loaded word among academics, to the point that many of them would probably hesitate to speak of a distinct "Japanese" or "Ainu" culture at all. If by "culture" we mean a static, objectively defined set of traits or behavior patterns, then this hesitation is well justified. But there is no denying the existence of cultural traits per se or that such traits can and do vary systematically by region (as well as by social class and other factors). Cultural variation—like genetic variation—can be smooth and gradual, or it can be sharp and rapid. The greater the level of discontinuity, the more justified it seems to speak of cultural "boundaries" (or, at least, "borders") that separate adjoining cultural "zones" or "areas." Is it possible to identify such cultural features within the Japanese archipelago? As I will argue below, the answer is "yes."

First, though, we need to ask, "what is culture?" In the West, the concept of "culture" has been around since at least the mid-1800s, although, like other concepts, it has changed in meaning over time. In the nineteenth century, "culture" (or alternatively, "civilization") referred to those aspects of society that improved the quality of people's lives. Societies, or countries, were ranked on the basis of how far they had progressed up the cultural ladder, the top rungs of which, of course, were thought to be occupied by the European societies doing the ranking.[33]

Later, in the early twentieth century, a more "scientific" approach to culture was developed by Franz Boas and other anthropologists. This concept has been summarized as follows by Elvin Hatch: "Culture is the way of life of a people. It consists of conventional patterns of thought and behaviour, including beliefs, values, rules of conduct, political organization, economic activity, and the like, which are passed on from one generation to the next by learning—and not by biological inheritance."[34] Culture, in other words, is everything that is not biological in human society.

This definition of culture seems perfectly straightforward at first glance but reveals problems when subjected to scrutiny. If culture is "the way of life of a people," what is "a people"? Can they have only one "way of life"? Hatch's definition, in other words, seems to assume the existence of a relatively homogeneous, well-defined social group. Moreover, by emphasizing that culture is "passed on from one generation to the next," Hatch implicitly treats culture as something static. Finally, and perhaps most fundamentally, the definition seems to imply that culture is something that can be objectively described—that it has an independent existence that looks the same (or should look the same) to all observers.

These and other issues have recently driven anthropologists and other scholars away from the "scientific" approach to culture. Most anthropologists today would probably agree with Renato Rosaldo that "social analysts can rarely, if ever, become detached observers."[35] Theoreticians and critics in the new field of "cultural studies" take an even more radical position. At the risk of oversimplification, the central propositions of "cultural studies" are that "culture serves power, and that it is (and should be) contested."[36] In general, "high culture" is reviled as a tool of the ruling class; mass-produced culture is "condemned as ersatz, if not irremediably corrupt"; while popular culture receives favorable treatment for its potential to "subvert" or "delegitimize" the existing hegemonic order.[37] In a sense, "cultural studies" seek not so much to *describe* "what is" as to *prescribe* "what should be."

What implication do these trends have for the study of historical cultures? There seems little point in adopting a prescriptive approach toward history, but the more basic insight of "cultural studies"— that culture serves power—seems as applicable to past societies as to the present. It is also good to keep in mind the possibility that cultures, and societies, may be fragmented rather than monolithic, dynamic rather than static, and diffuse rather than distinct—and to acknowledge the limitations of our own, subjective point(s) of view. All of which is simply to say that culture—or "way of life," to retain the old working definition—is a complex topic requiring subtle treatment.

In what follows, I will attempt to describe the culture(s) of premodern Japan from three different perspectives—those of cultural anthropology, archaeology, and historical linguistics—and then draw some broad conclusions about the nature of cultural borders in the archipelago and their relationship to the political frontiers and boundaries discussed in Chapter 1.

"Civilizations" and "Culture Areas"

To discuss the topic of cultural borders, we first need a way of thinking about culture in spatial terms. As it happens, this is not so difficult. Cultural traits of all kinds—material culture, forms of social organization, language, ways of thinking—have spatial distributions that can be identified by anyone with the will, the time, and the resources to do so. For example, French is spoken most commonly in France itself, to a lesser extent in former French colonies, and to a still lesser extent in other parts of the world. Chopsticks are used to eat in East Asia, and less commonly elsewhere. Extended families are the norm in some societies but uncommon in others. Christianity has a global distribution but has made more inroads in some societies than in others.

These banal observations lead naturally to the idea that the world can be divided into different cultural zones or regions. The largest of these are what are commonly referred to as "civilizations." Many attempts have been made to enumerate or classify the world's civilizations. As noted by Samuel Huntington, authors differ considerably on the total number of historical civilizations, but there is broad agreement on the identity of contemporary civilizations. Huntington himself identities seven: "Sinic" (i.e., Chinese), Japanese, Hindu, Islamic, Western, Latin American, and (possibly) African.[38]

A more sophisticated scheme for classifying civilizations has recently been proposed by geographers Martin Lewis and Kären Wigen. Based on their recognition that cultural cleavages range from the "superficial to the profound," these authors propose a hierarchy of divisions. The most important division is between the supercontinent of Africa/Eurasia and everywhere else. Within Afro-Eurasia, there is a second-order division between the "ecumene" north of the Sahara Desert and areas to the south. In the "ecumene" itself, the most important division is between the "Confucian realm" of East Asia and areas to the west. The next most important "cut" is between "Greater India" (in religious terms, the sphere of Hinduism and Theravada

Buddhism) and Europe, North Africa, and Southwest Asia (the sphere of the "peoples of the book," i.e., Jews, Christians, and Muslims). Finally, within the latter area is a further subdivision between "Christendom" and Islam. This basic "taxonomy" of civilizations is complicated by the presence of other geohistorical formations. On the one hand, civilizations are transcended by religious and imperial "super-regions" resulting from conversion or conquest; on the other hand, their borders are straddled by various subregional communities of identity.[39]

Where does Japan stand in the "roster" of world civilizations? As noted above, Huntington regards Japan as a distinct "civilization" separate from that of China. Indeed, this view would seem to be the consensus of most civilization theorists, including the likes of Arnold Toynbee, Carroll Quigley, and Schmuel Eisenstadt.[40] For Lewis and Wigen, by contrast, any cultural divide between Japan and China is fairly low down on the hierarchy; in the maps in their book, Japan appears together with Korea and China as part of the East Asian sphere of civilization.[41] Without getting bogged down in discussion of definitions, this seems to me the more reasonable position. China, Korea, and Japan all share a common cultural heritage centered on Buddhism, Confucianism, and the use of the Chinese writing system.[42]

What I am really interested in here, however, is the distribution of cultures *within* the Japanese archipelago, and for this we need to look at things on a finer scale. At the risk of appearing hopelessly antiquated, I think the best tool for the job is the old concept of "culture area," defined as a "geographical region which encompasses a cluster of societies possessing similar customs and social institutions, or similar material culture."[43] The idea that culture has a spatial dimension and that given cultures occupy discrete geographic territories originally grew out of anthropological interest in North American Indian societies. The idea of the "culture area" was developed most systematically by Clark Wissler and, later, Alfred Kroeber.[44]

For the concept of "culture area" (or, at a larger scale, that of "civilization") to have any meaning, we must accept the premise that cultural traits vary in tandem, rather than separately. If there is no correspondence between, say, the geographic distribution of language and that of material culture, or, at a finer degree of resolution, between one aspect of material culture and another, then there is no point in discussing "culture areas." Cultural traits would vary independently, and "culture areas" defined on the basis of any one trait would bear little resemblance to those defined on the basis of other traits. Of course, disparities in the distribution of cultural traits are easy to find. No one would claim that all speakers of English, for example, or Spanish, share a common lifestyle or material culture. Conversely, people sharing a common cultural identity, such as the Swiss, may speak a variety of different languages. But does this diversity represent the exception, or the rule?

I will explore this question in more detail later, but for now it is sufficient to note that at least *some* cultural traits clearly do vary in tandem. To see why this should be so, we need to briefly consider the topic of historical origins. According to Ōbayashi Taryō, "culture areas" are usually defined on the basis of either "ecological" or "historical" factors.[45] This is a roundabout way of saying that cultural traits themselves are the product of environmental constraints, on the one hand, and historical contingency, on the other. On the environmental side, climate or soil type may influence the development of agriculture, which in turn may influence various aspects of social organization, material culture, etc. On the historical side, the exercise of political power may influence the spread of languages, elite cultures, and other traits.

In other words, cultural traits result from broad underlying forces that act simultaneously upon a wide range of human activities. As a result, we should not be surprised to find significant correlations in the distribution of some, although by no means all, cultural traits. For example, Spanish-speaking societies in today's world may vary in many aspects of material culture and lifestyle, but they also share a common cultural legacy in the form of Spanish colonialism. All of which is to say that some aspects of culture do not vary randomly but come in identifiable "packages." And to the extent that they do, it makes sense to talk about "culture areas" and "cultural borders" or "boundaries"—so long as we avoid reifying these concepts and investing them with greater significance than they deserve.

How can the "culture area" concept be applied to the Japanese case? Here we can do no better than to refer to the work of the abovementioned Ōbayashi Taryō, a cultural anthropologist who has written a number of books and articles on the subject. Ōbayashi has observed that culture areas may be defined at three different levels or scales. At the top end of the hierarchy are subdivisions of large continental areas such as pre-Columbian North America. Continental masses contain a variety of ecological zones and language families, each of which can serve as the basis for defining a culture area. Second, culture zones can be defined on the basis of ethnic or other distinctions within large but subcontinental areas, such as Brazil. Finally, at the smallest scale, regional variations can be used to define culture areas within countries such as Japan that share a common ecological setting and a common national culture.[46]

Much of Ōbayashi's own research focuses on the third scale, that is, on regional culture areas within the Japanese archipelago. For the modern period, Ōbayashi uses similarities and differences in material culture, social organization, and dialect to subdivide "Japan" into various cultural zones. The most important distinction, according to Ōbayashi, is between the culture of the Ryukyus and "Yamato" culture, that is, the culture of the "interior" *(naichi).* Ōbayashi locates the boundary between these halfway down the Ryukyu chain between the Tokara Islands and Amami Ōshima.[47] However, the Japanese "interior" can also be subdivided into various "culture areas." Depending on the criteria used, these include a "northern" versus a "southern" region; a "Pacific Ocean" region versus a "Sea of Japan" region; and "coastal" region versus a "mountain" region.[48] More important than any of these, however, is the division between "eastern" and "western" Japan.[49] Interestingly enough, the boundary between these two cultural regions, as defined by Ōbayashi, corresponds roughly to the Fossa Magna, noted above in conjunction with the skewed distribution of "racial" or genetic traits within the archipelago.

As this brief description suggests, Ōbayashi is basically arguing for the existence of a "multicultural Japan." But this does not imply that the concept of "Japanese culture" is meaningless; quite the contrary. To Ōbayashi, "Japan" represents a culture area at the next level of organization, one that incorporates the various regional cultures into a larger whole. Despite local variations, Japanese culture has an underlying unity, as well as identifiable geographic boundaries.

What are these boundaries? According to Ōbayashi, "Japan" as a culture area is bounded in the "northwest" (actually, the west) by the Korea Strait between Tsushima and the Korean Peninsula, and in the southwest by the ocean separating the Yaeyama Islands (at the southern tip of the Ryukyus) and Taiwan. In the northeast, the boundary is less clear, but "for the sake of convenience," it can be placed at the Tsugaru Strait between Honshu and Hokkaido. To the south of this line, culture is basically Japanese; to the north, it is (or was, since Ōbayashi is writing on the basis of ethnographic materials) basically "Ainu." Among the hallmarks of Ainu culture cited by Ōbayashi are the Bear Festival *(kumamatsuri)*, traditional motifs *(mon'yō)*, and epic poetry *(Yukar)*.[50] It is interesting to note that "Japanese" culture is here defined in a negative sense, by what it is *not* rather than what it is.

Ōbayashi has also tried to apply the idea of "culture areas" to premodern Japan. In a study of the Nara and Heian periods, for example, he again portrays "Japan" as a second-order culture area subdivided by several third-order regional variations. Perhaps not surprisingly, the zone of "Japanese culture" itself was smaller than today. To the northeast, the Japanese culture area was bounded not at Tsugaru but in the Tōhoku region of Honshu, where it came into contact with the "Emishi" culture zone. To the southwest, the Japanese culture area extended not to the Yaeyama Islands nor even to the Tokara Islands, but only as far as southern Kyushu, where it came into contact with the "Hayato" culture area. Both the Emishi and the Hayato spoke different languages from those of the Japanese and also had different material cultures. With these broad outlines established, Ōbayashi then goes on to identify regional differences in the Japanese interior on the basis of spoken dialects, patterns of land use, and folk memories as recorded in myth cycles. Three culture areas are identified: "eastern Japan," centered on the Kantō; "western Japan," centered on the Kinai area; and "Kyushu," centered on what are now Fukuoka and Saga prefectures.[51]

Ōbayashi states that whereas culture itself changes over time, the physical boundaries of culture areas tend to be relatively stable.[52] This is manifestly not true for the boundaries of the Japanese culture area as a whole (more on that later), but it may be true of the division between "western" and "eastern" Japan. Ōbayashi is not the only scholar to have noticed long-standing cultural differences between these two parts of the country. Historian Amino Yoshihiko, for example, has produced a book-length study on this topic, in which he describes differences in dialect; material culture as seen in archaeological artifacts; transportation and military technology (ships in the west, horses and bows in the east); land use (rice paddies in the west, dry-field agriculture in the east); marriage customs and kin organization; and many other features.[53] According to both Amino and Ōbayashi, the east-west split has existed since the Jōmon period. Presumably the reason is ultimately ecological, although for historical periods Ōbayashi also emphasizes that Japan has had two politico-cultural "centers," one in the west at Nara and then Kyoto, and the other in the east at Kamakura and then Edo (Tokyo).[54]

Completely missing from this discussion—and indeed, from most of the discourse on "civilizations" as well—is an awareness that not all cultural variation is necessarily spatial. In stratified societies—which means virtually all societies since the invention of agriculture—culture varies not only by region but also by rank or class. The "way of life" of the elite is very different from that of the common people. Indeed, according to Ernest Gellner, the primary role of culture in agrarian society is "to reinforce, underwrite, and render visible and authoritative, the hierarchical status system of that social order." He adds, "Note that, if this is the primary role of culture in such a society, it cannot at the same time perform a quite different role: namely, to mark the boundaries of the polity."[55] In short, the most important cultural boundaries are vertical, between classes, rather than lateral, between regions.

Gellner is certainly correct to argue that culture played an important (perhaps the most important) role in maintaining and reproducing power relationships between classes in premodern times. And it is also possible that spatial variation in culture is relatively unimportant *within* regions sharing a common class structure or social organization. Indeed, I think this was the case for Japanese society for most historic periods. Ōbayashi and Amino notwithstanding, the cultural differences between eastern Japan and western Japan paled in comparison to the similarities: people in both areas spoke Japanese, paid taxes to the same government, farmed the land using similar technologies, wore the same types of clothing, and shared similar religious beliefs. The futility of trying to identify meaningful "third-order" culture areas within Japan is, I think, evident from the fact that Ōbayashi himself has come up with several mutually exclusive schemes of classification.

But at the next order of magnitude, spatial boundaries were important, and it does make sense to speak of "Japanese" culture as something distinct from "Ainu" or "Ryukyu" culture. Culture reflected and reinforced power relationships within Japanese society, but those relationships themselves had a spatial component and identifiable geographic limits. Ōbayashi's "second-order" culture areas are not mere figments of his imagination; they did exist, and they were coterminous with large-scale regional differences in social organization within the Japanese islands. To see how these differences came into being, let us now turn to a discussion of archaeology and "archaeological cultures."

Three "Archaeological Cultures"

Archaeology today is a mature academic field with a large and growing body of theory. Although the idea that material remains can serve as a guide to the past is a very old one, archaeology as an academic discipline dates from the early years of the twentieth century. It was given its theoretical foundations by, among others, V. Gordon Childe, an Australian who spent most of his career in Britain. Childe introduced the idea of an "archaeological culture," which he defines as "an assemblage of artefacts that recur repeatedly associated together in dwellings of the same kind and with burials by the same rite." He adds that "the arbitrary peculiarities of implements, weapons, ornaments, houses, burial rites and ritual objects are assumed to be the concrete expression of common social traditions that bind together the people."[56]

Childe's ideas served as the basis for the "culture-historical" approach that dominated archaeology from the 1930s through the 1960s, when it was replaced by the so-called New Archaeology of Lewis Binford and David Clarke. Whereas the "culture-historical" approach was empirical in orientation, emphasizing the description and classification of artifacts, the New Archaeology was more theoretical, stressing the need to explain change and to recognize the processes by which it came about. "Processual" studies ultimately derived from

New Archaeology remain popular today, but during the 1980s and 1990s other schools came to the fore. Known as post-processual (or anti-processual) archaeology, these feature an emphasis on cognitive factors, the subjectivity of knowledge, and the possibility of (or rather, need for) diverse views of the past. In short, archaeology is becoming postmodern.[57]

These very recent developments have yet to make much of an impact on archaeology as it is practiced in Japan. Japanese archaeology has traditionally concerned itself with the typology of prehistoric sites and cultural complexes. The result has been the familiar division of Japanese prehistory into a series of successive cultures (Paleolithic, Jōmon, Yayoi, and Kofun), each defined on the basis of a characteristic assemblage of artifacts. Similar considerations have led to the identification of chronological and also regional subdivisions within each major cultural period. In recent years, the influence of the "New Archaeology" has been seen in the form of increased interest in spatial analysis and social processes. However, it is fair to say that most Japanese archaeology is still of the descriptive, "culture-historical" variety, if only because of the prevalence of "salvage" excavations conducted by local boards of education. In most cases there is enough time to excavate the site and (eventually) publish a site report, but not enough time for detailed theoretical studies of the material.

At any rate, the present state of archaeological research in Japan is highly conducive to the analysis of cultural borders. If anything, there is a glut of pertinent information. In what follows, therefore, I make no pretense of offering a comprehensive treatment of the subject. Instead, I will simply introduce some of the major issues and research findings relating to cultural borders, again with special reference to developments in northeast Honshu and Hokkaido. Much of the discussion is based upon the work of archaeologist Fujimoto Tsuyoshi, author of one of the most important books on the subject.[58]

The basic thrust of Fujimoto's work is that throughout most of premodern history the Japanese archipelago was divided into three distinct cultural zones: one in the north, one in the center, and one in the south. In this sense, Fujimoto agrees with Ōbayashi, but with an important twist: whereas Ōbayashi reserves the term "Japan" for the central zone, Fujimoto applies it to the northern and southern zones as well, which he refers to as "two other Japanese cultures." On the one hand, this represents a laudable attempt to refute the idea of a homogeneous "Japan." On the other hand, it is anachronistic, because the "Japan" to which Fujimoto refers is synonymous with the boundaries of the modern nation-state, whereas the cultures he describes are premodern. In a sense, referring to the cultures of the north and south as "Japanese" represents a (probably unconscious) attempt to deny them autonomy and incorporate them within the framework of "national history." Fortunately, however, this viewpoint does not detract from the empirical value of Fujimoto's work.

The division of the archipelago into three culture areas, while ancient, is not primeval. Japan's first archaeological culture, the Paleolithic (or Pre-Ceramic), is found throughout the islands and was more or less identical to contemporary Paleolithic cultures on the Asian mainland. During the Jōmon period, by contrast, a distinctive culture emerged, named for its characteristic "cord-marked" pottery. Significantly, the remains of Jōmon culture are distributed throughout the area of present-day Japan, including Hokkaido and Okinawa. It was only during the succeeding Yayoi period that this larger area came to be divided into three separate cultural zones.[59]

The reason for this division, of course, was the introduction of rice cultivation from the Asian mainland. Although wet-rice farming spread rapidly outward from its initial point of introduction in northern Kyushu, it never reached the full geographic limits of Jōmon culture. In the northeast, the spread of agriculture was limited by the cold climate. Rice farming was never attempted in Hokkaido and indeed even disappeared from the northern Tōhoku region of Honshu following initial attempts at cultivation in the Yayoi period. In the south, poor soils and unsuitable topography prevented the widespread diffusion of rice cultivation into southern Kyushu and the Ryukyus. Japan's tripartite cultural landscape, in other words, emerged as a direct result of environmental constraints.

Nor were the differences limited to food production. Because rice cultivation came to Japan as part of a cultural "package," associated technologies such as the production of Yayoi-type pottery and the use of bronze and iron also remained limited to the "central" culture area. Nor did the material culture of the succeeding Kofun period spread beyond the practical limits of rice cultivation. The giant tumuli that give the period its name, for example, are unknown from northern

Tōhoku and Hokkaido, on the one hand, or from southern Kyushu and the Ryukyus, on the other.

Turning now to further cultural developments in the north, the Yayoi and Kofun periods of Japanese prehistory saw the flourishing of what is called the Epi-Jōmon *(Zoku Jōmon)* culture in northern Tōhoku and Hokkaido. As the name suggests, the Epi-Jōmon basically represents a continuation of Jōmon culture. Common Epi-Jōmon artifacts include stone tools such as arrowheads, spearheads, knives, and axes, together with a distinctive type of Jōmon-derived pottery. The people who made and used these artifacts are thought to have been hunter-gatherers who subsisted mainly on salmon, deer, and vegetable foods such as lily bulbs and walnuts. Although Epi-Jōmon culture initially exhibited significant regional variation, it later became quite homogeneous, at least judging from the increasing standardization of pottery styles.[60]

Around the seventh century, the Epi-Jōmon culture gave way to another archaeological culture, known as Satsumon after its distinctive "brushed pattern" pottery. These patterns were made by scraping the surface of wet pots with the coarse edge of a wooden board. Aside from surface decoration, Satsumon pottery is basically similar in form to the Hajiki pottery found in the Tōhoku region. As this suggests, the Satsumon culture is thought to have formed as a result of influences from mainland Japan in the late Kofun or early historical periods. Other characteristics of Satsumon culture—the use of iron as opposed to stone tools; the construction of pit dwellings and the large, mounded tombs known as Hokkaido-style *kofun;* and the development of agriculture—also bespeak of important influences from the south. Although buckwheat and barley were apparently farmed even during the Epi-Jōmon period, the Satsumon culture was characterized by the cultivation of many other crops such as wheat, sorghum, foxtail millet, barnyard millet, Chinese millet, green gram, perilla, melon, adzuki bean, hemp, and perhaps even rice. However, farming merely supplemented traditional forms of subsistence such as hunting, gathering, and fishing, particularly of salmon.[61]

Appearing slightly later than the Satsumon culture is the so-called Okhotsk culture of northeastern Hokkaido. Typical Okhotsk artifacts, which begin to appear in the ninth century, include a distinctive type of pottery; tools made of iron, bone, antler, and stone; and representations of women, bears, whales, and seals carved in bone and wood. Copper belt buckles, bells, knives, and coins—all obviously imports from northeast Asia—have also been found in limited quantities. Okhotsk sites, typically located on the coast, consist of large pentagonal or hexagonal pit-dwellings found in association with midden deposits of fish and animal bones. The people who inhabited them are presumed to have had a mobile lifestyle spent mainly in pursuit of sea mammals. Whereas the Satsumon culture was born as the result of "Japanese" influences on the preexisting Epi-Jōmon culture, the Okhotsk is thought to have diffused from the north via Sakhalin. The Okhotsk culture disappears throughout most of its range in the twelfth or thirteenth century.[62]

During the thirteenth or fourteenth century, a new archaeological culture, generally identified with that of the ethnographically attested Ainu, begins to appear in Hokkaido. Ainu culture is thought to have developed from a Satsumon base as the result of infusions from the north (Okhotsk) and the south (Japanese). The most important type of pottery, known as *naiji doki*, is a type of pan with inner lugs used for suspension over a fire in cooking. Other artifacts include knives and harpoons made of bone and antler. Later, particularly from the seventeenth century, artifact assemblages come to include many imported goods from Japan, including ceramic dishes, lacquerware, and iron kettles, axes, and knives. As a result of these infusions, local production of ceramics eventually disappears entirely. Pit-dwellings, which are commonplace during the Satsumon period, also disappear from the record, presumably in favor of surface dwellings, which are difficult to identify archaeologically. The most commonly excavated Ainu structures are graves, ritual sites, and "forts," or *casi*. The ritual sites are thought to be associated with the "Bear Festival" *(iyomante)* and other "sending-off" *(monookuri)* ceremonies, which represent influences from the Okhotsk culture to the north. The *casi* are generally thought to be military in nature, but other uses—for example, as sacred places, dwellings, or sites for negotiations—have also been proposed. Ainu sites of all types are generally found clustered around river basins in Hokkaido. Like the Satsumon culture before it, Ainu culture was associated with a hunting-gathering lifestyle supplemented by the cultivation of some grains and vegetables. The association of Ainu sites with particular river basins is thought to reflect the overriding importance of salmon fishing in these people's lifestyle.[63]

Although, as noted, post-thirteenth-century sites in Hokkaido are generally referred to as "Ainu," in general there is little correspondence between most of the archaeological cultures and the "ethnic groups" that appear in the Japanese historical record. As we shall see in the following chapter, Japanese texts refer to the peoples of the north as "Emishi" through about the twelfth century and as "Ezo" (confusingly, written with the same ideographs) thereafter.[64] The term "Ainu" also appears in some early modern texts. Comparing this with the chronology of archaeological cultures reveals some glaring discrepancies. A single culture, the Satsumon, was referred to in Japan by two different names, "Emishi" and "Ezo," while on the other hand a single name, "Ezo," was used for at least two different archaeological cultures, the late Satsumon and the Ainu. (How the Okhotsk culture was referred to, if at all, is unclear.)

And these are just the chronological discrepancies. Another important question is whether there was a one-to-one correspondence between the ethnic names used in Japan and the geographic distribution of any of the relevant archaeological cultures. This is a very problematic contention, but one that has been accepted without question in most of the Japanese literature, which simply assumes, for example, that if eighth-century sources refer to "Emishi" and if some archaeological sites from this period can be ascribed to the "Satsumon culture," then all "Emishi" must have belonged to the Satsumon culture area, and all residents of the latter were "Emishi." This may have been true, but there is no justification for assuming it a priori.

Nevertheless, the archaeological record, as summarized above, certainly supports the idea that several culture areas coexisted within the Japanese archipelago throughout much of premodern history. And, at least in the north, it is also clear that the roots of this division were basically climatic.[65] Areas suitable for intensive wet-rice cultivation were populated by immigrant agriculturists and incorporated within the Yayoi and Kofun culture areas and, later, the culture area of early historical "Japan." Areas too cold for this purpose were incorporated, successively, into the Epi-Jōmon, Satsumon, and Ainu culture areas. Differences in climate led to differences in subsistence, which in turn led to differences in material culture.

Language, Culture, and Genes

What sort of culture areas emerge when we look at other criteria—for example, language? Are culture areas defined on the basis of language or dialect similar to those defined on the basis of material culture, or are there significant differences? What, if any, relationship exists between culture areas, however defined, and genes or biological populations?

To answer these questions it is necessary to make another foray back into prehistory to look at the origins of the Japanese language. Unfortunately, there is little agreement among specialists regarding the affinities and prehistory of Japanese. Here I will simply present what seems to be a fair consensus position based on my reading of previous research, with particular reference to the work of Mark Hudson.[66]

First, with regard to affinities, a few scholars (mainly Japanese) assert that the Japanese language is unrelated to any other language, but this is not true. Among living languages, Japanese is most closely related to Korean. Both of these languages, in turn, bear many similarities to the so-called Altaic languages of north and northeast Asia, including Turkic, Mongolian, and Tungus. Some scholars classify Japanese (and Korean) as members of the Altaic "phylum" and some do not, but the syntactic resemblances are too strong to deny. Unfortunately, the picture is complicated by the fact that Japanese also exhibits some Malayo-Polynesian affinities, mostly in the area of vocabulary.

The question, of course, is how to explain these various affinities. At present, the most plausible scenario is as follows. During the Paleolithic and Jōmon periods, the Japanese islands were populated by Paleomongoloids, at least some of whom came from Southeast Asia and spoke a language genetically related to Malayo-Polynesian. (Of course, it is not necessary to assume that a single language was spoken throughout the islands during this period. It is equally possible that a variety of different, although probably related, languages were spoken by the Paleolithic and Jōmon inhabitants of Japan.)

Later, at the start of the Yayoi period, the northeast Asian immigrants who introduced wet-rice agriculture, new styles of pottery, and the use of bronze and iron also brought with them a new language—Altaic or a derivative thereof. At this point, the same language was spoken both in the Korean Peninsula and among the immigrant population in Kyushu. Geographic isolation led gradually to linguistic divergence and the development of two separate languages, proto-Korean and proto-Japanese. On the Japanese side, the immigrants interacted with the native Jōmon population, resulting in their adoption of some Malayo-Polynesian vocabulary items. The same process may have occurred in reverse among the Jōmon population. In the end, however, the language (or languages) spoken by the Jōmon people died out; the language of the immigrants survived and evolved into modern Japanese.[67]

The reason for this, according to Hudson, has to do with differential rates of reproduction among the two populations. Immigrant genes and immigrant language were able to spread rapidly throughout the islands because an agricultural lifestyle permitted a far higher population density than the hunting-gathering lifestyle of the Jōmon people. Hudson's "subsistence/demography model" of language replacement is ultimately based on the research of archaeologist Colin Renfrew into the origins and spread of Indo-European. According to Renfrew, Indo-European was the language spoken by early agriculturists in Asia Minor; their high rates of reproduction account for the rapid spread of their lifestyle and their language to other parts of the "Old World."[68]

How, then, are we to account for other languages spoken in the Japanese islands, such as Okinawan and Ainu? The answer is, in precisely the same way that we can account for the "racial" features of these people. As noted previously, the genetic input of the Yayoi immigrants was strongest in the center and weakest in the periphery. In terms of biological affinities, the Okinawans and the Ainu are essentially Jōmon. Similarly, in terms of linguistics, the languages they speak bear the stamp of pre-Altaic ancestors. It should be noted, however, that this is truer in the case of Ainu than in that of Okinawan. Because of the relatively strong historical ties between Japan and the Ryukyus, Okinawan bears such a heavy overlay of Japanese that it cannot really be considered a separate language. Ainu, by way of contrast, is probably best considered a relict Jōmon language.[69]

The idea that language correlates strongly with "race," or at least genetic background, may raise eyebrows in some quarters, but it is fully in line with the latest research on biological and linguistic evolution. Actually, the idea that linguistic change goes hand in hand with genetic change goes back to Darwin, who wrote in *On the Origins of Species:* "If we possessed a perfect pedigree of mankind, a genealogical arrangement of the races of man would afford the best classification of the various languages now spoken throughout the world; and if all extinct languages, and all intermediate and slowly changing dialects, were to be included, such an arrangement would be the only possible one."[70] This hypothesis has been verified by Luigi Luca Cavalli-Sforza and co-workers, who have found an extraordinarily high degree of correspondence between genes and language. The explanation for this correspondence is simple: when people move, they take their language with them. But distance and isolation lead to changes in both language and gene frequencies, with the result that major fissions in the history of human movements are mirrored in both linguistic and genetic data.[71]

Of course, when people move, they may take not just their language but also their lifestyle—witness the role of the Yayoi people in spreading the material culture associated with farming from the continent to Kyushu and then from Kyushu to other parts of Japan. This being the case, it seems reasonable to expect that in very early times, the spatial distributions of biological "populations," languages, and other aspects of culture exhibited significant correlations. In such a situation, geographic "barriers," either to population movement per se or to the spread of a "way of life," would have resulted in the formation of "compound" social borders between populations that differed not only genetically but also in terms of language (or dialect) and material culture.

As noted earlier, there is a lack of good skeletal material from northern Japan, but at the very least it is possible to demonstrate a general correlation between language and material culture. During early historic times, as noted above, the residents of northern Tōhoku were part of the "northern," "non-Japanese" cultural zone as defined on the basis of Epi-Jōmon and Satsumon pottery and other artifacts. But we also know that these people spoke a "foreign" (from the Japanese perspective) language, one that was apparently ancestral to Ainu.

Of course, there is little direct evidence concerning the historical development of the Ainu language, not least because it was a spoken language rather than a written one. However, Japanese sources from the eighth century and later state clearly that the residents of northern Tōhoku and Hokkaido spoke an unintelligible language and that interpreters were required to communicate with them.[72] The sources also record the personal names of many Emishi, and these, too, are clearly non-Japanese (although they are written with Chinese characters used for their sound value).[73]

The best evidence of all for the ancient languages of the northeast, however, comes from surviving place-names. Scholars such as Yamada Hidezō have noted the presence of many Ainu-like place-names in northern Honshu. Many of these are recognized by characteristic suffixes such as "*-nai*" or "*-betsu*," both meaning "river" in Ainu. The distribution of these place-names is largely confined to the area north of a line drawn between Sendai, Miyagi Prefecture, on the Pacific side, and the Yamagata-Akita prefectural boundary on the Sea of Japan coast. According to Yamada, these place-names date from the time of the ancient Emishi.[74] This conclusion seems likely enough, although it must be recognized that place-names as such are essentially undatable without specific evidence from the historical record.

The "Fuzzy Zone"

The general association among genes, language, and material culture does not in itself imply the existence of sharp borders. As discussed in the section on biology, the question is rather the "slope" of the transition, which can be gradual, abrupt, or anything in between. As noted earlier in this chapter, there is no strong evidence for an abrupt "racial" transition, at least in the north. Nor is there evidence for any abrupt cultural transitions—if anything, quite the reverse.

Let me give some examples. In terms of material culture, the biggest difference between "Japanese" society in the south and the "non-Japanese" societies in the north is in the area of subsistence; the residents of central Japan were basically farmers (specifically rice farmers), whereas the peoples of the north were basically foragers. But in fact, as we have seen, cultures like the Satsumon were engaged in farming as well as foraging—indeed, ancient historical sources identify "field barbarians" *(den'i)* as well as "mountain barbarians" *(san'i)* among the inhabitants of the north.[75] On the "Japanese" side of the border, meanwhile, the spread of agriculture in no way put an end to hunting and fishing, which remained part of the "Japanese" lifestyle throughout premodern times. The differences between the two cultures were of degree rather than kind, and even if we think in terms of "predominant" lifestyle rather than absolute differences, we will find a broad zone of overlap, where farmers coexisted with foragers or where the same people were codependent on both patterns of subsistence.

How about the distribution of artifacts and structures? Virtually all classes of material remains, for all periods, tell the same story. A good example is pottery. Typical Yayoi-style pots or Kofun-style pots have a limited spatial distribution, which in the north overlaps substantially with that of their Epi-Jōmon and Satsumon counterparts. Japanese-style tomb mounds *(kofun)* become less common (and also less typical in style) the farther one travels to the north, rather than abruptly giving way to some other type of burial style. In short, there is a broad zone whose culture was neither "Japanese" nor "non-Japanese" but some combination of the two. Using the terminology developed in the previous chapter, we might call this a cultural frontier as opposed to a cultural boundary.

This same idea has been developed by Fujimoto Tsuyoshi, although he refers to the intermediate region as a "fuzzy zone" *(bokashi no chitai)* rather than a "frontier." According to Fujimoto, the "fuzzy zone" between Japan's "central" and "northern" cultures extended from northern Tōhoku to the Oshima Peninsula. In other words, it consisted of a broad swath of territory straddling the Tsugaru Strait between Honshu and Hokkaido. To Fujimoto, the "point of contact" between the two cultures

> . . . shifted according to historical period and, as the expression "fuzzy" indicates, cannot be clearly defined by a single line. When various elements of culture are considered, one finds irregularities . . . with some elements extending further north and other cultural elements extend-

> ing further south. There is also an ebb and flow according to period, in which temporary movements to the north or south are followed by a return to the original [location].[76]

This is an apt description, with one major problem: unlike Fujimoto, I do not believe that the "fuzzy zone" remained more or less stable throughout the premodern period. To the contrary, while retaining its "fuzzy" nature, it gradually moved farther north, from the Tōhoku area in prehistoric and ancient times, into Hokkaido during the medieval and early modern periods of Japanese history.

For example, northern Tōhoku was culturally alien to the Japanese during Nara and early Heian times. Nine hundred years later, in the Edo period, it had been thoroughly assimilated, as is clear from the poet Matsuo Bashō's record of his 1689 journey to "the deep north."[77] To Bashō, this area was distant, sparsely inhabited, and even lawless, but it was still Japanese—people spoke the same language, the same gods were worshiped at shrines, and the landscape was dotted with comfortingly familiar Buddhist temples. To experience a truly alien cultural landscape, a seventeenth-century Japanese would have needed to travel not just to Hiraizumi (the "apex" of Bashō's journey) but much farther north, across the Tsugaru Strait, through the Matsumae domain of southern Hokkaido, and into the lands of the Ainu.

Culture and the State

This raises some interesting and important questions: How was this cultural "frontier" related to Japan's *political* frontier, which also moved northward during this same time frame? Was Japan as a state the same as Japan as a cultural region? Did an expansion in state power lead to the spread of Japanese culture, or vice versa?

The first point to make here is that cultural borders clearly emerged before their political counterparts. During Yayoi times, the introduction and spread of rice cultivation led to the emergence of an identifiable culture area throughout most of Kyushu, Shikoku, and Honshu, although of course there were regional variations. But politically this area was far from unified, and no state existed anywhere in the archipelago, only (presumably) a number of tribes or perhaps chiefdoms.

As noted in Chapter 1, scholars disagree as to when the first state appeared in Japan, with some arguing for the third century, others for the fifth, and still others for the seventh. In addition, scholars disagree as to whether there was originally one state, Yamato, which eventually expanded, or a group of several regional states, which were eventually incorporated by Yamato.[78] These doubts are symbolized by the varying interpretations given to the "Japanese"-style tomb mounds known as *kofun:* Does their widespread distribution indicate merely a common elite culture, or does it have political implications? If the latter, does the presence of *kofun* in a given area indicate control by Yamato or merely some degree of political influence?

There is no easy answer to these questions, but it is worth noting that the northern limit of *kofun* construction is more or less the same as the southern limit of proto-Ainu place-names—the line between Sendai on the Pacific Coast and the Yamagata-Akita prefectural line on the Sea of Japan[79] (see Map 6). This makes a great deal of sense, because the cultural divide reflected differences in subsistence, and the accumulation of wealth necessary to support the construction of *kofun* would have been lacking among the hunting-gathering communities of the north. To the south, however, agricultural surpluses would have facilitated not only the construction of *kofun* but also the formation of a ruling class (whose tombs they represent) and the emergence of a political apparatus, whether independent or subordinate to one degree or another to Yamato. Although this might be criticized as "environmental determinism," food production played an important role in the emergence of state societies worldwide, and there is no reason to doubt that this was also the case in early Japan.

These conjectures are strengthened by evidence from the early historical period, where documentary sources ease the task of distinguishing between political features and purely cultural ones. As discussed in Chapter 1, the extent of the provincial-district system of administration can serve as one proxy for the territory of the early historical state. The borders of this system are never clear, however, and it is possible to identify several zones between the area under full state control and that fully outside it. For this reason, scholars interested in the limits of state control have often chosen to focus on the

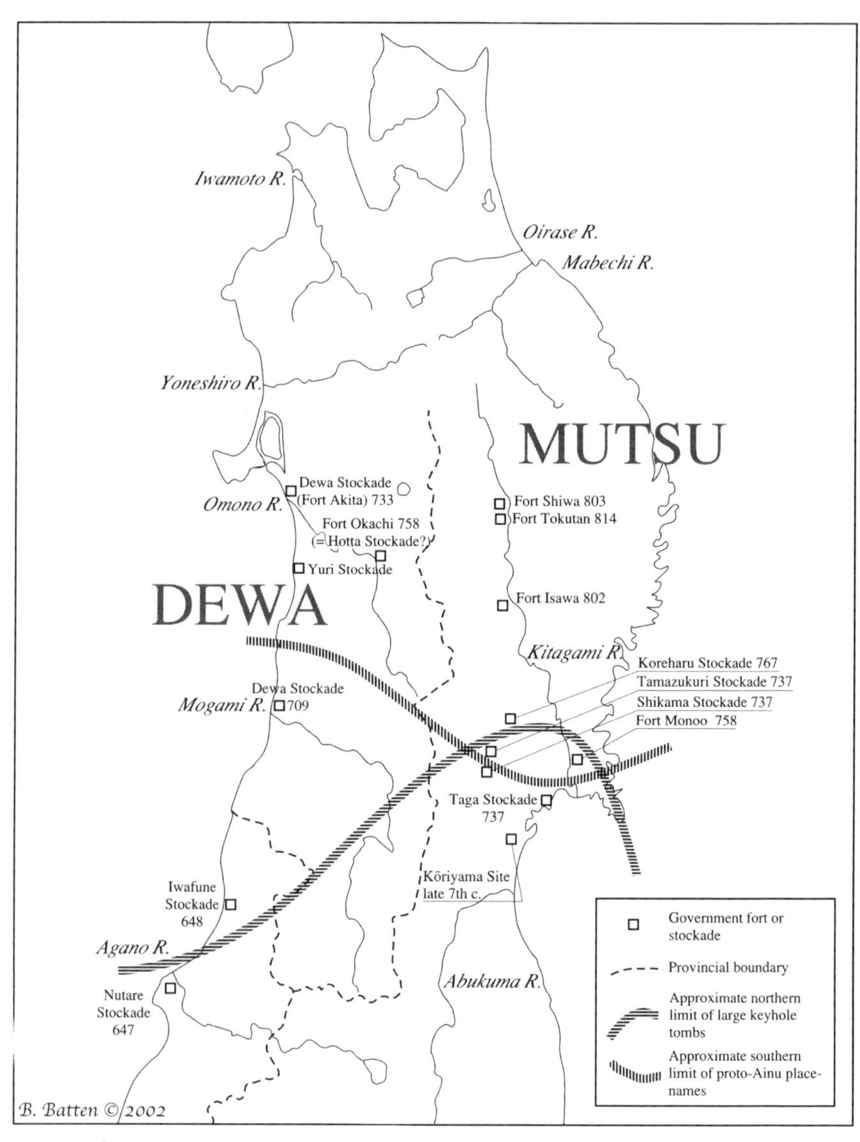

MAP 6. CULTURAL AND POLITICAL BORDERS IN ANCIENT TŌHOKU. BASED IN PART ON KUDŌ MASAKI, *KODAI NO EMISHI*, P. 44.

line of forts and stockades known collectively as *jōsaku*. These were colonial outposts used by the court as bases for military expansion. Significantly, the first *jōsaku* (dating from the late seventh and early eighth centuries) were built along the line marking the northern limits of *kofun* construction—which is to say they were built along the preexisting cultural frontier between Japanese-speaking farmers in southern Tōhoku and proto-Ainu-speaking hunter-gatherers in northern Tōhoku.[80] Political frontiers, in other words, were determined by cultural divisions, rather than vice versa.

During the subsequent Nara and Heian periods, however, this equation was reversed. As described in Chapter 1, during the eighth and ninth centuries the court pursued an aggressive policy of military expansion in the northeast. The line of active stockades marking the political frontier moved ever farther north, and in its wake followed waves of Japanese sodbusters. Surviving Emishi either moved north or, more often, stayed behind and were assimilated. Some indigenous leaders were given Japanese surnames and titles and served in government armies or as functionaries in district offices. (Culturally assimilated Emishi were known as *fushū*—literally, "captives"—and during the Heian period many of them were resettled in various provinces in the Japanese interior, where they formed ethnic enclaves that were eventually absorbed within the surrounding populations.)

As a result of these policies, the zone of Japanese culture moved northward, this time playing catch-up to the political frontier. But the process was slow—Satsumon pottery, for example, continued to be manufactured and used in northern Tōhoku well after this region was politically incorporated by the Japanese state. Even during the late Heian period, the culture of this area was not purely "Japanese" but rather a hybrid, where Buddhism and poetry mixed with "barbarian" customs and pedigrees. This juxtaposition of "Japanese" and "Emishi" cultural traditions was nowhere more evident than at Hiraizumi, the capital of the "northern Fujiwara" family who controlled northern Tōhoku in the twelfth century.[81]

Next, during Japan's middle ages, the relationship between politics and culture was reversed again. As described in Chapter 1, Japanese political influence spread into southern Hokkaido during the Kamakura and Muromachi periods. But at the same time, "Japan" itself became increasingly decentralized, eventually fragmenting into a host of independent, warring "statelets." Even during this "warring states" period of the late fifteenth and sixteenth centuries, however, the zone of Japanese culture remained largely intact—although as variegated and ill-defined as ever. At this point there existed a large culture area occupied by many competing polities—a situation much like that in the Yayoi period (with the exception that no true "state" or "states" existed at that time), but very uncharacteristic of Japan's historical experience as a whole.

What happened after this can be seen as a partial replay of events during the late prehistoric and early historic periods: when political unification came on the agenda again in the late sixteenth century, the borders of the emerging Japanese state were rapidly "pushed out" to meet the limits of the preexisting area of Japanese society or culture. This situation was very much like that during the initial period of state formation in Kofun times. The difference was that, unlike the ancient state, the Edo polity temporarily ceased to expand after reaching these cultural limits. Throughout the seventeenth and eighteenth centuries, the political and cultural borders between "Wajin" and Ainu remained fixed (and essentially identical) in southern Hokkaido. This situation changed only at the end of the Edo period, when fear of Russian encroachment and interest in the development of Hokkaido's natural resources prompted the shogunate to annex the entire island. Finally, during the subsequent Meiji period, a new cycle of colonization and assimilation resulted in Hokkaido's nearly complete incorporation within the Japanese cultural sphere.

This very brief account suggests two general conclusions about the relationship between political and cultural frontiers in the Japanese islands (or at least in the north). First, it is evident that these two things are by no means identical. At many times in Japan's history the territory claimed by the state has been much larger than the actual zone of "Japanese" culture. At other times the reverse was true, and no single political authority could claim jurisdiction over all the lands inhabited by the Japanese "people." Second, political and cultural frontiers have nonetheless evolved in tandem, exhibiting many of the same movements and historical trends. Political expansion paved the way for cultural assimilation, and vice versa.

3 Ethnicity

What Is "Ethnicity"?

The relationship between political and cultural boundaries may seem complicated enough, but it is necessary to take our analysis one step further: no study of boundaries would be complete without a consideration of ethnicity. What does it mean to refer to a Japanese "ethnic group" or "ethnic community"? Like other Western concepts such as race and culture, the idea of the ethnic group, or Volk, was imported into Japan in the Meiji period. During the late nineteenth and twentieth centuries, the idea of a Japanese ethnic group, or *minzoku*, came to play a large role in official, scholarly, and popular discourse. However, the meaning of the term was never clearly defined. To some people, "ethnicity" was a matter of blood: the Japanese people were defined by racial purity and common descent. To others, "ethnicity" was a creation of the nation-state: the Japanese were of mixed origins but united by a common history.[1]

Nor is this confusion unique to Japan or the Japanese language: in other countries, too, some people think of ethnicity in biological or racial terms, whereas others view it as a historical or ideological construct. I believe the latter approach to be more fruitful, and it is the one I will adopt here. Ethnicity, as the term is used here, is a matter of common identity, not common blood. In this sense, ethnicity is really a subset of culture. My reason for devoting a separate chapter to ethnicity is its highly subjective nature. Ethnicity is something felt by the individual, not something that can be independently verified by outside observers, like the "objective" cultural markers discussed in the last section. The presence of such markers may be a necessary condition for the emergence of ethnicity, but it is not a sufficient condition. Ethnicity is a matter of identity.

How does ethnicity emerge historically within a given population? This question has been addressed in countless studies by political scientists, anthropologists, and sociologists. For Japan, too, there is a substantial literature, with the current "state of the field" defined by the work of archaeologist Mark Hudson.[2] In this chapter, I intend to go over much of the same territory as Hudson, but from a rather different perspective—that of political science, not anthropology. Specifically I intend to apply the analytical scheme proposed by Anthony Smith to the Japanese case.[3] Smith's approach is useful because of the distinctions he draws among three stages in the emergence of ethnic consciousness: the "ethnic category," the "ethnic community" and the "nation."

Ethnic categories, by Smith's definition, are "human populations whom at least some outsiders consider to constitute a separate cultural and historical grouping." Smith continues, "But the populations so designated may at the time have little self-awareness, only a dim consciousness that they form a separate collectivity." In some cases, indeed, they may have no such consciousness at all, because "local identities of kin, village or region were often more important."[4] To put it another way, Smith's "ethnic categories" are the same thing we have been calling cultures: populations that can be "objectively" defined by third parties on the basis of shared language, material culture, or lifestyle.

This may also be true for the next stage, that of the "ethnic community" (or *ethnie*), but here we are dealing not just with objectively shared traits but also with a subjective sense of shared identity. According to Smith, "ethnic communities" have six main attributes:

1. a collective proper name
2. a myth of common ancestry
3. shared historical memories
4. one or more differentiating elements of common culture
5. an association with a specific 'homeland'
6. a sense of solidarity for significant sectors of the population[5]

As Smith notes, most of these traits are highly subjective. Even the relatively "objective" ones, such as the fourth, are important because of the diacritical significance with which they are endowed, that is, because they are taken to serve as markers of ethnic identification. To Smith, ethnic communities are not primordial entities but are formed as the result of historical circumstances and contingencies. Among the circumstances leading to the crystallization of ethnic identity, he states, "state-building, military mobilization and organized religion appear to be crucial."[6]

"Ethnic communities," according to Smith, are also to be distinguished from "nations." Smith defines "nation" as "a named human population sharing an historic territory, common myths and historical memories, a mass, public culture, a common economy and common legal rights and duties for all members."[7] On the surface, this looks very much like the definition of *ethnie*, the main differences being presence of a mass public culture and equality before the law. Smith (like most authors) argues that the nation is a purely modern phenomenon, and he is at some pains to shows that premodern ethnic states such as ancient Egypt, Greece, and Israel cannot have been nations, because their societies were fragmented along regional or class lines and lacked a unifying public culture.[8] To put it another way, a sense of ethnic community existed, but it was neither monolithic nor all-pervasive. In the modern nation, by contrast, most or all members of the population share a common sense of identity. The nation, in the memorable words of Benedict Anderson, is a pervasive "imagined community" of like-minded citizens.[9]

Before applying Smith's analytical framework uncritically to the Japanese case, it is perhaps useful to note some problem areas with this approach. First, Smith's is a "stage" theory of history, like the idea that political organization inevitably progresses from "bands" to "tribes" to "chiefdoms" to "states,"[10] or the idea that economic "modes of production" begin with foraging and go on to farming and then capitalism. All of these schemes envision a continuous, linear chain of progress from earlier, simpler forms of organization to later, more complex ones. It is certainly true as a generalization that, in most regions of the world, social organization has become more complex over time.[11] However, it does not follow that society in any given region necessarily goes through every single "stage" in precisely the same sequence. The question of continuity also deserves attention; Smith finds the origins of many contemporary nations in premodern ethnic groups, but many other researchers see a politically driven break between the two. In this view, nations are artificial creations based on "invented traditions," only tenuously derived from the pre-existing ethnic or cultural substrate.[12]

A larger problem with stage theories, and especially with Smith's model of ethnogenesis, is their failure to consider spatial (as opposed to temporal) variation in society. Foraging (or nomadism) may be not just a prelude to farming but a type of regional "specialization" complementing or existing in symbiosis with nearby agricultural societies.[13] In other words, if one looks at a broad region rather than a single "point," these differing lifestyles may evolve in tandem, rather than sequentially. Perhaps the same is true of Smith's "ethnic categories," "ethnic communities," and "nations."

A related issue, this time specific to Smith's analysis, is that of scale. Just how large does an identity group have to be to qualify as an "ethnic group" or a "nation"? Words like "homeland" and "historical territory" suggest that Smith is thinking of rather large social units, but this needs to be made explicit if we wish to exclude smaller units, like clans or villages, whose members may well share a common "identity," from consideration as "ethnic communities" or "nations." One reasonable criterion is suggested by Benedict Anderson's concept of the nation as "imagined community." To Anderson, a nation is *by definition* so large that "members of even the smallest nation will never know most of their fellow-members, meet them, or even hear of them, yet in the minds of each lives the image of their communion."[14] The idea of a group too large to allow for direct acquaintance between all individual members would also seem to be a useful refinement to Smith's definition of *ethnie.*

Japanese Ethnicity: A Historical Overview

The Japanese *Ethnie*

The above points notwithstanding, Smith's model does fit the Japanese case quite well. Residents of the "central," or core, area of Japanese culture constituted an "ethnic category" from the start—by definition, given that they shared (to a large extent) a common ancestry, a common material culture (albeit one divided by social class), and a common language. However, a sense of common identity as "Japanese" was not present until around 700 C.E., and then only among elite members of society. This *ethnie* evolved substantially over time, eventually forming the core of the Japanese "nation," which emerged at the end of nineteenth century.

Because there are no reliable indigenous sources on society in the Yayoi and early Kofun periods, we must turn to contemporary Chinese accounts, such as the justly famous *Wei History*. This text provides a third-century description of the "land of Wa," said to be located in the "mountainous islands to the southeast of Taifang."[15] The passage describes the geography, customs, political institutions, and history of Wa, which the Chinese evidently recognized as a discrete social unit. The scope and "territory" of Wa are never precisely defined, and so it is possible—even likely—that it was not wholly congruent with our "central" zone of culture. This is interesting because it illustrates that even "ethnic categories" are subjective, depending on the viewpoint (and knowledge) of the observer. In any case, the more important point I wish to make is that the *Wei History* contains no evidence that the residents of this region had a common sense of identity or belonging. The name "Wa" itself is of Chinese origin (C. Wo), and the only local names given are those of constituent political units—"countries" *(kuni)* in the terminology of the *History*—bearing names such as Matsura, Ito, Na, and, most famously, Yamatai. Judging from the passage, residents of Wa may have identified with their particular "country" but not with any larger ethnic group. The situation reminds one nothing so much as of native populations of the "New World" at the time of Columbus, peoples who were grouped together as "Indians" by white newcomers but who themselves perceived only local affiliations and identities.

When did an "ethnic community" first appear in the Japanese islands? There is a good deal of debate about this in the Japanese literature, but probably a majority of scholars would opt for the late seventh and eighth centuries, when a centralized, or semicentralized, state was created in response to a perceived threat from abroad. This view is well represented by Ōbayashi Taryō, who was discussed in Chapter 2 with reference to his view on culture. According to Ōbayashi,

> a large-scale armed conflict with a foreign people such as was experienced by the Japanese on the occasion of their defeat in the battle of Hakusukinoe [Paekchon River] in the mid-seventh century would have doubtless engendered an awareness of "We Japanese." The change in the name of Japan to be used for external purposes from "Wa" to "Nihon" and the birth of general histories such as the *Kojiki* and *Nihon shoki* all bespeak the establishment of a new ethnic identity. This we consider to have coincided with the final emergence of the Japanese people.[16]

The *Kojiki* and *Nihon shoki* are important not only because of the founding myths they record, which imply some sense of common identity, but also because of the descriptions they provide of the Emishi, the Hayato, and the various Korean kingdoms. These descriptions tend to be highly ethnocentric, suggesting the existence of some sort of Japanese self-image against which these "others" could be (unflatteringly) compared. Take, for example, this famous passage from the *Nihon shoki* (720 C.E.), which purports to describe the habits of the Emishi:

> Amongst these Eastern savages the Yemishi are the most powerful, their men and women live together promiscuously, there is no distinction of father and child. In winter they dwell in holes, in summer they live in nests. Their clothing consists of furs, and they drink blood. Brothers are suspicious of one another. In ascending mountains they are like flying birds; in going through the grass they are like fleet quadrupeds. When they receive a favour, they forget it, but if an injury is done them they never fail to revenge it. Therefore they keep arrows in their top-knots and carry swords within their clothing. Sometimes they draw together their fellows and make inroads on the frontier. At other times they take the opportunity of the harvest to plunder the people. If attacked, they conceal themselves in the herbage; if pursued, they flee into the mountains. Therefore ever since antiquity they have not been steeped in the kingly civilizing influences.[17]

Note the interesting parallel between this eighth-century Japanese worldview (based, ultimately, on the Chinese "middle kingdom" ideology) and nineteenth-century Western ideas of "culture." In both cases, societies were ranked according to their degree of cultural accomplishment. The Emishi, it would seem, failed to make the grade—

at least when judged against the Japanese self-image, which forms the necessary, although unstated, background to this description.

Assuming the emergence of a sense of Japanese "identity" in the seventh or eighth century, how far did it permeate society at large? Although this is a moot point, given the dearth of relevant source material, my view is that in the Nara period the sense of "we Japanese" was essentially limited to members of the central and local ruling elite. We know that the imperial family and other members of the central aristocracy had a more or less unified vision of state and society. This is clear from their role in creating a new, centralized state structure, in renaming the country "Nihon," and in authoring the *Kojiki* and *Nihon shoki*, which served as repositories for a "myth of common ancestry" and "shared historical memories." One could also plausibly argue that powerful families in the provinces "bought in" to this vision; according to Joan Piggott, for example, the spread of literacy and Buddhist culture throughout Japan in the Nara period shows that local elites were successfully incorporated within a "historical hegemonic bloc" centered on Nara.[18] At lower levels in society, it seems likely—although there is no evidence either way—that most people had little consciousness of being ethnically "Japanese." They were bystanders, rather than active participants, in the emergence of the Japanese *ethnie*.

If these speculations are true, Nara-period Japan is a classic example of what Anthony Smith has referred to as a "lateral" *ethnie*, so termed "because it was at once socially confined to the upper strata while being geographically spread out to form often close links with the upper echelons of neighboring lateral *ethnies*." Smith notes, "As a result, its borders were typically 'ragged', but it lacked social depth, and its often marked sense of common ethnicity was bound up with its *esprit de corps* as a high status stratum and ruling class."[19] Buddhism, writing, and the other elements of "high culture" that bound elites throughout the archipelago into a "hegemonic bloc" were also, of course, precisely the things that bound these elites to their peers in China and Korea—and precisely the things that separated them from low-ranking members of their own society.

Smith contrasts such "lateral" *ethnies* to another type, referred to as "vertical" ethnic communities. In the "vertical" *ethnie*, ethnic culture "tended to be diffused to other social strata and classes." According to Smith, "Social divisions were not underpinned by cultural differences: rather, a distinctive historical culture helped to unite different classes around a common heritage and traditions, especially when the latter were under threat from outside. As a result the ethnic bond was often more intense and exclusive, and barriers to admissions were higher."[20]

I would argue that the history of the Japanese *ethnie* after its inception in the Nara period was a history of transition from the original "lateral" type to something close to the "vertical" one. Specifically, during the Heian through Edo periods of Japanese history, we find (1) a gradual increase in ethnocentrism among elite elements in society, coupled with (2) a tendency for these ideas to diffuse outward and downward throughout Japanese society as a whole.

First, regarding the gradual increase in ethnocentrism among the elite, whereas the evidence for ethnic self-consciousness during the Nara period is at best indirect, that from the Heian and later periods is quite clear. After around 900 C.E., as noted in Chapter 1, the central elite became preoccupied with ideas of "purity" and "pollution," which were reflected in their increasingly circumscribed, inward-looking worldview. As Ishigami Eiichi, Murai Shōsuke, and others have shown, these changes resulted at least partly from problems on the foreign front, particularly in relations with Silla.[21] Diplomatic relations with Silla broke down toward the end of Nara period, but contact between the two countries remained close as a result of private trade. However, during the ninth century, Korean pirates began to conduct raids in northern Kyushu, encouraging xenophobic sentiments among the central elite (and also, presumably, among the residents of Kyushu). As Murai notes, this xenophobia was reinforced by other events of the late ninth century: pirate attacks from other directions (the "Southern Islands"), uprisings on the eastern frontier, and an outbreak of "coughing sickness" thought to have been transmitted by envoys from Parhae.[22] More generally, xenophobic tendencies were probably linked to the progressive weakening of Japan's central government, which rendered policymakers less willing and able to respond positively to internal and external threats.[23]

At any rate, these changes were all associated with increased ethnic consciousness. One excellent example is the Japanese monk Jōjin

(1011–1081), who made a pilgrimage to Song China in 1072. According to Robert Borgen, Jōjin's diary contains much evidence of his sense of "national identity." Jōjin's pride of country is evident throughout the diary, particularly in the record it makes of Jōjin's interview with the Song emperor, during which the monk was at pains to emphasize the divine origins of Japan's imperial family and the size and population of his country. Jōjin's sense of identity is perhaps best symbolized by the name he gives to his country—*Dainipponkoku*, or "Great Country of Japan" (a term that makes its first appearance in the historical record in 1046, just twenty-six years before it was adopted by Jōjin).[24] Incidentally, "Dainipponkoku" is just one of several new terms for Japan that appear in Heian sources: others include "Honchō ("this land," or more literally, "this court"); "Fusō" (a term for Japan borrowed from one of the Chinese dynastic histories); and "Shinkoku" ("land of the gods").[25]

The last of these terms, of course, is of the greatest importance in later Japanese history. In 1274 and 1281, Japan was invaded by the Mongol empire. The failure of both attacks was attributed to the "divine winds" *(kamikaze)*, which arose to destroy the Mongol fleets. These events, of course, served to reinforce the idea that Japan was a divine land protected by the gods—an idea that survived into the twentieth century, when it was co-opted by the Japanese government for propaganda purposes during World War II.[26]

By the sixteenth century, when Japan was first visited by Europeans, ethnic consciousness was quite firmly entrenched, at least among the elite. This is attested by the voluminous records left by these new foreign visitors. Consider the following statements:

> They look down on all other nations. (Cosme de Torres, S.J.)

> The Japanese have a high opinion of themselves because they think that no other nation can compare with them as regards weapons and valour, and so they look down on all foreigners. (St. Francis Xavier)

> The inhabitants of Japan, as men that never had greatly to do with other nations, in their Geography divided the whole into three parts, Japan, Siam, and China. And albeit the Japans received out of Siam, and China, their superstitions and ceremonies, yet they nevertheless contemn all

other nations in comparison with themselves, and standing in their own conceit do far prefer themselves before all other sorts of people in wisdom and policy. (Luis Frois, S.J.)[27]

Of course, the exaggerated sense of ethnocentrism seen in these statements was in part stimulated by the arrival of the Europeans themselves.[28] In this sense, the sixteenth century may represent one of the most important landmarks in Japanese ethnogenesis. And although direct contacts with Europeans decreased in volume after the imposition of the exclusionary acts of the early seventeenth century, knowledge about the West continued to filter in through the Dutch settlement in Nagasaki—particularly after 1720, when the eighth shogun, Tokugawa Yoshimune, lifted the ban on foreign books. Interest in astronomy, medicine, and other "Dutch learning" *(Rangaku)* and "Western learning" *(Yōgaku)* reached a peak in the late eighteenth and early nineteenth centuries.[29] Western knowledge was valued more for its "practical" use than its philosophical implications, but the specter of the European "Other" certainly played an important role in shaping Japanese images of "Self" throughout the Edo period.

A growing sense of ethnic identity is clearly evident in the realm of philosophical discourse.[30] The dominant intellectual trend in the early Edo period was undoubtedly Neo-Confucianism, which was used to legitimate the Tokugawa regime and, more generally, the privileges of the samurai class. Rather than accept Chinese teachings at face value, however, Japanese scholars were active in developing "nativized" or "universalized" versions of Confucianism. Hayashi Razan (1583–1657), Kumazawa Banzan (1619–1691), and Yamazaki Ansai (1618–1682), for example, attempted to identify Shintō with Confucianism. Yamaga Sokō (1622–1685), meanwhile, universalized Confucian values to argue that in terms of wisdom, humanity, and valor, Japan was in fact superior to China, deserving the title "Middle Kingdom" *(chūka)* on its own. Later, in the eighteenth century, these various trends culminated in the school of thought known as "Japanese learning" *(Wagaku)* or, later, "national learning" *(kokugaku)*. *Kokugaku*, most famously represented by the work of Kada no Azumamaro (1669–1736), Kamo no Mabuchi (1697–1769), Motoori Norinaga (1730–1801), and Hirata Atsutane (1776–1843), argued that alien Chinese teachings should be discarded in favor of Japanese values.

Closely related to "national learning" was Mitogaku, the nativist school of learning associated with Tokugawa Mitsukuni (1628–1700) and his intellectual successors, whose emperor-centered view of history was reflected in the multivolume *Dai Nipponshi* (History of Great Japan). Considered as a whole, these ideas represent an assertion not only of intellectual independence from China but also of ethnic identity on the part of Japanese scholars. From the perspective of ethnogenesis, they thus represent the culmination of trends first set in motion in the Nara period. And at the same time they also laid the basis for the modern Japanese nationalism of the nineteenth and twentieth centuries.

This brings us to the second point, namely the gradual diffusion of ethnic self-consciousness throughout society at large. In the Nara period, as we have seen, only the central elite and some members of the local aristocracy were full "members" of the Japanese *ethnie.* By the Edo period, however, this was no longer true. Ethnic consciousness was no longer limited to a few isolated "dots" but had diffused outward until it was common in most parts of the country; meanwhile it had also spread downward to ever lower levels in society. The well-known scholars of the Edo period, for example, came from all parts of Japan: Kumazawa Banzan, Yamazaki Ansai, and Kada no Azumamaro were from Kyoto; Yamaga Sokō, Kamo no Mabuchi, and Motoori Norinaga were from provinces located along the Pacific coast of eastern Honshu; and Hirata Atsutane was from Dewa in the far north. And although many of these scholars were born into the ruling samurai class, others were not: Kada no Azumamaro and Kamo no Mabuchi were the sons of Shintō priests, and Motoori Norinaga was from a merchant family. Also, some of these individuals had hundreds or thousands of disciples, again representing many different regions and social classes. The ideas of Hirata Atsutane, for example, were introduced to the imperial court, to various daimyo domains, and to commoners in towns and villages across Japan. This was made possible, in part, by the diffusion of literacy throughout society in the Edo period.[31]

By the eighteenth century, at any rate, Japan had become a "vertical" *ethnie*—a society with a well-developed sense of ethnic identity shared not just by members of the ruling class but also by a significant fraction of the population. But it was not yet a modern "nation." The difference is one of degree, but it is nonetheless crucial. In the eighteenth century, most residents of the archipelago probably thought of themselves as "Japanese," but this was only one of many possible identifications, and by no means the most important. Class affiliations, bonds of loyalty or service, village or domainal identifications, and blood ties—all of these would likely have played a more prominent role in daily life than some abstract sense of nationhood.[32] In a modern nation-state, such is no longer the case. Individuals continue to identify themselves in many ways, but the relative importance of national or ethnic identity has tremendously increased.

The Japanese "Nation"

When did the Japanese *ethnie* become a "nation"? A full discussion of this question would require a book in itself, but as a broad approximation it is safe to say that the transition occurred in the late nineteenth and early twentieth centuries.

At the end of the Edo period, Japanese ethnic consciousness was further stimulated by the (re)arrival of the western powers and the half-forced opening of the country. The result was a form of xenophobic proto-nationalism symbolized by the slogan *sonnō jōi*—"revere the emperor, expel the barbarian." Samurai, courtiers, members of religious orders, and commoners all became increasingly frustrated with foreign demands and the shogunate's inability to resist them. These frustrations ultimately took concrete form in the destruction of the Tokugawa regime and the "restoration" of the emperor to power in 1868.[33]

Following these revolutionary events, Japan's new leaders—a coalition of samurai and courtiers rallying around the new Meiji emperor—initiated a vigorous program of "modernization." Their vision of a new Japan was symbolized by three new slogans: *fukoku kyōhei*, or "rich country, strong army"; *shokusan kōgyō*, or "encouraging industry"; and *bunmei kaika*, or "civilization and enlightenment."[34] Japan, in other words, was to be re-created in the image of a modern Western nation-state. The Meiji leaders were largely successful in achieving this goal—although not immediately.

Many of the specific institutional reforms of the early Meiji period had the effect of eliminating social barriers and therefore homogenizing the patchwork of regional cultures and class differences characteristic of Edo society.[35] The old daimyo domains were dismantled and replaced by a centralized system of prefectures bound together by a network of railroads and post offices. The old status system was abolished, making most of the country's residents equal (at least in theory) before the law. These reforms had the effect of reducing (although hardly eliminating) regional and class loyalties.[36]

Further social homogenization—as well as a growing sense of national identity or "Japaneseness"—was achieved though the introduction of mass public schooling and universal military conscription. The education system, in particular, was used to disseminate the idea that Japan was a "family state" held together by the presence of an unbroken line of divine emperors.[37] The emperor's personification of the Japanese nation was also brought home through the invention of an elaborate "tradition" of state ritual and pageantry.[38] As a result, residents of Japan came to share a common (if perhaps skewed) view of their country's history, contributing to the growing sense of national identity.

Although most of these developments were initiated by the government, an emerging mass media also played an important role in disseminating ideas of "nationhood." Particularly significant in this regard were the journals *Kokumin no tomo* and *Nihonjin*, founded, respectively, in 1887 and 1888. The role of newspapers was also important; although newspapers had been published in Japan since 1861, it was only during the late 1880s that they began to attract a mass audience.[39] According to Benedict Anderson, the emergence of "print capitalism" plays an indispensable role in the creation of the "imagined communities" known as nations;[40] this would certainly seem to be the case in Japan as well.

These developments laid the foundation for the growth of Japanese nationalism during the final years of the nineteenth century and the early years of the twentieth. Nationalist sentiments, fanned by the newspapers, found their initial expression during the Sino-Japanese War of 1894–1895 and the Russo-Japanese War of 1904–1905. If any single decade marks a turning point in the emergence of the Japanese "nation," it is the 1890s.[41]

To briefly continue the story to the present, nationalism reached a peak during the 1930s and 1940s, when the Japanese military, acting in the name of the emperor, pursued fascist policies at home and imperialist expansion abroad. After the war, military nationalism essentially disappeared, but as many authors have observed, cultural nationalism remained. One of the most interesting examples of this is *Nihonjinron*, or "theories of the Japanese," which enjoyed great popularity during the 1970s and 1980s, partly as a by-product of national pride engendered by Japan's postwar economic success.[42]

Ethnogenesis on the Periphery

Core-Periphery Interactions and "Tribalization"

Although in the past it was commonplace to treat ethnogenesis as an internally driven process, this is no longer true. The consensus among anthropologists today is that ethnic consciousness often arises as the result of interactions between regions or societies. As David Chappell puts it, "In many cases, it is precisely contact with strangers that awakens communal identity by testing it against the competition."[43] Sometimes, this interaction is between roughly equal societies; perhaps more often, it is not.

Consider the origins of Japanese ethnicity, as described above. The Japanese, as an ethnic group, came into being over a period of many centuries, partly as the result of internal developments, but also as the result of interactions with the outside world in the form of Chinese civilization (and its derivatives in Korea) and, later, the West. The image being presented here is one of a relatively inchoate social group on the periphery of a larger, more advanced civilization, achieving ethnic identity as the result of stimulus from or, more precisely, interactions with the center. This is the ethnic equivalent of the political process known as "secondary state formation," where the appearance of a primary state (e.g., China) often results, through a process of interaction and emulation, in the formation of other, "secondary" states on the periphery.[44]

In this section I will argue that a similar process on a smaller scale occurred within the Japanese archipelago itself. Specifically, developments in the "core" area of Japanese society served as a stimulus to the formation of "non-Japanese" ethnic groups in peripheral areas to the north and south. This idea is by no means original. Archaeologist Mark Hudson, in his recent study of ethnogenesis in the Japanese islands, has argued:

> [A] variety of core/periphery systems—political and ideological as well as economic—were . . . present in ancient Japan. As it grew in power, the Yamato state began to define a system of ethnic relations whereby ethnic differences in the Inland Sea core region were played down to emphasize state unification, while ethnic differences with the non-Yamato periphery were stressed to provide further justification for Yamato expansionism. The latter process in turn appears to have led to heightened ethnic solidarity in those regions that actively opposed incorporation by Yamato.[45]

Later, around 1200 C.E., the "Ainu cultural complex" emerged in Hokkaido as a result of continued core-periphery interaction, this time on a more local level. Specifically, Hudson argues that "[i]n economic terms, in the early medieval era northern Tohoku can be seen as an autonomous periphery of the Kinai and Hokkaido as an attached periphery of north Tohoku." Ainu ethnicity, according to this model, was (at least partly) a consequence of increased trade between Hokkaido and powerful military leaders in northern Tōhoku.[46]

In the account that follows, I will make use of Hudson's insights in combination with another key concept, that of "tribalization." To give some brief background of this idea, one interesting result of recent anthropological studies is that historically known "tribal societies" are not necessarily pristine relics of a time gone by; rather, the process of "tribalization" (or in our terms, ethnogenesis) may have been stimulated from above and outside by the emergence of the European world-system in the relatively recent past.[47] Europeans coming to other parts of the globe *created* tribes by imposing European expectations, and political and economic needs, upon native societies. Only later did these partly artificial tribal identifications come to be internalized by the natives themselves. This idea, of course, throws into question generations of work by cultural anthropologists, who studied contemporary "primitive societies" for clues as to how our own ancestors lived in prehistoric times. If the new theories are right, however, this is not possible: historically known tribal societies were themselves recent creations of the expanding European world-system, not primordial relics from the past. "Stone Age" New Guineans are not really from the Stone Age at all.

Actually, this process is not unique to the expansion of the European world-system in recent centuries. As R. Brian Ferguson and Neil L. Whitehead have argued, it can occur and has occurred whenever one society expands or extends its influence into surrounding territories (provided, of course, that these are inhabited). According to these authors, "the frequent effect of such an intrusion is an overall militarization; that is, an increase in armed collective violence whose conduct, purposes, and technologies rapidly adapt to the threats generated by state expansion." Ferguson and Whitehead refer to the site of this activity as "the tribal zone" because "the wider consequence of the presence of the state is the radical transformation of extant sociopolitical formations, often resulting in 'tribalization,' the genesis of new tribes."[48] It can be argued that these authors overplay the role of war in ethnogenesis, but the larger point—that ethnogenesis is a frontier process that results from the interactions between groups—rings true.

These ideas have particular relevance to the emergence of ethnic groups on the Japanese periphery. As I will argue, we cannot automatically assume that the people in the northern (or southern) part of the archipelago always had a distinct "non-Japanese" sense of identity—in fact, we cannot automatically assume that they had an ethnic identity at all. Ethnic consciousness eventually emerged, to be sure, but only after a centuries-long process of interaction (much of it violent) with the core Japanese ethnic group (and state). Here again, as in previous sections, we will deal primarily with the peoples to the north—the "Emishi," the "Ezo," and the "Ainu"—with the understanding that with sufficient space, a similar story could be told for the peoples of southern Kyushu and the Ryukyus.

Emishi

Regarding the Emishi, as already noted, there is a vast scholarly literature on these early residents of Tōhoku/Hokkaido. According to a recent historiographical survey by Kaiho Mineo, most of these works fall into one of two categories: those that attempt to identify the Emishi with a particular ethnic group *(tokutei setsu)*, and those that do not *(hitokutei setsu)*.[49]

The first category of works can be further broken down into those that identify the Emishi as "Ainu" and those that identify them as "Japanese." Important proponents of the "Emishi = Ainu theory" *(Emishi Ainu setsu)* were the prewar scholars Kita Sadakichi and Kindaichi Kyōsuke. Kita mustered historical sources and archaeological findings in support of his view that the early residents of northern Honshu were related to the Ainu, while Kindaichi came to the same conclusion on the basis of linguistic arguments. Important proponents of the "Emishi = Japanese theory" *(Emishi Nihonjin setsu)* include postwar scholars such as Niino Naoyoshi and Itō Nobuo. According to Itō, the Emishi were just "backward" Japanese people who happened to live on the "periphery" *(henkyō)*.[50] Needless to say, all of these works, no matter which side they take, are flawed by their tendency to assume that modern categories such as "Ainu" and "Japanese" can be meaningfully projected back into the eighth century—the old fallacy of essentialism.

The second category of works, by contrast, tends to characterize the Emishi in political, not ethnic, terms. The "Emishi = Frontier Peoples theory" *(Emishi hōmin setsu)* popularized by the postwar scholar Takahashi Tomio portrays the Emishi as "*henmin*" or "*hōmin*," that is, residents of the "periphery" or "frontier." Although the terminology is similar to that used by Itō, the meaning is quite different. According to Takahashi, "Emishi" was simply a political term used by the court to refer to hostile people on the frontier, regardless of actual ethnic or racial affiliations.[51]

The "Emishi = Frontier Peoples theory" contains important seeds of truth, but it is not the final word on the subject. One problem with the theory is that eighth-century Japanese courtiers did not, in fact, make clear distinctions between what we would call "political" categories and "racial," "cultural," or "ethnic" ones. As is clear from the *Nihon shoki*'s description of the Emishi, quoted earlier in this chapter, all of these concepts were lumped together in their minds. Nonetheless, most Japanese writers on the subject have now lined up behind Takahashi, and it is generally agreed that "Emishi" should be understood as a political designation used by Japanese rulers for unincorporated peoples on the frontier.

Note, however, that this is not the same as saying that people referred to as "Emishi" had no ethnic identity. Indeed, proponents of the "Emishi = Frontier Peoples theory" often assume that they did. Some authors, like Itō Genzō and Torao Toshiya, argue that the Emishi as a group contained both people who were ethnically Japanese and people who were ethnically Ainu. Other scholars, such as Takahashi himself, have recently come to stress the "Ainu-like" character of the Emishi.[52] These authors thus also fall into the essentialist trap of mapping modern ethnic distinctions onto eighth-century realities. But even scholars who recognize the historical, contingent nature of ethnicity continue to use the old vocabulary to describe these residents of the north. A good example is Itō Jun, who argues that the only thing holding the Emishi together was state ideology—while at the same time referring to them as *iminzoku*, "a different ethnic group."[53]

The only relevant question here is how the northerners thought of themselves, and unfortunately there is not much to go on in this regard except the names by which they are called in Japanese historical sources. (There are, unfortunately, no native sources, because literacy was late to come to the north.) Here we are actually dealing with two separate issues: the ideographs that appear in the source materials, and the phonetic values that they were intended to represent.

Early Japanese sources used a variety of ideographs to refer to the northerners, but the most common name is a two-character combination meaning, literally, "shrimp barbarian." Kikuchi Tetsuo argues that this compound was read as "*kai*," which according to him, was the approximate sound value of an old Ainu ethnonym.[54] However, Kikuchi's theory has found little support among the other scholars, and the consensus is that the characters in question were pronounced not *kai* but *emishi*. Although little noted, the first character, "shrimp," may have been used for its sound value, given that the Japanese pronunciation of this word, *ebi-*, easily elides to *emi-*. The second character, "barbarian," is clearly a straight borrowing from Chinese vocabulary, used here for its meaning rather than sound value.

Granted that the ideographs in question were in fact read "Emishi," where did this word come from? Here again, there are several schools of thought. Some authors, such as Kindaichi Kyōsuke, have argued for an Ainu or proto-Ainu etymology, citing the Ainu word "*emciw*" or "*enciw*," a polite term for "person."[55] Other scholars, however, feel that the term "Emishi" was of Japanese origin, noting its similarity with the word "*yumishi*," or "archer."[56]

So the situation is far from clear. All we can really say is that although the Chinese characters used to write "Emishi" certainly reflect the internalized "middle-kingdom ideology" of the ruling class, at the same time they may have been used to represent the sound value of some proto-Ainu word, perhaps even an ethnonym of some sort. Even if this is the case, however, it does not necessarily follow that the "Emishi" as a whole shared some common identity. As evidence to the contrary, I would again cite the words of the *Nihon shoki:* "Amongst these Eastern savages the Yemishi are the most powerful . . . ," a phrase that would seem to imply that other tribes with other names also existed in the "untamed" areas of the Tōhoku region and Hokkaido.[57] I would suggest that the court later came to use the word "Emishi" as a catch-all for this entire group of tribes, which in reality might have had highly fragmented identities. That the court came to see them as one, however, reflected that they *did* share a more or less common culture, as we have already seen from the archaeological and linguistic evidence. In short, what we have here is another ethnic category—a group perceived as a single people from the outside (i.e., by the Japanese) but still probably lacking an overarching sense of subjective ethnic identity.

It was interaction with the Japanese polity that took this disparate group of villages or tribes and molded them into a unified "ethnic group." The process seems to have begun in the Nara and Heian periods. Certainly these centuries saw developments analogous to those noted by Ferguson and Whitehead in other cases of state expansion into peripheral "tribal zones." As we have seen, the political frontier of the early state was more or less congruent with the social border between the Kofun and Satsumon cultures. No doubt the frontier was a zone of conflict even at this stage, but the level of violence increased dramatically during the Nara and Heian periods as the result of Japanese expansionism. Significantly, it is during this period that we first find evidence of pan-Emishi social organization, although admittedly of a transient character.

According to Kudō Masaki, Emishi society was organized on the basis of *mura*, or villages, but in special circumstances (e.g., battles or wars) these might band together to form larger "leagues."[58] Certainly this is what happened during some of the major military conflicts of the time: the 780 "rebellion" of Koreharu (or Korehari) no Azamaro, which resulted in the burning of the government headquarters at Fort Taga; the wars fought in the late eighth–early ninth century between government general Sakanoue no Tamuramaro and Emishi leaders Aterui and More; and the 878 "Gangyō rebellion," when Fort Akita was attacked and burned to the ground by an assortment of Emishi "rebels."[59] There is even a tantalizing hint of ethnic consciousness in the circumstances surrounding the rebellion of Koreharu no Azamaro. Azamaro is said to have been provoked by the taunts of another frontier resident, Michishima Ōtate, who cast scorn upon Azamaro because of his Emishi background.[60]

It would be wrong to imagine that relations between the court and the residents of the north were purely hostile or that nascent ethnic consciousness among the Emishi resulted solely from the militarization of frontier society. Court policy toward the Emishi was a complex mixture of coercion and co-option, and ethnic consciousness may also have been stimulated by peaceful means. The regularization of tribute relations undoubtedly had the effect, whether intended or not, of imposing a kind of collective consciousness among the Emishi, or at least among the emissaries chosen to represent them at court. Participation in court ceremonies, particularly at New Year's and during the visits of foreign embassies, may also have had the effect of imposing a kind of common consciousness of submission by incorporating Emishi leaders as junior partners within the Japanese ritual order.[61]

At the same time it would be a mistake to imagine that the process of ethnogenesis proceeded very far in the Nara or Heian periods or that there was some sort of objective, universally recognized boundary between the "Japanese" to the south and the "Emishi" to the north. To the contrary, there was at best a subjective and ambiguous series of gradations: the ethnic equivalent of the political "frontier" discussed in Chapter 1. How things looked from the "Japanese" side is known from the record of a 659 visit to Tang China by a Japanese diplomatic mission. Apparently in order to impress their Chinese hosts with Japan's hold over "barbarian" societies on its frontier, these emissaries took with them a pair of Emishi from Mutsu. In response to questions by the Tang emperor, the envoys explained that the "land of the Emishi" lay to the northeast of Wa and that it was inhabited by three groups, the "Tsugaru," the "Ara [Wild] Emishi," and the "Nigi [Tame] Emishi."[62] (Other roughly contemporaneous references from the *Nihon shoki* describe yet a fourth group, the "Watarishima [Island-Crossing] Emishi," who may have lived in southernmost Hokkaido.[63])

The records do not tell us how this frontier looked from the other side, but my own view is as follows. Contrary to "common sense," consciousness of being "Emishi" probably developed earliest among those with the strongest geographic and cultural ties to court, not among the more "pristine" social groups to the north. The reason is that "barbarians" in constant contact with Japanese society were in the "best" position to internalize the worldview of their neighbors to the south. To cite one example, Koreharu no Azamaro was cognizant of, and "sensitive" about, his "Emishi" identity precisely because of his proximity to the court: prior to rebelling, he had fought on behalf of the Japanese (for which he was awarded with a court rank in 778) and served as the chief magistrate of Kurihara district in what is now Miyagi Prefecture.[64]

Nor was Azamaro's situation unusual; in the following centuries, "barbarian" ethnicity was always most highly developed in the "fuzzy zone" of the frontier. In the late Heian period, for example, the Abe family of Mutsu referred to themselves as "chief of the Eastern barbarians" *(Tōi no shūchō)* and "head of the assimilated Emishi" *(fushū no nushi).* The latter title was also used by the Kiyohara family, who succeeded the Abe as rulers of the Kitakami River Basin. Finally, the Northern Fujiwara, who inherited control over the area in the twelfth century, described themselves as the "leaders of the assimilated Emishi" *(fushū no jōtō)* and "distant chiefs of the Eastern barbarians" *(Tōi no enshū).*[65]

Ezo

Beginning in the twelfth century, Japanese people began referring to the residents of the north as "Ezo." Who were these medieval Ezo, and what, if anything, distinguishes them from the earlier Emishi? As might be supposed, there is little agreement among scholars in this regard.

One reason, of course, is the lack of consensus about the identity of the Emishi themselves, but even among scholars who take the increasingly common position that the Emishi were a political invention of the court, we find two different lines of thought regarding the Ezo. On the one hand are those scholars (probably the majority) who identify the Ezo with the ethnographically known Ainu, while on the other hand are those, like Kaiho Mineo, who argue that the concept of "Ezo," like that of "Emishi," was basically a creation of the court and that it is a mistake to equate the Ezo with any fixed ethnic group.[66] I personally find Kaiho's position to be the more persuasive, but if we follow him in arguing that there was little fundamental difference between the ancient Emishi and the medieval Ezo, we are left with explaining why there was a change in name. Regarding the origins of the word "Ezo," however, the consensus position seems to be that it represents an elision of "Emishi,"[67] which puts us within the realm of historical linguistics rather than ethnicity. In any case, there is no more (and no less) evidence that "Ezo" represents a genuine ethnonym than in the case of the earlier "Emishi," nor is there any evidence for a rapid diffusion of ethnic identity among residents of the north at this time.

Indeed, if anything there is continued evidence for fragmented, or geographically segmented, ethnicity during the medieval period of Japanese history. Consider the following quote, from a fourteenth-century Japanese source known as *Suwa daimyōjin ekotoba:*

> The "Thousand Isles of Ezo" [Ezogachishima] are located to the northeast of our country in the middle of the ocean. Three groups [known as] Hinomoto, Karako, and Wataritō inhabit three hundred and thirty three separate islands. . . . [The Wataritō] often visit Sotogahama in Mutsu Province to carry out trade. . . . The land of the two groups [known as] Hinomoto and Karako is contiguous with foreign countries. Their appearance is like that of demons, forever changing; as for their customs, they eat the flesh of fowl, beasts, and fish, and are unfamiliar with the cultivation of the five grains. It is difficult to understand their speech even with the aid of interpreters. The Wataritō resemble the people of Wakoku [Japan], but they have much hair on their faces and all over their bodies. Their speech is uncouth but for the most part comprehensible.[68]

This text contains some important information about fourteenth-century society in Hokkaido as well as some obvious distortions and prejudices. The author makes no attempt to conceal his opinion that the residents of the north were uncivilized and inferior compared with mainland Japanese. And yet there is no obvious reason to doubt his assertion that the Ezo consisted of three distinct groups. As in earlier times, northern society seems to have consisted of a series of zones ranging from the semi-Japanese to the truly "barbarian"—much the same structure as we saw in the seventh century, although of course the stage had shifted considerably to the north by medieval times. The consensus among Japanese scholars is that the "Wataritō" inhabited the Oshima Peninsula of southern Hokkaido and represent a creole society composed in part of Japanese refugees from the mainland. (Hokkaido was used as a place of political exile during the Kamakura period.) The "Hinomoto" and "Karako," respectively, are thought to have inhabited the eastern and western halves of the Hokkaido mainland.[69]

Do the Wataritō, Hinomoto, and Karako represent emerging ethnic groups (as opposed to social or cultural groups)? Unfortunately, it is impossible to say on the basis of the *Suwa daimyōjin ekotoba.* The text itself, as noted above, is written from a Japanese perspective, and what is more, the names of the three groups themselves are of obvious Japanese etymology. If these were genuine ethnic groups, they should have had their own ethnonyms—although, of course, the first stage in the emergence of ethnic consciousness is often recognition as an "ethnic category" from outside.

Ainu

Many Japanese and foreign scholars date the birth of Ainu ethnicity to the thirteenth and fourteenth centuries. This conclusion is based mainly on archaeological grounds. As described in the previous chapter, the "Ainu" archaeological culture was born after around 1200 C.E. as a hybrid of two previous cultures, the Satsumon and Okhotsk. Among the distinctive features of the "Ainu" archaeological culture are *naiji doki* pots, bone and antler tools, ritual sites, and "forts." Of these, the ritual sites and "forts" may have some implications for the emergence of Ainu (or at least, group) identity. But the evidence is indirect at best, and it is important to remember that people can share a common culture without sharing a common ethnic identity.

Probably the best evidence of the latter, again, is the use of a common name or ethnonym. In this regard it is interesting to note that the above-mentioned *Suwa daimyōjin ekotoba* does in fact contain the first known appearance of the term "Ainu."[70] However, "Ainu" appears here as a suffix to a personal name, not as an ethnonym per se. "Ainu," of course, means "man" or "human" in the Ainu language, and it is therefore likely that the word itself has quite ancient origins, well predating the fourteenth-century *Suwa daimyōjin ekotoba.* As we have seen, Ainu or a prototype thereof was spoken in Tōhoku during early historic times, and the language ultimately may have Jōmon roots.

So far as I know, the first recorded use of "Ainu" in the larger sense, as an ethnic name, is in a 1591 manuscript by Ignacio Morera, a Jesuit priest. On a visit to Toyotomi Hideyoshi's palace, Morera met an Ainu in the company of a Kakizaki delegation from southern Hokkaido. Morera learned from this man that he came from a place called "Aino-moxoriz," clearly a reference to "Ainu mosir," or "Land of the Ainu."[71] So here we have not just an ethnonym but evidence of a "homeland"—another of Anthony Smith's essential criteria for *ethnie.*

In very general terms, then, the Ainu *ethnie* probably emerged during the medieval period of Japanese history, possibly as early as the thirteenth century but possibly as late as the sixteenth. Here, as in other cases, ethnic consciousness seems to have emerged as a byproduct of frontier-zone interactions, many of them hostile. This was the period when Japanese settlers began moving into southern Hokkaido en masse, and the militarization of the frontier is attested by the construction of forts (known, respectively, as *tachi* and *casi*) on both the "Japanese" and "Ainu" sides. Indigenous resentment over territorial encroachment (and "unfair" Japanese trading practices) ran high during this period, eventually resulting in "Koshamain's War" of 1457. This was ignited when an Ainu youth was killed by a Japanese blacksmith in a dispute over the quality of a knife, or *makiri.* Ainu under the leadership of Koshamain, a local chieftain, attacked and destroyed ten of the twelve Japanese forts in southern Hokkaido before they were routed by Takeda Nobuhiro, a general representing the Kakizaki family.[72]

Cross-border interactions continued to reinforce Ainu solidarity during the following early modern period of Japanese history. A second major Ainu "rebellion" occurred in 1669. According to Brett Walker's analysis, "Shakushain's War" had its origins in intra-Ainu competition for trade resources but later developed into open ethnic conflict between "Ainu" and "Japanese."[73] Ethnic differences between the two groups were also highlighted by Matsumae domain's adroit use of administrative procedures and tribute relations, as both Walker and David Howell have shown. Particularly important in this regard was the rite of submission known as *uimam*, in which Ainu chieftains paid tribute to the lord of Matsumae at Fukuyama Castle.[74] In the end, as so often happens, these externally imposed perceptions were internalized by the native participants.

At the same time, it is worth noting that Ainu identity was by no means monolithic in the early modern period—or even, for that matter, in more recent, ethnographically attested times. Anthropologists normally divide the Ainu into three different groups: the Hokkaido Ainu, the Sakhalin Ainu, and the Kuril Ainu. Each spoke a different Ainu dialect and had a distinctive lifestyle and material culture. Each of these groups was itself culturally diverse as the result of environmental/ecological differences and varying degrees of influence from Japan and/or the continent.[75]

Even more important, the fundamental unit of Ainu society, at least in southwestern Hokkaido, was quite small—essentially the watershed of a single river. Ainu lived in villages called *kotan*, and according to Hans Dieter Ölschleger, the members of the several villages in each river valley "developed a deep feeling of unity and were identified by the name of the river followed by the words *un kur: Saru-un-kur* meant 'people of the Saru River valley.' The territory thus formed was called *iwor*, and *Saru-un-kur-iwor* was the stretch of land exploited by the Saru River Ainu."[76] The identity of each territorial group derived at least in part from shared dependence on subsistence resources and was expressed in hunting and fishing rituals that created "covenants" with the land and its gods, or *kamuy*.[77]

Further, it should be noted that interaction with Japanese society had centrifugal as well as centripetal effects. As I will describe in the final chapter of this book, Japanese encroachment on Hokkaido eventually led to a virtual collapse of Ainu society and culture during early modern times. This is illustrated, for example, by the third and final Ainu "rebellion," the "Kunashiri-Menashi Uprising" of 1789. In this incident, Ainu workers at a contract fishery in the southern Kurils and northeastern Honshu rebelled against poor working conditions, killing seventy-one of their Japanese co-workers. The rebellion was ultimately put down with the help of local Ainu chieftains dependent on the goodwill of Matsumae. "This action alone," as David Howell puts it, "testifies all too eloquently to the collapse of Ainu society."[78]

Conditions continued to worsen during the nineteenth century, following Japan's annexation and colonization of Hokkaido, which had the effect of turning the local Ainu into an ethnic minority in their own lands. Surviving Ainu suffered severe "racial" discrimination and socioeconomic subordination, despite the Meiji government's abolition of hereditary status differences and its official policy of assimilation. In the words of Richard Siddle,

> As the sense of "nation" took root among Japanese in the late Meiji period it became increasingly identified with the "Yamato race". In a racialized world both collective Self and Other, Japanese and non-Japanese, were perceived as hierarchically ordered "racial" communities. As a result, the dispossession and marginalisation of the Ainu during the colonisation of Hokkaido were paralleled by their categorisation as a subordinate and inferior "racial" population—a "dying race"—by all sectors of the Japanese immigrant community. Such perceptions directly influenced policies that furthered Ainu subordination. Moreover, in the context of debates over Japan's identity and place in a world dominated by Europe and the USA, the Ainu provided an initial "native" Other as a foil not only for Japan's own emerging national (and "racial") identity, but against which Japan's modernity and progress towards civilisation could be measured.[79]

The short- to medium-term effects of these developments on Ainu identity were probably negative, although this is difficult to document. In the very long term, however, the historical process of marginalization and subordination seems to have rekindled the fires of ethnic identity among surviving Ainu.

Ainu resistance was first expressed in the formation of self-help organizations such as the Ainu Kyōkai (Ainu Association) in 1930. In the postwar years, and particularly since the 1960s, these efforts were further stimulated by the prevailing climate of social activism. The end result, as noted in Chapter 2, was the Japanese government's official recognition of the Ainu as a separate ethnic group in the "Ainu New Law" *(Ainu shinpō)* of 1997. In Richard Siddle's analysis, it is now possible to speak of an actual Ainu "nation," which derives its self-identification not only from its status as a minority within the larger Japanese society but also from the lateral bonds it has formed with similarly positioned indigenous peoples in other parts of the world.[80]

Ethnogenesis, Ethnic Borders, and "Japan"

What conclusions can we draw from the above discussion about the process of ethnogenesis in the Japanese islands? If the analysis is sound, what implications does it have regarding the ethnic borders between the "Japanese" people and their neighbors to the north? And finally, what relation, if any, was there between these borders and their political and cultural counterparts? What, in other words, do we mean when we speak of "Japan" or "Japanese society"?

Ethnogenesis

Regarding the process of ethnogenesis, there are four major points I would like to stress. First, group identity is not an "either-or" proposition. People can simultaneously belong to—and identify with—any number of social groups, each performing a different function and operating at a different scale. For example, even after the emergence of an identifiable Ainu *ethnie* in medieval times, the essential units of society for most Ainu remained the *kotan* or, at most, the territory defined by the watershed of a particular river. Similarly, the existence of a Japanese *ethnie* did not preclude the existence of local or class-based affiliations.

Second, that having been said, it seems clear that the *relative* importance of these various identities has changed over time in a way that is more or less consistent with Anthony Smith's "stage" theory of ethnogenesis. At a gross level, in other words, subjective membership in very large-scale, abstract "communities"—the *ethnie* and the nation—has become more important, for more people, over the course of time. In Japan "proper," for example, one finds a systematic progression from a situation in which there was *no* overriding sense of ethnic affiliation to one in which most members of the community have a strong subjective sense of national identity. More or less the same trend, albeit on a smaller scale, can be seen in peripheral areas of the archipelago. Whether the Ainu today constitute a true "nation" (as claimed by Siddle) is perhaps a matter of debate, but at the very least they constitute what G. P. Nielsson calls a "nation-group," that is, an ethnic group "politically mobilized on the basis of ethnic group values."[81]

Third, although the general path of development was similar, the *pace* of ethnogenesis varied widely among between "core" areas and "peripheries." As I have argued, a Japanese *ethnie* was in existence by around 700 C.E., but no true ethnic community existed in the north until perhaps 1200. This should not be taken to mean that residents of the north were somehow "inferior" to Japanese society. Certainly, they have been *viewed* as inferior by the Japanese in many periods of history; we have already seen early manifestations of this in the *Nihon shoki* and the *Suwa daimyōjin ekotoba.* Still clearer examples could be given from the nineteenth and twentieth centuries. But notions of inferiority and superiority are inherently subjective, based as they are on values, not facts. Here I am merely trying to make an objective point—namely, that a widespread sense of ethnic identity was slower to develop in the north than it was in Japan "proper."

Fourth, these trends roughly mirror those we have observed for the development of political society in these different areas. For example, whereas a unified state emerged quite early in Japan "proper," social organization in Hokkaido remained at the level of the chiefdom until the island was annexed in the nineteenth century. I am not suggesting that the emergence of ethnicity is a direct consequence of political organization—although it is certainly one factor, as noted by Anthony Smith. Rather, it seems likely that different aspects of society evolve in tandem and that regions that are "behind" in one area are also likely to be "behind" in others.[82] The reasons behind the general "lag" in sociopolitical development between core and peripheral areas of the Japanese islands are complex and will be explored further in the final chapter of this book. Stated simply, however, the most important factors were differences in population size and density, which in turn were determined by ecological and environmental differences.

Ethnic Borders

What then, are the implications for the nature of ethnic borders? Quite simply, ethnic groups are not likely to have sharp boundaries, for several reasons, some of them obvious, some not.

First, group identity is based on the perception that "we" are different from "them," but the cultural or physical traits that form the basis of these comparisons also usually lack sharp boundaries, making it difficult to draw an unambiguous ethnic "line," even when people wish to do so. One apparent exception is language; most people do have but one "mother" tongue. This has some implications for ethnicity; according to archaeologists Colin Renfrew and Paul Bahn, "ethnic groups often correlate with language areas, and . . . ethnic and linguistic boundaries are often the same."[83] But even here, cross-border interactions—particularly intermarriage—inevitably result in a smearing of linguistic borders. An example—this time, not from the north—would be the diaspora community of Chinese merchants in the north Kyushu port of Hakata in the late Heian period, where we have good documentary evidence for intermarriage with local women, resulting in the appearance of (probably bilingual) individuals with Chinese surnames but Japanese given names.[84] Many similar instances are known from the Wakō of medieval times.[85] So even in the simplest possible case, where ethnicity is a direct function of language, ethnic borders would be inherently fuzzy.

Of course, the simplest case is not likely to hold, particularly in frontier situations. Social interactions expose individuals to a "matrix" of technologies, social practices, and belief systems from which they can pick and choose; in other words, people have a choice of identity positions.[86] As we all know from daily life, it is perfectly possible to adopt different (even mutually exclusive) postures, depending on the situation we find ourselves in. As a random example, one of my own students, a young woman with an Ainu father and a Japanese mother, happily identifies herself as Ainu in her dealings with other students and faculty at our school in Tokyo. Back home in Obihiro, however, she is much less willing to assume an Ainu identity, mostly because "racial" prejudice against the Ainu is much stronger in Hokkaido than in other parts of Japan. And when she goes abroad to meet indigenous friends in Canada, she considers herself a representative of both the Ainu and of Japanese culture in general. Presumably, this type of "situational" ethnicity also existed in premodern times.[87] Whatever the period, it would have resulted in a further smearing of ethnic borders.

Yet another important factor is the tendency for ethnic distinctions to be crosscut by distinctive "borderland" or "frontier" identities. This phenomenon, which is found in virtually all border situations, results from the fact that people living in proximity at the fringes of their respective societies may actually have more in common, and share more material interests, than they do with the more distant members of their own "ethnic" groups. It seems likely, for example, that the label *fushū*, which was worn so proudly by the Northern Fujiwara, represents a cross-border identity of this kind. Also relevant to this point are the many examples of "collusion" between subversives in northern Kyushu (especially Tsushima) and residents of Silla in the Heian period.[88]

One additional reason for the general fuzziness of ethnic borders is their subjective nature. Quite obviously, people on opposite sides of an ethnic border may have different ways of seeing it, or defining it, because ethnicity itself is subjective. So it would not be surprising to find, for example, that the border in northern Tōhoku in the Nara period might have looked considerably different, depending on whether the observer lived in the capital, say, or the Tsugaru area. What is not quite so obvious is that people on one side might see an ethnic border where those on the other saw none at all. However strange this assertion may seem, it follows directly from the concept of the "time lag" described above. In the Nara period, the "Emishi," unlike the "Japanese" to the south, were probably not an ethnic community at all in our sense of the term. True, residents of the far north would have seen linguistic boundaries, cultural differences, and possibly "racial" differences when gazing toward the south, but they might not have interpreted these in the same "ethnic" terms as did the "Japanese"—at least, not until they had internalized part of the latter's worldview.

What Is "Japan"?

Finally, how do the ethnic borders considered in this chapter relate to the cultural and political entities studied earlier? By now, the reader will not be surprised to hear me argue that although none of these things are precisely congruent, they are nonetheless closely related and evolved in tandem over the course of premodern history.

Current thinking on the relationship between ethnicity and culture owes much to the work of Fredrik Barth. In his landmark 1969 study of ethnic boundaries, Barth argued,

> It is important to recognize that although ethnic categories take cultural differences into account, we can assume no simple one-to-one relationship between ethnic units and cultural similarities and differences. The features that are taken into account are not the sum of "objective" differences, but only those which the actors themselves regard as significant. Not only do ecologic variations mark and exaggerate differences; some cultural features are used by the actors as signals and emblems of differences, others are ignored, and in some relationships radical differences are played down and denied.[89]

In a word, what matters in the formation of ethnic boundaries is not cultural differences per se but how these differences are perceived by the actors themselves.

In the years since Barth's work was published, anthropologists (particularly in the archaeological branch of the discipline) have expended much effort in the attempt to discover which features of "culture" are most likely to be used for ethnic identification. One conclusion, noted above, is that language (or dialect) is a reasonably good predictor of ethnicity (although, of course, it is easy enough to find counterexamples). Regarding material culture, the jury is still out. According to a recent survey of the topic by Michelle Hegmon, "a number of studies have found that various technological differences do seem to correspond to social differences or ethnic boundaries," while on the other hand, "[o]ther studies have found that technologies tend to cross-cut ethnic or other social boundaries."[90] Hegmon has nonetheless constructed a list of some of the important "regularities." Among her conclusions are the following: "Complex technologies (e.g., metallurgy) seem to be heavily loaded symbolically"; "[d]ecorations that cross-cut a number of media . . . are likely to be symbolically meaningful"; and "[m]aterial (including domestic ceramics and architecture) that is used in and that structures everyday domestic life may be particularly relevant to the concept of *habitus;* that is, such material plays an important role in defining who people are socially."[91] Admittedly, it is rather difficult to generalize from this list. A bold reading would be that aspects of material culture that either demand the individual's conscious attention or structure the basic patterns of his or her existence are more likely than others to be relevant to issues of identity and ethnicity.

Cultural features related to "mode of production" would seem to be an especially good candidate for this role. One example I have already mentioned concerns the Ainu, whose ethnic identity was based at least in part on shared respect for the land, its gods, and its natural resources. But subsistence issues played an important role in identity formation on the "Japanese" side of the border. The best example, of course, is the subjective importance assigned to rice agriculture.[92]

This concern with rice is evident from very early times and was codified in both law and myth by the Nara period. The system of local administration embodied in the *ritsuryō* law codes, for example, is predicated upon the idea that rice agriculture formed the basis of the Japanese economy, and the tendency to see the Emishi and Hayato tribes as non-Japanese "barbarians" stemmed at least in part from the fact that they were principally hunters and gatherers, not farmers. Several important court ceremonies of the Nara period also had their origins in harvest festivals. Among these are the *niinamesai*, an annual festival in which the emperor offered the "first fruits" of rice to the deities in thanks for an abundant harvest; and the *daijōsai*, a ceremony in which a new emperor shared a meal of "first fruits" with the heavenly deities as part of his official coronation. Rice agriculture also figures heavily in some of the myths recorded in the *Nihon shoki* and *Kojiki*, most notably the famous incident in which Susano-o, younger brother of the sun goddess Amaterasu, "sins" by his wanton destruction of rice fields and irrigation works.[93]

The idea that "Japanese" people were rice farmers, then, was part and parcel of the ethnic identity created by the ruling elite during the late seventh and early eighth centuries. And although this idea may have been stronger at the center than at the periphery, and stronger among elite groups than among the "common man," it—like other elements of Japanese ethnic consciousness—spread outward and downward through Japanese society throughout the remainder of the premodern period. Even at the beginning of the twenty-first century, when few Japanese make their living by agriculture, the idea that the Japanese have always been a rice-farming people is a central component in national identity. Social historian Amino Yoshihiko has criticized this as the "rice monoculture theory" *(inasaku ichigen ron)* and devoted a substantial portion of his career to emphasizing the importance of nonagriculturists—hunters, fishers, tradespeople, and others—throughout Japanese history.[94] Objectively, it is undoubtedly true that many Japanese throughout history have made their living without farming rice (or, indeed, anything else). Subjectively, it is not true: such is the power of ethnic (or national) identity.

The case of rice agriculture illustrates the role played by the state in *creating* ethnicity, in this case by authoring a "master myth" to define the identity of subjects, or citizens, within the reach of its territorial control. This is much the same phenomenon as we have earlier noted with respect to culture, in which political conquest frequently led to cultural assimilation. This being the case, it should come as no surprise to find examples of state involvement in the "demarcation" of ethnic boundaries that are more or less congruent with political ones.

One such example is provided by David Howell in his study of Ainu ethnicity. According to Howell, "the demarcation of an 'ethnic boundary' . . . between the Ainu and the Japanese was a critical element in determining the political boundaries of the early modern Japanese state."[95] Later in the same article, Howell states:

> Despite their small numbers and the remoteness of their homeland, the Ainu were important to the formation of a Japanese national identity during the Tokugawa and Meiji periods. The Tokugawa shogunate was the first regime in Japanese history to draw clear physical borders for itself. But rather than establish a dichotomy between Japan and the rest of the world, it surrounded itself with peripheral areas that were neither fully part of the polity nor completely independent of it. The resultant contrast between the dependent yet non-Japanese peripheral peoples,

> including the Ainu, and the inhabitants of the core spurred the formation of a Japanese identity even before the emergence of a modern nation-state in the mid-nineteenth century.[96]

Howell is certainly correct in stating that the Edo regime was actively involved in the creation of not just political but also ethnic boundaries. We need only add that it was hardly the first regime in Japanese history to do so: the same techniques used in the Edo period to maintain ethnic distinctions between "Japanese" and "Ainu" were earlier used in the Nara period to maintain distinctions between "Japanese" and "Emishi."

Why did the Edo and Nara regimes attempt to create ethnic boundaries along their peripheries? The answer has to do with identity and, ultimately, with power. If it is true that a sense of Self (either individual or ethnic) depends in part upon the existence of a contrasting Other, then ethnic groups have a built-in need for real or imagined counterparts and thus for ethnic boundaries of one kind or another. And if an ethnic group is charge of a powerful state apparatus, as was true in Japan during these two periods, then that group has the means, as well as the motivation, to maintain, or even create ethnic (and cultural) boundaries. Not all groups and societies are created equal, and in the past, as now, powerful actors had a tendency to impose their worldview over the not-so-powerful. As a result, the ethnic map of the Japanese islands bore many similarities to its political counterpart.

Of course, it would be foolish to look for a precise convergence between the borders of the Japanese *ethnie* and those of the Japanese state. As discussed in the previous chapter, Japan as a culture and Japan as a state were rarely one and the same. In some periods, most notably in the Sengoku era but also in late prehistoric and early modern times, the zone of Japanese culture extended beyond the boundaries of the Japanese state. (Indeed, for the Sengoku period it is difficult to speak of a Japanese "state" at all.) In other periods, such as the Nara and the Heian, the reverse was true, and Japan was quite literally a "multicultural" state. Similar disparities could be found between ethnic and political frontiers or between ethnic and cultural ones. In other words, not only did "Japan" have ragged borders, but it had a whole spectrum of ragged borders, each somewhat different from the others.

However, the key word here is "somewhat." The various "Japans" were not identical, but they were nonetheless closely related. With the exception of Hideyoshi's invasions of Korea in the 1590s (and, of course, the imperialist ventures of the modern period), the mismatch between the various "Japans" was never too great. In this sense, it is permissible to think not in terms of a political frontier, or a cultural or ethnic one, but of an amorphous, multifaced "frontier region" that encompassed all of these aspects, on the margins of a "Japan" that was not merely a state, not merely a cultural group or an ethnic group, but a mixture of all three. (See Figure 3.) So although the idea of a perfect congruence among state, culture, and ethnicity in premodern Japan is a myth, like many myths it contains a substantial grain of truth.

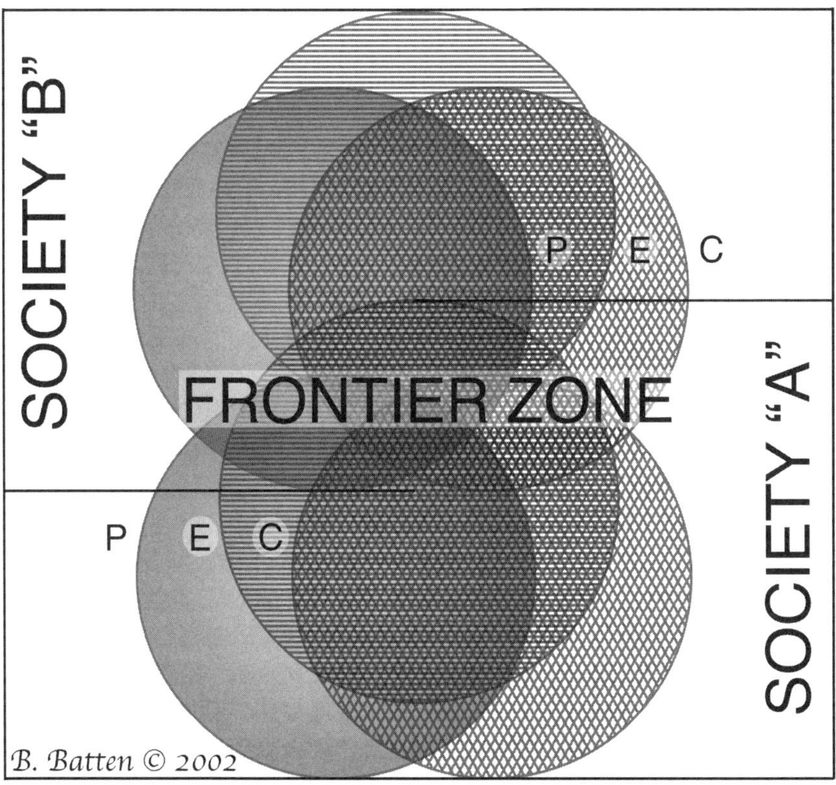

FIGURE 3. The frontier zone as a set of multiple, overlapping borders. P = polity; C = culture zone; E = ethnic group.

How are we to explain this overall congruity? All things being equal, cultural and/or ethnic unity probably facilitates the process of political incorporation. At the same time, political unification tends to facilitate cultural and ethnic integration by allowing the dominant culture to impose its worldview and lifestyle on newly assimilated groups on the periphery. As a result, there tends to be a dynamic interplay along frontiers, with cultural and ethnic developments paving the way for political ones and vice versa. When Japan expanded, it did so not just as a political unit but also as a cultural and ethnic one. Again, this begs the question of the ultimate reason for expansion, which, again, has to do with geographical disparities in social power. These, in turn, are related to ecological and environmental differences—a topic I explore more fully in the final chapter of this book.

In the meantime, we have another task. Assuming that "Japan" constituted a meaningful entity in premodern times, what was its place in the larger world? What role did its frontiers play in mediating external contacts? Did they serve to connect "Japan" to the outside world or to isolate it? As we shall see in the following chapters, these questions are best addressed through the application of "world-systems theory."

PART TWO

Interactions

4 Premodern Japan in World-Systems Theory

Japan's Borders: Barriers or Conduits?

In Chapter 3 we looked at several different ways of defining premodern "Japan," each of which results in a slightly different set of boundaries or frontiers. Japan may be thought of as a political entity, that is, as a state. If so, its borders represent the limits of territorial sovereignty, the lines or zones that separated areas under Japanese control from those ruled by neighboring states, chiefdoms, or tribes. "Japan" can also be considered a cultural entity, one whose borders are defined by the areal distribution of an identifiable way of life, forms of social organization, or linguistic characteristics. Alternatively, we may think of an ethnic "Japan," one defined by differences in identity positions, with self-consciously "Japanese" people on one side of the border and people of differing affiliations—Ainu, Okinawan, Korean—on the other. As I have argued, these various "Japans" are not necessarily identical—but neither are they wholly different.

What do all of these definitions have in common? They all follow from the same way of looking at the world, one that emphasizes the spatial distribution of social traits. The world is carved into discrete geographic units on the basis of observed (or perceived) similarities and differences. Regions that share common traits—political, cultural, or ethnic—are grouped together as part of the same entity; those with different characteristics belong to separate, adjoining entities. "Japan" is defined on the basis of characteristics shared by most of the people within its borders but not by residents of, for example, the Ainu homelands or Korea. In this view of the world, frontiers and boundaries are places of transition, where one relatively homogeneous social entity gives way to another. To the extent that the transition is abrupt, we are dealing with a "boundary"; to the extent it is gradual, a "frontier."

There is also another way of looking at the world, one that emphasizes not homogeneities but connections.[1] Scholars of this persuasion do not ask whether two locations, or groups, share a common political culture or are ruled by the same government. Nor do they ask whether people speak the same language, share a common lifestyle, or a common sense of ethnic identity. They ask instead to what extent the two regions are connected. Do they maintain formal or informal political relations? Do people from one region visit the other? Are there flows of material goods or information? Are their economies intertwined? In this view of the world, the meaningful units are social systems that display a high degree of internal "connectivity" but relatively few external links.[2] And borders represent not places of change but zones of high "falloff" in the density of social connections. This is the approach taken in this and the following chapters.

Of course, social units defined on this basis may turn out to be the same as those defined by the more traditional approach. Sharing a common culture in the form of language, beliefs, customs, and so on, can obviously facilitate interactions in some cases. Conversely, regular interaction may result in a certain degree of cultural convergence or homogenization. For example, the zone of "East Asian civilization" clearly developed out of historical interactions between China and societies in Korea, Japan, and elsewhere, which resulted in the transmission and adoption of Chinese ideographs, Buddhism, Confucianism, and other elements of Chinese culture.

On the other hand, interaction does not always lead to homogenization. Indeed, as argued in the previous chapter, interactions in frontier zones frequently lead to the crystallization of differences, as people on each side attempt to define themselves in terms of the other. The process of ethnogenesis in the Japanese archipelago is a case in point. It may well be, of course, that the degree of interaction across these frontiers is still less than that *within* the societies on each side: that a modicum of communication leads to the accentuation of differences, but completely unrestricted interaction leads to homogenization. However, this point is unproven, and it is probably wise not to assume any one-to-one correspondence between social units defined on the basis of homogeneities and those defined on the basis of connections.

The purpose of this and the following chapters is to explore these issues in greater depth. Specifically, I want to ask the following question: Was Japan, as defined on the basis of political, cultural, or ethnic homogeneities, relatively isolated during premodern times, or did it have strong ties to the outside world? Did Japan's borders, in other words, tend to function as barriers or as conduits for communication and exchange?

As noted in the introduction, there is already an enormous literature on this topic, both in Japanese and in English, but most of these studies either are too narrow in scope or suffer from a lack of theoretical and/or methodological rigor. In this section of the book, I will attempt to broaden the terms of the debate by considering *all* (or at least most) of Japan's external interactions during the premodern period, rather than focusing on some particular period or region. At the same time, I will try to make the analysis as rigorous as possible by explicitly adopting a single, consistent theoretical framework. To my mind, the candidate best suited for the task is "world-systems theory."[3] On the assumption that world-systems theory is probably unfamiliar to many readers of this book, I devote the remainder of this chapter to an overview of the approach and an explanation of why it is relevant to the question of Japan's historical isolation, or lack thereof.

The "Modern World-System"

World-systems theory received its original exposition in a series of books by American sociologist Immanuel Wallerstein concerning the origins and development of what he called the "modern world-system."[4] Wallerstein defined this system in essentially economic terms, equating it with the capitalist mode of production, which (according to him) emerged in western Europe in the late fifteenth and early sixteenth centuries. In his books, Wallerstein described how the European "world economy" came to expand in succeeding centuries, overtaking and incorporating earlier forms of production and accumulation, until, by the twentieth century, capitalism and its social consequences had come to encompass the entire globe.

As summarized by Peter Taylor, Wallerstein's modern world-system is composed of three basic elements.[5] First, it consists of a single world market, which, as noted above, is capitalist. The value of goods is determined by the market, and producers compete to sell goods and accumulate profit. Thus, "the world-market determines in the long run the quantity, type and location of production," Taylor notes. "The concrete result of this process has been uneven economic development across the world."[6]

Second, the world economy is characterized by a multiple state system. Economically, the modern world-system forms a single unit, but politically, it is divided into a large number of nation-states. Nation-states compete with one another for power, including economic power, within the basic framework of the capitalist world economy. Powerful states, or hegemons (see below), are able to distort the workings of the market well beyond their own borders, but they remain embedded within the overall economic logic of the system.

Third, the world-system embodies a three-tier structure. The most important example of this is the division of the world economy into a "core," a "periphery," and a "semi-periphery." As Taylor puts it, "core processes consist of relations that incorporate relatively high wages, advanced technology and a diversified production mix whereas periphery processes involve low wages, more rudimentary technology and a simple production mix."[7] These processes tend to concentrate in particular regions, so that it is possible to speak of "core" areas (e.g., western Europe, North America, and Japan) and "peripheral" areas (e.g., so-called Third World) in today's world. In general, the former regions tend to exploit the latter. The third and final tier is an intermediate category, the "semi-periphery," which consists of areas (e.g., the former Soviet Union, China, etc.) that display a mix of core and peripheral processes. As a result, "the overall social relations in such zones involve exploiting peripheral areas while the semi-periphery itself suffers exploitation by the core."[8]

In addition to these structural features, the modern world-system has also exhibited several important historical trends over the course of its existence. The first of these trends, already noted above, is geographic expansion. Between about 1500 and 1900, the European world economy gradually incorporated the Caribbean, North America, India, East Asia, Australia, Africa, and finally the Pacific Islands, in approximately that order.[9] This economic integration of the world was effected through a combination of plunder, colonization, and military conquest.

Of course, these were proximate means, which in and of themselves do not constitute a sufficient explanation for the expansion of the "modern world-system." One possibility is that capitalism itself had some sort of competitive advantage over earlier forms of production and accumulation. This is probably true as far as it goes, but other factors—technological, demographic, and perhaps ultimately environmental—were also undoubtedly involved.[10] Some of these will be examined in our discussion of social power in the final chapter of the book.

A second important historical trend concerns shifts in the spatial distribution of "core," "semi-periphery," and "periphery." Although the modern world-system has always exhibited a three-tier structure, there have been significant shifts in the location of core and peripheral processes. For example, core processes were originally located in western Europe, then expanded to include North America and now Japan. Partly these changes are a function of the overall expansion of the system, but even within areas that have always been incorporated, some important shifts have occurred. Within western Europe, for example, the highest concentration of core processes was originally in Iberia, an area that is hardly the most developed in Europe today.

A third, and again related, point has to do with shifts in political power, sometimes known as "hegemonic transitions." Just as the location of economic power may shift over time, so does the location of political power. Often, of course, the two go hand in hand: Iberia in the sixteenth century, Britain in the nineteenth, and the United States in the twentieth were all economic giants as well as political hegemons.[11] However, there are also exceptions: the Netherlands, which was the economic core of Europe in the seventeenth century, never exerted as much political power as its economic position would seem to have warranted. Probably the same could be said of Japan in the late twentieth century.

The underlying reasons for these shifts in the distribution of political and economic power have yet to be fully elucidated. It seems likely, however, that part of the explanation has to do with the "advantages of backwardness" and the "disadvantages of development." Semi-peripheral regions can take advantage of "pretested" models of development, bypassing a lengthy process of trial and error. Core regions, meanwhile, are burdened by numerous obligations—the "costs of empire." This structural imbalance may account, over time, for the tendency for semi-peripheral actors to overtake core areas and hegemons.[12]

Fourth and last, the world economy has tended to develop in a cyclic fashion, that is, in a series of fits and starts. This is best illustrated by the so-called Kondratieff cycles discovered in the early twentieth century by the Russian economist of the same name. Each Kondratieff cycle, consisting of a period of expansion (usually referred to as the "A" phase) followed by one of stagnation and/or contraction (the "B" phase), lasts roughly fifty years. Altogether, four such cycles have been identified, dating back to the late eighteenth century.[13]

As Peter Taylor notes, there is widespread agreement on the existence of these cycles but not on the explanation for them. Most world-systems researchers place the blame on capitalism, arguing that the "invisible hand" of the market produces distinctive spurts of investment. Individual producers do what is good for themselves but not for the system as a whole, resulting in overproduction during good times (the "A" phases) and underproduction during bad times (the "B" phases). The beginning of each "A" phase is associated with the adoption of a new "bundle" of technologies (e.g., cotton and steam, railroads and steel, oil and electricity, and aerospace and electronics), and the "B" phase commences when the economic possibilities for that particular "bundle" have been fully played out in the marketplace. Restructuring then occurs as a necessary preparation for the introduction of the next set of technologies.[14]

Kondratieff cycles are especially well documented, but they are probably not unique; a number of researchers have also pointed out the existence of longer "logistic waves" in the world economy. These seem to predate the Kondratieff cycles by a number of centuries, but as yet there is little agreement on their timing, still less on the reason(s) for their existence.[15]

The Premodern World-System(s)

Such is the "modern world-system" as portrayed by Wallerstein and his followers. Can any elements of this analysis be meaningfully applied to events predating the emergence of the "European world economy"? Wallerstein and other theorists such as Samir Amin are loath to apply world-system concepts to precapitalist societies, which—they say—were organized along fundamentally different lines.[16] These authors take pains to distinguish the modern capitalist mode of production from the "tributary" economies characteristic of premodern empires, in which resources were exploited and redistributed by overtly political means, not by the "invisible hand" of the market. This fundamental difference in social organization, argue Wallerstein and Amin, makes it difficult or impossible to apply world-system concepts to premodern societies.

In contrast to these so-called "post-1500ers" there is also a group of "pre-1500ers," scholars who believe that the world-systems paradigm, with appropriate modifications, can be usefully applied to premodern societies.[17] These scholars further divide into a number of competing camps; according to one apt description, "a hundred flowers bloom" in the area of premodern world-systems research.[18] Here we will merely examine some of the more important approaches.

One group of scholars, represented by Andre Gunder Frank and Barry Gills, argues that the current "world-system" has existed not for five hundred years but for five thousand.[19] Frank and Gills emphasize the similarities, rather than the differences, between modern and premodern societies. According to them, capital accumulation has been of fundamental importance for thousands of years, not just since the rise of Europe. They also find that many features of the modern world-system can be traced far back into the past. Among these are core-periphery differentiation, political alternations between hegemony and rivalry, and economic alternations between expansion and contraction. Frank and Gills identify a series of eight "A"/"B" cycles between 1700 B.C.E. and 1500 C.E., which they claim to be valid for most of Eurasia.[20] However, their data are by no means universally accepted by other scholars.

Other "pre-1500ers," represented by Janet Abu-Lughod, argue that there has been not one but "several successive world-systems, each with a changing structure and its own set of hegemons."[21] Abu-Lughod agrees with Wallerstein that the modern world-system began in sixteenth-century Europe. But she argues that "the fall of the East precedes the rise of the West,"[22] that is, that Wallerstein's European world economy arose following the breakup of an earlier, thirteenth-century world-system (see Map 7). According to Abu-Lughod, this earlier system can be visualized as

> one that stretched between north-western Europe and China at its geographic extremes and . . . was internally organized into eight overlapping circuits of trade that connected three (or possibly four) core regions that were politically and culturally distinctive. While each of these core regions had one or more hegemons, no single subsystem exercised hegemony over the entire system. Rather, a rough and somewhat stable balance existed—not necessarily of *detente*, but because, given the technological level of transport, as well as significant cultural-religious barriers, there were real limits to span of control that fell far short of the entire system's scale.[23]

Abu-Lughod argues that this world-system came into being when the various core regions (north-western Europe, West Asia, China, and possibly India) became linked by trade routes in the early thirteenth century, partly as a result of the Mongol conquests. The system broke down when these links were disrupted in the mid-fourteenth century following the devastations of the Black Death.

Abu-Lughod also notes that the thirteenth-century system had a precursor in classical times:

> Some two thousand years ago, an earlier incipient world system existed which involved almost all the regions (except northern Europe) participating in the thirteenth-century system. Geographically, its shape was very similar to the thirteenth-century one, although politically it was structured along more imperial lines, and economically its parts were much less well integrated.[24]

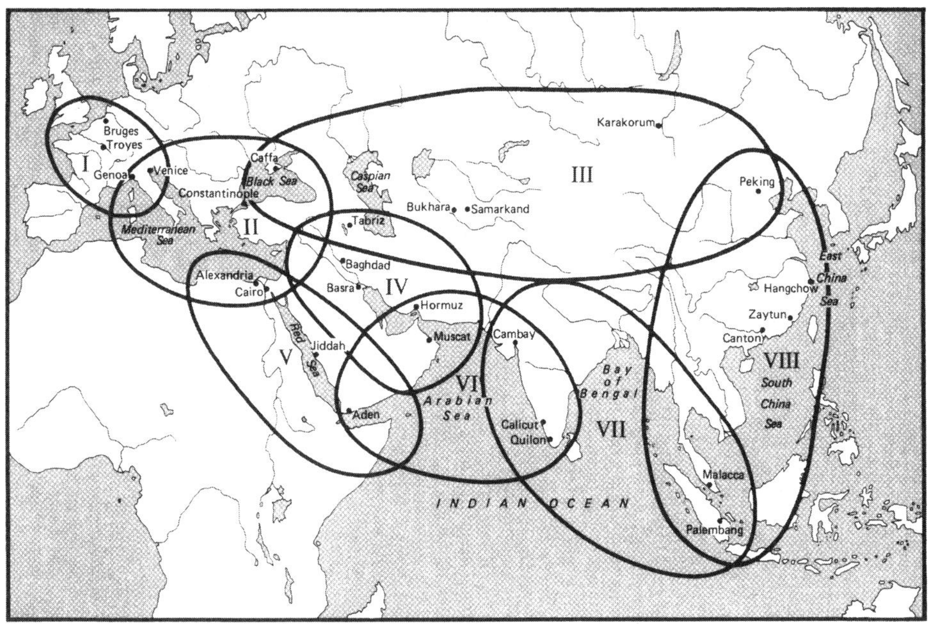

MAP 7. THE THIRTEENTH-CENTURY WORLD-SYSTEM. FROM JANET L. ABU-LUGHOD, *BEFORE EUROPEAN HEGEMONY*, P. 283; COPYRIGHT © 1989 BY OXFORD UNIVERSITY PRESS, INC. USED BY PERMISSION OF OXFORD UNIVERSITY PRESS, INC.

The links in this classical world-system, according to Abu-Lughod, were sustained by two great imperial powers, Rome in the West and Han China in the East. Accordingly, "that system also 'failed' after the fall of Rome and the loss of Han unity."[25]

Although Abu-Lughod's approach is very different from that of Frank and Gills, there is one point of similarity. Specifically, all of these authors reserve the term "world-system" for very large-scale social systems—not necessarily global but certainly continental or transcontinental in scale. The very radicalness of the position taken by Frank and Gills, in fact, comes from their assertion that such linkages have been important throughout history. Abu-Lughod, for her part, considers a "world-system" to have existed when most or all of Eurasia was linked by trade routes, but not in intervening periods when these interregional connections broke down. In her view, something that is merely regional is, by definition, not a "world-system."

Another approach to premodern world-systems, and the one I wish to adopt in the present study, is that of Christopher Chase-Dunn and Thomas Hall.[26] These authors, unlike Frank, Gills, and Abu-Lughod, do not set a lower limit on scale. Chase-Dunn and Hall define world-systems as "intersocietal networks in which the interactions (e.g., trade, warfare, intermarriage, information) are important for the reproduction of the internal structures of the composite units and importantly affect changes that occur in these local structures."[27] Taken literally, this means that any set of social structures, regardless of scale, can be considered a "world-system" so long as it has strong internal ties and is relatively autonomous of its external environment.

Although this may seem a distortion of the term "world," the definition is actually quite useful because it helps to focus attention on the essential character of "systemness"—that is, integration—without introducing any artificial constraints on scale. Applying this definition to world history, Chase-Dunn and Hall find not just one world-system (a la Frank), and not just a series of large-scale systems separated by historical blanks (a la Abu-Lughod), but rather a continuum in which a variety of world-systems, some of them large, some of them small, coexist (at least in premodern times). World-systems do not suddenly "emerge" or "disappear" at some arbitrary scale of organization; rather, systems of varying sizes undergo expansion and contraction, coalescence and fragmentation.

Admittedly, all of this sounds rather abstract. What helps to make the picture concrete is Chase-Dunn and Hall's attention to the nature of these links between societies. Specifically, they describe four different categories of intersocietal links:[28]

Bulk-goods network (BGN)

Prestige-goods network (PGN)

Political/military network (PMN)

Information network (IN)

According to Chase-Dunn and Hall, "All of these nets in combination constitute an entire world-system."[29] This approach is based upon the recognition that there are many different types of social interaction and that we should not assume prima facie that, for example, economic interactions are always more important than political ones, or that foodstuffs and other necessities are more important than luxury items.

Of course, as Chase-Dunn and Hall also note, "The use of multiple bounding criteria often will result in nested levels of system boundedness."[30] Just as there is no need to assume that one type of interaction takes precedence over another, there is no need to assume that all types of interaction take place on the same scale. Although the size of the various networks is of course a subject for empirical research, Chase-Dunn and Hall postulate:

> Generally, bulk goods will compose the smallest regional interaction net. Political/military interaction will compose a larger net that may include more than one bulk goods net, and prestige-goods exchanges will link even larger regions that may contain one or more political/military nets. . . . We expect the information net to be of the same order of size as the prestige goods net: sometimes larger, sometimes smaller.[31]

These various relationships can be depicted schematically, as in Figures 4–7.

In this analysis, system boundaries are not (necessarily) transitions from one "type" of society to another, but rather areas where there is a steep "falloff" in the density of social exchanges. Just because two regions are culturally similar or have the same type of economic organization does not mean they are part of the same "world-system." Conversely, it is possible for regions with very different cultures or political systems to be part of the same "world-system." The key criterion is regular, systemic interaction. Perhaps counterintuitively, these interactions do not even have to be peaceful. In the words of David Wilkinson, a "civilizations" specialist whose work on social networks prefigured that of Chase-Dunn and Hall, "[c]onflict, hostility, and even warfare, when durable (habitual, protracted, or inescapable), are forms of association that create a relationship between, and a social system composed of, the contestants, antagonists, and foes."[32] Two countries that are constantly at war, in other words, are as much part of the same system as if they were close political allies or trading partners.

Chase-Dunn and Hall have applied this methodology to three specific historical examples: a "very small world-system" located in northern California prior to the gold rush of 1849; the unification of

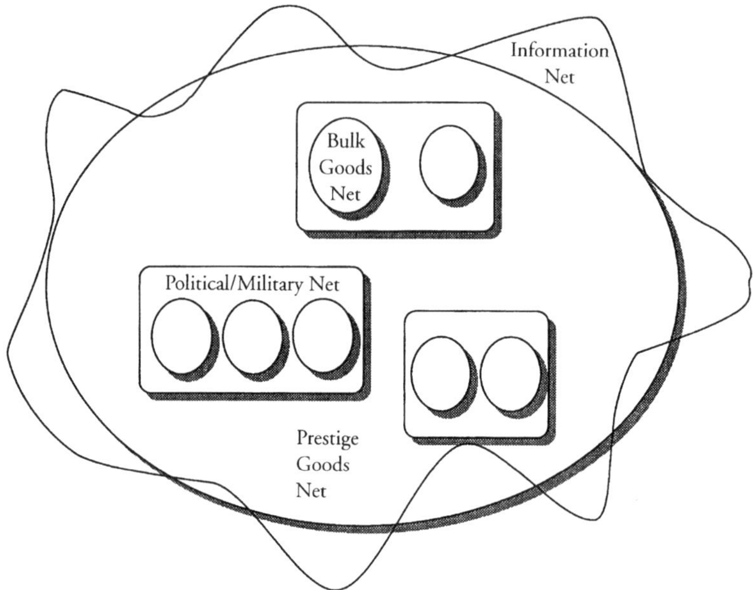

FIGURE 4. Nesting of the boundaries of the four networks of exchange. From Christopher Chase-Dunn and Thomas D. Hall, *Rise and Demise: Comparing World Systems,* p. 54; copyright © 1997 by Westview Press, Inc. Used by permission of Westview Press, a member of Perseus Books, L.L.C.

Afro-Eurasia that took place between 500 B.C.E. and 1400 C.E.; and finally, the Europe-centered system that emerged in the sixteenth century. The second of these is most relevant to the present study.

Drawing heavily on Jerry Bentley's masterly study of cross-cultural exchanges in the premodern world,[33] Chase-Dunn and Hill summarize the unification of Afro-Eurasia as follows:

> We argue that before the first opening of the Silk Road there were at least three major state-based world-systems on the Eurasian landmass: the Chinese, the South Asian, and the West Asian. These three core regions became involved in long processes of mutual incorporation that was uneven and sporadic, with periods of increasing and decreasing incorporation. At times they joined to form a single system constituted by the equal exchange of luxury goods and bullion among the three main core regions. . . . This system was tightly linked between 200 B.C.E. and 200 C.E., 500 and 900 C.E., and 1200 to 1400 C.E. At other times the system decoupled into largely autonomous smaller world-systems, but

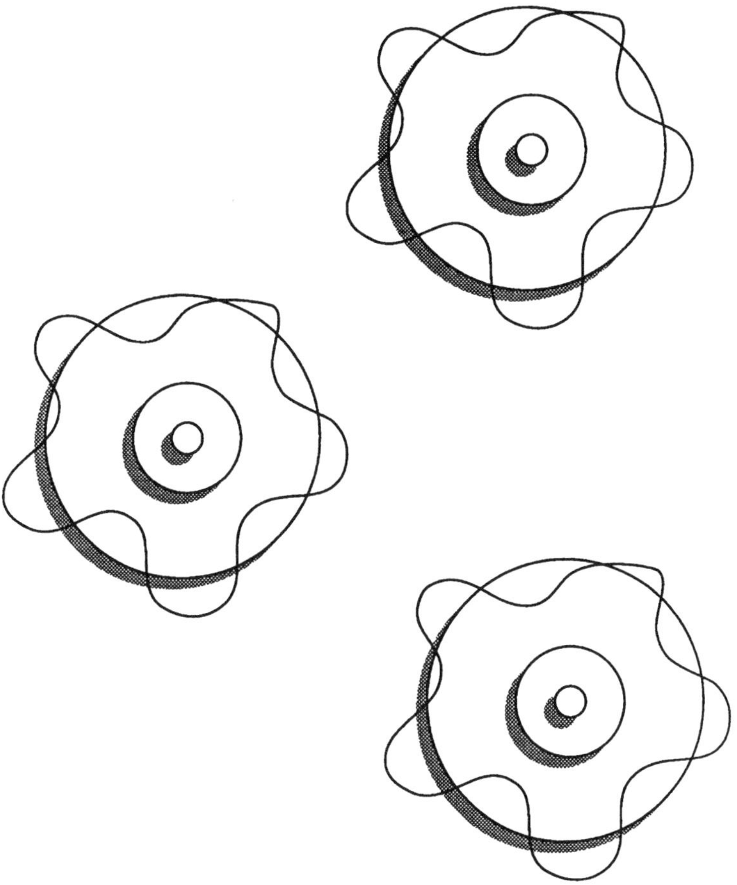

FIGURE 5. Three independent world-systems. From Christopher Chase-Dunn and Thomas D. Hall, *Rise and Demise: Comparing World Systems*, p. 60; copyright © 1997 by Westview Press, Inc. Used by permission of Westview Press, a member of Perseus Books, L.L.C.

> after each successive decoupling the separated regions were increasingly transformed by their interactions with the larger whole. What occurred was the merging of the largest networks, the information and the prestige-goods nets while the political/military and bulk goods nets remain distinct (except under the Mongols, when the military/political net also merged briefly).[34]

Although the terminology is different, there are many similarities between this picture and the one painted by Janet Abu-Lughod.

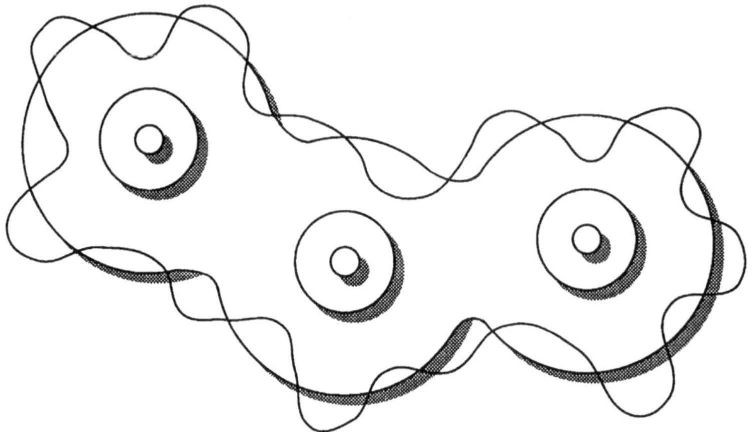

FIGURE 6. Three world-systems merged at prestige-goods and information networks. From Christopher Chase-Dunn and Thomas D. Hall, *Rise and Demise: Comparing World Systems*, p. 62; copyright © 1997 by Westview Press, Inc. Used by permission of Westview Press, a member of Perseus Books, L.L.C.

The first period of merged networks, 200 B.C.E. to 200 C.E., corresponds to Abu-Lughod's classical world-system, in which Rome to the west and Han China to the east were connected by long-distance trade across the silk routes. The third period of unification, 1200 to 1400 C.E., corresponds to her thirteenth-century world-system, when again long-distance trade was facilitated by the emergence of the Mongol Empire and other trends. The intermediate period, 500 through 900 C.E., is not discussed in detail by Abu-Lughod but is easily recognized as another period of empire building, not only in China (the Tang dynasty) but also in West Asia and North Africa (the Abbasid empire) and in western Europe (the Carolingian empire).[35]

Based on their three case studies, Chase-Dunn and Hall also draw some broad conclusions about the functioning of world-systems in general.[36] In my understanding, the most important points are as follows:

- Scale of social organization tends to become larger over time. The earliest world-systems, which had "kin-based, normative modes of accumulation," tended to be small-scale affairs. Later world-systems, most of them based on the tributary mode of accumu-

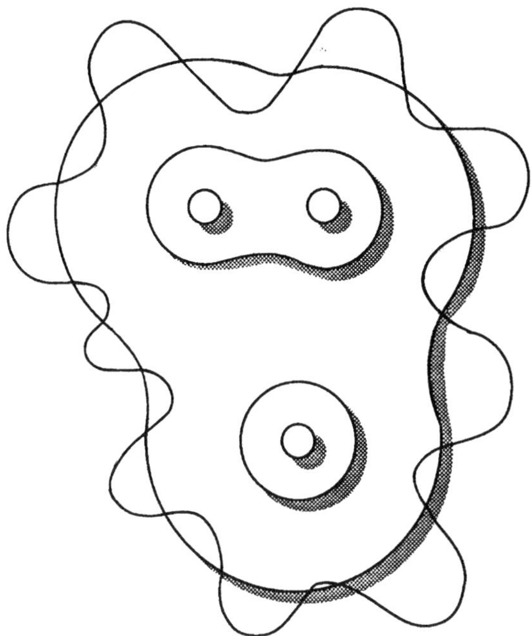

FIGURE 7. Three world-systems with merged prestige-goods and information networks, two with merged political/military networks. From Christopher Chase-Dunn and Thomas D. Hall, *Rise and Demise: Comparing World Systems*, p. 62; copyright © 1997 by Westview Press, Inc. Used by permission of Westview Press, a member of Perseus Books, L.L.C.

lation, were larger; and the current capitalist world-system is the largest of all.

- For the same reason, the number of world-systems tends to decrease over time. The globe can support many small, regional "world-systems" but not so many larger ones. Over time, systems tend to merge together, a trend that eventually culminates in the formation of the present global world-system.
- "All world-systems pulsate in the sense that the spatial scale of integration, especially by trade, becomes larger and then smaller again."[37] This tendency is obvious in the cyclic expansion and contraction of the Afro-Eurasian world-system(s).
- All world-systems "rise and fall," that is, they undergo "sequences of centralization and decentralization of economic, political, and

social power."[38] Politically, for example, state-based world-systems in premodern times tended to oscillate between periods of centralization, characterized by the presence of a "core-wide empire," and periods of decentralization, characterized by an "interstate system." One good example of this is the alternation between political unification and fragmentation in Chinese history.

- Chase-Dunn and Hall agree with Frank and Gills that capital accumulation is not unique to the modern world, but they stress that "capitalism only began to predominate over the tributary modes of accumulation"[39] in the seventeenth century. Earlier societies were organized not on the basis of capitalism but along lines of kinship or tributary relations.
- Nonetheless, Chase-Dunn and Hall find some limited support for Frank and Gill's argument that parallel cycles of growth and decline can be identified across much of Eurasia since the Bronze Age. The match is best for West Asia/Europe and East Asia; correlations between these regions and South Asia, however, are poor to nonexistent.
- Finally, these authors argue that the hierarchical, core-exploits-periphery structure of the modern capitalist world-system is not necessarily characteristic of earlier systems. Although core-periphery structures were present in many premodern world-systems, interregional exchanges tended to be more equal in character than is the case today.[40]

Chase-Dunn and Hall are hardly the only workers in the field of premodern world-systems studies, and many of their ideas will undoubtedly be refined or refuted in coming years. However, their definition of world-systems in terms of social networks of exchange represents a significant advance that defines the current state of the field. These ideas also provide us with the needed tools to answer the question posed at the beginning of this chapter regarding Japan's historical isolation, or lack thereof. In light of the above discussion, this question can now be reframed as follows: Did, or did not, premodern Japan constitute a "world-system" in some sense of the term?

A Japan-Centered "World-System"?

Given that world-systems theory has been around for a while, it is surprising that few attempts have been made to apply it to the case of Japan. The most systematic study in English is by Alvin So and Stephen Chiu, who attempt to explain how Japan (and more generally, East Asia as a whole) became integrated within the world economy in modern times.[41] Sociologist and world-systems theorist Stephen Sanderson has also written extensively on Japan, but his main interest is in explaining the origins of capitalism, which according to him first appeared in Europe and Japan.[42] Finally, archaeologist Mark Hudson's discussion of ethnogenesis in the Japanese islands (see Chapter 3) draws heavily on world-systems theory (especially the notion of core-periphery differentiation) but makes no real attempt to identify the spatial extent of the system, or systems, in question.[43]

Japanese scholarship on this topic is also sparse, although there have been a few cursory discussions in some of the recent literature. So far as I know, the first Japanese scholar to apply world-systems theory to Japanese history was political scientist Tanaka Akihiko, who wrote in 1989:

> We must note that world-systems in this sense do not necessarily have to cover the entire globe. Several world-systems can exist on the globe, and in fact, until quite recently (the nineteenth or twentieth centuries) many world-systems did exist on the globe. Social systems with almost no interaction with other parts of the globe can themselves be seen as world-systems. Ancient Greece and ancient China were clearly separate world-systems. In pre-Columbian America, there existed a world-system [which was] clearly separate from Europe. There is debate over how much interaction must be present in order to view [two regions] as being part of a single social system, but for example, there may be nothing strange about viewing Japan in the age of seclusion as a world-system of its own.[44]

Another view, admittedly pertaining to a different historical period, is presented by Murai Shōsuke. In a 1997 book aimed a semi-popular audience, Murai examined Japan's overseas contacts during the Sengoku, or "warring states," period of the sixteenth century. At the start of the book, Murai asks rhetorically,

> Prior to the appearance of the Europeans, what type of world-system, based on what kind of political and economic relationships, existed in the East Asian region, including the Japanese archipelago? How was it transformed through contact with the "European world economy"?
>
> Needless to say, China was located at the center of this regional world-system; Japan and surrounding areas, which were located on its periphery, can be thought of as forming, or aspiring [to form], a sub-system with a certain degree of autonomy from China. What did its structure and logic have in common with, and how did they differ from, the China-centered world-system? Again, one would expect that this sub-system displayed unique aspects in its contact with the "European world economy," but what concrete form did these take?[45]

Here we have two explicit, albeit cursory attempts, to understand premodern Japan within the context of world-systems theory. Which, if either of them, is correct? Was Japan an independent world-system, or was it a subsystem of a larger Asian system? Is there just one answer, or does it depend upon the period being discussed?

These are not easy questions, partly because of the sheer glut of relevant information available in the primary and secondary sources—far too much for any single individual to read through, let alone master. My purpose, of course, is not to give a complete account of all of Japan's overseas contacts in premodern times, but only to ascertain their broad outlines. To do even that much, however, I have had to rely extensively on secondhand and even thirdhand information, on semipopular, synthetic works rather than scholarly monographs or original documents. As a result, specialists will undoubtedly find much to complain about in the chapters that follow: omissions, oversimplifications, and probably more than a few outright mistakes. But these flaws, I hope, will not affect the overall flow of the argument. With this brief apologia, then, let me attempt to assess Japan's status, or lack thereof, as a "world-system" by using the criteria developed by Chase-Dunn and Hall. I will examine each type of exchange network in turn, beginning for the sake of convenience with political/military relations.

5 Political and Military Interactions

Japan as an Autonomous "Political/Military Network"?

The idea of a "political/military network" is in fact not original with Chase-Dunn and Hall but goes back to earlier work by David Wilkinson.[1] Wilkinson is a student of comparative civilizations, but unlike most of his colleagues, who define "civilization" in terms of cultural homogeneities, he identifies them with political/military networks—that is, areas that maintain regular, systemic relations of these kinds. For this reason, Wilkinson's roster of "civilizations" (to the extent he correctly identifies them) may be considered equivalent to the political/military aspect of "world-systems" as defined by Chase-Dunn and Hall.

According to Wilkinson, it is possible to identity fourteen such civilizations in world history. The earliest to appear (around 3000 B.C.E.) were Egyptian civilization and Mesopotamian civilization, which fused around 1500 B.C.E. to give birth to what Wilkinson calls "central civilization." After this seminal event, central civilization went on to evolve and expand until by the twentieth century it had absorbed all of the world's remaining civilizations. In East Asia, our area of interest, Wilkinson identifies two major civilizations: an "East Asian" political/military network centered on China and originating around 1500 B.C.E., and a separate "Japanese" civilization originating around

650 C.E. Both of these are said to have been subsumed within central civilization during the mid-nineteenth century.[2]

Is it really true, as Wilkinson asserts, that Japan constituted an autonomous political/military "system" in premodern times? Of course, the real question here is what we mean by "autonomous." How much foreign contact does it take before a society loses its independence and becomes part of larger "system"? Here I think the best approach is to follow the lead of Chase-Dunn and Hall and agree that "integration" takes place at the point where cross-border interactions become "important for the reproduction of the internal structures of the composite units and importantly affect changes that occur in these local structures."[3] To put it another way, Japan can be said to constitute an autonomous "civilization" (in Wilkinson's terms) only if political/military contacts with other societies were not important enough to materially affect the functioning, or the historical development, of any of the participants. By this criterion, as I will argue in the rest of this chapter, society in the Japanese islands did *not* constitute an independent political/military network, except perhaps in prehistoric times. In short, Wilkinson's interpretation is wrong.

Factors Affecting Cross-Border Interaction

Before examining the case of Japan in detail, however, it is necessary to consider some of the factors that influence the level of social interaction in general. Not surprisingly, perhaps is a great deal of previous research on this question, much of it by mathematically inclined geographers. One of the results of this research is the concept of "social gravity," which, as the name implies, is modeled on the theory of gravity in physics. (Indeed, this whole line of research is known as social physics.) Although some readers may object to seeing human behavior reduced to a formula, the model "has been found to accord with empirical data on all manner of human movement" irrespective of historical period or cultural setting.[4]

What is "social gravity"? Readers who studied physics in high school will recall that the gravitational attraction between two bodies is proportional to the product of their masses divided by the square of the distance between them. The social gravity model similarly proposes that the level of movement or social interaction between two given regions is roughly proportional to the product of their respective sizes or populations divided by some power of the distance between them.[5] In other words, the degree of interaction between two areas tends to increase with the size of the populations involved and to decrease as a function of distance. All things being the same, the more people there are, the more chances they have for interaction; the farther apart they live, the harder it is for them to meet.

This much seems intuitive. However, things are not quite this simple, because the inhibiting effect of distance (the power to which it is raised) can vary according to geographic or sociohistorical circumstances. For example, the presence of a geographic barrier (such as an ocean or a mountain range) can impede human movement, increasing "distance friction." Of course, the effect of such "barriers," and more fundamentally, of distance itself, also depends greatly upon the level of technology available. Clearly, an ocean presents less of a barrier to people with seaworthy boats than to people without, and even less to people with airplanes. Finally, "distance friction" also varies according to social characteristics other than technology, such as political circumstances. Political restrictions on movement, for example, may multiply the inhibiting effect of distance alone, in some extreme circumstances reducing the level of cross-border interaction to nearly zero.

All of this may sound unnecessarily complex, but the implications for the present study can be summarized as follows:

- In *all* periods of history, the absolute level of cross-border traffic (at least with areas outside the archipelago) was probably low by world standards because Japan was an island-country. The reason is simple: all other things being equal, it is easier to walk across a land border than to travel across an ocean.
- At any given time, all other things being equal, we would expect to find more interaction with nearby regions, both inside and outside the archipelago, than with distant regions.
- The "natural" tendency would have been for the volume of cross-border interactions, and their geographic scope, to increase over time. There are two reasons for this. First, population generally

tends to increase over time, and this was certainly the case for Japan, which had five million residents in the eighth century C.E. but more than thirty million in the eighteenth.[6] Second, as noted above, the level of transportation technology also tends to increase over time. As a result of these two factors, we would expect people to be traveling in greater numbers, and over longer distances, with each passing century.

- Any deviations from this "default" pattern probably resulted from period-specific sociopolitical circumstances hindering (or, alternatively, promoting) human movements across frontiers.

Of course, these predictions apply equally to all forms of cross-border movement. For that reason we will be returning to them again and again during the next few chapters. For now, however, let us see whether they are borne out by an examination of Japan's political/military interactions in premodern times.

Political/Military Relations with the Continent: A Brief Survey

Let me note at the start that the following survey will focus largely on Japan's political/military relations with continental Asia. This does not constitute a full accounting of Japan's external contacts, because it ignores relations with the (semi-)autonomous societies in southern Kyushu/Ryukyu and northern Honshu/Hokkaido. These areas were relatively accessible for geographic reasons, and as a result, political and military contacts with them existed throughout the premodern period, as I have already shown in previous chapters. This fact alone is sufficient to demonstrate that Japan, as a state, was *never* isolated in political or military terms but was always embedded within a web of relations, including at a minimum the surrounding "tribal zone." Precisely for this reason, however, further discussion of relations with Kyushu/Ryukyu and northern Honshu/Hokkaido would tell us little about the overall scope of Japan's political/military network in premodern times. For this, we need to go outside the archipelago.

Most introductory works on Japan treat foreign relations as a subset of cultural history. Japanese leaders, it is argued, engaged in foreign relations with Asian states, and later the West, in order to gain access to luxury goods, ideas, and other aspects of "advanced" culture. There is an element of truth to this, but the argument fails to note that these items were desired not only for their intrinsic value or interest but also because they conferred prestige on those who had access to them. In other words, differential access to foreign goods improved the position of political leaders vis-à-vis their domestic rivals. More generally, I would argue, the desire for prestige and/or political legitimacy was the primary motivation for *most* foreign relations—diplomatic, military, and commercial—initiated by Japanese leaders during premodern times. The precise form these relations took depended on the configuration of domestic and international power—that is, on geopolitics. In the most general terms, weak leaders had a stronger need for external props but fewer means to achieve them. Strong leaders were able to carry out foreign relations on their own terms but had relatively fewer incentives for doing so.[7]

The history of Japanese political/military interactions with the outside world can be divided into several distinct phases. First, in very early times we find a pattern of progressive engagement with the Korean Peninsula and China. This culminated in the Nara period with Japan's full integration into what Nishijima Sadao refers to as the "East Asian world" *(Higashi Ajia sekai).*[8] Second, during the Heian period we find a pattern of progressive disengagement. Third, during the Kamakura and Muromachi periods, Japan again became actively involved in political/military relations with the continent, although not all of these were state-driven. Finally, during the Edo period, the trend was again toward partial disengagement.

Phase 1: Engagement

Regarding the first phase, political leaders in Kyushu and other parts of western Japan were in direct contact with their counterparts on the Asian mainland from very early times. Chinese dynastic histories, for example, chronicle the arrival of envoys from "Wa" (presumably meaning some polity in Kyushu) during the Later Han dynasty in both 57 and 107 C.E. More famously, the *Wei History* describes several missions sent by "Queen Pimiko" of Wa in the mid-third century to Taifang, the site of a Chinese commandery on the Korean Peninsula. Also known from Chinese records are the "five kings of Wa," who sent tribute missions to the southern dynasties during the fifth century.[9]

Relations with Korean polities per se were also intense during these early centuries, at least to judge by the archaeological record (described in Chapter 7). There are also a number of historical sources on the Japanese side, but most of the information is suspect, because it comes from the *Nihon shoki* and is premised on the eighth-century view that southern Korea originally "belonged" to Yamato. Nonetheless, the very frequency of the records suggests that Yamato leaders were heavily involved in Korean affairs, particularly during the fifth and sixth centuries. The records suggest a pattern of shifting strategic alliances with the various Korean kingdoms, coupled with occasional military forays by Japanese troops into southern Korea.[10]

During the late sixth and seventh centuries, the emergence of the Sui and Tang empires in China initiated a cycle of competitive state-building throughout East Asia. Interstate relations took the form of multilateral diplomacy among the Korean states, China, and Wa, but the level of tension gradually increased until all parties became involved in a full-scale war for control of the Korean Peninsula. Japan and its Korean allies, Paekche and Koguryŏ, were defeated at the hands of Tang and Silla, which gained control of the entire peninsula in the 670s. Remnants of the Koguryŏ elite fled northeast to Manchuria, where they founded a successor state, Parhae.[11]

Japan's political/military engagement with Silla and Parhae continued during the eighth and ninth centuries.[12] Relations with Silla improved temporarily in the late seventh century but deteriorated again in the eighth. Open warfare was avoided, although Korean sources do mention a Japanese "attack" in 731, and Japanese sources record the details of another, aborted plan to attack Silla in the 760s. A chronic state of military tension is also indicated by the defense network maintained by Japan in Kyushu under the supervision of the Dazaifu.[13] Despite (or perhaps because of) their mutual mistrust, Japan and Silla also periodically exchanged ambassadors until 779. Japan's relations with Parhae, unlike those with Silla, were peaceful, with no military incidents of any kind. Japan and Parhae exchanged diplomatic missions every few years between 727 (when Parhae sent its first embassy to Japan) and the early tenth century.

Relations with China were somewhat more intermittent (and also one-sided). Here there is no hint of military interaction, although we know that Japanese officials were aware of the 755 An Lu-Shan rebellion in China and concerned (unnecessarily, as it turned out) that it might have direct consequences for Japan. Japanese contact with Tang was carried out almost exclusively by diplomatic channels, specifically via *kentōshi*, or Japanese "missions to Tang," which were sent approximately once every twenty years during the Nara and early Heian periods. The last party of *kentōshi* was the one dispatched in 838; it was accompanied by the Tendai monk Ennin, who left a detailed record of the embassy's activities in his diary.[14]

Phase 2: Disengagement

A dramatic and long-lasting change in the scale of Japan's political and military relationships occurred in the early tenth century. Japanese embassies to China were suspended in the late ninth century, and the Tang empire itself fell in 907 as the result of an internal rebellion. Japan retained diplomatic ties with Parhae until the latter state was destroyed by a Khitan invasion in 926. As noted, Japan's formal ties with Silla ended during the Nara period, but the two countries remained in a state of military tension characterized by rampant Korean piracy in the East China Sea. However, "connections" of this kind also came to an end in the tenth century when a new regime, Koryŏ, restored order to the peninsula. Manchuria and China also came under the control of new states (the Khitan Liao empire and Song, respectively), but Japanese leaders stubbornly resisted diplomatic overtures from all of these new polities on the Asian mainland.[15]

Thus began a period of relative isolation that lasted for three and a half centuries, until the first Mongol invasion of 1274. I do not deny that there were *some* political and military contacts between Japan and the continent in this period. Some pirate raids continued to occur in Kyushu, most notably in 1013, when a huge fleet of Jurchen marauders laid waste to Tsushima, Iki, and the area around Hakata (the "Toi Invasion").[16] One can also find examples of semi-official messages exchanged between political figures in Kyoto and the Koryŏ and Song governments via priest or merchant intermediaries. But no full-scale diplomatic missions were either sent or received—a radical departure from the pattern of foreign relations that prevailed through Nara and early Heian periods.

Phase 3: Reengagement

The Mongol invasions of 1274 and 1281 mark the beginning of another phase of involvement with the continent. Although the invasions themselves were unsuccessful, they forced Japanese authorities to create and maintain coastal defenses in Kyushu and ultimately contributed to the downfall of the Kamakura shogunate.[17] Military interactions with the continent remained intense during the subsequent Muromachi period, although they were initiated by pirates rather than state-level actors. Wakō, or "Japanese brigands," from the Gotō Islands and other parts of coastal Kyushu ravaged coastal Korea and northern China for a number of decades beginning around 1350.[18] Their raids for grain and slaves came to a temporary halt, however, in the fifteenth century, when they were suppressed by the Muromachi shogunate at the request of Ming China and Yi-dynasty Korea. (Appeasement measures instituted by Korean officials also played a role in the disappearance of the Wakō.)

The fifteenth and sixteenth centuries also saw intense political/military ties with the Korean Peninsula and China. Under the third Ashikaga shogun, Yoshimitsu, the Muromachi government reestablished tributary ties with China, sending a total of nineteen trade-motivated embassies to Ming between 1401 and 1547. As the Muromachi power structure weakened, however, this system gradually broke down.[19] Control over the tribute missions was usurped by powerful military families such as the Hosokawa and Ōuchi, while at the same time the Wakō made a reappearance. These "later Wakō," who operated freely in the East China Sea throughout the entire sixteenth century, are said to have been largely Chinese, not Japanese, in composition (so much as these terms have meaning at all in this period). Their depredations eventually ceased as the result of a 1567 Ming ban on overseas travel, combined with suppressive measures instituted by the Japanese hegemon Toyotomi Hideyoshi in the 1580s.

Although Hideyoshi played an important role in the disappearance of the Wakō, it should not be concluded that he was responsible for a reduction in the scale of Japan's political/military networks;

far from it. After Hideyoshi succeeded in reunifying the three main islands in 1591, he turned his attention to the continent and invaded Korea on two separate occasions, in 1592 *(Bunroku no eki)* and 1597 *(Keichō no eki).* Korea was merely a stepping-stone to Hideyoshi's greater ambition of conquering Ming China, but this plan was never realized, and Japanese troops rapidly abandoned Korea following the warlord's death in 1598.[20] In sum, then, the three hundred years beginning with the Mongol invasions saw nearly continuous military and political interaction with the Korean Peninsula and China, although of course the nature of the involvement varied significantly from time to time.

The late sixteenth century, of course, also saw the first European visitors to Japan, and there is some justification for considering these contacts within the context of Japan's political/military network. For example, Europeans took part in Wakō-like piracy in the East China Sea, and the adoption of Western firearms by Oda Nobunaga and other daimyo certainly helped to accelerate the pace of reunification.[21] There is also the "official" mission (the so-called *Tenshō ken'ō shisetsu*) sent to Europe by a group of Christian daimyo under the sponsorship of the Society of Jesus in the 1580s.[22] But overall, contacts with Europe in the sixteenth century were essentially commercial and religious, and it would probably be an exaggeration to say that Japan's political/military network had expanded to global proportions at this point. This is all the more true, of course, during the subsequent Edo period, when direct contact with Europeans was limited to the Dutch at Nagasaki.

Phase 4: Disengagement

The "seclusion" edicts of the early seventeenth century, which placed severe restrictions on the arrival of foreign ships and a total ban on Japanese travel abroad, symbolize the greatly reduced scope of Japan's political/ military interactions during the Edo period.[23] I am not arguing that Edo Japan was a "closed" country—quite the reverse, as we shall see below in our discussions of trade and information flow. But it is clear that Japan's military/political network was smaller in the Edo period than at any time since before the Mongol invasions. There were no external wars or invasions, no significant pirate activity in international waters adjoining Japan, and no diplomatic contacts except for Yi-dynasty Korea (Chosŏn) and the Ryukyu kingdom. Of course, this contraction was merely temporary; beginning in the late eighteenth century, Russian expansion to the north broadened Japan's political/military horizons, which became fully global following the arrival of the American "black ships" and the "opening" of the country in 1853–1854.

Patterns and Explanations

Thus ends our highly simplified survey of political and military interactions between Japan and overseas countries during the premodern period. How well do actual events, as presented here, match my earlier "predictions" about cross-border interaction? Since I have not made comparisons with other countries, it is impossible to evaluate whether the overall level of cross-border contacts was lower for Japan than for other, land-bound countries. The other points, however, are borne out well by the historical record.

First, it is clear that frequency of interaction has normally correlated inversely with distance in Japanese history. As an illustration, let us consider once again Japan's external connections during the Nara period, this time taking into account not only continental Asia but also peripheral societies in the north and south of the archipelago.

Regarding diplomatic relations, both the Emishi and the Hayato sent tribute missions to the imperial court for most of the period in question: one every six years in the case of the Hayato and perhaps as many as one per year for the Emishi.[24] On the Asian continent, Silla sent seventeen embassies to Japan, and Japan sent twelve to Silla. During the same period, Parhae sent eleven embassies to Japan, and Japan sent nine to Parhae. Slightly farther afield, Tang sent one embassy to Japan, while Japan sent six *kentōshi* missions to China.[25] In sum, during the Nara period, Japan's political interactions were continuous with the tribes on its periphery, regular with its nearest continental neighbors, and intermittent with China. Very occasionally visitors from farther afield made an appearance in Japan; one well-known example is Bodai Senna, a monk from "Tenjiku" (possibly meaning India), who performed the "eye-opening ceremony" for the

Great Buddha at Tōdaiji in 752. However, there is no evidence of systemic diplomatic ties with any region more distant in China.

Much the same can be said for military interactions, although here the distance gradient appears steeper (because military campaigns involved more people, more materiel, and more time than diplomatic missions). In the Nara period, troops were sent to quell "rebellions" by the Hayato in 720 and the Emishi in 720 and 724. This marked the end of Hayato resistance to the state, but the Emishi rebelled again in 774, initiating three decades of nearly continuous warfare on Japan's northern frontier.[26] As noted above, there may have been a Japanese attack on Silla in 731, but if so, this was the only occasion during the Nara period when Japan (or Japanese individuals) exchanged hostilities with another Asian state. Again, as was the case for diplomacy, the intensity or frequency of interaction decreased as a function of geographical distance.

Second, the prediction that scale and frequency of interactions should generally increase over the long term is also borne out by the historical record. As we have seen, Nara-period Japan had no political or military ties with any land more distant than China. Eight centuries later, however, during the Sengoku period, Japanese warlords were sending diplomatic missions to Europe, and still later, during the nineteenth century, Japan was fully exposed to the political/military dynamics of the modern world-system.

Despite this very long-term trend, however, it is also obvious from the above discussion that the scale of Japan's military and political interactions fluctuated wildly during premodern times. Relative maximums are seen in the early centuries C.E., the Nara period, and the Muromachi period (all involving systemic interaction with China), with an absolute maximum (including the European powers) occurring in the sixteenth century. Relative minimums occur in the sixth century and the Edo period (which saw systemic interaction with Korea, but not China), with an absolute minimum (no systemic relations outside the archipelago) occurring in the late Heian period.

This pulsation is not particularly surprising, given Chase-Dunn and Hall's research on comparative world-systems. The question we must ask, however, is, Why? What caused Japan's political/military network to "pulsate" so conspicuously? Of course, there is no single answer to this question; each change in scale undoubtedly resulted from a unique constellation of events and processes. All the same, it is still possible to identify some of the major factors. To state my conclusion first, the pulsation of Japan's political/military network resulted from an interplay of domestic and external political conditions, but with definite emphasis upon the latter.

First, let us consider domestic factors. Certainly, Japanese politics played a strong role in determining the *type* of interaction that was most common in each period: periods of relatively centralized rule were characterized by formal diplomatic relations and, in some cases, state-level hostilities, whereas periods of decentralized rule were characterized by "privatized" relations and maritime piracy. With regard to *scale* of interaction, however, no clear pattern emerges. Certainly, it is possible to find many individual cases where changing political conditions in Japan resulted in an expansion or reduction in network scale. The problem, however, is that factors that had one effect in a particular period might have the opposite effect in another. For example, some periods of relatively centralized rule, such as the Nara period, were associated with "up" phases, while others, such as the Edo, were associated with "down" phases. Periods of relative decentralization could likewise see either a reduction in overseas contacts, as occurred in the late Heian period, or an expansion, as occurred in the early Muromachi period and again in the sixteenth century.

By contrast, some of the broad features of the pattern are easily explained with reference to external conditions, specifically those in China. For example, the timing of most of the "up" phases correlates well with periods of imperial expansion in China. The most obvious case, of course, is the rise of the Mongols in the thirteenth century, which had a direct, although short-lived, impact on Japan. Less obvious, but in the long run probably more important, were the rise of the Later Han dynasty in the first century C.E.; that of the Sui and Tang in the late sixth and early seventh centuries; and that of the Ming in the fourteenth. In all of these cases, imperial expansion in China resulted in the emergence (or reemergence) of direct political and, in some cases, military contacts between suzerains in the Japanese archipelago and their counterparts in China.

Admittedly, there are exceptions as well; one has to ask, in particular, why the emergence of the Song dynasty in the tenth century and that of the Qing in the seventeenth did not produce similar changes. The case of the Song is not hard to explain, given that this particular Chinese dynasty, unlike most of the others, lacked expansionist tendencies. A similar argument could be made with respect to the Qing dynasty, which in the seventeenth century remained shackled by domestic problems (e.g., the Revolt of the Three Feudatories) and later was prevented from pursuing imperialist policies by the encroachment of the European powers. So perhaps here we simply have a case of the exception proving the rule.

This leads to the corollary point that periods of decentralization or disorder in China were often, although not always, associated with a tendency for Japan to become politically "decoupled" from the continent. Probably the best example here is the long period of Japanese "isolation" that followed the breakup of the Tang dynasty at the start of the tenth century. And yet, here too we find some exceptions. The most important of these came quite early in the game: the breakup of the Later Han dynasty saw, if anything, an expansion in diplomatic ties between rulers in Wa and their counterparts in China. The reason for this, evidently, is that the former remained insecure in their rule and desired the political legitimacy that could accrue from relations even with minor Chinese kingdoms, such as those that emerged after the fall of Han.

As should be clear from the previous paragraph, my argument is not that most of Japan's overseas relationships were unilaterally imposed from abroad. Quite the reverse: most of Japan's formal contacts with China, at least, were initiated by Japanese rulers in search of specific goals such as political legitimacy, security, or access to luxury goods. Rather, what I am arguing is that their inclination and ability to achieve these goals were strongly affected by the dynastic cycle in China. Chinese expansion tended to create links of all kinds throughout Asia as well as to raise the general level of interregional consciousness and tension. Conversely, political fragmentation and disorder in China allowed relatively distant countries, such as Japan, to sever links with it if they so chose.

Another important point, already implicit in the above discussion, concerns the effect of these various interactions upon Japan: although interactions with distant partners such as China and later Europe were hardly continuous, when they did exist they could have a decisive impact on the course of Japanese history. As just one example, tributary relations with the Han dynasty and its successors were not "just" superficial diplomatic contacts. Rather, they actively stimulated state formation in Japan by conferring political legitimacy on Wa chieftains, both directly, through diplomatic recognition, and indirectly, by giving them access to prestige goods (see Chapter 7) that could be redistributed within the archipelago. This classic case of secondary state formation is but one example of how contacts with China influenced political developments in Japan.[27] So above, in asking whether pulsations in Japan's political/military network can be explained on the basis of domestic circumstances, we were really asking the wrong question; if anything, domestic circumstances can be explained on the basis of foreign contacts, not vice versa.

If political interactions with China were so important to Japan, what about the reverse? Is it possible, in other words, to argue that political interactions with Japan played a decisive role in Chinese history before the modern period? Probably not. Of course, one could say that early tributary relations with Japan were important to China because they reinforced Chinese ideas of superiority (i.e., the "middle kingdom ideology") and hence political legitimacy. However, Japan was only one of many tributaries, and it is hard to believe that loss of contact with it would have made much of a difference in the long run. In other words, although Japan and China were embedded in the same political/military network for much of premodern history, interactions and influence between the two were quite one-sided. This one-sidedness is typical, I might add, of core-periphery relations and supports the idea that during phases of integration, Japan may be considered a periphery of China—at least in political/military terms.

Questions of Scale

While Japan may be considered a political "periphery" of China for much of premodern history, a very different picture emerges when we look at other partners and other scales of interaction. Looking first at societies to the north in Tōhoku and Hokkaido, in general I think it is fair to say that the timing and scale of their military and political interactions with Japan were determined by developments in Japanese society, not the reverse. As just one example, the wars of the Nara and early Heian periods resulted fundamentally from Japanese expansionist tendencies, not the activities of Emishi chieftains. Similarly, as a general rule these interactions had more of an impact upon northern society than they did upon Japan. As we saw in Chapter 4, ethnogenesis in the north was greatly stimulated by contact with Japan (although it is also true that presence of a barbarian Other was important to the development of Japanese ethnicity). The relations of Japan with northern societies mirrored its relations with China—but in microcosm, and with the signs reversed. Here, then, we have another classic, although relatively small-scale, example of core-periphery relations.

If true, this argument has important implications for the theory of frontiers. By far the most influential of all frontier historians was Frederick Jackson Turner, an American active in the late nineteenth and early twentieth centuries. Turner's writings, although sometimes contradictory and hard to understand, argued that the development of the American people and the American character had been essentially shaped by the frontier experience. In Turner's words, "American history has been in a large degree the history of the colonization of the Great West. The existence of an area of free land, its continuous recession, and the advance of American settlement westward, explain American development."[28] This idea, dubbed the "Turner thesis" by later historians, has been widely criticized, not least because it is so abstract as to defy proof or disproof. Still, it has been and remains highly influential, not only in American history but also in comparative frontier studies.[29]

Indeed, one Japanese historian, Takahashi Tomio, has attempted to apply some of Turner's ideas to Japan. In a semipopular book on Japanese frontiers, Takahashi presents the following argument:

> [T]he ancient Japanese state, based in the west, matured into a unified Japanese state by conquering, assimilating, and developing the frontier (undeveloped land) of Eastern Japan. In terms of modern regional divisions, this region comprised all of Chūbu, Kantō, Tōhoku, and Hokkaido, corresponding to about 65% of the entire Japanese archipelago.

> Contrary to the American case, we must speak of a "Great East." Moreover, I think we can also say that this eastward expansion (conquest or colonization) created the Japanese state and the Japanese nation.[30]

Fortunately, Takahashi is careful to temper what sounds like a paean to Japanese "manifest destiny" by noting that, just as the American expansion extracted a terrible price from native Americans, so did the Japanese expansion from the Emishi and their descendents.

And this, I think, is the important point, and one that refutes the "Turner thesis" for both Japan and America. Frontier expansion in both cases had a tremendous and ultimately disastrous effect on peripheral native societies; the impact those native societies, or the frontier itself, had on the expanding core, was far less wrenching. The issue, as I have repeatedly stressed, is one of power; core societies had it, but peripheral ones did not—at least not to the same extent.

I am not arguing that bilateral relationships are always unequal, however. This becomes clear when we look at the intermediate group of contacts—for example, those between Japan and the various Korean kingdoms. Here, I think it is fair to say that the direction of causality and influence ran both ways, at least after the initial period of state formation in Japan.[31] Among many examples of geopolitical developments in Korea that had a significant impact on Japan are the unification wars of the seventh century (which stimulated the emergence of a centralized state apparatus in Japan) and the decline of public order in ninth-century Silla (which led to pirate attacks on Kyushu and, ultimately, to the xenophobia of the late Heian period).[32] Examples of the reverse kind, in which Japan decisively influenced events in Korea, include the Wakō attacks of the medieval period and, even more obviously, Hideyoshi's invasions in the sixteenth century.

In general, I think that political and military relations between Japan and the various Korean states are best understood as a form of "peer-polity" interaction.[33] This concept, formulated by archaeologist Colin Renfrew, refers to interactions between societies of near-equal status, to which the ideas of core and periphery or dominance and subordination do not necessarily apply. According to Renfrew, peer-polity interaction can take many forms, including competition, competitive emulation, warfare, transmission of innovation, "symbolic entrainment" (the tendency to share symbolic systems including iconography, religion, etc.), ceremonial exchange of valuables, flow of commodities, and linguistic and/or ethnic commonalities.[34] Many of these fall outside the political/military sphere and thus outside the present discussion, but even a cursory examination of the history of Japanese-Korean relations reveals the ubiquity of many of these forms of interaction and, hence, the utility of the "peer-polity" concept.

A Web of Overlapping Systems

In sum, during premodern times Japan's military and political interactions with the outside world displayed considerable variation across space and time (see Figure 8). First, interactions with other societies within the archipelago were intense, continuous, and normally hierarchical in nature, with the Japanese "core" exercising "dominance" over a weaker "periphery." In other words, Japan as a polity was *never* isolated from the outside world but always embedded within a web of political/military interactions that extended well beyond its actual borders. Next, at various times in history this network merged with other political/military spheres of interaction in continental Asia. Historical developments either in Japan or Korea could cause a temporary fusing of networks and mutual influence in the form of "peer-polity" relations. More distant developments could sometimes lead to integration on a much greater scale, in which regional networks in Japan, and of course Korea, were subsumed as peripheries within a continental political/military network centered on China. This occurred most commonly during periods of imperial expansion in China—which, not coincidentally, correspond closely to the phases of maximum integration for Eurasia as a whole, as identified by Chase-Dunn and Hall: roughly 200 B.C.E.–200 C.E., 500–900 B.C.E., and 1200–1400 C.E.

I hasten to add, however, that this picture, as complex as it may seem, is still vastly oversimplified. One important reason for this is that our discussion has been highly "Japanocentric," focusing only on bilateral relationships involving Japan. This is fine as far as it goes, but by ignoring multilateral and third-party relationships, it gives a distorted view of how the system, or systems, may have functioned as a whole.

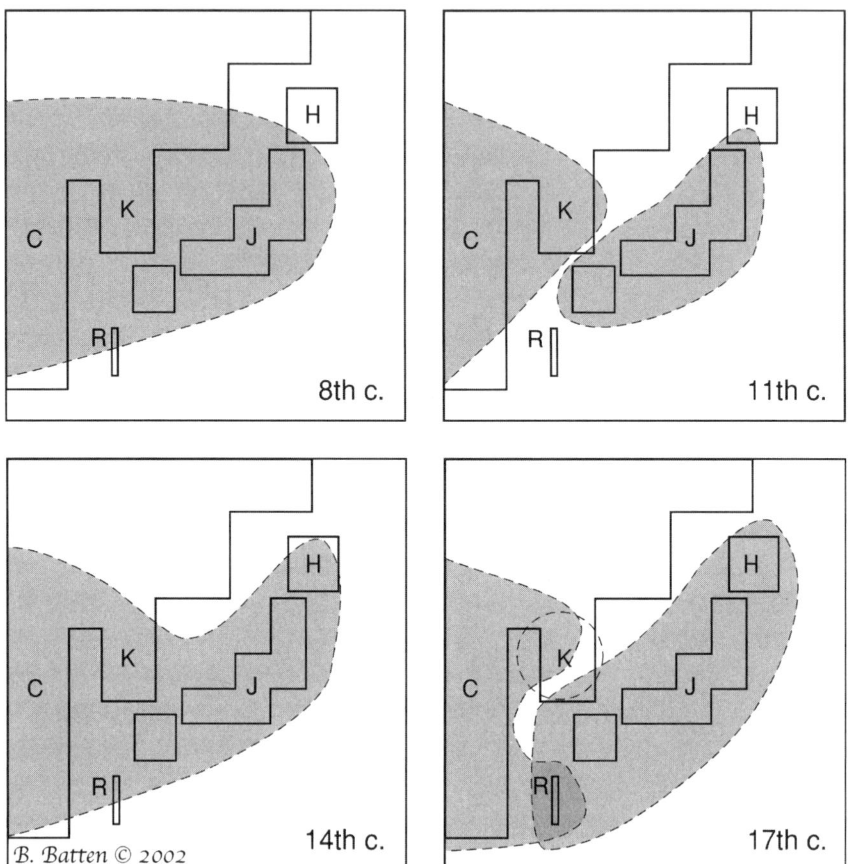

FIGURE 8. Evolution of Japan's political/military network, showing shift from engagement with East Asian network (eighth century), to disengagement (eleventh century), reengagement (fourteenth century), and partial disengagement (seventeenth century). J = Japan "proper"; H = Hokkaido; R = Ryukyu; K = Korea; C = China.

Consider, for example, the case of the Ryukyus, which I have all but ignored for the sake of simplicity. From a Japan-centered point of view, Okinawa has been a "periphery" throughout recorded history—much like Hokkaido. Okinawa, however, was not just a periphery of Japan but also of China, with which it simultaneously maintained tributary relations. At the same time, because of its role as a trade entrepôt, Okinawa was able to maintain a degree of independence from both of these "cores" and indeed to develop an autonomous state structure around the fifteenth century. Presumably, in microcosm, the Okinawan state also contained its own "cores" and "peripheries."

In short, it is not enough to conceive of Japan as being at the center of a pulsating political/military network that from time to time became subsumed within larger Asian networks. We must remember that each of the regions with which Japan was in contact was also at the center of its own local (or in some cases, large-scale) network and that these regional networks overlapped and interfingered in highly complex ways.

Still more important, there was *local* continuity at nearly all points. Even in periods when Japan had no direct political/military interactions with China, it did with the Ryukyus—or Korea or Ezo—and these polities had their own, independent connections with China. China, in turn, had connections with polities on its own frontiers—and so on and so forth. It is this "down-the-line" continuity that accounts for some of the large-scale (albeit indirect) interactions we will encounter later with respect to the flow of prestige goods and information. For now, however, we turn to a rather different picture, that presented by the circulation of bulk goods.

6 Bulk Goods

Japan's Bulk Goods Network

What are "bulk goods"? How do they differ from the "prestige goods," which also figure in Chase-Dunn and Hall's classification of world-systems? The first point to make is that these are not objective, precisely defined categories. Rather, they are rough-and-ready labels for two partly overlapping categories of goods. In this study I will use the term "bulk goods" to refer to utilitarian items used in quantity—for example, daily necessities such as food and clothing, and the like. "Prestige goods," by contrast, refers to high-value, non-utilitarian items, that is, luxuries.

Obviously, there is no sharp dividing line between bulk goods and prestige goods, not only because many products fall somewhere between the two extremes but also because the categories themselves are subjective. Differences in valuation and perceived need, as we all know, can coexist even within a single culture. For example, many of the tribute products imported to Nara from the Japanese countryside would have been considered luxuries by farmers; but to the aristocrats who consumed them they constituted "necessities." Just as important, the role played by a given product may change over time. For example, Chinese ceramics and textiles were first imported to Japan in the ancient period as high-prestige, high-value items for consumption by the court elite; later, however, as volume increased and the composition of society changed, they became items of mass consumption (although more so in Japan's cities than in the countryside). In what follows, I shall treat these and similar items as prestige goods, while acknowledging that this classification is somewhat arbitrary.

Perhaps more fundamentally, some items do not fit Chase-Dunn and Hall's categories very well to begin with. Take money, for example. Money is certainly an economic "good," but it is not one that is usually consumed directly; rather, it serves as a standard of value, a means of storing wealth, and a medium for transactions of all kinds, especially the acquisition of other goods. Is money, then, a bulk good or a prestige good? Arguably, neither. This is an important point, because it shows that the networks described by Chase-Dunn and Hall are hardly all-inclusive; they omit some important categories of exchange. Of course, the status of money is most likely to become an issue when attempting to apply the theory to modern, capitalist societies, but it cannot be ignored even in premodern times.[1] As we shall see, Japan was a major importer of Chinese currency (copper coins) throughout the medieval period. Later, beginning in the fifteenth century, Japan assumed an equally important role as an exporter of bullion (first silver and later copper) to world markets. These exchanges were of major systemic importance: the influx of Chinese coins was both cause and effect of economic growth in medieval Japan, and the outflow of Japanese silver was sufficient to affect world markets during the early modern period. However, such transactions are not easily accommodated within Chase-Dunn and Hall's framework. Here, again largely for the sake of convenience, I will discuss coins and bullion under the category of "prestige goods" in the next chapter.

Even when we have agreed upon what to include (and what not to include) in our discussion of "bulk goods," some obvious difficulties remain in identifying the "networks" in which these items circulated. For one thing, it is possible—even probable—that volume and extent of circulation varied significantly from item to item. As a hypothetical example, fresh foodstuffs might all be consumed locally, whereas textiles or items of clothing might have a countrywide or even larger circulation. Second, the apparent size of the network might vary greatly, depending upon where we choose to "center" our analysis. Residents of large urban areas are likely to have access to more types of goods from a wider geographic area than are farmers living in isolated areas of the countryside.

It is, of course, impossible to give full consideration to these issues in a study such as this. Fortunately, for our purposes, it is not necessary to give a complete description of the circulation of bulk goods in premodern Japan. The reason is that we are mainly interested in the maximum size of the network, not in all the local variations and minimums. In the discussion that follows, therefore, I have chosen to look mainly at widely circulated goods that were available in urban centers of consumption, particularly Heijō-kyō (present-day Nara), which served as Japan's capital from 710 through 784; Heian-kyō (Kyoto), which was founded in 794 and has remained an important city until the present; and Edo (present-day Tokyo), Japan's military capital after 1600. Heijō-kyō and Heian-kyō are both located in west-central Honshu; Edo is located much farther east on the Pacific coast of the same island. These cities also represent a range of populations. Heijō-kyō in the eighth century had a population of perhaps 100,000, and Heian-kyō in the ninth century had 150,000 at most. Edo in the early eighteenth century, by contrast, was home to a million urban residents.[2] These differences disappear somewhat, however, when we consider these figures as a percentage of the country's total population, which was approximately five million and thirty million, respectively, in these two periods.[3] Both Heijō-kyō and Edo, therefore, were home to some 2 to 4 percent of Japan's population.

Circulation of Bulk Goods in Ancient and Medieval Times

The early eighth century represented an important landmark not only in Japan's political history but also in its economic history. The reason is the elaborate tax system set up as part of the *ritsuryō* reforms.[4] Peasants throughout the country were counted in official censuses and required to pay taxes known variously as *so*, *chō*, *yō*, and so on, as well as to provide labor and military services for the government. Tax collection was supervised by provincial and district officials; some of the goods were used to pay for local administrative expenses, and others were shipped to the capital to pay for the expenses of the central government, most importantly the official salaries and stipends of government workers. The tax system, in other words, created a tribute economy in which the labor of the masses was used to support the "lifestyles of the rich and famous"—that is, the central and, to a lesser extent, the local elites.

At any rate, this is how the system functioned in theory, as described in the Yōrō Code of 757.[5] The question, of course, is to what extent the system actually functioned in practice. At the risk of oversimplification, Japanese scholars have traditionally assumed that anything written in the codes must have actually taken place. Western scholars, by contrast, have tended to assume that the *ritsuryō* tax system existed largely on paper or that, if it was in fact implemented, it neither worked well nor survived long.[6] It was not possible to address this issue authoritatively when our main sources of information about the Nara period were the codes themselves and the (possibly equally biased) official histories such as the *Shoku Nihongi*. Now, fortunately, that is no longer the case, thanks to a veritable explosion of archaeological research in the past several decades.[7]

On the whole, archaeological research strongly supports the view that the Nara-period tax system functioned not only on paper but also in practice. Indirect evidence comes from excavations of provincial and district headquarters and government roads.[8] These show that infrastructure necessary to collect and ship taxes actually existed as the result of an early eighth-century building boom. Direct evidence comes from the discovery of huge numbers of wooden shipping tags *(mokkan)* found in Nara (Heijō-kyō) and elsewhere. These tags list the type, quantity, and place of origin of the tax shipments to which they were attached.[9]

To be sure, there are some discrepancies between the tax system as described in the law codes and that revealed by the shipping tags. For one thing, many of the surviving tags were attached to *nie*, a type of levy that does not appear in the *ritsuryō* codes but was evidently used to provide foodstuffs and other items for consumption by the imperial family and the high nobility.[10] Despite this difference, however, most of the actual items collected (as opposed to the category to which they were assigned) provide a close match with the lists in the codes. A second difference, to be discussed in more detail below, concerns the geographic scope of the shipments, which was somewhat more restricted than would appear from the paper codes.

What, then, were the tax goods shipped to the capital and where did they come from? Judging from previous research, the single most important item was "white" (polished) rice, which was shipped from at least twenty-four provinces ranging from Higo (central Kyushu) in the west to Kaga (along the Sea of Japan) and Mikawa (along the Pacific coast) in the east (see Map 8).[11] Both Kaga and Mikawa are relatively close to Nara in central Honshu, and it is perhaps notable that no polished rice was shipped to the capital from the eastern half of the island. Another very important item was salt, which came from at least ten provinces in western and central Honshu and Shikoku. (Kyushu was not represented, nor, again, was eastern Honshu.) Why were these products not shipped from eastern Japan? One possibility is that they were simply not produced there: upland farming, as opposed to wet-field farming, was more common in the east, and perhaps less of the population was concentrated near the sea, where salt production took place. Probably the main reason, however, had to do with transportation costs. Access to eastern Japan was primarily by land, meaning that it was difficult and expensive to ship heavy goods like rice and salt over long distances. Locations in western Japan, by contrast, could easily be reached by sea, resulting in reduced shipping costs.[12]

This point is confirmed when we consider other, lighter, marine products. The most important of these was the seaweed known as *wakame* (*Undaria*, brown kelp), which was shipped to the capital from twelve provinces ranging from Chikuzen in northern Kyushu to Shimōsa and Hitachi, both located in the Kantō to the east of Tokyo Bay. Other marine products show a similar distribution, although none were as pervasive as *wakame*. In addition to other types of seaweed, such as thick-haired *Codium (miru)* and laver *(nori)*, we find fish such as skipjack *(katsuo)*, "red fish" (*akō*, possibly referring to *madai*, or red sea bream), sardines *(iwashi)*, black porgy *(kurodai)*, mackerel *(saba)*, sea bass *(suzuki)*, and shark *(same)*, mollusks such as abalone *(awabi)*, hard-shelled mussel *(igai)*, horned turban *(sazae)*, and squid *(ika)*, and other seafoods such as dried sea cucumbers *(iriko)* and jellyfish *(kurage)*.[13] Unidentified "dried seafood" *(himono)* is also recorded from a number of provinces.

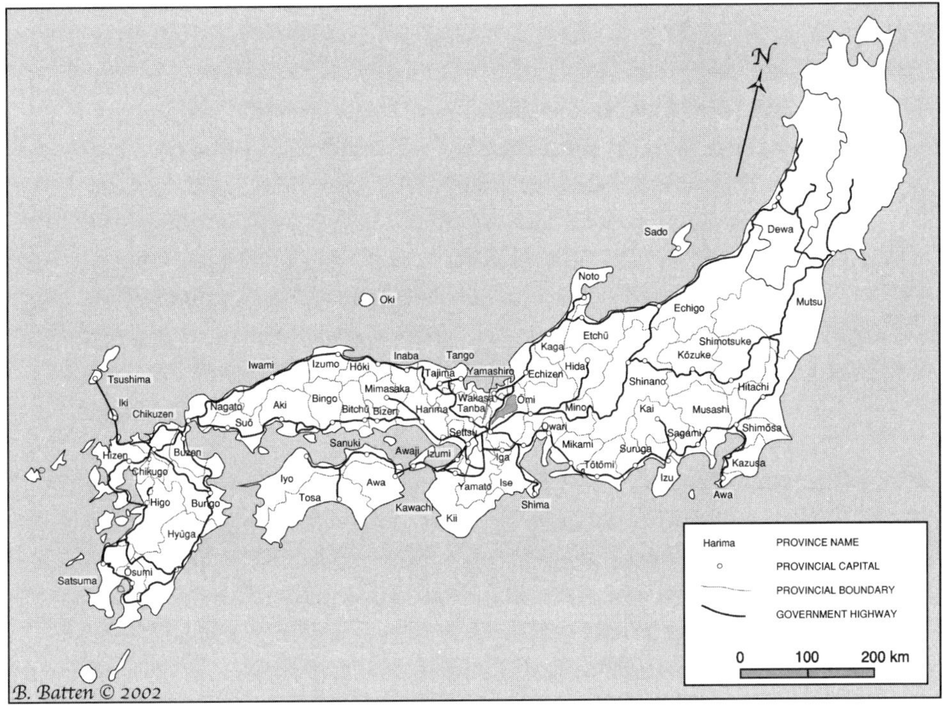

MAP 8. ANCIENT PROVINCES AND GOVERNMENT HIGHWAYS. ADAPTED FROM MAP IN ASAO ET AL., *KADOKAWA SHINPAN NIHONSHI JITEN.*

Other items are also in evidence. These include non-marine foodstuffs: freshwater fish such as sweetfish *(ayu)* and crucian carp *(funa)*; but also game such as wild boar *(inoshishi)*, deer *(shika)*, and pheasant *(kiji)*; and fruits and vegetables such as tangerines *(mikan)*, walnuts *(kurumi)*, soybeans *(daizu)*, cowpeas *(sasage)*, *Pueraria (kuzu)*, and sesame *(goma)*. Nonfood items included raw iron and iron hoes; silk floss and thread; oak boards and elm bark *(nirekawa)*; and various other products.

The *ritsuryō* system of tax collection broke down early in the Heian period, but many of the same products continued to be collected by different means.[14] A mid-eleventh century source known as the *Shinsarugakuki*, for example, describes a retainer in the service of a *zuryō*, one of the professional tax farmers entrusted with provincial administration in this period.[15] During the course of his duties, according to the *Shinsarugakuki*, the retainer was able to collect (perhaps "extort" would be a better word) the following:

> . . . silk fabric from Awa; silk floss from Echizen; Hachijō [silk] and rice-dumplings wrapped in bamboo leaves *(chimaki)* from Mino; twill *(aya)* from Hitachi; *katori* silk fabric from Kii Province; spotted cloth *(madara-nuno)* from Kai; pongee *(tsumugi)* from Iwami; paper from Tajima; ink from Awaji; needles from Harima; swords from Bitchū; small boxes, whetstones, bamboo screens, and sardines from Iyo; straw mats *(mushiro)* from Izumo; round mats *(waraza)* from Sanuki; saddles and cruppers *(shirigai)* from Kazusa; stirrups from Musashi; kettles from Noto; pots and bean paste *(miso)* from Kawachi; boards from Aki; iron from Bingo; oxen from Nagato; horses and paper from Mutsu; pears from Shinano; chestnuts from Tanba; rice from Owari; acorns *(shii)* from Wakasa; crucian carp and rice cakes *(mochi)* from Ōmi; salmon and lacquer from Echigo; opossum shrimp *(ami)* from Bizen; mackerel from Suō; gizzard shad *(konoshiro)* from Ise; abalone from Oki; eggplants from Yamashiro; gourds *(uri)* from Yamato; *wakame* seaweed from Tango; rice cakes from Hida; and rice from Chinzei [Kyushu].[16]

Although many of the items in this list are also known from eighth-century shipping tags, there is at least one important difference. The *Shinsarugakuki* specifically mentions many products from eastern Japan, up to and including the frontier province of Mutsu, which provided "horses and paper." Whereas in the Nara period the bulk goods network that was centered on the capital had extended only to the edge of the Kantō region, by the late Heian period it had evidently come to encompass all of Honshu. It will not escape the reader's attention that this territorial expansion roughly parallels that of the Japanese state itself. Military campaigns in the east resulted not only in political but also economic integration.

So far we have been discussing the tax system, but it is important to note that by the Heian period this was no longer the only, nor perhaps even the primary, means by which bulk goods achieved widespread circulation. Also of great importance was the so-called *shōen* system, by which members of the central power elite gained title to provincial estates, from which they extracted tribute directly.[17] The nature of the tribute is known in detail for many *shōen*, thanks to the survival of voluminous written documents. Koyama Yasunori, in a classic study of the estates belonging to Hōshōgon'in, an "imperial vow temple" founded by ex-emperor Toba in the early eleventh century, offers this comparison of the estates in three regions: central Honshu, Saigoku (western Honshu, Shikoku, and Kyushu), and Tōgoku (eastern Honshu):

> *Shōen* from central Honshū produced mostly "heavy freight" such as rice and oil, together with miscellaneous dues in the form of reed mats *(komo)*, perfume, rice-cakes, and sundry utensils. These are roughly the same items which were collected from estates in the Kinai. By contrast, goods from the Saigoku were limited to rice, oil, and silk floss . . . while from estates in the Tōgoku basic annual dues consisted of cloth and other "light freight." (Although not apparent from the Hōshōgon'in document, silk fabric and floss were also levied as annual dues from many Tōgoku estates.) Under the *shōen* system, in other words, there was a clear regional difference between estates in the Kinai, central Honshu, and Kyushu, which supplied "heavy freight," and those in the Tōgoku, which produced "light freight."[18]

This is the same difference we have already noted for Nara-period tax dues, and as Koyama is at pains to demonstrate in his article, it occurred for the same reason: differential costs in transportation between overland routes (in the east) and maritime routes (in the west). Koyama's categories of "heavy freight" and "light freight" both fall within our concept of bulk goods, but this is not to say that no prestige goods were obtained through the *shōen* system. In the same article, this author goes on to describe how estates in northernmost Honshu paid their dues in the form of gold, lacquer, eagle feathers, and sealskins, some of which were ultimately obtained from the Ezo in Hokkaido, while estates in northwest Kyushu paid dues in the form of luxury goods imported from the continent.[19]

We would also be remiss in failing to mention the activities of merchants in this general period. Professional shippers and agents of one kind or another were involved in the transportation of tax goods from very early times (certainly by the Nara period), and they played a similar role in transporting goods from *shōen* during the Heian period and later.[20] It is not hard to imagine that shippers of this type became involved in the buying and selling of goods on their own account. A good example, again, comes from the *Shinsarugakuki*, which provides a vivid description of a "merchant prince" *(akindo no shuryō):*

> He values profit, knowing neither wife nor child. He thinks of himself, without a care for others. He multiplies one [thing] into ten thousand, and turns lumps of earth into gold. He deceives others with his words and plays tricks on their eyes with his plots. His travels take him from the land of the *fushū* in the east to Kikaigashima in the west. There is no limit to the goods he trades and the things he sells.[21]

The text goes on to give a long list of products, to which we will return in the next chapter, because most of them are luxury items. However, there can be little doubt that private shippers and merchants were involved in selling bulk goods as well. A good example, well supported by archaeological evidence, is provided by the ceramic vessels used for cooking and storage.

An influx of high-quality Chinese porcelain in the Heian period (see Chapter 7) stimulated the emergence of a domestic ceramics industry that produced utilitarian goods. Important kilns were founded in the twelfth century at Tokoname and Atsumi on the Pacific side of Honshu in modern Aichi Prefecture, and in Suzu on the Sea of Japan coast in present-day Ishikawa (see Map 9). Ceramics produced in these areas quickly achieved wide circulation, respectively, along the Pacific and Sea of Japan coasts. In western Japan, by contrast, the market for domestic ceramics was dominated by the Tōban ware produced in present-day Hyōgo Prefecture.[22] (Much later, during the fifteenth and sixteenth centuries, respectively, new kilns in Bizen and Echizen took over the roles formerly played by Tōban and Suzu.) There are several theories regarding how these ceramics were distributed; the most widely accepted is that of Wakita Haruko, who argues that ships bearing taxes and tribute from the provinces carried ceramics back as return cargo.[23]

With merchant activity of this kind came the development of established shipping routes along all stretches of coast; in fact, by the end of the Heian period "hop, skip, and jump" routes connecting one local port with another had been expanded and integrated into what was in effect a countrywide shipping network. The major routes, as exemplified by the distribution of ceramics, were up and down the Sea of Japan coast, along the Pacific seaboard of eastern Honshu, and

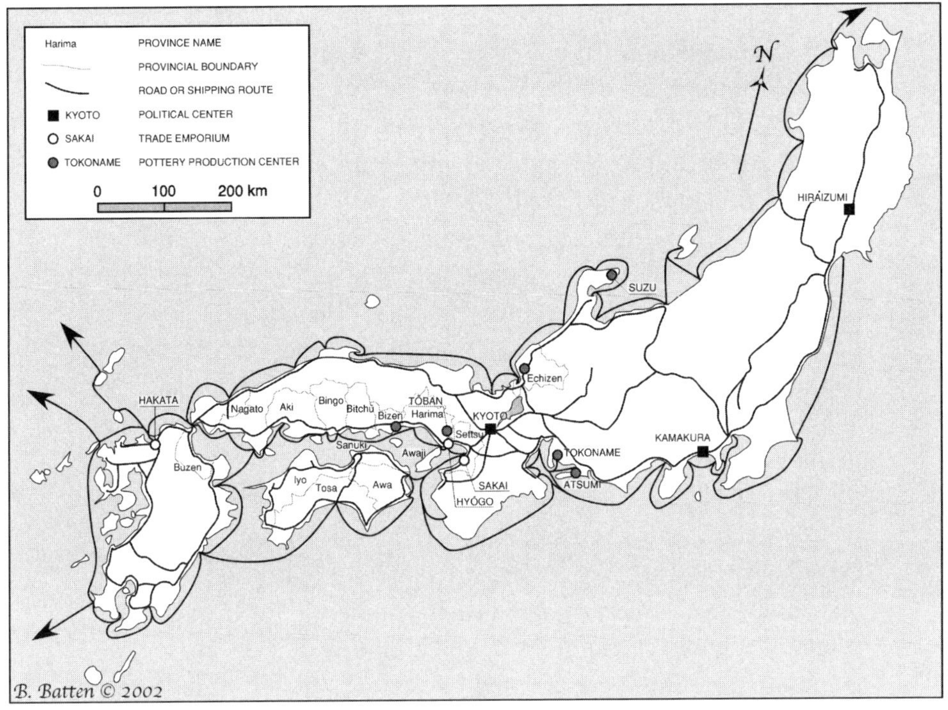

MAP 9. MEDIEVAL TRADE ROUTES AND POTTERY PRODUCTION CENTERS. ADAPTED IN PART FROM SASAYAMA HARUO ET AL., EDS., *YAMAKAWA NIHONSHI SŌGŌ ZUROKU (ZŌHOBAN)*, P. 56.

above all, along the Inland Sea, which connected Kyoto and other major population centers to western Honshu, Shikoku, and Kyushu.[24]

The scale of merchant activity in the Inland Sea in the medieval period is suggested by a remarkable document called the *Hyōgo kitaseki irifune nōchō* (Tax Register for Boats Entering the North Checkpoint at Hyōgo).[25] This document provides a comprehensive list of ships that docked at Hyōgo (modern Kobe) at the eastern terminus of the Inland Sea during a one-year period beginning in the first month of 1445. The entries for each ship list port of origin, nature and quantity of cargo, shipping taxes assessed on the cargo, date collected, name of captain, and name of wholesaler responsible for consigning the goods at Hyōgo. Judging from this document, during the fifteenth century Hyōgo played host to ships from all provinces along the Inland Sea in Honshu and Shikoku, from the Pacific coast of

Shikoku, and even from the northern part of Kyushu. Altogether 104 ports are mentioned: 10 in Settsu, 19 in Harima, 12 in Bizen, 4 in Bitchū, 7 in Bingo, 4 in Aki, 5 in Suō, 1 in Nagato, 9 in Awaji, 16 in Sanuki, 3 in Iyo, 9 in Awa, 4 in Tosa, and 1 in Buzen (see Map 9).[26] Among the many items of trade brought by these ships to Hyōgo were polished rice, low-quality "red" rice *(akagome)*, barley *(ōmugi)*, wheat *(komugi)*, salt, lumber, indigo *(ai)*, ramie *(karamushi)*, straw mats, cloth, paper, iron, ceramic vessels, sesame, sardines, sea bream, shrimp, and seaweed.[27] Most of these, of course, are already familiar from our earlier discussions of tax shipments. It would seem that there was strong continuity in the types of commodities consumed by the capital elite, although, of course, these were obtained through different channels in different periods.

During the ensuing Sengoku period, political decentralization proceeded apace, but this seems to have had little effect on commercial activity in general or on the circulation of bulk goods in particular. Individual *sengoku daimyō* were in competition with each other, economically as well as politically and militarily. For this reason protectionist measures were adopted by some daimyo in order to prevent the "export" of important resources (precious metals, materiel, etc.) from their domains. However, export controls were hard to enforce, and on top of this, most daimyo faced a fundamental contradiction in the sense that their domains were too small to ensure economic self-sufficiency. What this meant was that they had to purchase needed goods from outside, and they had to raise the cash to do so—partly by taxing the local peasantry but also via trade. *Sengoku daimyō* thus were ultimately dependent on the existence of a countrywide market and for the most part actively promoted long-distance trade—for example, by guaranteeing the safety of merchants, protecting guild rights, and reducing transport and enterprise taxes.[28]

The Early Modern Period

Economic growth continued in the early modern period, partly as a "peace dividend" and partly as the result of government policy. The Tokugawa shogunate, like the Nara government nine centuries earlier, spared no effort in creating (or re-creating, in this case), a national network of roads, this time one centered on the new capital of Edo.[29] One of the main reasons for this was the "alternate attendance system" *(sankin kōtai sei)*, by which local daimyo were required, as a security precaution, to spend half of their time in Edo (where their families were kept permanently as semi-hostages). Daimyo, of course, did not travel alone but in the company of large numbers of retainers, and so one important result of this system was to stimulate urbanization, and also hence consumption, at Edo.[30]

Goods consumed by the warriors and "city dwellers" (*chōnin;* artisans and merchants) in Edo came by several routes. First, there was tax rice *(nengu)* collected by the shogunate on its own landholdings, by the daimyo on their domains *(han)*, and by lesser shogunal retainers called *hatamoto* on their own estates, mostly located in the vicinity of Edo. (Although taxes were collected in the form of rice, not all of this rice was brought to Edo; some was sold locally or in Osaka, with the resulting profits sent to Edo in the form of cash, where it could be used to buy goods brought in by other means.) Second, there were goods collectively known as *kudarimono*, which large-scale merchants in Osaka (or elsewhere) shipped to Edo by sea for sale to urban consumers. A third and final category was *jimawarimono*. These were goods produced locally in the Kantō and surrounding regions and brought to Edo by horse, overland, or by boat, down any of the various rivers that flowed into Tokyo Bay.[31]

Although consumption patterns in Edo are also well known from historical records,[32] a new body of evidence has recently come to light through the efforts of urban archaeologists. Ceramics of one kind or another are among the most common finds in Edo, and most excavations reveal fragments of imported vessels as well as domestic wares from kilns located in Hizen, Seto-Mino (present-day Aichi and Fukui prefectures), Shigaraki (Shiga Prefecture), and other regions. The number of ceramic artifacts is said to increase greatly from the second half of the eighteenth century, probably reflecting improvements in supply, transportation, and, most importantly, demand, as Edo grew in population and as urban residents grew richer. Many of the vessels were used as tableware, but others were used to store or transport food. Prominent among the storage vessels are jars used to ship salt from the Kinai region, which have been recovered from former daimyo residences at Iidamachi and Hakuō and on the University of Tokyo campus. Excavations at daimyo residences also yield wooden containers and tubs used to ship items such as dried skipjack *(katsuobushi)* from Arai, fermented soybeans from Odawara, and so on. More direct evidence of samurai eating habits comes from the food and animal remains also found at these sites. Bones of deer, wild boar, raccoon-dog *(tanuki)*, dog, and rabbit are quite common, and garbage pits at samurai sites also yield quantities of fish bones and mollusk shells. Among the fish represented are red sea bream, Pacific cod *(madara)*, *Sillago (kisu)*, sea bass, trout *(masu)*, sweetfish, skipjack, yellowtail *(buri)*, tuna *(maguro)*, Japanese flounder *(hirame)*, flatfish *(karei)*, horse mackerel *(aji)*, mackerel, and sardine. Shellfish include various species of clams as well as horned turbans and abalone.[33]

Obviously, many of these are the same products that were being consumed a millennium earlier in the imperial capitals of the Kinai region. But there are also important differences, aside from the obvious fact that the Kantō region had emerged as a new "core" region alongside the old Kinai hub. (Within the Kinai, incidentally, the major center of population was now not Nara or even Kyoto but Osaka, known as the "kitchen of the realm" for its role as a commercial center.[34]) First, scale of consumption, and thus flows of bulk goods, had increased exponentially: as we have seen, eighteenth-century Edo was ten times as large as Nara in its heyday. Second, methods of procurement had changed from the largely political to the largely commercial. Goods flowing into eighth-century Nara were mostly tax and tribute items procured through bureaucratic channels; those consumed in eighteenth-century Edo, by contrast, were often obtained through commercial—one might even say capitalist—channels.[35]

Third, and most important for our purposes, bulk goods were now being procured from a vastly larger region than in Nara times. As we have seen, northern Honshu was incorporated within Japan's bulk goods network as early as the Heian period. Hokkaido, however, remained outside for many centuries, indeed throughout the entire medieval period. Prestige goods, as we will see in the next chapter, were another matter: Japanese elites valued, and had access to, luxury products from the north since at least the Heian period. But there is no evidence that bulk goods flowed in quantity between

Hokkaido and the rest of Japan. However, during the Edo period, this situation changed dramatically as Ainu territory was incorporated within the greater Japanese economy. As the reader will recall, Ainu lands were still politically autonomous at this time. Economic integration preceded—and laid the ground for—the political integration that came at the end of the Edo period.

Economic integration was achieved through the "trading fief system" *(akinaiba chigyō sei)* and "fief-contracting system" *(basho ukeoi sei)*, which were established, respectively, in the seventeenth and eighteenth centuries. During the Edo period, the lords of Matsumae domain, located at the southern tip of Hokkaido, were assigned monopoly trading rights with the Ainu by the Tokugawa shogunate.[36] This trade took several forms. First, during the whole Edo period, Ainu chiefs were required to travel to Matsumae for "audiences" *(uimam)* with the lord of Fukuyama castle, to whom they presented "tribute."[37] In the early Edo period, groups of Ainu also traveled to Fukuyama once a year for the purpose of trade, setting up temporary huts along the beaches to purvey their wares.[38] Far more important in terms of volume, however, were the trading fiefs *(akinaiba, basho)* assigned to important Matsumae vassals within Ainu territory after Shakushain's War in 1669. During the seventeenth century, these fiefholders dispatched ships each year to carry out trade with the *kotan* (Ainu villages) in their area of jurisdiction. As Brett Walker has argued, the "trading fief system" introduced market forces into the Ainu homelands, undermining native autonomy and subsistence patterns.[39] Even so, it was still far less invasive than the later "fief-contracting system," under which trading rights were subcontracted to Japanese merchants, many of them from Ōmi, who paid fees in cash (called *unjōkin*) for the privilege of conducting trade with the Ainu. Under the "fief-contracting system," merchant contractors established direct control over their jurisdictions, using Ainu residents as a pool of cheap labor to run fisheries, factories, and other commercial activities. As a result, according to David Howell, Hokkaido was incorporated within an expanding web of proto-capitalist economic relations, and Ainu society lost whatever autonomy it still had.[40]

What products did the trading fiefs supply to Japan? Prestige goods were certainly part of the trade, particularly in the seventeenth century, but bulk goods were also very important.[41] Of these, the most important were unquestionably Pacific herring *(nishin)*, salmon, and kelp *(konbu)*.[42] Salmon had always been consumed in Hokkaido by the Ainu and their ancestors; the fish were generally caught in the rivers and smoked for preservation. During the Edo period, however, the scale of salmon fishing increased dramatically, partly as the result of commercial demand from Japan "proper" and partly as the result of new techniques of fishing and preservation. The demand for herring, if anything, was even greater.[43] Kippered herring, herring roe, and above all, fertilizer made from pressed died herring, were mainstays of the Hokkaido trade from the end of the seventeenth century. The demand for herring fertilizer was vast; by the middle of the eighteenth century, commercial farmers throughout western Japan depended on it to produce rice and cotton.

Hokkaido's integration within the Japanese bulk goods network is also evident in reverse flows from Japan to the Ainu. Judging from historical records, many bulk goods from Japan were imported to Hokkaido during the early modern period; among the most important items were rice, sake, tobacco, and salt.[44] There are some nice ironies (or perhaps congruities) here. Fertilizer from Hokkaido was being used to produce rice in Honshu, some of which went back to Hokkaido as food and some of which was used to produce rice wine for the same market! Or, in reverse, salt from Honshu was used to produce salted salmon in Hokkaido for reexport to Honshu.

A similar picture is also evident from the archaeological record. Items of Japanese manufacture appear in Hokkaido from a fairly early date, but prior to the seventeenth century there is no evidence that they were important to Ainu subsistence activities. Implements used in hunting and fishing, e.g., knives and harpoon tips, were produced locally out of bone and horn, and the clay pots used in cooking were also of local manufacture. Some iron was imported, but it was often reworked. Iron cauldrons from Japan were also in use, but when there were not enough of them, the Ainu produced imitations in clay rather than trying to import more. The economy, in other words, was for all intents and purposes autarchic. However, beginning in the seventeenth century, ceramic vessels, lacquerware, and iron cauldrons, axheads, and knives from Japan began to appear in quantity. At the same time, products of local manufacture began to decrease in number, or in some cases, such as that of Ainu-manufactured pottery, to disappear altogether.[45]

An extension of Japan's bulk goods network is also evident at the other end of the realm, in the Ryukyus. Okinawa, unlike Hokkaido, never became completely dependent on Japan for any items of daily use. However, as is clear from archaeological investigations, large quantities of Japanese ceramics and iron tools were imported beginning in the so-called Gusk period, corresponding to the Kamakura and Muromachi periods in Japan.[46] Although it is not clear how to classify all of these finds, some of the more utilitarian items can probably be considered "bulk goods." Reverse flows, from Okinawa to Japan, consisted at this time mainly of prestige items (many of them actually manufactured in China or elsewhere, as described in the following chapter). By the Edo period, however, at least one Okinawan product was being imported to Japan in bulk quantities: sugar.

Sugarcane was originally native to New Guinea and other parts of Southeast Asia, but during the seventeenth century it was transplanted to Okinawa, rapidly becoming a staple crop. Okinawan sugar was imported to Japan (for sale in Osaka) by Satsuma domain, which enjoyed the same type of monopoly privileges with regard to Ryukyu as Matsumae did in Ezo. However, the end result of this particular story was somewhat different from what occurred in Hokkaido. In an early example of "import substitution," domain officials in Satsuma learned how to cultivate sugarcane and began planting it on the nearby island of Amami Ōshima. To prevent sugar prices in Osaka from falling in response to the increased supply, Satsuma then turned to Ryukyu and ordered it to limit its own production. As a result of these events, Amami Ōshima developed a monocultural economy that was highly dependent upon the Japanese market.[47] Ryukyu itself retained a fairly diversified economy, although one that continued to center on external trade.

But although Ryukyu enjoyed a more independent standing than Hokkaido, there is no denying that economic exchanges between it and Japan were unequal and operated in favor of the latter. Despite differences in degree, the incorporation of both of these regional economies within Japan's bulk goods network took the form of exploitation. In other words, here we have the economic dimension of the core-periphery relationship discussed in the previous chapter. Hokkaido and the Ryukyus functioned as peripheries in Japan's bulk goods network, just as they did in its political/military network.

So far we have considered the circulation of bulk goods within the Japanese archipelago. What about relations with the continent? Is there any evidence of flows of bulk goods between the Japanese archipelago and other countries? Certainly diplomats, traders, and armies must have carried bulk goods in all periods, if only for their own provision, but these were isolated, small-scale "flows," not evidence of systemic linkages. Better examples are provided by some continental imports, which—like Okinawan sugar—were converted over the course of time from luxuries to quasi-necessities. Three further examples, to be discussed in the next chapter, are Chinese coins, ceramics, and textiles. Depending on definitions, some of these items might qualify for "bulk" status in Japan's middle ages.

But for a true systemic linkage in bulk goods between Japan and the rest of East Asia, we have to wait for the Edo period. During this period, some of the foodstuffs produced in Hokkaido began to find their way out of Japan entirely through the foreign trade in Kyushu. By around 1700, in fact, foodstuffs from Hokkaido made up about 60 percent of Japan's exports. (Most of the remainder was copper.) Foodstuffs were divided into two categories: *tawaramono*, or "baled goods," and *shoshiki*, or "miscellaneous items." "Baled goods," named after the straw bags in which they were shipped, consisted of three items: dried sea cucumbers *(iriko)*, dried abalone, and shark fins (as in shark-fin soup). These made up the bulk of the trade. "Miscellaneous items," which were numerically less important, included kelp, squid jerky *(surume)*, and other marine products.[48]

Bulk Goods and the State

In sum, Japan's bulk goods network started out small and got substantially larger over time (see Figure 9). During the ancient period, bulk goods circulated only within the confines of the Japanese polity itself (aside, perhaps, from some minor spillover effects along the frontiers). During the medieval and early modern periods, the bulk goods network expanded until it was substantially larger than the polity at

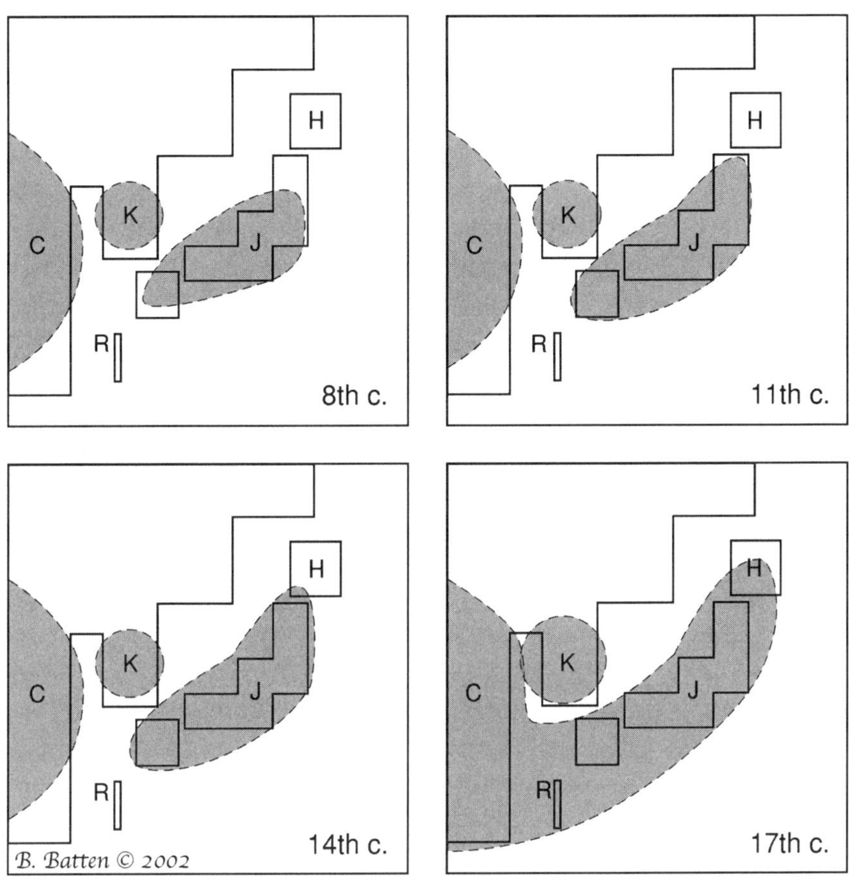

FIGURE 9. Evolution of Japan's bulk goods network, showing gradual expansion in the eighth, eleventh, and fourteenth centuries and a partial merger with the Chinese bulk goods network in the seventeenth century. J = Japan "proper"; H = Hokkaido; R = Ryukyu; K = Korea; C = China.

its center. Hokkaido, in particular, was fully subsumed within the larger Japanese economy, even though it remained politically "independent." Ties with Okinawa and, farther away, the Asian continent, were less intense, but nonetheless of systemic importance by Edo times.

How does the bulk goods network compare with the political/military network discussed previously? Obviously, there are similarities as well as differences. One similarity is that both networks tended to expand over time; another is that they both exhibited marked core-periphery differentiation. However, to my mind, at least, these similarities are far less important than the differences.

One of these differences is size. Although, depending on definitions, the political/military and bulk goods networks may have been roughly coterminous during the Edo period, this was the exception, not the rule. More commonly, flows of bulk goods took place on a much more limited scale than political/military interactions. In most periods of history, Japan had political or military relations with some or all of its Asian neighbors but remained essentially autarchic with respect to daily economic necessities.

A second difference relates to the historical evolution of the two networks. One of the most significant features of Japan's political/military network, as we have observed, was its tendency to "pulsate." Such pulsation, however, is not evident for the bulk goods network. As we have seen, the political/military network evolved in response to outside events, specifically processes at work in the larger Eurasian world-system. The flow of bulk goods, by contrast, was fundamentally determined by internal events, specifically the growth of the Japanese state. But though the historical development of Japan's bulk goods network followed the beat of a domestic drummer, this was not true for all categories of material goods. A counterexample is provided by prestige goods, the subject of the next chapter.

7 Prestige Goods

Japan's Prestige Goods Network

As noted at the beginning of Chapter 6, "prestige goods" in this study refers to high-value luxury items, as opposed to bulk items of daily consumption. Individuals may desire prestige goods, but they do not need them to survive. However, access to prestige goods may well be necessary to for an individual to achieve or maintain a particular rank or position in society. In hierarchical societies (which means almost *all* societies since the invention of agriculture), luxuries serve as vehicles for the accumulation of wealth and, even more importantly, as symbols of power or authority. As such they play an important role in the functioning of society as a whole. In fact, it has been argued that loss of access to prestige goods can cause crises of legitimation or even total political collapse in some premodern societies.[1]

According to Christopher Chase-Dunn and Thomas Hall, networks defined by the circulation of prestige goods tend to be larger than those associated with the circulation of bulk goods or even political/military interactions. To state my conclusion first, this hypothesis is certainly borne out by the historical record from Japan. As we have seen, until the Edo period, Japan's bulk goods network was generally limited to the area under central control or, to put it another way, was essentially coterminous with the Japanese polity. Political and military interactions generally involved a larger region, including the entire Japanese archipelago as well as, in most periods, parts of continental Asia. As I shall argue in this chapter, prestige goods circulated on an even larger scale. Prestige goods from many parts of Asia were available to Japanese courtiers as early as the eighth century; by the sixteenth, the scale of exchange had expanded to include all of Eurasia, and quite possibly the New World as well.

"Tribute Trade," "Maritime Regions," and "Networks"

Before examining the "facts," it may be helpful to touch briefly on some of the recent Japanese literature on this topic. Although foreign relations have always attracted the interest of some Japanese historians, in the postwar period most scholars turned their attention inward, producing volume upon volume of Marxist-inspired analyses of domestic socioeconomic and political institutions. It may be that painful memories of Japan's all-too-recent wartime excesses in Asia caused scholars to subconsciously avoid the topic of foreign relations. During the 1980s, however, the historiographic tide begun to turn and foreign relations once again became a hot topic—a situation that has continued until the present. One reason for the shift was the simple passage of time; as wartime memories faded, the topic of international history once again became "safe." More fundamental, however, was a realization of Japan's growing importance in the contemporary global system. It can be no coincidence that the boom in international history started precisely when the Japanese media began touting the buzzword "internationalization" *(kokusaika)* in the 1980s.

While some of the new research focuses on traditional concerns such as diplomacy, much of it also focuses on trade. Possibly this trend is not unrelated to the fact that Japan's postwar successes in the international arena have been mostly economic ones. In any case, the point I wish to make here is that most of these studies are concerned, by default, with prestige goods, because in most periods of history the circulation of bulk goods was purely domestic in scale. For reasons of space, it is impossible to give a full review of the literature here. In the remainder of this section, my goal is more modest: to introduce and discuss three key concepts that have played an important role in recent debates among Japanese historians about foreign trade in premodern times.

The first concept is that of "tribute trade," which has been developed most systematically by Hamashita Takashi, a historian of early modern and modern China.[2] Although Hamashita himself might disagree, I think his work is best described as the economic analogue of Nishijima Sadao's earlier work on the "East Asian world." Nishijima focused on the political relationship of investiture, by which sovereigns throughout East Asia were confirmed in their status by the Chinese emperor in exchange for their recognition of Chinese suzerainty.[3] Hamashita, by contrast, focuses on the economic aspect of this relationship. When diplomatic envoys arrived in China, they brought local products, or "tribute," from their home country; in exchange, the Chinese emperor entrusted them with a variety of "return gifts." Typically, the return gifts were of greater value than the original "tribute," because they were supposed to express the magnanimity and benevolence of the "son of heaven." In addition to these official exchanges of presents, tribute missions were also the occasion for a great deal of trade conducted by the visiting diplomats either at their initial port of call or at the foreign capital.

The main criticism to be made of Nishijima's research is that it is heavily Sinocentric, and to a certain extent the same criticism could be made of Hamashita. Fortunately, Hamashita further generalizes the idea of "tribute trade," noting:

> The tribute system, being based on bilateral tribute–return gift relationships with China, did take a radial, Sinocentric form, but not everything was unitarily subsumed within this relationship. There also existed multiple satellite-like tribute relationships, whose location on the Chinese periphery resulted in the formation of a single system. Accordingly, a compound region was formed, including relations of competition as well as relationships of subsumation.[4]

In other words, we are dealing with a single economic "system" but one that also included a number of partially overlapping subsystems. This was also true, of course, of the political system upon which these economic relationships were predicated. Despite Nishijima's emphasis on the unitary, centripetal nature of the "East Asian world," politics in premodern Asia was always a complex, multilateral affair involving a number of competing subsystems, each with its own ethnocentric "worldview."

A second important concept is that of the "region," usually understood in economic terms as an area over which goods are circulated. In the recent Japanese historiography, the greatest attention has been focused on "maritime regions," or *kaiiki*. We have already met this idea in Chapter 1, where I discussed Murai Shōsuke's concept of a "Pan-East China Sea Region" that "straddled the borders" of Japan and Korea. More recently, a number of authors, Hamashita Takeshi included, have generalized this idea and applied it to Asia as a whole. In a recent discussion, Hamashita argues:

> When thinking of Asia, a perspective which concentrates power only on "land" does not necessarily suffice to give a full understanding of this region. Rather, from a historical point of view, a major characteristic of this vast region is the existence of a history in which a number of maritime regions existed from Northeast Asia to East Asia, and further from Southeast Asia to Oceania, and that maritime regions mediated the mutual influences among the countries, regions, and trading cities located on their fringes. . . .
>
> These maritime regions were surrounded by . . . continents, peninsulas, and islands, and were also separate from other maritime regions. Regarding the mutual relationships between the regions located on the fringes of these various seas, we can say that they were located close enough to influence each other but at the same time were distant enough to avoid homogenization, maintaining their mutual identities. . . . Further, [each] maritime region formed a trading sphere, and trading ports and cities arose on the margins of the trading sphere. At points of intersection between trading countries, urban transit points were formed, and these cities satisfied the [necessary] conditions for trade by developing markets, creating residential wards for trading groups, issuing currency, etc. This is why these seas are thought to be inseparably tied to the structure of the tribute trade.[5]

Among the important "maritime regions" identified by Hamashita, from north to south, are the Sea of Okhotsk, the Sea of Japan, the Yellow Sea, the East China Sea, the South China Sea, the Sulu Sea, the Java Sea, the Banda Sea, the Arafura Sea, the Coral Sea, and the Tasman Sea.

Interestingly, Hamashita's approach to "regions" bears considerable resemblance to that in Janet Abu-Lughod's analysis of the "thirteenth-century world system." As the reader may recall, Abu-Lughod describes a world-system comprising eight overlapping trade "circuits," most of them centered on bodies of water. The main difference between the two authors in this regard is that Abu-Lughod is more of a "lumper" than Hamashita; whereas Hamashita sees a number of maritime regions in Southeast Asia, Abu-Lughod sees only one, the South China Sea.[6]

A third concept that has received much attention in Japan is that of "networks." However, usage of this term has been far from consistent. The ubiquitous Hamashita, for example, seems to use "network" as a synonym for the entire system of tribute trade. In the article quoted above, he refers to the "tribute trade" as a "regional network," stating (in tortured prose), "The tribute trade may be called the network, and the concept, that made the Asian region, and particularly the East Asian region, into a region."[7] A more graphic image is offered by Arano Yasunori, Ishii Masatoshi, and Murai Shōsuke, who describe the tribute-trade system as a "spiderweb-like network" connecting the various Asian polities.[8] These same authors, however, also use "network" in a different, more limited, sense, as a synonym for the "Pan-China Sea trading region."[9]

It is useless to look for uniformity in the existing literature, but it is not useless to try to synthesize these concepts into a coherent picture. Here is what I suggest: The "continents, peninsulas, and islands" described by Hamashita correspond to political entities and also, if Japan is any guide, to bulk goods networks. The "maritime regions" surrounding and connecting them represent, in the language of the present study, frontiers, that is, interstitial zones between polities. The "tribute trade" involved the exchange of prestige goods over a broad region, encompassing not only various land-based polities but also the "maritime regions" between them. However, these exchanges were fundamentally predicated on the political relationship of investiture. For that reason, although Hamashita is certainly correct in calling the tribute system a "network," it should not be automatically equated with a prestige goods network. Rather, it is best viewed as one aspect of the China-centered political/military network discussed in Chapter 5. If Chase-Dunn and Hall are correct, prestige goods networks are likely to have been still larger in scope, encompassing not only the area of "tribute trade" but also other, politically unconnected polities and regions. Both within and outside the area of "tribute trade," maritime economic regions ("circuits") as well as equivalent land-based structures probably constituted important links in the network. Janet Abu-Lughod's "thirteenth-century world system" provides a good model of how such a prestige goods network might have looked in one period of world history.

Of course, this formulation raises as many questions as it answers. First, was "tribute trade" really the principal medium for long-distance exchanges of prestige goods in Asia, as Hamashita's work would seem to imply? Or was private, commercial activity also important in its own right? If so, what was the balance between the two and how did it change over time? Second, what was the actual geographic scope of exchange in different periods? Did Abu-Lughod's "thirteenth-century world system" represent a typical state of affairs? Or did it represent a maximum point of extension within a broader pattern of pulses? Finally, what specific routes or circuits were utilized to convey prestige goods in these international exchanges? Were these links static and permanent, or did they tend to change in location or importance over time? Obviously, to fully answer these questions would require us to review Eurasian history as a whole, which is beyond the scope of the present work. But it is still possible to draw some interesting conclusions on the basis of Japan's historical experience, to which we now turn.

"Public" vs. "Private" Exchange

First, regarding the balance between "tribute trade" (more broadly, official trade) and private commerce: it is apparent that both mechanisms were at work in the case of premodern Japan, although the precise mix varied substantially from period to period.[10] Broadly speaking, tribute trade was the more important of the two early in Japan's history, if only because private commercial networks, both in Japan and in East Asia generally, were relatively undeveloped; only political actors had sufficient resources to carry out systematic long-distance trade. From the early Heian period, however, both official and private trade played important roles. Tribute trade, of course, took place only in periods when Japan maintained official relations with other countries or societies. Private trade existed in all periods (at least after the Heian), but it particularly flourished during times of weak central government, which were associated with a reduction or cessation of official trade. In periods of strong government, by contrast, central authorities attempted (not always with complete success) to monopolize foreign contacts through tribute trade and other mechanisms.

As noted earlier with reference to political/military relations, leaders in Wa actively pursued diplomatic relationships with continental polities from a very early date. The fundamental purpose of these ventures, as I have argued, was to enhance their legitimacy and/or social standing with respect to domestic rivals and/or underlings. This could be achieved in several ways. Diplomatic recognition by a prestigious foreign power, of course, was effective in its own right. Equally important, however, was the monopolistic access to foreign prestige goods that accrued from such recognition. Prestige goods acquired through diplomacy could be redistributed to vassals and other domestic notables, underlining the authority and legitimacy of the paramount.[11]

As is well known, one of the best early examples of this kind of "tribute trade" in Japan comes from the Chinese *Wei History*. In 239 C.E., according to this source, "Queen Pimiko" of Wa sent an envoy to the Chinese outpost of Taifang in Korea and from there to the capital of Luoyang. After meeting with the emperor, the envoy was given a gold seal and one hundred bronze mirrors. The seal is not extant, but possible candidates for the mirrors have been excavated from a number of early *kofun* in various parts of Japan. If the mirrors are authentic, this is prima facie evidence for domestic redistribution of the type mentioned above.[12]

Despite this example, most of the prestige items entering the Japanese islands during the Yayoi and Kofun periods probably came not from China but from Korea. Because the Korean kingdoms are best considered peer polities of Yamato (and each other),[13] the term "tribute trade" may not be entirely appropriate to relations with them. Nonetheless the fact remains that Yamato (and later, Japan) maintained more or less continuous official relations with these countries and that diplomatic visits were normally occasions for official trade and/or the exchange of gifts.

One very important import from Korea was iron.[14] Iron sounds more like a bulk good than a prestige item, but this is a subjective judgment that does not necessarily apply to Kofun-period Japan. Iron was consumed principally by the Wa elite, who used it for high-status goods such as weapons, armor, and horse trappings. Iron was also used for farm tools, but again these are known only from elite graves—even as late as the ninth century, most peasants had no access to iron and used wooden tools to farm their fields.[15] Japan does have important native sources of iron (particularly near Okayama on the Inland Sea coast of Honshu), but the technology for exploiting them was not available during this period, and the insular elite were dependent upon foreign sources, specifically iron ingots from the Kaya region of southern Korea. (The need to obtain iron accounts for the Yamato court's strong and lasting political and military interests in Korea; and its monopolistic control over import channels—although *not* over sources of production in Korea—was one reason why Yamato was able to "outcompete" other regional power centers in the archipelago to emerge as the one legitimate government of Kofun-period Wa.[16])

Occasionally, Yamato lost its monopoly over access to imported goods. The best example comes from the early sixth century, when Iwai, a regional warlord in Kyushu, established independent ties with Silla.[17] As a result, Yamato was temporarily deprived of access to prestige goods from the peninsula, resulting in a crisis of legitimacy. The situation was soon "righted," however, when a Yamato-led army successfully deposed Iwai in 528.

Following Iwai's defeat, access to prestige goods from the continent was again largely monopolized by Yamato. As before, most goods were obtained through tribute trade and other official relationships—a situation that prevailed through the end of the Nara period in the late eighth century. During the Nara period, as we have seen, Japan maintained diplomatic ties with Tang China, Silla, and Parhae. Most of the prestige goods available to courtiers in Heijō-kyō (such as those preserved today in the Shōsōin, an imperial repository located within the Tōdaiji temple precincts) probably originated as "return gifts" obtained by Japanese envoys *(kentōshi)* in China or as "tribute" brought by visiting Korean dignitaries.[18] Among the more important imports in this and subsequent periods were cultural artifacts (books, objets d'art, Buddhist images), textiles (particularly silk), precious woods, and aromatics and spices of various kinds. All of these will be discussed in more detail in the following section of this chapter.

A major change in procurement channels occurred in the following Heian period, as commercial relations came to supplement, and then supplant, official trade.[19] Judging from historical records, Korean, and later Chinese, merchant vessels began to ply the waters off Kyushu in the early ninth century. Although the Japanese court placed a number of restrictions on their activities around 900 C.E., the volume of trade, if anything, increased thereafter. Most likely this reflects a deep-seated Japanese demand for foreign wares, which were no longer available through diplomatic channels. (As the reader will recall, Japan entered a long period of diplomatic isolation in the tenth century.) Under law, trade with Chinese merchants was supposed to take place at the Kōrokan, an official guest lodge maintained by the government on the west side of Hakata Bay. Later, however, private, unsupervised trade became the norm. A "Chinatown" grew up at Hakata, several kilometers east of now-defunct Kōrokan, and some merchant vessels began to avoid Hakata altogether, choosing instead to dock at private *shōen* elsewhere along the north Kyushu coast.[20] But whatever the specific circumstances, most of the prestige goods imported through this trade were consumed by the local elite in Kyushu and, more importantly, by their central counterparts in Kyoto, who not only controlled the official trade but also owned the various coastal estates in Kyushu.[21]

Foreign trade continued to be of great importance during the subsequent Kamakura and Muromachi periods. The total volume of commerce is difficult to estimate, although judging from archaeological finds of imported porcelain and copper coins (see next section, below), it increased substantially between the twelfth and sixteenth centuries. Be that as it may, at least three other important trends deserve our attention.

First, foreign merchant vessels came to dock at more and more ports in Japan. As early as the eleventh century, some merchant vessels were avoiding Kyushu altogether to dock at Echizen or other provinces along the Sea of Japan coast in Honshu. During the late twelfth century, they also began to enter the Inland Sea for perhaps the first time in Japanese history. During the mid-thirteenth century, the Hōjō regents in charge of the Kamakura government made some attempts to regulate foreign traffic on the Inland Sea linking Hakata and Kamakura.[22] By and large, however, Japan became ever more "open" to foreign commerce, and by the sixteenth century, foreign vessels could routinely be found at major and minor ports throughout the Japanese archipelago. This trend was made possible by two important facts. First, the growth of a domestic commercial network provided foreign merchants with more geographic opportunities to "plug in" to existing channels of distribution. Second, and ultimately more important, the long-term trend toward political decentralization resulted in a loosening of central control over "boundary functions" of all kinds.

The second major trend was for Japanese merchants to venture abroad on their own. Initially, the only commercial source of foreign prestige goods were the Korean and Chinese merchants stopping at Hakata. Eventually, however, Japanese merchants also began to take an active part in the trade. The traditional view among historians is that Japanese merchants first began to travel to Koryŏ and Song China in the eleventh century.[23] Recently, Enomoto Wataru has convincingly argued that these "Japanese" merchants were actually members of the Chinese community in Hakata.[24] Nonetheless, by the Muromachi period, at the latest, Japanese vessels were routinely docking at Korean ports for the purpose of trade, and during the Sengoku period their radius of activity expanded to include other parts of East and Southeast Asia. By the early seventeenth century, Japanese merchants—and even diaspora communities—could be found as far afield as Luson, Cochin China, Tongking, Siam, Cambodia, and Taiwan.[25]

Third, as is perhaps already obvious, the roster of Japan's trading partners expanded greatly over time. During the ancient period, trade was only conducted with China and Korea. During the medieval period, however, Japan came to have commercial relations with countries in Southeast Asia and also, of course, Europe. As is well known, missionaries and traders from Portugal and Spain began to arrive in Japan during the sixteenth century; later, they were joined by visitors from two other European states: England and Holland.[26]

Although I have emphasized the role of private trade in the preceding paragraphs, it would be an exaggeration to assert that foreign items of prestige value were obtained exclusively through private channels in the medieval period. The most obvious counterexample is the "tally trade" with Ming China established by the third Ashikaga shogun, Yoshimitsu.[27] It must be recognized, however, that the separation between "public" and "private" is exceedingly ambiguous during these centuries. This is well illustrated by the later history of the "tally trade" itself, which eventually fell under the control of daimyo families such as the Ōuchi and Hosokawa and their respective merchant backers in Hakata and Sakai. The situation during the "warring states" period of the late fifteenth through sixteenth centuries is even more complex. In a sense, this was the heyday of private trade, with Japanese merchants, other Asian merchants, and Europeans mixing in ports throughout Japan and Asia. On the other hand, *sengoku daimyō* in Kyushu and elsewhere were deeply involved in this trade, and to the extent they may be considered emerging local "sovereigns," the foreign trade also had a distinctly "official" face.

In any case, there is no denying that the pendulum began swinging back to the "public" side of the spectrum at the end of the sixteenth century. During the Edo period, of course, there was a distinction between the "tribute trade" that accompanied political relations with Korea and Ryukyu and the nontributary trade conducted with Holland and China. But even the latter was conducted under government rules and government auspices and was most definitely a type of official trade.[28] The only purely private overseas trade during the Edo period was that conducted by the occasional smuggler.[29]

The disappearance of private trade, of course, was accompanied by a reversal of all of the trends discussed above. Foreign trade was restricted to the port of Nagasaki and the other three "mouths" of Edo Japan: Tsushima, Satsuma, and Matsumae. "Maritime prohibitions" *(kaikin)* were enacted to prevent Japanese from traveling abroad. And, course, the number of trading partners dropped sharply: direct trade ceased, not only with Spain, Portugal, and England but also with many regions of continental Asia.

In short, the balance between official trade and private commerce shifted over time in direct proportion to the degree of political centralization in Japan. There were also important shifts over time in the identity of Japan's trading partners. Trade with the Korean Peninsula and China (whether public or private) was almost uninterrupted from the Yayoi period on. During the medieval period, interstate trade routes also came to link the Japanese islands with Southeast Asia and, ultimately, Europe. Some of these ties were cut after the emergence of the Tokugawa regime in the seventeenth century, but the geographic scale of exchange remained virtually unaffected, thanks to the continued presence of the Dutch in Nagasaki. The long-term trend, then, is one of gradual expansion followed by (temporary) stasis during the Edo period—much like the situation we have already observed for political/military relations, but with most of the "rough edges" smoothed off. Trade relations were less subject to pulsation than their political/military counterparts because the former could flourish even in the absence of direct state involvement. Private trade stepped in to take up the slack when official trade faltered.

Imports

Unfortunately, this is only part of the picture. As a moment's reflection will make clear, making a list of Japan's trading partners in different periods is not sufficient to establish the scope of its prestige goods network. The reason is that many luxury items were traded down the line, not obtained directly from the producing country. All we have done so far, in other words, is to set a lower limit on the size of the network. As I will argue below, Japan was actually part of a pan-Asian prestige goods network from at least the Nara period.

The best way to establish this point is to take a look at what goods were actually imported and where they originally came from. I have already discussed two very early categories of import, bronze mirrors from China and iron ingots from southern Korea. Accordingly we will here focus on imports from a slightly later date. Actual samples of many imported prestige goods from the Nara period, of course, survive in the Shōsōin repository at Tōdaiji.[30] Japanese historical sources from the Nara and Heian periods also contain much information on goods brought to Japan through diplomatic channels and, later, by Korean and Chinese merchants visiting Hakata.[31] Because the types of items imported seem to have changed little over time, I choose here to focus on a list of products contained in the eleventh-century *Shinsarugakuki*, that veritable encyclopedia of late Heian life and society. As noted in Chapter 6, the *Shinsarugakuki* describes a "merchant prince" whose travels take him "from the land of the *fushū* in the east to Kikaigashima in the west"—that is, from one end of Japan to the other. The text goes on to give the following list of "foreign goods" *(karamono)* handled by the merchant:

> . . . aloeswood, musk, perfume, cloves, spikenard, frankincense, birthwort, camphor, pride-of-India, "chicken-tongue" [a type of clove], sandalwood, sanderswood, *Bischofia*, sappanwood, alum, "red snow," "purple snow," gold elixir, silver elixir, purple gold salve, croton oil, orpiment, myrobalans, betel nuts, gamboge, indigo, cochineal, verdigris, azurite, minium, cinnabar, ceruse, leopard and tiger skins, wisteria stems, tea cups, wicker baskets, rhinoceros horns, water-buffalo scepters, agate belts, glass urns, twill, brocade, scarlet raiments, "elephant eye" damask, "cloud-patterned" brocade, soft Koryŏ brocade, Tonkin brocade, "floating-line" twill, silk gauze and crape, Chinese bamboo, sweet bamboo, and hollow glass balls.[32]

Frankly, some of these items are all but unidentifiable. Modern commentators tell us, for example, that "red snow" and "purple snow" were medicines, but who is really to know? Fortunately, such items are in the minority; what we are left with is a remarkably coherent list of aromatics (aloeswood through "chicken-tongue"), precious woods (sandalwood through sappanwood), medicines (alum through betel nuts), dyes and pigments (gamboge through ceruse), household goods and accessories (leopard and tiger skins through glass urns), textiles (twill through silk gauze and crape), and miscellaneous items (Chinese bamboo through glass balls). Of course, some things had more than one use, rendering any classification somewhat arbitrary, but nonetheless the general outlines are fairly clear.

Regarding the provenance of these goods, some are definitely of Chinese or Korean origin: "Chinese bamboo" is an obvious example of the former, and "tea cups" (see below for further detail) as well as most of the textiles were also probably from China. An example of a Korean manufacture, at least judging from its name, is "Koryŏ brocade." It is hardly surprising to find goods of this kind in a trade dominated by Chinese and Korean merchants.

What is perhaps surprising is that most of the identifiable items come from other areas entirely. Among the fabrics, "Tonkin brocade" presumably came from Indochina. Even more strikingly, most of the aromatics, precious woods, and medicines are clearly from tropical Asia. A few can even be identified with fairly specific locations, for example, cloves from the Moluccas and camphor from the islands of Borneo and Sumatra. Likewise, gamboge, a yellow pigment made from the sap of a tree related to the mangosteen, could only have come from Cambodia. Still other items came from even farther afield. Frankincense, for example, was imported from either Persia or Somaliland, depending on which specific plant was used. "Glass urns," at least to judge from surviving examples in the Shōsōin, were also of Persian origin. Alum might also have come from the same source, although in this case Central Asia is also a possibility.[33]

In sum, in the eleventh century (indeed, by the Nara period), elite members of Japanese society had access to luxury products not only from Korea and China but also from all parts of Southeast Asia, India, Central Asia, West Asia, and perhaps even eastern Africa. Given what we know about Japan's international contacts, of course, imports from these latter regions could not have come to the archipelago directly: they were obtained indirectly, through China or Korea, which represent penultimate steps in a chain (or chains) of transactions connecting distant "producers" with the ultimate "consumers" in Japan.

The *Shinsarugakuki*, of course, provides no direct evidence on how spices were brought from Southeast Asia or glass vessels from West Asia, but previous research on international trade routes in premodern Eurasia supplies most of the answers. The most basic distinction, of course, is between land routes and sea routes. Of the former, the most important were the so-called silk routes which connected China to West Asia and Europe via the deserts of Central Asia. These routes, which were traversed by caravan, were of primary importance in the first phase of Eurasian integration, that it, at the time of the Han dynasty in China and the Roman Empire in Europe. They were also heavily utilized during later phases of integration, particularly under the Mongols.[34] However, in general there was a long-term shift in favor of transportation by sea. The reason for this shift is simple: kilogram for kilogram, it is cheaper to transport goods by sea than by land. During very early periods of world history, shipbuilding and navigational skills were not up to the task of long-distance shipping, but once these technologies had been developed (primarily by Arab merchants), maritime routes began to take precedence over land routes in international trade. A maritime equivalent of the silk routes (extending from the Red Sea and the Persian Gulf in the west to the China Sea in the East) emerged in the south as early as the seventh century C.E.[35] However, it was not until the "age of commerce" (roughly 1480–1680) that maritime trade came to reign supreme. This was also the period when many Asian sea routes fell under European domination and became linked with Portuguese routes around the Horn of Africa, on one hand, and Spanish routes across the Pacific, on the other.[36]

This background information allows us to make more sense of the list in the *Shinsarugakuki*, but it also raises some new questions. Most of the spices, precious woods, and medicines that figure so prominently in the text must have come by the southern sea routes to China or Korea, which served as bases for transshipment to Japan.[37] Frankincense might also have come by ship, via either the Persian Gulf or the Red Sea. Or it could have come overland, via the silk routes. Alum, depending upon its exact provenance, most likely came overland, via the silk routes; the same was true for Persian glass. But whatever the precise routes these products followed, their availability in Japan in the eleventh century is of some significance. For this period, falling as it does midway between the Tang and the Mongol empires, does not represent one of the high points of Eurasian integration. Either the basic idea of pulsation is wrong or, more likely, it applies more to political/military interactions than to the circulation of prestige goods.

Of course, it would be a mistake to conclude that vast quantities of luxury items from the far reaches of Asia were making their way into eleventh-century Japan. The great bulk of items listed in the *Shinsarugakuki* are from China and Southeast Asia, and these regions remained the most important sources of imports in subsequent centuries as well. The importance of China and Southeast Asia is attested archaeologically by a sunken merchant vessel discovered in 1979 near Sinan on the southwest coast of Korea. This ship, which is thought to have been sent from Japan to raise money for the rebuilding of Tōfukuji temple in Kyoto, apparently sank on its way back from China in 1323. A series of underwater excavations ending in 1984 recovered huge quantities of artifacts from the 28–by-9–meter hull. Among the finds were nearly a thousand pieces of sanderswood and numerous spices and medicines such as pepper, crotons, oleaster, jasmine, and betel nuts. Most important in terms of sheer volume, however, were Chinese coins and porcelain. Altogether twenty thousand pieces (including fragments) of porcelain were recovered, together with twenty-eight tons of coins.[38] All this from a single vessel!

Both porcelain and coins, of course, are also known archaeologically from Japan. Chinese trade ceramics begin to appear in the ninth century, coincident with the beginnings of government-supervised trade at the Kōrokan in Kyushu (from which most of the early finds come). A recent statistical survey of porcelain finds shows that the volume of imports remained fairly small through the eleventh century, underwent an explosive increase in the twelfth century, and then remained at a high level until the sixteenth.[39] Most probably, the increase in the twelfth century reflects the breakdown of government control over foreign trade in the late Heian period. The decrease in the seventeenth century may be a result of the "closed-country" policies instituted at this time, but it probably also reflects a decline in demand for Chinese porcelain, owing to the increased availability of high-quality domestic wares. We might also note that although porcelain finds from the Heian period tend to concentrate in Fukuoka (the location of the Kōrokan) and in Kyoto, later ones, while still skewed in favor of these two areas, come from all over the country, including Hokkaido and Okinawa.[40] This trend toward geographic diffusion probably reflects the growth of domestic trade networks as well as the increased ability of foreign traders to "plug in" to the domestic network at different points along the coast.

The other major item, Chinese coins, begin to appear archaeologically in the late Heian period.[41] Most of the coins are found as buried caches; altogether 135 such hoards have been found, ranging in age from the late thirteenth century through the late sixteenth. The largest number of hoards seems to cluster around the beginning of the sixteenth century, although this finding may well reflect vagaries of preservation and discovery.[42] Like the porcelain finds described above, these coin hoards disappear in the Tokugawa period.

Why were coins hoarded? Some scholars have argued that these caches served magical purposes, for example, as offerings to placate the gods.[43] However, this seems unlikely, at least as a general explanation. We know from a plethora of historical sources that the coins were imported for use as money, not as tokens or trinkets. (This period saw an extensive monetization of the Japanese economy, although whether the influx of coins was responsible for the growth of market relations or vice versa is a moot point; undoubtedly both factors were present.[44]) And if the coins were used as money, it only makes sense to assume that hoarding was an attempt to store wealth for the future, and that surviving hoards represent attempts that failed, either because memories were lost over the generations or, more likely, because the owners died or were forced to leave in a hurry without their wealth.[45] Such circumstances cannot have been uncommon in the political turmoil of Japan's middle ages.

Another interesting fact about the coin hoards is their geographical distribution, which is heavily skewed toward eastern Japan. Again, this may be an artifact of preservation, or it may reflect geographical biases in the state of research.[46] If the difference is real, it might conceivably reflect regional variations in the development of a market economy. However, that seems unlikely, because by all other measures western Japan was more economically "advanced" than the east. A more logical explanation is that unstable political conditions in the east led to a greater need for hoarding and thus a greater chance of a hoard, once buried, being lost to posterity. It is noteworthy in this regard that the largest of the known caches, containing nearly 400,000 coins, was buried at the end of the fourteenth century in Shinori near modern-day Hakodate in southern Hokkaido—a frontier environment if there ever was one.[47]

As noted above, hoards of foreign coins disappear in the Edo period. One reason for this may simply be that life was now more stable and there was no need to store wealth underground. However, this was only one factor, and perhaps a minor one at that. Banking institutions were also better developed in the Edo period, and even more important, money was now being minted domestically by a central government for the first time in nearly a millennium. This would have rendered foreign coins superfluous, and in any case import restrictions would have reduced their availability, even if demand had still existed.[48]

Other imported luxury items do not preserve so readily as ceramics and coins, and so they are largely absent from the archaeological record. However, historical sources show a remarkable continuity, with spices from Southeast Asia and silk products from China figuring prominently in accounts from all periods. It is impossible to be comprehensive, but as an illustration I cannot resist quoting the following passage by Englebert Kaempfer, a German physician who spent two years at the Dutch settlement in Nagasaki in the last years of the seventeenth century. According to Kaempfer,

> Our cargo consists of the following goods: raw silk from China, Tunkin, Bengal, and Persia; a variety of woven cloth without gold or silver threads and some other fine woolen material from the above and other countries: especially taffachelas from Bengal and Coromandel, large white rolled pelangs, white gilams, armozeens, sumongis, sestiens, and florette yarn. There are variety of chintzes, some half-silken, but also some rough, cotton ones (but no delicate, printed, or painted ones), white gunnies, salempores, and percales. From Europe there is woolen cloth and some other woolen and silken pieces, especially ordinary serge and fine serge. From Siam and Cambodia there is sappan or dyewood, which is called brazilwood in Europe. Also wild buffalo and deer hides, ray skins, wax and buffalo horns, cordwains, and treated skins from Persia, Bengal, and other localities (but under no circumstances from Spain or Manila), pepper and sugar, powdered as well as candy, from a variety of East Indian countries. From Ambon and Banda come cloves and nutmeg (cinnamon is no longer desired), white sandal from Timor, camphor de Baros from the islands of Borneo and Sumatra. On occasion quicksilver, cinnabar, and saffron are sent from Bengal. Also from the latter location and from Siam come tin, lead, salt-peter, borax, and alum. Musk from Tunkin, gum benzoin from Atjeh, gum-lac from Siam. From Mocha in Arabia come rose-mallows, or liquid storax, and catechu, commonly called *terra japonica*, from Surat and Siam the root putchuk or costus amara. Again from Europe there is coral, amber, rough molten glass, used for coloring porcelain, mirrors (which are broken here and used for telescopes, magnifying glasses, and spectacles). Less important items are Masang de Vaca (this is a ball of gall from cows from Mozambique), snake-wood, atjar of bamboo, mangoes and other unripe fruits preserved in Turkish pepper, garlic and vinegar, lead and red ochre for writing,

> sublimate mercury (but not calomel), delicate files, sewing needles, spectacles, cut drinking glasses, fake coral, foreign birds, and a variety of foreign natural and manufactured, new and rare curiosities.[49]

Kaempfer concludes this passage by reaffirming, "Among the imported goods, the Japanese like nothing better than raw silk."[50]

Although many of the items noted by Kaempfer would have been available to the Japanese in earlier periods as well (albeit through different channels of procurement), there are also some important exceptions. Chief among these, of course, are items or European manufacture. Western merchants in Japan served primarily as intermediaries in intra-Asian trade, but they also brought prestige goods from their own countries, which were entirely new to Japan. Among those brought by Spanish and Portuguese in the sixteenth century were religious icons, maps, scientific instruments, and (perhaps most important) guns. After the imposition of the "seclusion" policies in the seventeenth century, the flow of Western goods partially dried up. But, as is clear from Kaempfer's account, it did not stop entirely. Kaempfer's statements are backed up by recent archaeological excavations at Dejima, which have produced a variety of European artifacts, including Dutch and German ceramics, buttons, thimbles, copper pins, combs, hairpins, rings, glass bottles, and clay pipes.[51] Few of these items achieved wide circulation outside the Dutch community, but there were exceptions. Western books, for example, were widely sought in elite circles, particularly after the ban on their import was repealed by the eighth Tokugawa shogun, Yoshimune.[52] (See Chapter 8 in this volume.)

According to Conrad Totman, the total value of Japan's foreign trade at the end of the seventeenth century was less than 1.5 percent of total domestic agricultural production.[53] This does not sound like a lot, but as John Lee has observed, "This and similar figures belie the importance of foreign trade throughout the century as a source of revenue for the rulers and as a channel of supply for luxury consumer goods and for raw material for handicraft industries."[54] After around 1700, however, there seems to have been a real decline in the volume of trade as a result of government controls and a policy of what has been called "import substitution."

In the previous chapter we saw how sugar, originally available only as an import, came to be cultivated by Satsuma in the Edo period. Later, at the urging of the shogunate, sugarcane came to be planted (although not always successfully) in many parts of the country. Similar policies were followed for a variety of other products—most importantly, for silk, ginseng, cotton, and tobacco.[55] Why did the shogunate pursue import substitution with such vigor? The most important reason was quite simple: it could not afford to pay for imports anymore. This brings us to an important question, which we have hitherto ignored: If all of these goods were coming in, what was going out?

Exports

At the end of Chapter 6, I noted that bulk goods (e.g., *tawaramono*) were exported to continental Asia in Edo period, but this was the exception rather than the rule. During most periods of history, Japanese exports, like Japanese imports, consisted almost wholly of luxury goods. Further, as in the case of imports, the nature of these goods showed considerable continuity over time. For purposes of convenience, Japanese exports can be divided into two major categories: manufactured goods and raw materials.

Outgoing manufactures included handicrafts and objets d'art as well as weapons of various kinds. In the late Heian period, for example, exports to Song and Koryŏ included lacquerware boxes, mirror and inkslab cases, writing stands decorated with mother-of-pearl, incense burners, folding fans, painted screens, deer-hide baskets, and dyed hides, as well as swords, bows and arrows, armor, bronze and steel stirrups, and saddles and bits decorated with mother-of-pearl.[56]

As an aside we might note that the materials for some of these were prestige goods obtained from within the archipelago—most frequently from frontier regions. Mother-of-pearl came from the snail *Turbo (Lunatica) marmoratus*, the "marble turban" *(yakōgai)* of Yaku, an island located south of Kyushu. "Dyed hides" appear in eighth-century *mokkan* as a tribute item from Hyūga, located on the Hayato frontier in southern Kyushu.[57] And we can guess with some confidence that arrows destined for export—like those used by high-ranking warriors within Japan itself—were fletched with eagle feathers from the far north. Most of these probably came from Hokkaido or the Kurils, but others were obtained from Manchuria through the same channels as "Ezo brocade" (see below).[58]

Although the above list refers to the Heian period, many of the same items continued to be exported, or taken abroad as gifts, during later centuries. Items exported sold to the Dutch at Nagasaki in the seventeenth century, for example, included lacquerware, furniture, tableware, and other manufactures.[59] Or to take another random example, the party of Japanese Christian converts sent to Europe in the 1580s under the sponsorship of the Society of Jesus presented King Philip II of Spain with a set of folding screens and a desk. Francesco dei Medici, Grand Duke of Tuscany, received an inkpot made of black wood (possibly camphor) and various other trinkets, while Pope Gregory XIII was given two folding screens and a writing desk.[60] Aside from stylistic and technical differences—and, of course, their ultimate destination—none of these manufactures would have been out of place in the Heian period.

Of course, there were exceptions too. Probably the most important of these was Japanese porcelain, which was exported in quantity after the seventeenth century. As noted in Chapter 6, a domestic pottery industry existed in the medieval period, but most of the ware was of relatively low quality. After Hideyoshi's invasions of Korea, however, Korean craftsmen brought over to Kyushu discovered and developed a rich deposit of kaolin at Arita in Hizen province. After a period of experimentation, they began to produce high-quality porcelain, and millions of pieces of Arita ware were shipped to Southeast Asia and Europe by the Dutch in the late seventeenth century.[61]

Be that as it may, exports of manufactured products were relatively modest in all periods compared with those of raw materials, our second category. Here the most important items were minerals and precious metals. Interestingly, a large proportion of these also came from Japan's frontier regions. One example is sulfur, valued (strangely enough) as a medicine and also, in later centuries, as an ingredient in gunpowder. Sulfur was an important export throughout Japan's early history, particularly in the Muromachi period. Although this mineral was found in various parts of the volcanic Japanese archipelago, the best source was Iōjima ("Sulfur Island") off the southern coast of Kyushu.[62] As noted in Chapter 1, this island may be one and the same as Kikaigashima, which medieval Japanese considered to be the southern boundary of their realm.

Sulfur was overshadowed in importance by a variety of metals, particularly gold, silver, and copper. The first of these to be exported in quantity was gold. This again came from a frontier region, Mutsu, where placer gold was discovered in 749. Gold from Mutsu paid for many of Japan's imports from the Heian through the Muromachi periods, leading to the belief in China, as reported by Marco Polo in the fourteenth century, that "Zipangu" was a "land of gold."[63] Gold also enriched "boundary powers" such as the Northern Fujiwara, whose wealth is symbolized by the gilt Buddhas of Chūsonji temple and the hoards of imported porcelain recovered by twentieth-century archaeologists from the Fujiwara capital of Hiraizumi.[64] In later centuries, mines on Sado Island in the Sea of Japan became the main source of Japanese gold.[65] However, the metal did not again become a major export item, except for a short time in the late seventeenth century, when silver exports were temporarily banned and the Dutch began to export gold coins called *koban*, mostly to India.[66]

Over the long run, Japanese exports of silver far exceeded those of gold. Silver was first discovered on the island of Tsushima in 674. However, it did not become an important item of export until the mid-sixteenth century, when additional reserves were discovered in Iwami, on the Sea of Japan coast in western Honshu, and when a new method of refinement, known as cupellation, was introduced from Korea. Silver rapidly became Japan's largest export, and merchants from throughout Asia and Europe vied to obtain the metal in exchange for Chinese silk and silk thread. By the early seventeenth century, silver ingots made up nearly 90 percent of Japan's exports, and Japan was supplying fully one-third of the world's demand for silver. (Much of the rest came from Spanish-run mines in the New World.) However, because of intensive mining, domestic silver reserves were exhausted in about a century.[67]

The result was the balance-of-payments crisis referred to at the end of the previous section. Unable to pay for the imports it needed, the shogunate cut the volume of trade and put more effort into import substitution. This is not, of course, to say, that trade stopped. Import substitution notwithstanding, there was still a need for foreign goods, and these were paid for with gold, as noted above, and later and more importantly with copper. Copper was Japan's most important export in the late seventeenth century. Large reserves of copper ore existed in many parts of Japan, particularly along the Honshu coast of the Inland Sea, but intensive mining resulted in their rapid depletion. By the end of the seventeenth century, copper, like silver before it, was becoming a scarce item.[68] Once again, the shogunate scrambled to find new items for export. This time, the lack was made up not with metals but with foodstuffs, specifically the dried marine products known as *tawaramono* and *shoshiki*, which were discussed in the previous chapter.

In sum, Japan exported—both through political channels and trade—a wide variety of manufactured goods and raw materials, most of them luxury or prestige items, throughout the premodern period. What was the final destination of these goods after they left the country? Unfortunately, this is not an easy question to answer in most cases. But at least it is clear that Japanese metals, particularly silver, were circulating throughout Eurasia by the sixteenth century and that certain manufactures, such as Arita ware, were widely available in Europe by the seventeenth century.[69] Political efforts to the contrary, Japan's borders were hardly "closed" in early modern times.

Transshipment and Scale of Exchange

This chapter has by no means provided a full account of Japan's prestige goods network in premodern times. Among other things, I have only touched in passing upon interactions between Japan "proper" and its archipelagic neighbors to the north and south. But these interactions must have been quite important throughout premodern times.

To briefly sum up the evidence, Japan imported many prestige goods from the Ryukyus and Hokkaido, both via political means (tribute) and via trade. From the south, one item we have already encountered is mother-of-pearl obtained from the large snail shells known as *yakōgai.* Other prized imports from the Ryukyus were "red tree" *(akagi)*, or *Bischofia*, a kind of precious wood, and betel nuts *(binrōji)*, which were used as medicine.[70] In the north, as noted above, Tōhoku served as a source of gold in the Heian period, while Hokkaido produced eagle feathers and furs for Japanese consumption throughout premodern times. In the Edo period the Ainu also supplied many pharmaceuticals to the Japanese, including bear gallbladder, dried seal penis, and various medicinal plants.[71]

Nor were these flows of prestige goods entirely one-way. Although details are lacking for the south, in Hokkaido many of the items received by the Ainu from the Japanese were valued as "treasures" that conferred status and prestige upon their owners. This was true even of such "utilitarian" objects as iron kettles, but also of sword hilts and pommels, gold utensils, and lacquerware. As noted by Brett Walker, some of these objects remained prized family heirlooms well after the Meiji Restoration of 1868.[72]

To my mind, however, what is really significant about prestige goods exchanges within the archipelago is their systematic linkage to larger, Eurasian networks. For example, many of the furs and feathers that found their way to Japan ultimately came from Manchuria, not Hokkaido. This was also true of the silk robes known as "Ezo brocade" *(Ezo nishiki)*, which were so prized by the military classes in Edo times. Despite its name, "Ezo brocade" was not made in Hokkaido but in China. Both the brocade and the robes were originally obtained by various tribes in Manchuria through "tribute trade" with the Qing dynasty. The silks were then traded to the Sakhalin Ainu in exchange for lacquerware, furs, rice, and liquor and finally made their way to Japan as tribute presented by the Ainu to the lords of Matsumae.[73] At the other end of the archipelago, the Ryukyus provided shells and precious woods to Japanese rulers, but their more important historical role was as an intermediary in intra-Asian trade.

This role may be considered a special case of transshipment, or down-the-line trade, which was characteristic of virtually all exchanges involving prestige goods. Consider, for example, how goods from West Asia were brought to Japan in ancient times by ship (or, alternatively, over the silk routes) in a series of transactions involving merchants and political authorities from many separate regions. Transshipment from one trade "circuit" to another was one reason why the prestige goods traveled such great distances. Another, of course, was their high value-per-weight ratio, which made them much cheaper to ship than, for example, bulk goods. Transshipment also explains why prestige goods "carried" farther than political/

military relationships, which typically took the form of direct, face-to-face interactions.

As we have seen, the total scale of Japan's prestige goods network can be measured in two ways—in terms of the ultimate provenance of imports, or the ultimate destination of exports. We know a great deal more about the former, and based on this information it is clear that from the eighth century at the latest, elite members of Japanese society were already part of a vast exchange network (or, more precisely, a collection of interconnected networks or "circuits") encompassing all of Asia, and possibly Africa as well. The scale of the system remained more or less constant for many centuries thereafter, until the 1500s, when Europeans first began to visit the archipelago.

At this point Japan's prestige goods network was fully Eurasian, and quite possibly global, in scale. After all, the Spanish traveled to Asia, including Japan, via their outposts in Mexico and Peru, and so there must have been interchanges, of a sort, with the New World as well as the Old. I have not been able to discover any concrete examples of prestige goods from the Americas reaching Japan (or vice versa) in the early modern period, but if we look beyond Chase-Dunn and Hall's categories, it is easy to find connections of other kinds. For example, many Western food crops, mostly from the Americas, were introduced to Japan during the Edo period. The most important was the potato, which came from South America, but other examples include green beans, corn, red peppers, pumpkins, watermelon, spinach, peanuts, asparagus, lima beans, marjoram, peppermint, sage, and lemons.[74]

Whether we include the New World or not, however, it is clear that throughout Japan's premodern history prestige goods not only traveled farther than bulk goods but also well beyond the limits of political/military interactions. This leaves us with just one more category of social exchange to consider: information flow, the subject of the next chapter.

8 Information

Information and Frontiers

What types of information were available in premodern Japan about the outside world, and vice versa? What was the quantity of information, and what was the quality? How was information transmitted, and what factors (geographic, technological, or social) determined access or lack thereof? How did these variables change over time?

These are not easy questions to answer, in part because the topic is so broad. The word "information" itself simply means "knowledge communicated or received,"[1] but this would seem to include virtually everything that goes on inside the human brain—or, more accurately, that can be conveyed from one brain to another. The topic of information flows between Japan and the outside world, therefore, encompasses all aspects of foreign relations, including but not limited to cultural and intellectual exchanges. Obviously this is a rather large bite to chew. It would be difficult or impossible for any one person to read everything written on these subjects, still less to summarize it for the purposes of a book chapter.

Although the field of information is too large, it is also, paradoxically, too small, in the sense that few studies have been specifically devoted to this topic. The student will search long and hard in the library before finding a book or article on Japanese history with the word "information" in the title.[2] Nor is this a problem limited to Japan; indeed, much the same point could be made for world history.

But given that the field is larger, so is the cumulative number of titles. One excellent recent book, which I would like to introduce here for its relevance to the present study, is A. D. Lee's *Information and Frontiers: Roman Foreign Relations in Late Antiquity*.

In this study, Lee examines flows of information between the later Roman Empire and its neighbors to the north (i.e., the various tribes in what is now Germany) and east (i.e., the Persian empire). Although the author for the most part avoids drawing sweeping conclusions, some of his arguments are nonetheless highly suggestive. Lee finds, for example, that "information of strategic importance moved across both the eastern and northern frontiers of the Roman empire and in both directions," leading him to conclude that "the suggestion that the empire's frontiers were information barriers needs qualification."[3]

This having been said, Lee also argues that in general the eastern frontier was more permeable to information flow than the northern. In order to explain the difference, he introduces the idea of "social gravity" and then describes some of the key factors affecting the circulation of information between premodern societies, specifically "cross-frontier interactions, mutual linguistic intelligibility, settlement density, and 'newsworthiness.'"[4] Lee concludes,

> The more sophisticated degree of organisational complexity in Persia encouraged a higher level of diplomatic interchange with the Roman empire (with all the attendant consequences in terms of opportunities to gather intelligence and increase knowledge of one another), and also made the task of detecting military preparations and the like easier for envoys and spies, while the greater degree of urbanisation meant that information circulated more widely and intensely within Persia. By contrast, the relative absence of these conditions in the north meant that it was inherently more difficult to gather information there, no matter how energetic the efforts. Differing levels of urbanisation, together with the various socio-cultural and economic factors making for more intense interaction across the empire's eastern frontier, also meant that information was more likely to traverse the eastern frontier than the northern through informal channels.[5]

Last but not least, this book argues for a direct relationship between level of information flow and political stability. Specifically, the author suggests that mutual availability of accurate information is largely to account for "the greater stability which tended to characterise Roman relations with Persia compared with the situation along the northern frontier."[6] (Although Lee draws no modern parallels, it is hard not to see in this assertion shadows of the old Cold War argument that a stable nuclear balance of power is best maintained by open, verifiable treaty arrangements within a strategic context of "mutually assured destruction.")

All of this is highly suggestive in view of what we already know about foreign relations in premodern Japan. One is tempted to speculate, for example, that the situation along Japan's northern frontier may have paralleled the experience of Rome with the German tribes. Sparse population and low levels of social organization, in other words, may have hindered the flow of information across the frontier, contributing to political instability. (More generally, this argument might be relevant to Ferguson and Whitehead's finding that warfare and violence are associated with "tribal zones" throughout world history.[7]) Conversely, relations with more populous state-based societies—for example, in Korea—might have followed the Rome-Persia pattern, where relatively good information flow contributed to stability.

Unfortunately, these ideas are not easily verified. Lee's study involved a painstaking search of Roman sources, including what he calls "classicising" histories, ecclesiastical histories, and chronicles for scattered references to foreign contacts, military engagements, and so on.[8] The same methodology could be attempted for Japan in a full-scale study of the problem, but I do not have time for it here. So for the moment the hypothesis that poor information flow contributed to sociopolitical instability on Japan's northern frontier must remain precisely that—a hypothesis.

However, this does not mean that we can say nothing about the topic of information flow in premodern Japan. Even without combing primary sources for evidence, it is possible to assess the major channels by which information was conveyed and the changing geographic scale of Japan's information network. Following the same strategy used to analyze prestige goods, I will first look mainly at information coming into Japan, saving a discussion of information leaving Japan for somewhat later in the chapter.

"Formal" vs. "Informal" Channels

In his study of information dispersal across Roman frontiers, Lee first of all distinguishes between "formal" and "informal" channels. In effect, this is more or less the same distinction we have already made between "official" and "private" channels for the acquisition of prestige goods; it is useful again here so long as we remember that the boundary between the two categories is not always hard and fast.

Two examples of "formal channels" mentioned by Lee are diplomatic embassies and spies.[9] I cannot think of any good examples of Japanese "spies" collecting information abroad, but embassies are another matter. Diplomatic contacts have been described in some detail in previous chapters, and although there is no need to repeat any of that material here, it is worth emphasizing that such missions, both to and from Japan, played a vital role in the transmission of information throughout history. Diplomatic missions in all periods, of course, featured exchanges not only of goods ("tribute" and "return gifts") but also of information (broadly defined) in the form of written greetings (state letters) and oral exchanges (audiences) between envoys and their hosts.[10] Of course, these ritualized exchanges were only the tip of the iceberg; diplomatic missions provided myriad opportunities for envoys to observe and collect information about their hosts, and vice versa. In some cases, indeed, collecting information was the primary goal of the mission. This was certainly true of the seventh-century Japanese embassies to Sui and Tang, whose purpose was to acquire knowledge about Chinese civilization, partly by direct observation but also, and more importantly, through the acquisition of texts such as Buddhist sutras and legal codes.[11]

Diplomatic contacts did not even have to be direct to provide useful information. One fascinating example is the Tokugawa shogunate's use of Ryukyuan diplomats to obtain up-to-date information about conditions in Qing China during the mid-seventeenth century. Worried that China's Manchu rulers might, like the Mongols five centuries earlier, attempt to invade Japan, government officials instructed Satsuma on several occasions to obtain information from Ryukyu via diplomatic channels. The shogunate, which maintained no official relations with China, thus exploited Ryukyu's dual allegiance to Qing and Japan for its own purposes.[12]

In addition to spies and diplomats, it is possible to think of several other examples of "formal channels." One would be information obtained by government armies, such as the Japanese forces sent to aid Paekche in the 660s, the various expeditions sent against the Hayato in the seventh and eighth centuries and against the Emishi in the seventh through ninth centuries, and (much later in history) Hideyoshi's invasions of Korea in the 1590s. Of course, countless other examples could be given.

Government-sponsored missions of exploration, although not always clearly distinguishable from military expeditions, were another important source of information in some periods. An early example would be the expedition sent by the imperial court in 698 to "search for countries" in the "Southern Islands" (i.e., the Ryukyu chain), which seems to have been undertaken for the purpose of exploring Japan's territorial surroundings and fixing its place in the greater world with more precision than had heretofore been possible.[13] Much better known are the various expeditions sent to the far north by the Edo shogunate in the late eighteenth and early nineteenth centuries, partly in response to security fears about Russia. Among the various explorers who participated in these missions were Mogami Tokunai, the first Japanese official to reach Etorofu and Uruppu (in 1786), and Mamiya Rinzō and Matsuda Denjūrō, who showed that Sakhalin was an island (and not part of the Eurasian landmass) in 1808. The work of these individuals, and others, resulted in the first accurate maps of Hokkaido and adjacent regions and also produced a wealth of detailed information about Ainu society and customs.[14]

As we move on to discuss "informal channels," among the important ones cited by Lee in his study of Rome are "pilgrims, students, clerics, merchants, mercenaries, and the like."[15] With a few exceptions, most of these categories also apply to the Japanese case, although some of them cannot clearly be separated from the "formal channels" discussed above. For example, members of religious orders sometimes served as proxies for diplomatic envoys during the late Heian period, when there were no "formal" relations with China or other states. In other cases, merchants might be enlisted to carry official messages. But in general, these channels were perhaps more "private" in character than "public."

Certainly pilgrims and clerics served as an important conduit of information between Japan and the outside world in all periods of history. Japanese sources from the Heian and Kamakura periods, in particular, are replete with stories of Buddhist monks coming to Japan from China to propagate Buddhist teachings and of Japanese priests making pilgrimages to China for the purpose of study. An excellent example is Ennin, the Tendai monk who spent the years 838–847 in Tang China studying Buddhism and also, not incidentally, acquiring a wealth of up-to-date information on Tang China, which he left to posterity in the form of a diary.[16] Of course, the role of clerics in transmitting information was not limited to the ancient period or to members of the Buddhist faith. One has only to recall names such as Francisco Xavier, Luis Frois, and Alexandro Valignano of the Portuguese Society of Jesus to realize how important Western missionaries were in disseminating information to and from Japan during the sixteenth and early seventeenth centuries. These missionaries brought Christian teachings and miscellaneous information about the West to Japan and, just as important, left voluminous writings describing Japan to their countrymen back in Europe.[17]

It should probably be emphasized, however, that clerics did not generally travel on their own but availed themselves of existing means of transportation—sometimes public but more often private. Ennin, for example, went to China in the company of a Japanese diplomatic mission but was forced to find other means for his return; through contacts with Korean communities in coastal China he eventually found passage on a merchant vessel bound for Kyushu. Most later pilgrims also made use of commercial vessels, particularly those belonging to members of the Chinese diaspora community in Hakata. (Incidentally, these Korean and Chinese settlements provide good examples of the important role that diaspora communities played in mediating "cross-cultural" trade throughout world history.[18]) Western missionaries were also dependent upon traders. When Francisco Xavier came to Japan in 1543, he came on a Chinese merchant vessel—although in this case one based in Malacca.[19] Xavier's successors generally came on Portuguese or other Western vessels, but they were merchant ships all the same. The reason was simple: throughout premodern history, merchants—whether of Korean, Chinese, or Western ethnicity—were responsible for the bulk of international traffic in Asia. And of course, this was true in other parts of the world as well.

This does not necessarily mean, however, that merchants themselves played an unduly large role in disseminating information. Certainly, they would have been exceptionally well informed about countries they resided in or visited, but it also seems likely that much of this information was retained within diaspora communities. It must be remembered that merchants were in business to make a profit, not to convey information per se (unless, presumably it could be sold). It would not be surprising to find, therefore, that data about other countries, winds and tides, and commodities were considered trade secrets to be protected, not shared.

Although above I denied the existence of government spies, it is true that foreign merchants were sometimes accused of spying on Japan. (And presumably, Japanese merchants were subject to the same accusations abroad.) One reason for this is that, at least in some periods, there was very little distinction between merchants and pirates. Some good examples of this kind again come from the Heian period. At precisely the same time that Ennin was visiting China, for example, officials at the Dazaifu in Kyushu were regularly accusing Korean merchants in Hakata and/or Tsushima of spying on Japan. Whether this was true or not is unclear, but we do know that pirates had access to important strategic information in this period. In 869, for example, Korean pirates entered Hakata Bay and made away with a year's worth of tax goods from Buzen province, which at the time was waiting shipment to Kyoto.[20] Many other examples of pirate activities, of course, can be found in Japanese history, particularly during the medieval period, when the East China Sea was dominated by the Wakō. So perhaps "pirates" should be added to our list of informal channels for the transmission of information, although here again, as in the case of merchants, these individuals were more likely to possess information than to actively seek to convey it to others.

Another category not mentioned by Lee is immigrants. As described in Chapter 2, the entire population of the Japanese islands originally came from outside, but immigration remained important through at least the early Heian period. Many of these immigrants, probably the majority, came to the islands because of "push" factors that forced them to leave their home countries. Political turmoil on the peninsula and in China was responsible for the influx of so-called *kikajin (toraijin)* of pre-Nara times. A particularly good example comes from the 660s and 670s, when many aristocrats and soldiers from Koguryŏ and (particularly) Paekche fled to Japan after the destruction of those countries by the combined forces of Tang and Silla. As many authors have stressed, immigrants from the Korean Peninsula played an essential role in transferring advanced continental culture and technology to elites in Japan. Later, in the early Heian period, there are many records of immigrants from Silla, who apparently came to escape socioeconomic turmoil in their homeland. During later periods of history, the pace of immigration seems to have slowed down considerably, particularly during early modern times, when foreign contacts were harshly regulated by the shogunate.[21]

This by no means exhausts the list of possible informal channels for the exchange of information. Another category, few in number but occasionally important, was castaways. Several incidents involving castaways have been described by Donald Keene in his classic study, *The Japanese Discovery of Europe.* In one case, "Denbei," a Japanese shipwrecked in Kamchatka, was discovered in 1697 by Russian conquerors and taken to St. Petersburg, where he met Peter the Great and founded a Japanese-language school. Even more interesting is the case of "Kōdayū," a Japanese merchant carried to the Aleutians in 1783 by a freak storm. After spending several years on an island in the company of natives and Russian trappers, Kōdayū and his companions were rescued by a Russian sealing vessel and taken to Kamchatka. Kōdayū then made his way to Siberia and eventually to St. Petersburg, where he met Empress Catherine. The empress ordered Kōdayū to be taken home to Japan, and a Russian ship carrying him arrived in Ezo in 1792. Government authorities redirected the ship to Nagasaki, but it failed to comply, depositing Kōdayū and his one surviving companion in Ezo before returning to Russia. Kōdayū was immediately summoned to the shogun's court, where he proved to be a veritable gold mine of information about contemporary Russia, most of which found its way into a multivolume official report. Kōdayū, incidentally, spent the rest of his days under virtual house arrest, because government officials did not want him spreading information about the world beyond Japan to the general public.[22]

As this last example suggests, government officials often tried to monopolize cross-border flows of information, even those involving informal channels. (This was true not just in the Edo period but throughout premodern times.) Officials tried to discourage information from leaving the country because it was thought to represent a security risk. Information entering the country, meanwhile, was a scarce resource to be kept from other elements of society who might use it to their own advantage, undermining the position of the ruling class. Not surprisingly, the degree to which the government was able to achieve these goals depended upon how much political power it wielded in the first place. As was the case for other types of cross-border interaction, central controls were relatively effective in times of strong government (i.e., the ancient and early modern periods) and relatively ineffective in times of weak government (i.e., the medieval period).[23]

Inflows

This brings us to the next question: From what regions or countries was information available to the Japanese in different periods of history? What, in other words, was the geographic scope of Japan's information network, as measured in terms of inflows? To answer this question, we have to define more precisely what we mean by "information flow."

I would submit that there are at least three important cases to be considered. First would be the transmission of specific skills or technologies (including cultural traditions) from particular regions. An example (although relating to outflows rather than inflows) would be the teaching of Japanese in St. Petersburg by the above-mentioned Denbei. A second, closely related category would consist of general information about specific countries or peoples—for example, geographic information or knowledge about customs. Much of the information gleaned by the Edo shogunate from Kōdayū probably fell into this category. Kōdayū also provided officials with considerable information about current events, in other words, "news"—our third category.

I think that we can agree that "information" of the first two kinds is likely to be more widely distributed (at least in premodern times) than that of the third, because—in ideal circumstances—only a single "transmission" is required for the first two. Knowledge of current events, by contrast, requires sustained, systemic links. For that reason, regular availability of "news" is probably the best practical gauge of the scope of a country's information network.

By this standard, what was the size of Japan's information network in different periods of history? In order to simplify matters, let us organize the discussion by region, using the following (loose) categories: (1) peripheral societies within the archipelago; (2) other countries in East Asia; and (3) more distant parts of the globe.

Peripheral Societies within the Archipelago

Although the Ryukyus and Hokkaido were both part of the Japanese archipelago, good information about them was relatively scarce in premodern Japan. To focus again on the case of Hokkaido, some geographic information may have been available to the court as early as the late 650s, thanks to the military expedition or expeditions commanded by Abe Hirafu against the Emishi.[24] However, despite rather intense (at times) interaction with the peoples of the north over subsequent centuries, Japan's stock of cumulative information about them was not terribly impressive.

As evidence, I refer readers to the passages from the eighth-century *Nihon shoki* and the fourteenth-century *Suwa daimyōjin ekotoba*, which were discussed at length in Chapter 3. The *Nihon shoki* passage is entirely fanciful, although it was written by courtiers presumably familiar with the expeditions of Abe Hirafu and more recent events on the frontier, such as the construction of Dewa Stockade in 709. Of course the purpose of this passage is to contrast the "barbarian" Emishi with the "civilized" Japanese, so whatever knowledge was available may well have been omitted from this particular text. The *Suwa daimyōjin ekotoba* is somewhat more concrete but still contains elements of fantasy, such as the following: "Their appearance is like that of demons, forever changing; as for their customs, they eat the flesh of fowl, beasts, and fish, and are unfamiliar with the cultivation of the five grains." The medieval residents of Hokkaido were neither demons nor unacquainted with the cultivation of grain.

Nor was information about the geography of the north much better. As late as the 1590s, the warlord Hideyoshi—presumably one of the best-informed individuals in Japan—could believe that Ezo (Hokkaido) was part of the Eurasian continent. Apparently, Hideyoshi thought that Hokkaido could serve as a northern route to Korea, which at that time was the focus of his imperialist ambitions. This belief was based, at least in part, on maps received from European missionaries—showing that ignorance about northeast Eurasia was hardly limited to Japan.[25]

It was not until early modern times, at the earliest, that Hokkaido and adjacent islands were fully incorporated within Japan's information network. Information and news about Hokkaido itself became available as a natural consequence of the establishment of "trading fiefs" throughout the island in the seventeenth century. But it was not until the expeditions of Mogami Tokunai, Mamiya Rinzō, and Matsuda Denjūrō toward the end of the period that information about the Kurils and Sakhalin became readily available. Even regarding Hokkaido itself, knowledge of current events (except in the case of crises such as Shakushain's War or the Kunashiri-Menashi Uprising) remained quite limited in Japan until the island was formally annexed, first on a temporary basis at the end of the Edo period (1799–1821 and 1855–1867) and then permanently, following the Meiji Restoration of 1868.

Other East Asian Countries

Next, regarding other countries on the Asian mainland, clearly elites in the Japanese archipelago had access to various aspects of Chinese and Korean culture from very early times; the transmission of irrigated farming and metallurgy (in the Yayoi period) as well as the Chinese writing system and Buddhism (in the Kofun period) are all cases in point.

Regarding historic periods, probably the best study of the subject (albeit one that largely ignores Korea) is by Masayoshi Sugimoto and David Swain. According to these authors, Japanese borrowing of culture and technology from the continent occurred in two historical "waves." "Chinese Wave I," which began circa 600 C.E. and lasted until 894, saw the importation of Tang-style learning and institutions, including Confucianism, law, literature, history, mathematics, calendrics, divination, and medicine, not to mention various traditions associated with Buddhism (including Buddhist art and architecture). This was followed by a "Semi-Seclusion Era," circa 894–1401, when little new information came in from the continent. A second wave of borrowing began circa 1401 and continued until the opening of the country in 1854. This "Chinese Wave II" was mainly associated with the importation of Neo-Confucian learning.[26]

It will be noted that the "waves" postulated by Sugimoto and Swain correspond very well with phases of expansion in Japan's political/military network, which I described in Chapter 5. And indeed, this is no coincidence, since most of the borrowing described by Sugimoto and Swain occurred through official or "formal" channels, most notably diplomatic contacts. But is it really fair to say that Japan was in an era of "seclusion" with respect to information flow during Heian and Kamakura times? I think not. It is true that fewer technologies were being imported during these centuries, but the presence of "informal channels" such as merchants, and even more important, Buddhist clerics, in fact kept up a steady flow of information from the continent to Japan. Priests such as Jōjin sent back important information about Song China in the late Heian period, and the level of contact was even higher in the Kamakura period, thanks to thirst among high-ranking warriors for up-to-date information about Chinese Zen Buddhism.[27]

I think the real question, for *all* periods and not just the supposed "Semi-Seclusion Era," is whether information flow from China (and the Korean Peninsula) was sustained enough to constitute "news" in the sense I have described above. The answer to this question is a qualified "yes"—by which I mean that although "news" did not automatically flow into Japan, government officials were generally capable of getting it when they saw the need. Many of the early diplomatic missions were dispatched for precisely this reason, and as Tōno Haruyuki has shown, returning envoys from Tang were often required to prepare detailed reports on current events in China.[28] Even during the

"Semi-Seclusion Era," a crisis would cause officials in Kyoto or Kamakura to exploit available contacts in search of information abroad. Such was certainly the case after the "Toi Invasion" of 1019 or during the prolonged Mongol crisis of the late thirteenth century.[29] And the sustained political and commercial relations with continental Asia during "Chinese Wave II" virtually guaranteed that up-to-date information was available when required. During the Ming-Qing transition of the seventeenth century, worried officials in Edo successfully kept abreast of current events using both "formal" and "informal" channels. A good example of the former, mentioned earlier, was the gathering of information via Ryukyuan diplomatic contacts. An example of the latter was the requisitioning of written reports on current conditions, known as *fūsetsugaki*, from Chinese merchants visiting Nagasaki.[30]

More Distant Regions

What about more distant regions? One obvious question here relates to knowledge about India, the birthplace of Buddhism. But while detailed knowledge about Buddhism as a religion, including Chinese translations of important sutras, was available in Japan from the seventh century, knowledge of the historical Buddha's homeland was quite sketchy indeed. The term "Tenjiku," customarily translated into English as "India," had no such concrete referent for the Japanese who actually used it. "Tenjiku" was "the Land of the Buddha," but in geographic terms all this really meant was "somewhere beyond China."[31]

In human terms, "Tenjiku" was almost completely off limits to Japan, and vice versa. Once every few centuries (to judge from surviving records), a man from "Tenjiku" might find his way to Japan; the two best-known examples are a monk from the eighth century (who presided at the opening ceremonies for Tōdaiji temple) and a merchant from the fourteenth century (who resided near modern Osaka and fathered two sons, one of whom entered the service of Kōfukuji temple and took part in two trade missions to China).[32] Equally rarely, someone from Japan might attempt a pilgrimage to the Buddhist holy land. One well-known example is Prince Takaoka (also known by his Buddhist name, Shinnyo), who died *en route* to Tenjiku (reputedly on the Malay Peninsula) in 865, three years after his initial crossing to China. Interestingly, news of the prince's death did eventually reach Japan—but not until 881, when the court received a letter from another monk, Chūgon, then studying in China.[33]

In short, throughout most of the premodern era, Japan's information network was for all practical purposes limited to the archipelago itself (excluding, as we have seen, some of the more distant regions), the Korean Peninsula, and China. It is possible, of course, that knowledge of Southeast Asia became gradually available with the expansion of trade in medieval times. But no fundamental change occurred until the sixteenth century, when the arrival of the Europeans led to a drastic and permanent resizing of Japan's "world." Because the facts of the European arrival are well known, I will limit myself here to a brief listing of some of the implications for the availability of information in Japan.

Here again it seems reasonable to cite the work of Sugimoto and Swain, who postulate two "waves" of Western cultural and scientific borrowing as a counterpoint to the two earlier Chinese "waves." "Western Wave I," according to these authors, consists of the period from 1543 to 1639, which saw the introduction of Christian doctrine and Scholasticism via the efforts of Jesuit priests. Some Western techniques (for example, the use of firearms), as well as astronomy and mathematics, were also introduced but for the most part were abandoned or forgotten after the imposition of the final "seclusion" edict in 1639. During "Western Wave II," circa 1720–1854, a boom in "Dutch learning" *(Rangaku)* was initiated when Tokugawa Yoshimune relaxed the ban on Western books. At first, Japanese scholars were attracted mostly to anatomy and medicine, but later, interest spread to other fields of science. In the nineteenth century, as security threats from abroad multiplied, the greatest focus was on the acquisition of Western military techniques.[34]

Although this approach tells us what kinds of knowledge *came from* the West in Sengoku and early modern times, it does not answer the equally important question of what contemporary Japanese knew *about* the West or other parts of the world as the result of the European presence. In what follows, I would like to give a brief summary with respect to the two categories of background knowledge about culture, geography, and so forth, and actual "news" of current events.

Regarding general knowledge about the world, the arrival of the Portuguese and Spanish caused the "scales to drop off the eyes" (to use a Japanese proverb) of their hosts. In a historical instant, Japanese leaders and even commoners became aware that the world consisted not just of "Japan," "China" (and Korea), and "Tenjiku" but also of "myriad realms" inhabited by people of many different races, languages, and cultures. Their new knowledge found expression in the production of large numbers of European-influenced world maps and globes in the sixteenth and seventeenth centuries. Many world maps of the Edo period were accompanied by "pictures of the peoples of the world," which showed men and women from each country clad in typical garb and engaged in culturally distinctive activities. This is not to say that all the information in these maps and pictures was accurate; to the contrary, some of it was wildly stereotyped, and mythical countries such as the "land of the giants" and the "land of the dwarves" received the same treatment as real locations like "Ingeresu" (England) and "Amerika" (America). Nonetheless it is clear that in broad outline, literate Japanese of the Edo period were familiar with the "shape of the world" and the location and characteristics of its major countries.[35]

Nor was this all. Elites in Japan had access to current news of world affairs, not just in the sixteenth century, when European visitors had virtually the run of the land, but even during the Edo period, when the Western presence was limited to the Dutch at Nagasaki. The Dutch, like the Chinese, were required to submit reports called *fūsetsugaki* in exchange for the privilege of trading at Nagasaki. The shogunate first required Dutch merchants to submit *fūsetsugaki* in 1639, primarily in order to obtain information about Spanish and Portuguese activities in Asia. These reports were translated (sometimes poorly) into Japanese by government interpreters in Nagasaki, and then submitted to Edo. The information they contained was supplemented in question-and-answer sessions held with the Dutch captain, who after 1633 was required to visit Edo every year to pay his respects to the shogun. (In 1790 this was changed to once every four years.) Although this system was by no means perfect, it did give the government access to relatively accurate news about world affairs throughout the early modern period.[36]

In sum, Japan's information network, viewed from the perspective of inflows, was pan-Eurasian in scale by the end of the sixteenth century. Indeed, it may have been global. Although it would be an exaggeration to say that early modern Japanese had detailed knowledge of the Americas, they were not totally ignorant of it either. The New World was more or less properly depicted on Japanese-made world maps, and as noted at the end of the previous chapter, American food crops, including but not limited to the potato, were widely introduced in the Edo period.

Outflows

Next, let us briefly examine outflows of information from Japan. Throughout premodern times, information about the country was transmitted to its nearest neighbors by the same kinds of formal and informal channels used by the Japanese themselves. It is difficult to assess the level of knowledge about Japan in peripheral societies within the archipelago (particularly in the north, where there are no written records). Regarding China, a glance at the various dynastic histories shows that at least some information on society in the Japanese islands was available from very early times.[37] The quantity and quality of this information can only have increased over time with the growth of diplomatic, and then commercial, contacts in the ancient and medieval periods.

Here I would like to touch briefly instead on the information available about Japan in other parts of the world, particularly Europe. According to Donald Lach, Persian writings from the ninth century make refer to the land of "Wakwak," a term presumably derived from the Chinese "Woguo" or "Country of Wa." Half a millennium later there is the famous description of "Cipangu," the "land of gold," in Marco Polo's *Travels*. The country of "Jampon" also appears in a 1513 work, *Summa Oriental*, by the Portuguese sailor Tome Pirés. But all of these early mentions are cursory and based entirely on secondhand information.[38]

All of this changed, of course, after 1543, when the first Europeans arrived in Japan. As is well known, the Jesuit missionaries active in Kyushu and elsewhere sent back voluminous letters and reports to their superiors in Rome. Many of these were later collected and published, so that, by the end of the sixteenth century, educated Europeans had access to a wide variety of firsthand reports on Japan, written both in Latin and the major vernaculars.[39] The level of interest in, and knowledge about, the country also increased significantly following the arrival in Europe of the Japanese legation of 1584–1586. "Their persons, gifts, and samples of writing," according to Donald Lach, "all helped to make Japan more real for Europeans."[40]

As it happened, however, this situation was only temporary. Following the expulsion of the Jesuits in the early seventeenth century, new sources of information about Japan became quite scarce. Partly this was because fewer Westerners were now visiting the country, but more fundamentally it was a result of the stringent controls imposed by the shogunate on their movements and access to information. Kaempfer, from his vantage point on Dejima, noted,

> All those who are in contact with us especially are bound by an oath and sign with their blood not to talk or entrust to us information about the situation of their country, their religion, secrets of government, and various other specified subjects. They are all the more prevented from doing so since the above oath requires all to act as their neighbor's informer. To make an even deeper impression this blood oath must be repeated and renewed annually.[41]

Kaempfer himself was able to circumvent these rules in part, with the help of a young Japanese servant. Kaempfer trained this individual in anatomy and medicine and paid him a "handsome" salary.

> In return he had to look for good information about the situation of the country, the government, the court, their religion and the history of past ages, their families as well as daily events and pass it on to me. There was not a book I endeavored to see which he did not obtain for me and explain and translate the passages I indicated.[42]

Others, however, were not so lucky. The best-known example is Franz Balthasar von Siebold, another German physician in the service of the Dutch mission at Dejima. In 1828, as Siebold was about to depart from Japan, prohibited items, including a copy of a map of Japan's coastlines by Inō Tadakata and another map of Hokkaido and Sakhalin, were discovered in his luggage. After a lengthy investigation of the affair, Siebold was expelled from the country (although he returned in 1859–1862). His principal Japanese conspirator, a government astronomer named Takahashi Kageyasu, was sentenced to death and died shortly thereafter in prison.[43]

Nature and Scale of the Network

What conclusions can we draw about the nature and scale of Japan's information network in premodern times? I can think of three.

First, as is clear from the case of the Edo period, just because information flows in one direction, we should not automatically assume that there is an equal flow the other way. Ichimura Yūichi, in a very interesting book on this topic, has argued that during the Edo period the government tried, more or less successfully, to prevent information from leaving Japan while at the same time maximizing (through the use of *fūsetsugaki* and so forth) intelligence about the outside world. Information flow, in other words, was essentially one-way; in Ichimura's words, Japan "received" *(jushin)* but did not "transmit" *(hasshin)* information.[44] I think this is an exaggeration; quite a lot of new information about Japan reached the world through the writings of Kaempfer, Siebold, and others. But it is probably true that the "balance of trade" in information operated in Japan's favor, thanks to the efforts of the shogunate. When government officials operated from a position of power, they were indeed able to influence the nature and volume of information crossing international borders.

Second, by whatever measure is used, the absolute scale of Japan's information network expanded greatly over time, as was the case for the other social networks we have observed. Although the information network was essentially limited to East Asia in ancient and medieval times, after the arrival of the Portuguese and Spanish in the sixteenth century it suddenly expanded to global proportions. (In addition to its tendency to expand over time, the network may also have exhibited small- or medium-scale "pulsations," but it is not possible to establish this without more detailed study.)

Third, in most periods the relative scale of the information network vis-à-vis that of other social networks generally bears out the predictions of Chase-Dunn and Hall—with one possible exception. According to the model, information networks are generally much larger than bulk goods networks, somewhat larger than their political/

military networks, and on the same order of magnitude as prestige goods networks. For the most part, this seems to have been true for Japan. The exception relates to the status of Hokkaido, Sakhalin, and the Kurils. Arguably, indigenous peoples in these islands were (at least indirectly) susceptible to political and military influences from Japan, and vice versa, in most periods of history. And yet it is clear that the level of information flow between these regions and Japan was relatively low, both in terms of quantity and quality. In this one region, at least, Japan's political/military network may have exceeded its information network in scale.

9 Japan, East Asia, and the World

Japan and East Asia

After the extended discussion in preceding chapters, it is time to return to our original question: Did premodern Japan (or, more broadly, the Japanese archipelago) constitute a "world-system" in its own right? Or is Japan more properly considered part of a larger, China-centered "East Asian world-system"? Let us review the evidence and attempt to draw a conclusion.

Take a look at Figure 10, which summarizes the information presented in previous chapters about Japan's connections with other parts of East Asia. (More distant regions are omitted for the sake of simplicity.) The figure shows the extent of the four networks of exchange at four "slices" in time spaced at intervals of three hundred years, from the eighth to the seventeenth centuries. Note that the information is presented in schematic form, with no attempt to map geographic relationships accurately.

Perhaps the most obvious conclusion to be drawn from Figure 10 is that Japan was *never* isolated from its external environment. As I have argued, "Japan" can be defined as a polity, a cultural zone, an ethnic unit, or all three. No matter which definition one prefers, however, cross-border interactions were the rule, not the exception, throughout premodern history. Japan was always part of a larger web of social relations connecting it to other parts of the archipelago as well as to the Eurasian continent.

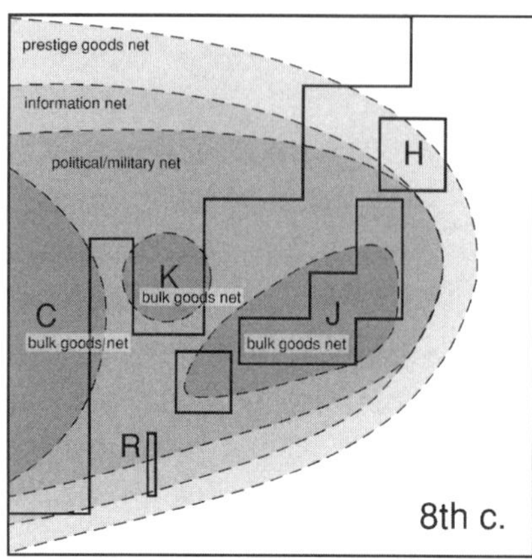

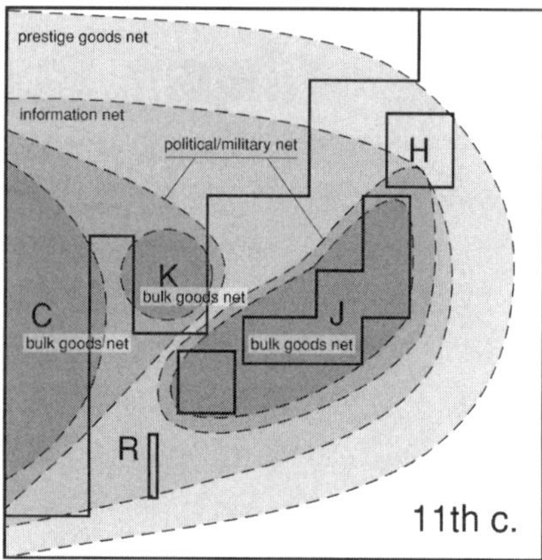

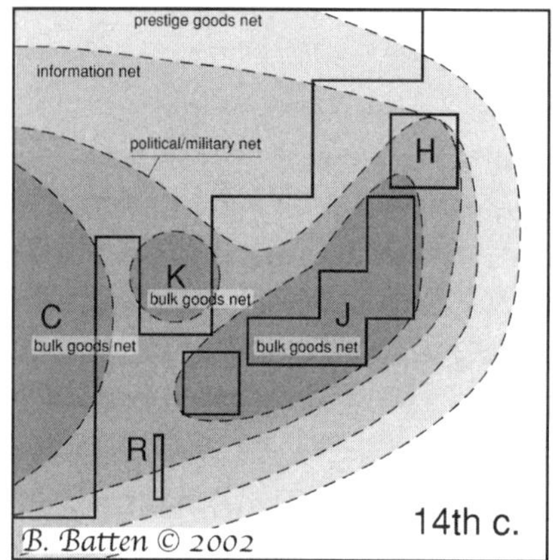

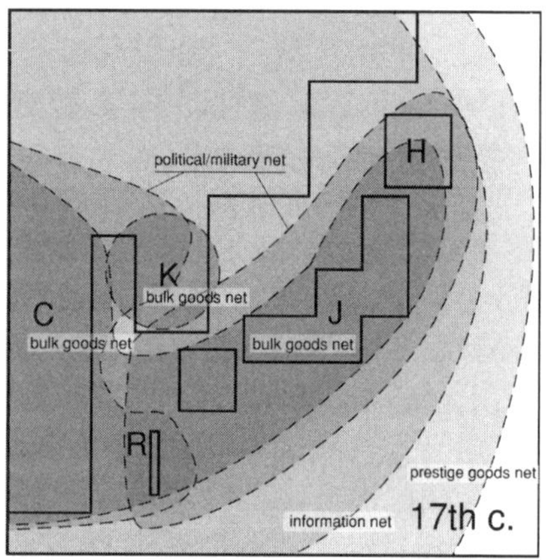

FIGURE 10. Evolution of Japan's four networks of exchange over the eighth through the seventeenth centuries. J = Japan "proper"; H = Hokkaido; R = Ryukyu; K = Korea; C = China.

The presence of external connections, however, does *not* in itself disqualify Japan, or the Japanese islands, from consideration as a world-system. According to Chase-Dunn and Hall, partial mergers, involving one or more of the four networks, often occur between neighboring world-systems. If that is true, the extended networks shown in Figure 10 may simply represent overlap between a Japan-centered world-system, located in the archipelago, and another system or systems located in continental Asia.

To evaluate this possibility, let us quickly review the nature of Japan's connections with China. As we saw in Chapter 4, China was the core of the East Asian world-system, one of the three major Eurasian systems identified by Chase-Dunn and Hall. (The other two, again, were centered in West Asia and South Asia.) How pervasive were Japan's ties with China in premodern times?

As a glance at Figure 10 will reveal, Japan's ties with China were quite close during all periods. At the level of the prestige goods and information networks, Japan was fully merged with China and the rest of East Asia no later than the eighth century. Even at the level of the political/military network we find a substantial (albeit intermittent) degree of integration. In short, we find important systemic connections between Japan and China in all periods of history, although the nature and scope of these contacts varied considerably over time.

On the other hand, it is also clear that Japan was never, or almost never, completely subsumed within the Chinese system. Most obviously, the Japanese archipelago was autarchic with respect to bulk goods until the seventeenth century. And even in the area of political/military relations, ties with China were by no means continuous. So although Japan had close relations with its large neighbor throughout history, it was never completely subsumed within a China-centered world-system.

What are we to make of this? One possible interpretation is that the Japanese islands were basically part of the Chinese world-system, but occasionally became partially decoupled to form an incipient world-system of their own. Another is that the Japanese islands basically constituted their own minor world-system, which by accident of geography was sometimes partially absorbed by its larger, China-centered neighbor. Which of these scenarios is nearer to the truth? In a sense, neither, because they both describe different aspects of the same phenomenon. But if I had to pick one, I would choose the first, for the following three reasons.

First, Japan's ties with China were closer than ties between any of the major state-based world-systems recognized by Chase-Dunn and Hall. To reiterate information presented in Chapter 4, prior to the emergence of the "modern world-system" in the sixteenth century, the Chinese, West Asian, and South Asian systems were almost completely autonomous in terms of bulk goods and political/military interactions. This contrasts significantly with Japan's much closer ties to China, which frequently involved political/military interactions and even (from the seventeenth century) extended to bulk goods flows. This higher degree of integration seems like a good reason for regarding Japan as part of the China-centered East Asian world-system, rather than an independent entity.

Second, and related to the first point, Japan, like other regions of East Asia, can be regarded in many periods as a periphery of China. Not only were the two countries part of the same political/military network, but power relations took an unequal, hierarchical form, with China playing the role of core and Japan playing that of periphery. This type of relationship can be found among none of the major systems, which were essentially equals in terms of power or, if not, sufficiently distant from each other that no hierarchical relationship could form.

Third, there is the matter of size. This is related to the previous point, because Japan's smaller size and population help explain its unequal relationship with China. More fundamental, however, is the question of how large a society must be to qualify for consideration as a world-system. Recall that in Chase-Dunn and Hall's formulation, any society, no matter how small, can be a world-system so long as it is sufficiently autonomous. I am in basic philosophical agreement with that position, but as was noted above, autonomy is a matter of degree. In the case of Japan we have a partial merger with the larger, Chinese system to the west. When systems are partially "nested" like this, the prudent course, it seems to me, is to reserve the term "world-system" for the larger one (or, better yet, for the whole). Japan, following this approach, would be a subsystem of the East Asian world-system.[1]

This approach is also useful because it saves us from the danger of infinite regression. For if the Japanese islands, despite their relatively small size and peripheral status vis-à-vis China, can be considered a world-system in their own right, why not apply the same logic to peripheral regions within the islands themselves? Why not, for example, treat Hokkaido or the Ryukyus as independent world-systems? Why not Sakhalin or the Kurils? Of course, there is nothing objectively "wrong" with such an approach, since we can define terms however we like, but to me, it seems more useful to think in terms of nested or partially nested subsystems, reserving the term "world-system" for the highest level in the hierarchy. Through most of the premodern period, Japan was a second-tier player in East Asia, not a fully developed world-system in its own right.

Japan and the World

As described in detail in previous chapters, Japan's ties were not limited to East Asia in premodern times. As early as the seventh century C.E., Japanese elites were aware of a land "beyond China," and they had access to prestige goods from all over Eurasia (with the probable exception of Europe). However, it was not until the sixteenth century, with the arrival of the first Europeans, that Japan's prestige goods and information networks became truly global in scale. In retrospect, the arrival of the Europeans marked the beginning of Japan's incorporation within Wallerstein's "modern world-system."

Although the actual process of incorporation is beyond the scope of this book, it seems appropriate to make a few brief comments. The most important point I wish to make is that incorporation did not take place overnight—indeed, it was an extraordinarily drawn-out affair, for Japan as well as for East Asia as a whole. According to Alvin So and Stephen Chiu,

> The core states in Western Europe had naturally made many attempts to incorporate East Asia into the capitalist world economy since the 16th century. The Portuguese were the first to send warships and trading boats to China to request the expansion of foreign trade. Then arrived the Spanish, the Dutch, the British, and the Americans. However, it was not until the mid-19th century that East Asia began to be incorporated into the world economy.[2]

So and Chiu identify various reasons for this lag, but they place the greatest weight on internal "resistance" or "antisystemic movements." In their words, "the East Asian states quickly adopted an exclusive policy to shut them off from foreigners."[3]

One way to judge the success of this policy is to look at economic cycles. One important feature of the modern world-system, as mentioned in Chapter 4, is the presence of Kondratieff waves, that is, system-wide alternations between "A" phases of economic expansion and "B" phases of economic contraction or stagnation. Here are the four commonly recognized Kondratieff cycles:[4]

I —— 1780/1790——A——1810/1817——B——1844/1851

II —— 1844/1851——A——1870/1875——B——1890/1896

III—— 1890/1896——A——1914/1920——B——1940/1945

IV—— 1940/1945——A——1967/1973——B——?

Unfortunately, no one can agree on whether these cycles can be pushed back further than the late eighteenth century. As noted in Chapter 4, Andre Gunter Frank and Barry Gills argue for a five-thousand-year sequence of "A"/"B" phases.[5] Most authors, however, are not prepared to go this far. A "middle of the road" position is presented by Taylor, who describes two "logistic waves" preceding the first Kondratieff cycle:[6]

c. 1050———A———c. 1250———B———c. 1450

c. 1450———A———c. 1600———B———c. 1750

To what extent do Japanese data from the Edo period match the "up" and "down" phases of the Europe-centered economy? Several studies have argued that Japan (and/or East Asia in general) experienced an economic "crisis" in the first half of the seventeenth century.[7] The mechanism is uncertain; both climatological factors (poor weather) and monetary issues (decreased availability of silver) have been invoked. Note, in any case, that this period corresponds to the start of the "B" phase in Taylor's second "logistic wave." If Japan (or, more generally, East Asia) experienced economic problems at this time, then perhaps that is evidence for some degree of integration within the Europe-centered world economy.

However, if this linkage was real, it was only temporary. If the chronology given above is to be trusted, the world economy was in a state of decline from around 1600 to 1750, after which it began to pick up again with the start of the first Kondratieff cycle. How does this correspond to events in Japan? Not well at all. As any student of

Japanese history can vouch, the period from around 1630 to 1710 was one of unprecedented growth, whereas after 1710 the economy entered a period of "stasis" (or, at least, slower growth).[8] The most charitable interpretation of these trends is that Japan may have been on the "verge" of integration into the world economy during the sixteenth century, but this trend was later reversed.

Mark Metzler, in a study of this issue, has argued for a pattern of "disengagement and re-engagement with the world-economy."[9] According to Metzler, Japan's domestic economy was closely linked to the world economy in the seventeenth century but became decoupled in the early eighteenth century, as a result of increased import restrictions and reduced bullion flows. Metzler goes on to argue, "The re-opening of Japan to foreign trade in the 1850's thus came as a radical monetary shock, and the price revolution of the 1860's . . . represented Japan's jarring reintegration into the world-economy. Since then, the rhythms of the Japanese economy have become synchronized with those of the West."[10] In conclusion, despite some tentative movements toward integration in the sixteenth and early seventeenth centuries, Japan retained a high degree of autonomy from the "modern world-system" until the end of the Edo period.[11]

But again, this does not mean that Japan was isolated during this period of time. All of the discussion about integration, or lack thereof, into the modern world-system is really about *economic* integration. In the language of this study, what this really amounts to is a discussion of bulk goods networks. When Metzler describes Japan's "jarring reintegration into the world-economy," therefore, all he is really saying is that in the mid-nineteenth century the country's bulk goods network, which had been relatively limited in scope, suddenly expanded to global proportions as the result of merging with (or, more accurately, being subsumed within) the Europe-centered network.

Of course, I do not mean to trivialize the events of the nineteenth century. As we all know, Japan's economy became opened to the West as the direct result of political/military pressure. In other words, it was not just Japan's bulk goods network that suddenly merged with its Europe-centered counterpart; so did its political/military network, which up to that point had also been merely regional in scope. These were tremendously important developments, for they deprived Japanese society of its last vestiges of autonomy. As we have seen, Japan's other two networks—those of prestige goods and information—had already been global in scope since the sixteenth century. When the bulk goods network and the political/military network also merged with their global counterparts in the nineteenth century, therefore, Japan lost all claims to systemic integrity, probably for the first time in its history.

PART THREE

Dynamics

10 Social Power: Causes and Consequences

The Frontier as "Contested Ground"

To recapitulate, premodern "Japan" and its borders can be defined in any of a number of ways. A political emphasis reveals the outlines, fuzzy but nonetheless recognizable, of a state distinct from less organized tribes and chiefdoms to the north and south and from other states on the Asian mainland. "Racial," cultural, and ethnic definitions produce related, but not identical, configurations. Viewed in this way, "Japan" emerges as a composite of superimposed entities, each with its own ill-defined border.

These borders, by definition, represent the geographic limits of certain social characteristics or forms of organization. But as we have seen, this does *not* mean that they represent limits to social intercourse or exchange. Japan's frontiers did often function as barriers to the circulation of bulk goods such as foodstuffs and clothing, but throughout history they were generally permeable to other forms of interaction: political and military exchanges, trade in luxury goods, and the flow of information. By these criteria, Japan was never isolated from its external environment but always functioned as part of a larger system—East Asia for much of premodern history, and the world as a whole in more recent times.

However, to acknowledge that Japan was embedded in a larger web of relations is *not* to say that its frontiers were irrelevant or unimportant. To the contrary, they mediated and structured the country's external relationships throughout history, serving as crucial interfaces between Japan and its various neighbors. It was precisely for this reason that Japan's rulers—not just in the Edo period but throughout history—actively sought to control their borders. External links of some kinds were desirable or even necessary for state survival; government officials tried to encourage and/or monopolize these. Other forms of interaction were destabilizing or inimical to state survival; authorities attempted to limit, or when possible, eliminate these. The Edo period provides one example of a relatively successful attempt to meet these goals.

But—precisely because Japan was part of a larger network of social relations—political actors could not pursue their goals in a vacuum. Their counterparts on the other side of the border also sought control, often for the very same reasons. In the words of Donna Guy and Thomas Sheridan, frontiers are "contested ground," places where "different polities contended for natural resources and ideological control, including the right to define categories of people and to determine their access to those resources."[1]

However, the results of such "contests" varied considerably, according to location. In the north (and, to a lesser extent, in the south), the contest was quite uneven, and Japanese society expanded more or less continuously at the expense of native populations. The process of "conquest" came to a halt only when the indigenous residents of Hokkaido were more or less fully incorporated within the Japanese "body politic" in the early modern and modern periods. (Of course, Japan's "victory" in this frontier "contest" did not erase all ambiguities. The Ainu today both are and are not "fully Japanese," having retained their identity as an ethnic minority within the larger Japanese nation-state.) In the west, by contrast, we see neither expansion nor assimilation. With the exception of Hideyoshi's invasions in the 1590s, Japan never crossed the East China Sea to encroach upon Korean ground (or vice versa). This particular frontier "contest," in other words, took the form of a stalemate—at least, until modern times.

How can we account for these different outcomes? I have already touched upon this issue in Chapter 1, with specific reference to political frontiers and boundaries. There I borrowed some ideas from

Robert Gilpin to argue that frontiers represent lines (actually, zones) of approximate equilibrium between factors encouraging expansion and "countervailing forces." The most important countervailing forces are distance and the presence of rival powers—which face their own, similar limits to expansion. Looked at in this way, borders are located in places where the ability of neighboring polities to project power at the *local* level, after subtracting the effects of distance, is approximately equal.

If at each point in time a frontier represents a zone of equilibrium between two opposing states or societies, why do some frontiers stay in the same place while others shift location? Geographic factors may provide some explanation. One could argue, for example, that the East China Sea and Japan Sea represented "natural" barriers to expansion that did not exist in the north or south, and that this is why Japan's western frontier remained static while other frontiers were more mobile. To an extent this is probably true, but the difference is only relative; had enough of a power imbalance existed, geographic factors could presumably have been overcome. After all, the Tsugaru Strait or the sea south of Kyushu also represented geographic barriers to expansion, albeit less significant ones. And even assuming that geographic constraints were less important in the north and south, we are still left with explaining the fact of expansion itself. If a frontier represents a zone of equilibrium, then a shift in its location can mean only one thing: something has happened to upset the equilibrium.

As this discussion suggests, systematic shifts in the location of a frontier reflect shifts in the underlying balance of power between two neighboring polities (or, more generally, societies). Perhaps one society has become stronger while the other has stayed the same or become weaker; or perhaps both societies have evolved in the same general direction but at differing rates, resulting in a significant power differential. As argued in Chapter 1, therefore, the northward movement of the Tōhoku-Hokkaido frontier is best explained as the result of a structural imbalance of power between "Japanese" society to the south and indigenous societies to the north. The western maritime frontier, by contrast, remained more or less stable because (taking allowance for geographic barriers) this type of power imbalance did not exist between Japan and neighboring states in Korea, Manchuria, or China.

Of course, this explanation may strike some readers as too deterministic or mechanical, and for good reason: I have simply referred to "power" in the abstract, without discussing its nature, causes, and effects, or its specific manifestations in the "contested ground" of the frontier. The purpose of this chapter is make up for these omissions.

"Power" has been defined as "the ability to pursue and attain goals through mastery of one's environment,"[2] which of course includes the human environment, i.e., other people or groups. The author of this definition, Michael Mann, has also attempted to identify what he calls the "sources of social power." According to Mann, there are four such sources: ideological, economic, military, and political relationships. These relationships can be conceived as "overlapping networks of social interaction," although at the same time they are also "organizations, institutional means of attaining human goals."[3]

If this sounds familiar, it is; we have already seen how the concept of "networks" may usefully be applied to human society in our examination of world-systems theory. But although the network approach is useful for analyzing existing social relationships, it cannot provide a full explanation for why some groups are more powerful than others. The reason is that some "sources of power" are in fact external to the workings of society; power also has a geographic or environmental component.

Jared Diamond, in an important recent work, has attempted to explain the underlying reasons for Europe's domination of the globe in modern times.[4] Diamond's explanation revolves around a nexus of social, technological, and environmental factors—"guns, germs, and steel," in the author's shorthand phrase. Although Diamond's focus is global, I believe that a similar approach can help us understand the differing fates of societies in and around the Japanese archipelago.

In this concluding chapter we will look at four sets of factors that have affected the outcomes of frontier "contests" in Japanese history: (1) the strategies and actions of people on either side of the border; (2) differences in the level of sociopolitical organization; (3) technological differences; and (4) environmental and ecological factors.[5] In discussing these issues, I will once again focus primarily on Japan's northern frontier, where systemic power imbalances are most evident and where the reasons for them can be seen in starkest relief.

Actors and Strategies

On the surface, of course, the outcome of frontier "contests" is determined by actual historical "events," that is, by the actions of people living on either side of (or within) the border zone. What type of actors are present? How do they perceive their roles? What types of strategies do they pursue, and how successful are they in implementing them? Clearly, power relationships along the frontier are determined, at least in part, by the answers to these questions.

Although frontiers are indeed "contested ground," social relationships in border areas are actually far more subtle than this simple formulation would suggest. In macro-historical terms, Hokkaido (for example) was certainly "contested" by the "Japanese" and the "Ainu," but we should not imagine that either society always acted as a bloc or that relations between the two were exclusively competitive. Most societies are fragmented, not monolithic, and cross-border relations are as often peaceful or cooperative as they are antagonistic. Border zones are inhabited by people of all sorts who are pursuing all types of goals, some of them at cross-purposes and some of them complementary.

Who are the actors in the frontier zones? No matter what type of classification we choose, most types of people normally present in a society will also live near its geographical margins. In addition, there may be other groups unique or peculiar to the frontier. A visitor to northern Tōhoku in the eighth century, for example, would have encountered a rich mix of male and female, young and old, rich and poor, noble and base, free and unfree, local and immigrant, colonist and colonized—all engaged in one or more nonexclusive activities such as government administration, religious work, fighting and/or guard duty, commerce, entertainment, farming, hunting, fishing, mining, and banditry. Some of these people would have been "Japanese," by whatever definition; some of them would have been "non-Japanese"; and others would have been difficult to place in either category.

In the course of their lives, these actors pursued a bewildering variety of goals, private and public, individual and collective, freely chosen and imposed.[6] These in turn found expression in social relationships of all kinds, ranging from the amicable and cooperative to the competitive and antagonistic. People traded, but they also raided; they made friends, but they also made enemies. Some relationships involved just a few people, others hundreds or even thousands; some were purely local, others long-distance; some took place between people of similar backgrounds, while others were interracial or intercultural.

It is important to realize that social relationships between "Japanese" and "non-Japanese" were not necessarily antagonistic. Neighboring societies, or elements thereof, may share an interest in trade or other peaceful relationships. Cross-border cooperation can exist even within a prevailing climate of hostility. The reason for this phenomenon is that societies are composed of different groups, each with its own values and goals. Proximity to another society may offer some groups new opportunities to seek support or otherwise advance their own parochial interests.[7] Elites on either side of the border may have a common interest in controlling their subordinate populations. Non-elites may share a common interest in subverting elite objectives. People of all social stations may find opportunities to enhance their own position by forming alliances or collaborating with members of the other society. Cross-border ties of these kinds are common and help account for the wide variety of social exchanges described in previous chapters. Frontiers are porous precisely because, in almost all situations, some people on one side have shared interests with some people on the other.

In some cases, the need for cross-border support is so great that one society will help to create counterpart organizations in the other where none existed before. The best example is the process of "tribalization" described by Ferguson and Whitehead:

> States have difficulty dealing with peoples without authoritative leaders and with constantly changing group identity and membership. All expanding states seek to identify and elevate friendly leaders. They are given titles, emblems, and active political and military support. . . .
>
> State agents, whether they be Roman governors in North Africa or Roman Catholic missionaries on the Upper Amazon, also seek to identify or, if need be, to create clear political boundaries ("polity") in place

> of the multilayered and constantly shifting allegiances they actually encounter ("anarchy"). Tribal identification then becomes a means of relating to the political apparatus of the state. . . . So it is that the needs and policies of states create tribes.[8]

Cross-border ties not only serve to bind societies together but also have the effect of further confusing the already murky identity positions of frontier residents. The multiple, overlapping nature of frontier zones in itself created social ambiguities, because people who were "Japanese" by one definition (e.g., culturally) might be "non-Japanese" by another (e.g., ethnically). This situation, however, is rendered even more complex by the cooperative relationships that tended to form between the two "sides." Cross-border ties further eroded the already fuzzy boundary between "us" and "them."

For these and other reasons, frontiers can be places of mutual accommodation, where people of varying backgrounds together created a "middle ground" of shared meanings and practices.[9] And yet, to overemphasize this aspect of frontier relations is to engage in historical tunnel vision. The "middle ground" existed, but, at least in Tōhoku and Hokkaido, it was historically transient. Over the long run, the sum total of human relationships in and around the frontier operated to the clear benefit of the "Japanese" to the south and the clear disadvantage of the Emishi, Ezo, and Ainu to the north. The single most important fact about the frontier was the structural cleavage of interests between people on one side and those on the other. In this sense, the frontier was indeed "contested ground."

This brings us back to the initial question: Can the outcome of such contests be explained solely in terms of the success or failure of strategies pursued by local (or intrusive) actors in the frontier zone? Obviously, local events and processes do have considerable bearing on the historical evolution of frontiers. For example, the balance of power in northern Tōhoku was certainly affected by the arrival and activities of Japanese soldiers and colonists in the seventh and eighth centuries. Some Emishi chose to collaborate with the Japanese intruders; others chose to flee; and still others chose to resist, either by force of arms or by subterfuge, foot dragging, and other "weapons of the weak."[10] One event led to another, and hostilities ensued, not once but many times, over a course of decades. When the dust had settled in the ninth century, the Japanese found themselves in possession of territories formerly belonging to the Emishi. Many of the latter were now gone, having died or moved farther north. Those who remained were *fushū*, part of an ethnic minority of acculturated "barbarians" within Japanese society. In a very real sense, this outcome was the cumulative result of the countless human interactions that had occurred to date in and around the frontier zone.

And yet, to describe the overall development of the frontier in terms of the accumulated success or failure of local events is merely to replace one set of questions with another. Why do we find Japanese soldiers and colonists in Emishi territory but not the reverse? Why were the Emishi vulnerable to such incursions? Why, in the final analysis, were the Japanese able to deprive the Emishi of their land? To answer these questions, we must look beyond the panorama of historical "events" to the larger social and ecological context. What was the nature of the two opposing societies? What relative advantages or disadvantages did each bring to the "contest" in the frontier zone? And what, ultimately, were the reasons for these strengths and weaknesses?

Sociopolitical Organization

One important factor, of course, is relative level of sociopolitical organization. Japan in the eighth century was already a state society with relatively efficient, centralized mechanisms for gathering information, formulating political decisions, and carrying them out. Important decisions, such as to build a military stockade or put down an Emishi "uprising," were based on relatively current, reliable information obtained by local officials and transmitted to the central government in the form of written documents. Decisions themselves were made by the emperor following debate among top-ranking nobles within the Great Council of State *(daijōkan)*. Once a decision had been made, it could be transmitted back down the bureaucratic pipeline for implementation by the appropriate civil or military officials. If it was necessary to appoint new officials, such as a general to oversee military operations, this could be accomplished using existing procedures. Whatever resources were necessary for implementing the decision were either available on hand or could be procured fairly swiftly through existing channels of tax collection, military conscription, and so forth. Throughout, formulation and implementation of state policy was facilitated by a clear chain of bureaucratic and military command, a clear set of legal and administrative procedures, a sophisticated infrastructure for transportation and communication, scrupulous reliance on written (as opposed to oral) communications, and relatively firm central control over human and material resources at the local level.

Or at least, this is my view. Admittedly, what we know about the workings of government in this period is based largely on court histories (e.g., the *Shoku Nihongi*) and collections of official documents (e.g., *Ruijū sandai kyaku*). Because of their official nature, these sources contain some important biases. In particular, they go out of their way to present the actions of the emperor and the government in a positive light, either by omitting or embellishing relevant information. So it may well be that Japan's sociopolitical system in the Nara and early Heian periods was less centralized, and less organized and efficient, than I have suggested. This, in fact, is the line taken by some American scholars, among them Joan Piggott. According to Piggott, the Nara state was a "segmented" polity that was "centered, rather than centralized."[11]

The problem with these terms is that they are relative. Polities are not "centralized" or "segmented" in some absolute sense but only by comparison, either with the same polity at earlier or later stages of development, or with other polities in different places and/or times. In this sense it is meaningless to argue about whether eighth-century Japan was, or was not, a "centralized" state. What is *not* meaningless is to ask how it compares with the earlier Yamato polity or later Heian polity or, alternatively, with contemporary societies in continental Asia or peripheral areas of the archipelago. I have already discussed long-term trends in the degree of political centralization within Japan, and the reader will understand my contention that the Nara period represents a relative high point in this regard. This leaves us with the question of how the Nara polity compares with contemporary, neighboring societies.

To put my conclusion first, there was a rough parity in level of sociopolitical organization between Japan and continental polities such as Silla and Parhae, but a great disparity, operating in Japan's favor, along the Emishi and Hayato frontiers. What we are dealing with here, of course, is the difference in organization between state societies, on the one hand, and tribes (or, perhaps, chiefdoms) on the other. As is clear from even biased Japanese sources, Silla was a state like Japan and had the same general degree of organization and ability to procure and deploy resources. This organizational parity, I believe, goes a long way to explain the geopolitically static nature of the border between these two states. Peripheral societies within the archipelago, by contrast, were no organizational match for the Japanese state. This is not to cast aspersions on the inherent abilities or worth of these people; it is merely a plain statement of fact.

Take the Emishi, for example. Here again, what we know is based largely on the same biased Japanese sources, which describe the Emishi as inferior savages. On the other hand, as in the case of Silla, the authors of these documents and chronicles presumably also had an interest in portraying the Emishi as enemies to be feared, because if they were not, Japan's ability to subordinate them would not seem so impressive. So the Emishi do appear as powerful rivals who are continually causing mischief and damage along the northern frontier. Be that as it may, there is no hint in the sources or elsewhere that these people ever had a very sophisticated political or military organization. In times of crisis there are references to leaders—such as Koreharu no Azamaro in the war of 780, or Aterui at the beginning of the ninth century—who seem to have commanded a significant number of troops. But in times of peace the highest level of political organization seems to have been the "village."[12] There is no evidence of anything that might be called a "government," no evidence of an apparatus for tax collection, no evidence of a legal system—and in fact, no evidence of a written language at all.

Of course, this may overstate the Japanese advantage. Karl Friday, in a perceptive discussion of the Japanese-Emishi wars, has argued that while Japanese forces appeared to be superior on paper, they were frequently ineffective in the field. Friday notes that Japan had "greater organizational power," which "enabled it to field armies of far more than ten times the size of *emishi* forces." These large Japanese armies, "numbering in the thousands or tens of thousands," were largely composed of foot soldiers who "fought with bow and arrow from behind portable standing wooden shields"; the Emishi, by contrast, "fought almost exclusively as light cavalry and seldom in groups of more than a few hundred." According to Friday, this should theoretically have given the advantage to the Japanese, because bowmen on foot are better protected and can give undivided attention to their shooting, whereas those on horseback are unprotected and must also pay attention to their mounts. In many cases, however, the Emishi were able to negate this supposed advantage by refusing to engage the Japanese on a fixed field of battle. According to Friday, they adopted "hit-and-run raiding tactics"—an early, and often very effective, type of "guerrilla warfare."[13]

All of these are good points, but they do not alter the fact that during these centuries Japan was able to encroach—slowly, but also surely—into Emishi territory and that one important reason for this ability was the great disparity in organization between the two societies. Although there were undoubtedly advantages to small size and mobility, in general the Emishi (to the extent this label represents a social entity at all) were at an organizational disadvantage compared with the Japanese. The Emishi had no centralized political apparatus for making and implementing decisions, nor could one easily be created. The general lack of social stratification precluded the formation of efficient organizational structures and chains of command. And the fragmented nature of political society made it difficult to organize large-scale resistance, when such was necessary, and also rendered the Emishi susceptible to "divide-and-conquer" tactics.[14]

This discussion, for convenience, has focused on the eighth and ninth centuries, but I think the conclusion also applies to other—probably most—periods of Japanese history. Of course, the Japanese polity itself varied from period to period in terms of social complexity and political organization—witness the cycles of centralization and decentralization that we have repeatedly discussed. It is also true that the societies bordering Japan to the north and south tended to increase in complexity over time, partly as a result of a "challenge and response" pattern of interactions with Japan. One result of this dialectic, as discussed in Chapter 3, was the emergence of a pan-Ainu *ethnie* in late medieval and early modern times; another was that of a unified Ryukyuan kingdom in the fifteenth century. Note, however, that these were levels of organization that had been reached in Japan many centuries earlier. The peripheral societies to the north and south never "caught up," in organizational terms, to the Japanese center. Throughout all of premodern—and indeed, modern—history, Japan remained more highly organized and more capable of formulating and executing coherent policies, than its neighbors to the north or south.

Technology

The organizational advantage, however, was just one factor in Japanese "superiority": another, closely related one was technological. In the broadest sense of the word, "technology" refers to all "ways in which social groups provide themselves with the material objects of their civilization."[15] Some examples of technology in this broad sense have already been introduced for their relevance to the topic of sociopolitical organization. Probably the most important is the knowledge of writing, which made possible the adoption of Chinese-style law codes and administrative institutions and facilitated their smooth functioning once adopted. Here is a clear example of a "technology" that conferred a significant competitive advantage on Japan vis-à-vis its neighbors to the north. Note, by way of contrast, that such a disparity did *not* exist between Japan and its continental neighbors in Korea and Manchuria, at least after written language disseminated from the continent to Japan in the early centuries C.E.

Of course, the term "technology" is usually used in a somewhat narrower sense. To most people, the word refers to the techniques used to produce or obtain "things" for human use or consumption, such as food, clothing, tools and weapons, buildings, fortifications, roads, and so on. Is it fair to say that Japan's level of technology, in this sense, was more "advanced" than that of peripheral societies to the north and south? And if so, did this "superior" technology constitute a competitive advantage in the "contested zone" of the frontier? Although there is a danger in making sweeping generalizations of this kind, I believe that the answer to both questions is yes.

What do we mean by "level" of technology? Admittedly, this concept is not easy to define. However, in general terms it seems reasonable to define technological level in terms of the total *complexity* of inputs (knowledge, materials, labor, production techniques and processes, etc.) required to achieve a given end. In this sense, rice farming represents a higher level of technology than hunting and gathering, because it involves a more complex agenda of tasks that must be coordinated to achieve the final result (obtaining food). Similarly, metallurgy represents a higher level of technology than stone- or woodworking. True, it takes a great deal of skill to make an obsidian arrowhead, but craftsmanship is not the same thing as technology. An arrowhead can be made out of naturally occurring materials by a single individual. The same cannot be said of an iron kettle or a steel sword.

Alert readers will not have failed to note the relevance of these examples to the question at hand. Both farming and metallurgy were widely practiced in Japan from very early times, but these technologies never "took root" in the northern part of the archipelago. As described in Chapter 2, the residents of Hokkaido cultivated grain and other crops as early as the Satsumon period (seventh through thirteenth centuries), but farming never replaced hunting and gathering as a way of life. Ironworking also came to Hokkaido during Satsumon times; fragments of bellows have been discovered at a number of archaeological sites.[16] But residents of the island apparently limited themselves to the small-scale reworking of iron imported from Japan "proper"; they never learned how to extract iron from ore, and they never began to produce iron implements, far less steel implements, in bulk. Excavations of late medieval Japanese forts in southernmost Hokkaido yield an impressive variety of iron and steel artifacts—saws, sickles, braces, nails and pins, bullets, armor plates, fishhooks, arrowheads, knives, and swords—together with large quantities of raw iron.[17] Contemporary Ainu sites yield far fewer items, principally consisting of iron pots, knives, arrowheads, and fishhooks, the first directly imported from Japan and the rest either imported or, more commonly, fashioned locally of Japanese materials.[18]

Before discussing the reasons for the Ainu "failure" to adopt agriculture and metallurgy, I would like to point out the tremendous competitive advantages these technologies conferred upon the Japanese. Regarding metallurgy, the most obvious advantage is in the area of weaponry. Japanese blacksmiths could produce virtually unlimited numbers of steel arrowheads, swords, suits of armor, and helmets, not to mention bits, stirrups, and other items of saddlery. Later, following contact with the West, guns were also added to the Japanese arsenal. Few if any of these items were directly available to the residents of the north. This technological disparity may have been partially offset by other factors—skillful use of guerilla tactics, familiarity with local climate and terrain, and the like. But over the long run, there can be no doubt that the superior weapons wielded by the Japanese played a significant role in the conquest of the north—just as the superior weapons wielded by white settlers played a significant role in the conquest of the American West, despite tactical and other advantages enjoyed by the defending native Americans.

Another, less obvious advantage of metallurgy is in the area of trade. As noted above, Ainu sites in Hokkaido do yield some iron artifacts, most or all of them derived from imported metal. During the late middle ages and the Edo period, the Ainu became quite dependent upon imported goods, including iron kettles and other metal implements. This dependence is important because it allowed Japanese "suppliers" to exploit Ainu "consumers," exacerbating the "imbalance of power" along the frontier.

Metallurgy was also a factor in the second crucial difference between Japan and northern society: the technology of food production. Specifically, Japanese farming technology relied heavily on hoes, plows, and other implements made of iron. But regardless of what tools were used, the prevalence of agriculture in Japan—and its relative lack among the Ainu and other northern societies—was in and of itself a major determinant of power relations on the frontier. The competitive advantages conferred on Japan by agriculture were legion. For one thing, trade in agricultural commodities such as rice and sake, like trade in iron, fostered Ainu dependency. But above and beyond that, agriculture was simply more productive, hectare for hectare, person for person, than hunting, fishing, or gathering. Agricultural societies are larger and more densely populated than nonagricultural ones, providing the necessary manpower for colonization, conquest, and other activities. Surplus wealth generated through agriculture encourages the formation of class society and, in general, sociopolitical complexity of all kinds, resulting in the advantages described in the previous section. Surplus wealth also, of course, directly finances colonial and military activities on the frontier. All of these factors were of direct relevance to competitive relations between Japan and the residents of the north. Again, the Ainu were not entirely ignorant of farming techniques, nor was Japan an exclusively agricultural society. But there is no doubt that the relative importance of agriculture was greater in Japan and that this had important implications for the balance of power between the two societies.

If agriculture and iron production were so critical, why were they not adopted by the Ainu or earlier residents of the north? It was probably not for lack of information; as we have seen, the frontier was relatively permeable to information flow and other types of social exchange throughout history. One possibility is that these technologies were rejected for cultural reasons, that is, because they did not fit into the northern "lifestyle." Although this may be true for some technologies, it probably does not apply to rice or iron. After all, in early modern times the Ainu clearly wanted these items enough to purchase them from Wajin traders. Of course, wanting to consume goods and wanting to produce them are two different things. But if production had been a real possibility, one would expect the Ainu to have taken steps in this direction, if only in order to reduce their growing dependence on Japan.

There is some evidence that the spread of these technologies was hindered by political factors. During the Nara period, for example, the Japanese court issued laws against the export of weapons and the establishment of smitheries in northeastern Honshu.[19] Also, during the Edo period, the rulers of Matsumae domain prohibited the Ainu from producing iron. Such laws probably helped stifle a technology that was already known and (to a limited extent) practiced. The same is true of rice farming, which was subject to strict, and apparently quite effective, prohibitions by Matsumae.[20] In neither case, however, do political constraints explain why these important technologies were not already flourishing in Hokkaido during early historic times, as they were in Japan to the south.

In the case of iron production, the immediate "culprit" was probably sociopolitical development or, rather, the lack thereof. As noted, the use of iron was known in Japan "proper" from a very early date—the Yayoi period. However, early blacksmiths relied for their raw material on iron ingots imported from the Korean Peninsula—a rather precise analogue of the later relationship between Ainu blacksmiths and the Japanese. It was not until the fifth or sixth century that the Japanese began to extract the metal from native sources, mainly concentrated in the Inland Sea region.[21] It is no coincidence that this same period was also one of rapid state formation in Japan. The large-scale extraction of iron requires not only access to ore (including iron sand) and charcoal but also the presence of a specialized labor force and a capacity for "top-down" management or political direction. The natural resources had always been present in Japan. The sociopolitical factors, however, were not present until the emergence of state-level organization in the Kofun period. The raw materials for iron production were also available in Hokkaido (although not in such abundance as in some parts of Japan "proper"). What was permanently lacking was the requisite level of sociopolitical development.

The lack of sociopolitical development, in turn, was a direct result of the nature of local subsistence, which emphasized foraging over farming. So the real question is why agriculture never took hold in Hokkaido. And the answer to this is quite simple: as I have already noted many times, the climate in Hokkaido was too cold to permit the widespread cultivation of rice.

Environment and Ecology

Viewed in this perspective, many of the differences we have observed between Japan's western and northern frontiers appear to be environmental in origin. As a result of its temperate, wet climate, Japan was able, over time, to develop levels of sociopolitical organization and technology commensurate with those of its continental neighbors; this in turn led to a relatively stable balance of power along Japan's western, maritime frontier. In contrast, the cold climate of Hokkaido acted as a brake on sociopolitical development and technological innovation, resulting in a permanent, structural imbalance of power between Japan and indigenous societies to the north. In other words, the presence of a significant ecological boundary at the Tsugaru Strait, and the lack of such a "barrier" to the west, are of fundamental importance in explaining the differing nature of Japan's relations with its closest neighbors in premodern times.

To fully appreciate the importance of differences in subsistence, it is helpful to look at some numbers. Ethnographic and archaeological studies show that typical population densities in pre-agricultural societies range from 0.1 to 1 person per square kilometer. In Europe, the introduction of agriculture led to populations on the order of 40 to 60 persons per square kilometer by the end of the eighteenth century—a 100-fold increase.[22] In the Japanese archipelago, the population rose from a pre-agricultural high of perhaps 300,000 around 6000 B.C.E. to more than 1 million around 300 C.E., 5 million in the eighth century, and 31 million in the early seventeenth century.[23] This last figure—coincidentally, almost precisely 100 times larger than the maximum pre-agricultural population—remained more or less constant until around 1800. (The reasons for this cessation of population growth in the Edo period are complex and are subject of vigorous debate among historians. Older works generally stress "negative checks" such as famine and disease, whereas more recent authors focus on "positive checks," that is, deliberate population control by economically rational peasants eager to maintain their standard of living.[24]) At any rate, it is clear that the introduction of agriculture led over the centuries to enormous population growth in Japan, as well as in Europe.

These figures are for Japan "proper." What about Hokkaido? The Ainu population is given as about 20,000 in a document from 1670s, and other early estimates range up to about 40,000.[25] Even assuming the higher figure to be correct, however, we find that the Japanese outnumbered the Ainu by nearly 800 to 1 during the seventeenth century. Of course, the Ainu also inhabited a smaller territory than the Japanese: the land area of Hokkaido (83,452 km^2) is less than 30 percent of that of the other three islands combined (294,267 km^2). Even when this is taken into account, however, the population densities of agrarian Japan and non-agrarian Hokkaido differed by a factor of at least 200—even more than we would expect on the basis of the time-series data from preindustrial Europe and Japan. No wonder there was a power imbalance on the northern frontier!

Moreover, these figures actually *underestimate* the magnitude of Japan's ecological advantage over the Ainu. For although there may have been 40,000 Ainu in the late seventeenth century, this number soon shrank further as the result of intensified contact with Japanese (particularly merchants) during the Edo period. The reason was not outright conquest or genocide so much as it was epidemic disease. Disease, together with climate, was a crucial "natural" source of competitive advantage for Japan in its relations with native societies in Hokkaido.

First, some background information: although historians have long displayed interest in the black death that affected fourteenth-century Europe, the more general role of epidemic disease as a force in world history was not recognized until the 1970s, following the publication of a seminal work by William McNeill.[26] Although it is impossible to do justice to McNeill's study in a few short lines, his basic argument is as follows. During the very early phases of human history, people were relatively healthy and disease-free; although communicable diseases may have been present, there were no large settled communities in which they could spread or take permanent root. This, however, changed with the introduction of agriculture and the emergence of dense settlements of farmers and, later, city dwellers. Viral and other infections, mostly derived from the diseases of domestic animals, began to multiply in human populations, and by around 500 B.C.E., the "major civilized regions of the Old World [had] each developed its own peculiar mix of infectious, person-to-person diseases."[27] During the period 500 B.C.E.–1200 C.E., these disease pools began to mix, resulting in a partial epidemiological unification of Eurasia. The tentative equilibrium was disrupted between 1200 and 1500, when the emergence of the Mongol empire facilitated the spread of bubonic plague from its original home on the Asian steppes to Europe. Finally, during the period 1500–1700, the various diseases of the Old World were transmitted with devastating effects to other parts of the globe via European-initiated "transoceanic exchanges." Best known, of course, are the tremendous demographic losses (up to 95 percent of precontact populations, according to some estimates) suffered by native populations in the Americas following infection by smallpox, measles, influenza, typhus, and other Eurasian diseases.[28]

As Alfred Crosby has shown, the European "conquest" of the globe was accompanied (and made possible) by the spread, not just of communicable diseases, but of entire ecosystems, including domesticated plants and animals as well as weeds and pests of all kinds.[29] Crosby aptly describes this process as "ecological imperialism" perpetrated by Eurasia's human, animal, vegetable, and microbial biota—a "team effort by organisms that had evolved in conflict and cooperation over a long time."[30] This of course begs the question of why the biological "exchange" was so one-way: why Eurasian pathogens, animals, and plants were able to "invade" local ecologies in other parts of the globe but not vice versa. Jared Diamond has attempted to answer these questions in evolutionary and geographic terms.[31] Among the important points he raises are the following. Not only humans but also many of the plants and animals most suitable for domestication evolved in the Old World, giving that region an important "head start." Moreover, large-scale ecological exchanges within Eurasia were facilitated by the continent's sheer size and by the east-west axis of its principal landmass. By contrast, the north-south orientation of the Americas had the effect of impeding biological exchanges, because differences in latitude (unlike those of longitude) translate directly into differences of temperature and climate.

Whatever the ultimate reasons, the biological "unification" of the world bears a striking resemblance to the process of social and economic unification that we examined in previous chapters. Indeed, it would be fair to say that the gradual integration of the various Eurasian "world-systems" in the premodern period, and their collective "conquest" of other world-systems during recent centuries, is simply one aspect of this larger, underlying process of biological expansion.

These arguments, of course, have important implications for our study of Japan and its relations with neighboring societies. The history of infectious disease in Japan was touched on many years ago by William McNeill. In very early times "Japan's geographical position . . . tended to insulate the archipelago from disease contacts with the world beyond," McNeill asserts. "This was, however, a mixed blessing, for insulation allowed relatively dense populations to develop which were then vulnerable to unusually severe epidemic seizure when some new infection did succeed in leaping across the water barrier and penetrating the Japanese islands."[32] At the same time, the population was not yet dense enough to sustain such infections indefinitely, meaning that "a number of important and lethal diseases that became chronic in China could not establish themselves lastingly among the Japanese until about the thirteenth century." McNeill concludes, "Consequently, for more than six hundred years, before Japan's population density surpassed the critical threshold that allowed these epidemics to subside into endemic infections, the islands suffered a long series of severe disease invasions."[33]

This general scenario has been confirmed by more detailed research by William Wayne Farris, Anne Bowman Jannetta, and others. Farris' study of the Nara and early Heian periods led him to conclude:

> Virulent epidemics of heavy mortality entered Japan from the continent approximately every generation, and seriously retarded population growth. Plagues of smallpox, measles, and other viruses killed off young adults, who had no resistance to infection and who were also the primary source of labor. The smallpox pestilence that lasted from 735 to 737 is the most completely documented example of such an epidemic. It reached Japan from Korea, and carried off from 25 to 35 percent of the populace with disastrous economic and political consequences.[34]

Like McNeill, Farris believes that smallpox and measles reached endemic status in the thirteenth century, when they became "chronic in the Japanese populations as infections of childhood." Farris continues, "Adults no longer commonly died from either disease. The decline of smallpox and measles plagues by the early medieval period is probably associated with a rise in population density and a sizeable increase in agricultural productivity."[35]

Anne Bowman Jannetta's study covers a later period and a slightly different configuration of diseases.[36] Regarding smallpox, Jannetta agrees that this disease was endemic in Japan by the early medieval period. Regarding measles, however, she finds—contrary to McNeill and Farris—a continuing pattern of once-in-a-generation epidemics lasting well into the nineteenth century. And regarding other diseases, such as bubonic plague and typhus, which played important—if negative—roles in European history, Jannetta finds no real evidence that they were introduced to Japan at all until the opening of the country in the late nineteenth century.

All in all, this research seems to show that although Japan was to some extent incorporated within a larger, Eurasian disease ecology no later than the seventh or eighth century, full integration did not take place until at least the middle of the nineteenth century—following much the same pattern as we have already observed with respect to Japan's social integration within the "modern world-system." According to Jannetta, the failure of many Eurasian diseases to take hold at any earlier date stemmed from "Japan's geographical position and her limited contact with other population centers before 1850." However, as Jannetta is also quick to note, "Some diseases had no difficulty getting to Japan, whereas others were unsuccessful. The characteristics of each individual disease seem to have been the determining factor."[37] In addition, "the Japanese may have played an active role in keeping foreign diseases out of the country," Jannetta speculates. "For example, Japanese port officials may have tried to identify and quarantine ships that had visibly sick persons aboard. Certainly the tendency for measles and other infections to enter Japan by way of Nagasaki was general knowledge at the time."[38]

If the history of disease in Japan "proper" follows these broad outlines, what effect did disease have on cross-border relations in different periods of history? Here, again, a distinction must be made between the western (and to a lesser extent, southern) frontier, which mediated exchanges with the continent, and the northern frontier, which mediated exchanges with the indigenous residents of Hokkaido. Diseases, like "culture" and technology, tended to come in from continental Asia. At first they had a devastating impact on the "virgin" populations they encountered in Japan, which had no natural resistance. A case in point, of course, is the devastating smallpox epidemic of the 730s, which Farris studied in detail. Later, as smallpox became endemic, a rough epidemiological "parity" between Japan and the continent emerged—yet another important element in the relative stability of the western frontier.

Although disease ecology was a source of stability in the west, it played a very different role in the north, further serving to tip the balance of power in favor of Japan at the expense of the residents of Hokkaido. As noted above, it is unclear how many Ainu originally lived on the island, but according to Brett Walker, "In the late eighteenth century, more accurate data became available as shogunal officials in Edo grew alarmed by the Ainu demographic slide. In 1807, officials estimated the total population of Hokkaido Ainu at 26,256. Forty-seven years later that number had been reduced to 17,810, a 32 percent decline."[39]

The chief culprit, of course, was epidemic disease—specifically measles, smallpox, and syphilis. All of these were initially spread as the result of increased trade between Matsumae and "Ezochi" during the second half of the Edo period. Diseases were introduced to

Hokkaido by Wajin traders conducting business in Hokkaido, by Ainu chieftains and elders returning from visits to Matsumae, and by Ainu and Wajin prostitutes in port cities such as Esashi.[40] Beginning in the early nineteenth century, diseases were also sometimes transmitted directly from Eurasia as when, for example, the arrival of a Russian vessel reportedly caused an outbreak of smallpox on two islands off northwestern Hokkaido in 1805–1806.[41] Finally, after the opening of Japan to Western trade in the mid-nineteenth century, the Ainu (like the residents of Japan "proper") were exposed for the first time to the complete spectrum of Western diseases—not least because Hakodate was one of the five ports (along with Kanagawa, Nagasaki, Niigata, and Hyōgo) opened for trade in 1858.

To Japanese merchants operating in Hokkaido in the Edo period, smallpox and—less certainly—measles were not terribly serious diseases. People either experienced these diseases in childhood, in which case they usually survived and were protected from further infection by acquired immunity, or they never contacted them at all, because of genetic immunity. The Ainu who came in contact with these diseases were not so fortunate: without either acquired or genetic immunities, adults and children alike succumbed to these diseases in huge numbers.

Syphilis presented a slightly different story. This disease did not create natural immunities, but on the other hand, it did not kill, either—at least not for many years after initial infection. So the Ainu, in theory, were no more—and no less—susceptible to syphilis than the Japanese who introduced the disease to Hokkaido. (How the disease first came to Japan "proper" is not entirely clear; the first known historical reference is from 1512, meaning that its introduction predates the arrival of Western traders in Kyushu.[42])

The effect of these various diseases was not limited to immediate morbidity and mortality. People in the prime of life got sick and died—and this brought down the birth rate, because sick or dead adults could not produce further children. It also increased the death rate among survivors, because the sick and dying could no longer care for previously born children or elderly family members. Nor could they carry out subsistence-related activities such as fishing and hunting. All of this caused a sudden drop in population—and this, in turn, caused families and other institutions to become dysfunctional or break down completely, rending the fabric of society and leaving it far weaker than would be suggested by the drop in population alone. Moreover, the loss of village elders and others in positions of authority made it difficult or impossible to pass on cultural traditions—or even basic knowledge of sustenance-related technology—to surviving members of the younger generation.[43] This general breakdown in society bears many resemblances to what happened in medieval Europe following the ravages of the Black Death.[44]

Epidemic disease, in short, decimated Ainu society—and it did so approximately once every generation from at least the seventeenth century. According to Brett Walker, Hokkaido was struck by more than twenty recorded epidemics of smallpox and/or measles in the period 1624–1862.[45] Because the population in Hokkaido was not dense enough to sustain endemic pockets of disease, each infection "burned out" rapidly; children born in the aftermath of each epidemic thus had no natural immunities, leaving them completely susceptible when the next deadly virus was introduced from Matsumae—or Russia, or the West.

What about earlier periods? There are very few records of disease outbreaks in Hokkaido prior to the smallpox epidemic of 1624; the only known examples are from the late fifteenth century, in 1469 and 1471. Both of these epidemics are also thought to have been caused by smallpox.[46] Were these exceptional cases, as the historical record would seem to indicate? Or did epidemics from Japan periodically sweep through Hokkaido from very early times, but without leaving any written record for later historians to ponder?

Certainly, if the indigenous residents of Hokkaido had no natural immunities to smallpox or measles in the seventeenth or eighteenth century, they would not have had immunities in earlier centuries either. Given that both of these diseases were causing epidemics in Japan from very early times, and that smallpox, at least, was endemic in the main islands by the thirteenth century, it is certainly possible that infections spread periodically to Hokkaido. If this is true, the pattern of once-in-a-generation epidemics might possibly go back well past 1624, and even 1469, to a very early—but ultimately unknowable—date.

However, this is mere speculation. It might just as well be the case that no major outbreaks of epidemic disease occurred in Hokkaido prior to the Edo period. Although Hokkaido was never truly isolated from Japan "proper," the actual volume of cross-border contact was rather small until Japanese merchants began entering the island in the seventeenth century. Opportunities for the introduction of infectious disease would thus have been limited. It is also possible that, at least in very early periods of history, population density was so low that any introduced infections would have been essentially self-limiting, "burning out" locally before spreading to other parts of the island. Unfortunately, we will probably never know the truth of the matter. Nor are we ever likely to learn whether epidemic disease spreading from Japan played a role in the demise of other indigenous populations within the archipelago, such as the Hayato of southern Kyushu, who disappeared without a trace in the eighth century C.E.[47]

As Murai Shōsuke has shown, Japanese of the ancient and (particularly) medieval periods believed that epidemics were things that came into their country from outside. The outside world was "impure," inhabited by "devils" who were a source of contamination.[48] This belief was grounded in fact, as Japan's experience with smallpox and measles illustrates quite clearly; until at least the thirteenth century, epidemic diseases from abroad *did* repeatedly sweep the country, with devastating results. But all of these epidemics would seem to have come from the west; the Japanese, in a classic example of overgeneralization, came to associate disease with "outsiders" in all directions. With regard to indigenous populations of the archipelago, however, the situation was, if anything, the reverse. In the north, and perhaps also in the south, diseases spread *out* from Japan with devastating results for native populations; almost certainly, the reverse was never true. Although the facts are not clear for early periods of history, by the early seventeenth century at the latest, *Japan* was the source of "contamination"; among the victims of this tragic "exchange" were the Ainu.

A Socioenvironmental Feedback System

By this point the reader may have concluded that I am arguing for a form of environmental determinism. Historical events are "surface" phenomena played out against a background of institutions, whose character is determined by available technologies, and ultimately by geography and biology. Such a view is not completely wrong, but it is not the whole truth either.

It would be a mistake, for example, to view "natural" factors as "givens" that influence, but are not influenced by, human society. Clearly, humans can and do change their environment, either intentionally or otherwise. Well-known contemporary examples include the destruction of tropical rain forests, acid rain, global warming, ozone depletion, and many others. However, modern society has no monopoly on large-scale environmental destruction (or alteration), which is in fact a recurring theme in human history.[49] One example from Japan, already mentioned, is the overhunting of eagles and fur-bearing mammals in Hokkaido and Sakhalin during the Edo period to meet increased consumer demand. Another, from earlier times, is the extensive deforestation that occurred in central Honshu because of "monumental construction" (e.g., of capital cities) in the Nara and early Heian periods.[50] One might also point to the way disease ecologies in Japan and elsewhere have been changed by human activity, specifically, population growth and urbanization.

To extend this line of argument, *all* of the factors we have considered in this chapter are dependent in one degree or another upon all of the others. Social power, in other words, does not result from the individual words and deeds of historical actors, or from the strength or resilience of institutions, or from better weaponry or tools, or from climatic and ecological factors. It results from all of these things acting in combination. In short, there is no "prime mover" but rather a feedback system (see Figure 11).

The interaction of these various factors can produce, via positive feedback, a type of "ratcheting" effect whereby the society in question becomes progressively "stronger" or more competitively effective. This was the case in Japan for much of its premodern history. If some of the feedback is of the negative variety, however, "ratcheting" may occur at a slower pace, or not at all. This was the situation in Hokkaido, where a colder climate—among other factors—tended to retard technological and sociopolitical "progress" of all kinds. Because all of these factors influence each other, a very small difference between two regions may rapidly be magnified into a tremendous difference in social power. Not only that, but the very existence of a

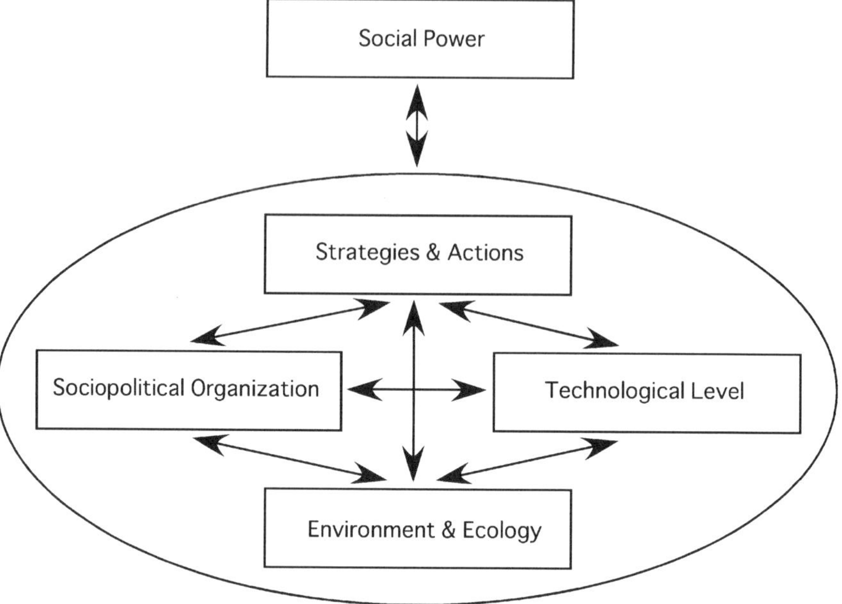

FIGURE 11. Factors contributing to social power.

power differential may in and of itself also contribute to further magnification, because the strong can exploit the weak, becoming still stronger in the process. This, in essence, is what happened on Japan's northern frontier.

One important point to note is that none of the factors discussed here has a fixed or absolute meaning; their significance varies according to specific historical context. This is true even for something as apparently fundamental as population size. In this chapter I have argued that having a large, dense population generally contributed to social power in premodern times. However, this is certainly not the case today. Far from being a source of competitive advantage, a large and growing population is frequently a liability for poor nations in the "Third World." To take another example, access to natural resources such as petroleum or uranium is of vital importance for nations in today's world; two hundred years ago, this was not the case.

Viewed in this context, Hokkaido's conquest and exploitation by Japan was perhaps not so such much an inevitability as it was the result of an unfortunate series of coincidences. Hokkaido's climate was, and is, not particularly suitable for wet-rice cultivation, but it is eminently suitable for other types of agriculture—witness the very large quantities of potatoes, corn, wheat, and other crops grown there today. Hokkaido is also rich in marine resources and timber. Many important mineral resources, particularly coal, were found there in the past, although most of these have been exhausted as the result of intensive mining since the late nineteenth century. Some of these resources could have served as sources of power for indigenous residents of the island, but they did not—partly because society was not sufficiently developed to exploit them, partly because the requisite technology was not available, and partly, one suspects, because of historical accident. Far from serving as a source of indigenous social power, therefore, these resources became actual liabilities: targets for Japanese exploitation. True, the Ainu are making somewhat of a "comeback" today, as the result of increased awareness in Japan of the importance of human rights and ethnic identity. But they will certainly remain a small ethnic minority within a vastly larger Japanese nation-state for the foreseeable future.

The End of Geopolitics?

In cases where the power imbalance is not so extreme, however, different outcomes are sometimes possible. A case in point, on a much larger geographical scale, is Japan's own rise to prominence within Asia and, indeed, the world as a whole. As we have seen, despite an initial lag in development, Japan achieved a degree of sociopolitical parity with neighboring states in Asia quite early in its history. Later, following its "opening" by the West in modern times, Japan was not only able to avoid "peripheralization" but was eventually able, in the twentieth century, to advance to "core" status within the "modern world-system."

Japan's transition to "core" status had important implications for its relations with continental Asia. In the premodern period, as I have argued, Japan's relatively rapid development resulted in the emergence of a more-or-less static maritime frontier. In modern times, Japan's ability, (temporarily) unique in Asia, to play "catch-up" with the West led to a dramatic shift in power relations. Where there had once been a rough parity in social power, now there was a profound imbalance, and one that operated in Japan's favor.

Geopolitically, then, it is easy to see why the nineteenth and early twentieth centuries witnessed an outward movement of historically static frontiers between Japan and continental Asia. Japanese influence, and later actual political control, began to extend beyond the archipelago itself to Korea, Manchuria, China, and Southeast Asia. A conscious strategy of imperialism is to blame for most of these intrusions. But Japanese imperialism was possible only because of Japanese power.

These imperialist ventures ended with Japan's defeat by the Allied Powers in the Pacific War; at that time, the country was dispossessed of its wartime colonies and possessions, and even of some areas—such as the so-called Northern Territories—that it had ruled since the late nineteenth century. After the war, however, Japanese power began to manifest itself again, this time in economic, as opposed to military, form.

Unlike previous cycles of growth, however, this postwar trend has not been accompanied by an outward movement of Japan's frontiers. Today, Japan's territory—with a few notable areas of dispute, such as the "Northern Territories"—is essentially fixed as the result of international treaties and the "delegitimization" of the idea that war and territorial expansion are acceptable instruments of national policy.

Throughout most of Japan's history, there has been a close relationship between social power and state territory—and hence, the location of Japan's frontiers. That is no longer the case. Whether the present situation represents a temporary aberration or—one hopes—the "end of geopolitics," remains to be seen.

Notes

Introduction

1. This point is also made by Hall, *Japan*, p. 1.

2. For an excellent discussion of how foreign scholars have used (and misused) Japan's geography to explain its history and/or social characteristics, see Wigen, "Geographic Imagination."

3. On Reischauer's life, see his autobiography, *My Life*.

4. Reischauer, *Ennin's Diary* and *Ennin's Travels*.

5. Reischauer, *The Japanese Today*, p. 3.

6. Ibid., p. 31.

7. Ibid., p. 32.

8. Ibid., p. 33.

9. Beasley, *Japanese Experience*, p. xv.

10. Ibid., p. 1.

11. There is a close relationship between the view of history being discussed here and the postwar Japanese discourse on national identity. For a brief but cogent introduction to the latter topic, see Befu, "Nationalism."

12. For a list of some of Amino's most important works, see the Works Cited.

13. McCormack, "Introduction," p. 3.

14. Ibid., p. 12.

15. The concept of "paradigm shift," of course, derives from Kuhn, *Structure of Scientific Revolutions*.

16. See, for example, the words cited in note 83 to Chapter 1.

17. See Chapter 5, and more generally, Part II, for details.

18. This is discussed in Chapter 1. A recent overview is provided by Toby, "Rescuing the Nation from History."

19. Amino, "Deconstructing 'Japan,'" pp. 122–132. (Note that this section of the article is a direct translation of Amino, *Nihonron no shiza*,

pp. 5–20.) Amino also makes the same point in *Nihon no rekishi o yominaosu*, pp. 191–235. An English translation of this will also soon be available from the University of Michigan's Center for Japanese Studies.

20. Amino, *Higashi to nishi.*

21. Morris-Suzuki, "Creating the Frontier," p. 1.

22. For an excellent recent introduction to the topic, written from an anthropological perspective but containing an extensive survey of the literature on borders in other fields, see Donnan and Wilson, *Borders.* An earlier, but still valuable, survey of the literature is Strassoldo, "Study of Boundaries."

23. It is impossible to be comprehensive, but a list of some of the best recent works (omitting those on the American frontier, which are discussed below) would include Barfield, *Perilous Frontier;* Bartlett and MacKay, *Medieval Frontier Societies;* Bowman, *Life and Letters;* Davis and Prescott, *Aboriginal Frontiers;* Drummond and Nelson, *Western Frontiers of Imperial Rome;* Elton, *Frontiers;* Ferguson and Whitehead, *War in the Tribal Zone;* Gaubatz, *Beyond the Great Wall;* Green and Perlman, *Archaeology of Frontiers and Boundaries;* Guy and Sheridan, *Contested Ground;* Hay, *Boundaries in China;* Hershatter et al., *Remapping China;* Isaac, *Limits of Empire;* Reynolds, *Frontier;* Sahlins, *Boundaries;* Stark, *Archaeology of Social Boundaries;* Thongchai, *Siam Mapped;* and Whittaker, *Frontiers of the Roman Empire.*

24. See the works by Bowman, Elton, and Whittaker cited in the preceding note.

25. Turner's best-known work is *The Frontier in American History.*

26. Others include William Cronon and Donald Worster; for representative works, see the Works Cited.

27. Limerick, *Legacy of Conquest.* Also see her recent collection of essays, *Something in the Soil.*

28. See Limerick, *Something in the Soil,* pp. 20–21. Note also that Limerick is by no means the only author to reject the idea of the "frontier"; in American history, there is now such a taboo surrounding the term that some scholars—only half-jokingly—refer to it as the "'f' word." See Klein, "Reclaiming the 'F' Word."

29. White, *Middle Ground.* Also see the same author's *"It's Your Misfortune."*

30. White, *Middle Ground,* p. x.

31. E.g., Murai, *Ajia no naka no chūsei Nihon; Chūsei Wajin den; Umi kara mita Sengoku Nihon; Kokkyō o koete; Chūsei Nihon no uchi to soto;* and most recently, "Boundaries of Medieval Japan."

32. Oguma, *"Nihonjin" no kyōkai.* Also see the same author's earlier *Tan'itsu minzoku shinwa no kigen.*

33. There is also an important literature in French. An outstanding recent example, written from the standpoint of political geography, is Pelletier's *La Japonésie.*

34. As well, of course, as many others whose works are cited in later chapters.

35. Howell, "Ainu Ethnicity" and *Capitalism from Within.* Other works by Howell include "Prehistory of the Japanese Nation-State"; "The Meiji State"; "Territoriality"; "Kinsei Hokkaidō"; and "The Ainu."

36. Morris-Suzuki, "Creating the Frontier"; "Descent into the Past": *Re-inventing Japan; Henkyō kara nagameru;* and "Northern Lights."

37. Siddle, *Race, Resistance and the Ainu;* "Ainu: Japan's Indigenous People"; "Ainu and the Discourse of 'Race'"; "Ainu History"; and "From Assimilation to Indigenous Rights."

38. Walker, "Reappraising the Sakoku Paradigm"; "Early Modern Japanese State"; "Foreign Contagions"; and *Conquest of Ainu Lands.*

39. Toby, *State and Diplomacy.*

40. Recent works in English (Toby has also published extensively in Japanese) include "Contesting the Centre," "Leaving the Closed Country," "And the Twain Did Meet," "The 'Indianness' of Iberia," and "Imagining and Imaging 'Anthropos.'"

41. Smits, *Visions of Ryukyu* and "Ambiguous Boundaries."

42. Yiengpruksawan, *Hiraizumi.*

43. Hudson, *Ruins of Identity.*

44. Howell has also explored the possibility of a "middle ground" in early modern Hokkaido in his Japanese article, "Kinsei Hokkaidō."

45. Note that this is the same position taken by White, *"It's Your Misfortune,"* pp. 3–4. White is here criticizing the tendency of other New Western Historians to define the "West" on the basis of purely geographic criteria such as aridity.

46. Paraphrased from Limerick, *Something in the Soil,* p. 333.

47. Howell, *Capitalism from Within,* pp. 16–19; Walker, *Conquest of Ainu Lands,* pp. 6–12.

Chapter 1. State

1. Asahi Shimbun, *Asahi Shimbun Japan Almanac 2002,* pp. 56, 63.

2. Ibid., p. 1. For a good description of Japan's physical geography, see Collcutt et al., *Cultural Atlas of Japan,* pp. 12–31.

3. For a balanced discussion, see Ishiwatari, "Northern Territories."

4. The dispute over the Senkaku Islands is the subject of a recent monograph by Suganuma, *Sovereign Rights.*

5. Serida, "Kokusai hō," pp. 462, 465–467. Regarding maritime boundaries, see the exhaustive treatment by Prescott, *Maritime Political Boundaries.*

6. For background, see Stephan, *Kuril Islands,* and Kimura, *Nichiro kokkyō kōshōshi.*

7. Some earlier Japanese boundaries were also defined on the basis of mutual negotiation, despite the absence of modern ideas of territorial sover-

eignty. For examples, see pp. 33 and 46. In world history, the idea of territorial sovereignty emerged together with the "modern state-system" in western Europe during the fifteenth through eighteenth centuries. For details, see Anderson, *Frontiers*, pp. 12–36.

8. Giddens, *Sociology*, p. 301 (emphasis in original removed). For a detailed explication of Gidden's view of the state, see his *Nation-State and Violence*.

9. Note, however, that whereas the presence of a state implies the existence of a territory, the reverse is not necessarily true. Many other social formations, large and small, are also associated with specific geographic territories.

10. Tsude, "Kofun Period." Tsude himself comes down in favor of state formation in the third century. Other important works in English on the topic of state formation in Japan include Kiley, "State and Dynasty"; Barnes, *Protohistoric Yamato;* Amino, "Deconstructing 'Japan'"; and Piggott, *Emergence of Japanese Kingship*.

11. See Batten, *Kokkyō no tanjō*, esp. the concluding chapter.

12. It should be noted that while the *conceptual* distinctions I am making are (presumably) universal, the *labels* for them are certainly not. My discussion generally draws on the political geography literature from the United States and Australia; works published by scholars in other fields or from other countries sometimes assign different meanings to the same words (or vice versa). When languages other than English are taken into account, of course, the problem of labels becomes even more complex. For example, in Japanese, *kokkyō* means state boundary, but there is no good word for what I call "frontiers"—*henkyō*, which is frequently used as a translation, means something closer to "periphery" in English.

13. Prescott, *Political Frontiers and Boundaries*, pp. 1, 13.

14. Kristof, "Nature of Frontiers and Boundaries," pp. 270–274.

15. Giddens, *Sociology*, p. 303. Again, readers wishing a fuller explication of Giddens' views are also urged to consult his *Nation-State and Violence*.

16. Anderson, *Imagined Communities*, p. 19.

17. In addition to the sources listed in note 23 to the Introduction, see Brauer, *Boundaries and Frontiers;* Lattimore, *Inner Asian Frontiers of China* and *Studies in Frontier History;* and Waldron, *Great Wall of China*.

18. Thongchai, *Siam Mapped*.

19. Ibid., pp. 75, 77.

20. For similar examples from other parts of the world, see Anderson, *Frontiers*, and Prescott, *Political Frontiers and Boundaries*.

21. Jones, "Boundary Concepts," p. 242.

22. Davis and Prescott, *Aboriginal Frontiers*.

23. Luttwak, *Grand Strategy*, p. 60.

24. E.g., Drummond and Nelson, *Western Frontiers of Imperial Rome*.

25. Whittaker, *Frontiers of the Roman Empire*.

26. I realize, of course, that the distinction between "religious" and "secular" is an arbitrary one. By "religious" I refer specifically to Shintō and Buddhist worldviews. Judging from research by Edwina Palmer, the indigenous Shintō "world" consisted of four separate realms of existence: the present, everyday world; a heavenly realm in the sky; an overseas land of eternal youth; and a subterranean underworld (Palmer, "Beyond Geography"). In the Buddhist cosmography, the "real world" (consisting largely of India, with China and Japan as appendages) was located on the periphery of a larger, sacred realm centered on the fabled (and imaginary) Mount Sumera (Ishigami, "Kodai Higashi Ajia chiiki," pp. 83–84; Unno, "Cartography in Japan," pp. 370–376).

27. Sakayori, *Bokkai to kodai no Nihon*, pp. 435–472. In English, the classic study is Fairbank, *Chinese World Order.*

28. Ishimoda, *Nihon kodai kokkaron*, part 1, pp. 311–328; Sakayori, *Bokkai to kodai no Nihon*, pp. 435–472.

29. Tsunoda et al., *Sources of Japanese Tradition*, vol. 1, p. 8. For a Japanese version, see Ishihara, *Shintei Gishi Washinden hoka sanpen*, pp. 92–93. (The original Chinese text is also reproduced in the same work by Ishihara, p. 125.) "King Bu" is generally identified with "Emperor Yūryaku" of the Japanese chronicles. For general background, see Yoshimura, "Wa no goō to wa dare ka," and Piggott, *Emergence of Japanese Kingship*, pp. 44–65.

30. The literature on *kentōshi* is vast. In Japanese, some of the more important studies are Mori, *Kentōshi;* Saeki, *Saigo no kentōshi;* Mozai et al., *Kentōshi kenkyū to shiryō;* Tajima, "Kentōshi wa naze haken sareta ka"; and Tōno, *Kentōshi to Shōsōin* and *Kentōshi sen.* (For Japan-Tang relations in general, see the various essays in Ikeda, *Kodai o kangaeru: Tō to Nihon.*) In English, the best sources are probably Reischauer, *Ennin's Diary* and *Ennin's Travels;* Borgen, "Japanese Mission to China"; Wang, "Sino-Japanese Relations"; and Tōno, "Japanese Embassies." In French, see the comprehensive study by von Verschuer, *Les relations officielles du Japon avec la Chine.* The same author also has a review article in English of recent Japanese-language studies, "Looking from Within and Without."

31. On the imperial ideology, see Ishimoda, *Nihon kodai kokkaron*, part 1, pp. 329–359; Ishigami, "Kodai kokka to taigai kankei," pp. 270–277; and Kumata, "Iteki, shoban to tennō." Mori, *Kodai Nihon no taigai ninshiki to kōtsū*, pp. 28–65, and *"Hakusukinoe" igo*, pp. 6–11 and 212–224, argues that Japanese perceptions of Tang were in fact ambivalent (or, perhaps, situational), alternating between "realism" (the view that Tang was superior to Japan) and "ethnocentrism" (the view that Japan was superior to China). On relations with Silla and Parhae, the best single-volume work is probably Lee Sungsi, *Higashi Ajia no ōken to kōeki.* For more details on relations with Silla, see Suzuki, *Kodai taigai kankei shi no kenkyū.* On Parhae, see Sakayori, *Bokkai to kodai no Nihon*, and Ishii, *Nihon Bokkai kankei shi no kenkyū.*

32. For general background on the Emishi, see Yiengpruksawan, *Hiraizumi*, especially pp. 9–27. Hudson, *Ruins of Identity*, pp. 175–205, discusses the

Emishi and the Hayato (a peripheral society in southern Kyushu; see below) from a world-systems perspective. In Japanese, there are hundreds, or perhaps thousands, of works on the Emishi. Probably the most accessible are the various books by Kudō, including *Jōsaku to Emishi*, *Kodai no Emishi*, and *Emishi no kodaishi*.

33. Okazaki, "Japan and the Continent," pp. 312–316. In Japanese, see the collection of essays in Oda, *Kodai o kangaeru: Okinoshima*.

34. Batten, "Kodai Nihon no kokkyō to Dazaifu," p. 63.

35. On early relations between Yamato and the Korean Peninsula, see Hirano, "The Yamato State and Korea," and Farris, *Sacred Texts*, pp. 55–122. Recent works in Japanese include Yamao, *Kodai no Nitchō kankei;* Suzuki, *Kodai no Wakoku to Chōsen shokoku;* and Azuma, "Chōsen sankoku to Wakoku."

36. On which, see the discussion in Chapter 8.

37. Kudō, *Jōsaku to Emishi*, pp. 25–39.

38. Described in detail by Friday, "Pushing beyond the Pale." In Japanese, see the various works by Kudō, cited above, and Kumata, "Kodai kokka to Emishi, Hayato."

39. Itō, "Kodai kokka no ryōdo, ryōiki." This should not be taken to mean that northernmost Honshu came under *direct* central control, since most of the new districts were in fact controlled by local chieftains from (successively) the Abe, Kiyohara, and Fujiwara families. Yiengpruksawan, *Hiraizumi*, describes the Fujiwara sphere of influence as a quasi-independent "nation," but I disagree. For the reasons, see note 65 to Chapter 3.

40. Until recently most authors lumped the Hayato together with the Emishi under the category *iteki*. Itō, "Emishi to Hayato wa doko ga chigau ka," however, argues convincingly that the Hayato were more completely assimilated than the Emishi—that the Hayato were, in effect, more of an ethnic minority *within* the Japanese state than an independent regional society.

41. Several works cited above in connection with the Emishi also contain descriptions of state interactions with the Hayato: Hudson, *Ruins of Identity*, esp. pp. 193–197; and Kumata, "Kodai kokka to Emishi, Hayato" and "Iteki, shoban to tennō." Readers wishing further detail are urged to consult Nagayama, "Hayato to ritsuryō sei," and the many books by Nakamura, including *Shintei Hayato no kenkyū; Kumaso, Hayato no shakaishiteki kenkyū; Kodai Hayato shakai; Hayato to ritsuryō kokka;* and *Hayato no kodaishi*.

42. On the Southern Islands, see Yamazato, *Kodai Nihon to Nantō no kōryū*.

43. Gilpin, *War and Change*, p. 112.

44. Ibid., p. 146.

45. Ibid., pp. 146–154. Note that this strictly geopolitical analysis ignores cultural and ethnic factors, which may also be important. For example, it is possible that cultural similarities facilitate political integration, while cultural differences impede it. To simplify the discussion, however, consideration of these and related issues is postponed to Chapters 2 and 3.

46. Batten, "Foreign Threat and Domestic Reform" and *Kokkyō no tanjō.*

47. Murai, "Boundaries of Medieval Japan," p. 82.

48. Shils, *Center and Periphery*, p. 80.

49. This idea comes from Elvin, *Pattern of the Chinese Past*, p. 19. Elvin's reference is to polity "size" rather than "distance" per se, but the principle is the same.

50. By comparison, the communication radius of Ming China (so far as I am aware, no figures for earlier dynasties have been published) was about six to seven weeks: Blunden and Elvin, *Cultural Atlas of China*, p. 94. In this sense, then, China was only about twice as "large" as Japan.

51. Ōishi, "Sotogahama, Ezo kō"; Murai, *Ajia no naka no chūsei Nihon*, pp. 565–598, and "Boundaries of Medieval Japan," p. 72; Amino, "Deconstructing 'Japan,'" p. 139 (Figure 9).

52. The case of Kikaigashima is explored by Murai in "Boundaries of Medieval Japan," pp. 74–77.

53. Amino, "Emperor, Rice, and Commoners," p. 238.

54. Murai, *Ajia no naka no chūsei Nihon*, p. 111. (Here and below, all translations from Japanese are by the author, unless otherwise noted.) Also see Murai, "Boundaries of Medieval Japan," p. 73.

55. See, for background, Kaiho, *Chūsei no Ezochi*, and Kikuchi and Fukuda, *Yomigaeru chūsei 4 Kita no chūsei.*

56. Murai, *Chūsei Nihon no uchi to soto*, pp. 176–180; also see Robinson, "Tsushima Governor and Regulation."

57. Murai, "Boundaries of Medieval Japan," pp. 82–84, and "Kikaigashima kō."

58. The concept of "boundary functions" comes from Boggs, *International Boundaries.*

59. On the Dazaifu, see some of my previous works, such as "State and Frontier in Early Japan" and, more recently, *Kokkyō no tanjō.*

60. On the Chinjufu, see Friday, "Pushing beyond the Pale," and Yiengpruksawan, *Hiraizumi*, esp. pp. 21–22, 32–36, and 41–45.

61. The term "boundary powers" *(kyōkai kenryoku)* comes from Kikuchi, *Ainu minzoku to Nihonjin*, pp. 35–53.

62. In the Japanese edition of this book I argued, following Kaiho Mineo, that the ultimate expression of this independence was an embassy sent to Chosŏn (Yi-dynasty Korea) by the self-proclaimed "King of the Thousand Isles of Ezo" in 1482. The "Thousand Isles" refers to Hokkaido, the Kurils, and vicinity, and according to Kaiho Mineo, the "king" responsible for sending the embassy was Andō Masasue, the strongman who controlled some (but by no means all) of this territory at the time (Kaiho, *Chūsei no Ezochi*, p. 198). It was pointed out to me by Hashimoto Yū, however, that this identification is not accepted by all authors. Osa Setsuko, for example, has argued that the "King of the Thousand Isles of Ezo" was a specious title dreamed up by unidentified persons on Tsushima as a pretext for carrying out trade with Chosŏn (Osa,

"Ezogachishima ō Kasha," pts. 1 and 2). If so, the incident illustrates the autonomy not of the Andō family but of the residents of Tsushima. But in any case it supports my larger point that the central government had very little control over "boundary powers" in the late medieval period. For a more detailed discussion of these issues in English, see Robinson, "Jiubian and Ezogachishima Embassies." On other "imposter embassies" sent to Chosŏn by Japanese elites during the Muromachi/Sengoku periods, see Robinson, "Centering the King of Chosŏn," pp. 116–122, and "Imposter Branch of the Hatakeyama Family."

63. On Tsushima, see Robinson, "Tsushima Governor and Regulation."

64. Murai, *Chūsei Wajin den*, p. 39. On the Wakō, see Tanaka with Sakai, "Japan's Relations with Overseas Countries," pp. 161–163; Kawazoe, "Japan and East Asia," pp. 405–408, 423–432; and Elisonas, "Inseparate Trinity," pp. 239–265. Another old but useful reference is So, *Japanese Piracy*.

65. Murai, "Boundaries of Medieval Japan," p. 89. The Chikama case is also covered in Murai, "Kikaigashima kō," pp. 7–10.

66. Much has been written on this process; perhaps the best account remains Berry, *Hideyoshi*, pp. 8–40. For more detailed background on the Sengoku period, see the various essays in Hall et al., *Japan before Tokugawa*, as well as Nagahara, "The Lord-Vassal System."

67. Katsumata, "15–16 seiki no Nihon," pp. 27–33.

68. See the many references to "Japan" and the "Japanese" in Cooper, *They Came to Japan*.

69. Machida shishi hensan iinkai, *Machida shishi*, vol. 1, pp. 564–565. On the Later Hōjō, see Birt, "Samurai in Passage."

70. On which, see the essays in Bartlett and MacKay, *Medieval Frontier Societies*.

71. See Asao, "Sixteenth-Century Unification."

72. Ōishi, "Bakuhan System"; Hall, "*Bakuhan* System."

73. E.g., Fairbank et al., *East Asia*, pp. 392–434; Reischauer, *The Japanese Today*, pp. 64–77.

74. Ravina, *Land and Lordship*. Other recent works emphasizing local autonomy include Brown, *Central Authority*, and Roberts, *Mercantilism*. An older, but classic, work is Bolitho, *Treasures among Men*.

75. See Toby, "Rescuing the Nation from History." In this review article, Toby argues that some of the recent scholarship goes overboard in its eagerness to write the shogunate out of the picture. Another relatively recent work emphasizing the power of the central government is White, *Ikki*.

76. Berry, *Hideyoshi*, pp. 207–217; Elisonas, "Inseparable Trinity," pp. 265–293.

77. Toby, "Imagining and Imaging 'Anthropos,'" "Kinsei shoki no aidentitii kiki," and "Tō no kanata yori."

78. On the "Japanese-style middle kingdom order," see Arano, *Kinsei Nihon to Higashi Ajia*, pp. 3–65, and "Kinsei no taigai kan"; Toby, *State and*

Diplomacy, pp. 217–219; Wakabayashi, *Anti-Foreignism*, pp. 17–57; Morris-Suzuki, *Re-inventing Japan*, pp. 15–20; and Kang, *Diplomacy and Ideology*, pp. 153–166.

79. Arano, *Kinsei Nihon to Higashi Ajia*, pp. 161–162; Tsuruta, "Kinsei Nihon no yottsu no 'kuchi.'"

80. On the Nagasaki magistracy and its supervision of foreign trade see Jansen, *China in the Tokugawa World*, pp. 5–14, and (for a contemporary account) Kaempfer, *Kaempfer's Japan*, pp. 148–157, 207–228. Regarding Dutch-Japanese relations in general, see Blussé et al., *Bridging the Divide.* On Tsushima, see Tashiro, "Tsushima-han's Korean Trade," and Tsuruta, "Establishment and Characteristics of the 'Tsushima Gate.'" Satsuma's relationship with Ryukyu is described in Smits, *Visions of Ryukyu*, pp. 15–34. Regarding Matsumae and the Ainu, see Howell, "Ainu Ethnicity" and "The Ainu"; Siddle, *Race, Resistance and the Ainu*, pp. 32–38; Walker, "Reappraising the Sakoku Paradigm," and *Conquest of Ainu Lands*, pp. 21–47.

81. Kamiya, "Japanese Control of Ezochi"; Kaiho, *Chūsei no Ezochi*, pp. 265–267; Walker, *Conquest of Ainu Lands*, pp. 36–37.

82. Arano, *Kinsei Nihon to Higashi Ajia*, pp. 191–222; Toby, *State and Diplomacy*, pp. 76–83.

83. Toby, *State and Diplomacy*, pp. 3–22; Arano, "Entrenchment of the Concept of 'National Seclusion'"; Katō, "Research Trends." In Japanese, see Arano, "Kaikin to sakoku," and the various essays in Nagazumi, *"Sakoku" o minaosu.*

84. Again, this point will be discussed in detail in later chapters.

85. Kaiho, *Chūsei no Ezochi*, pp. 241–244; Edmonds, *Northern Frontiers*, pp. 49, 88.

86. Kaiho, *Chūsei no Ezochi*, pp. 15, 26–27, 30, 275–282; Edmonds, *Northern Frontiers*, pp. 85–112.

87. The failure of Gyōki-zu maps to depict a clear state boundary is discussed in Li, *Hyōshō kūkan no kindai*, pp. 203–204. On the history of mapmaking in Japan, see the authoritative treatment by Unno, "Cartography in Japan."

88. On Japanese notions of territoriality (and status) in this period, see Howell, "Territoriality."

89. Kikuchi, *Ainu minzoku to Nihonjin*, pp. 65–147; Siddle, *Race, Resistance and the Ainu*, pp. 32–38; Morris-Suzuki, "Creating the Frontier," pp. 4–8; Howell, *Capitalism from Within*, esp. pp. 24–49.

90. Again, on Satsuma's relationship to Ryukyu, see Smits, *Visions of Ryukyu*, pp. 15–34.

91. For general background on these events, see Kikuchi, *Ainu minzoku to Nihonjin*, pp. 233–259.

92. For details, again, refer to Smits, *Visions of Ryukyu.* Among the many excellent surveys of Okinawan/Ryukyuan history in Japanese, see in particular Takara, *Ajia no naka no Ryūkyū ōkoku*, and Hamashita, *Okinawa nyūmon.*

93. This is the thesis of my book *Kokkyō no tanjō.*

Chapter 2. "Race" and Culture

1. Nielsson, "States and 'Nation-Groups,'" p. 28.

2. Ibid., pp. 30–31 (Table 2.1).

3. Ibid., p. 33 (emphasis in original removed).

4. For a short, authoritative survey of this topic, see Howell, "Ethnicity and Culture."

5. Kodansha, *Japan*, vol. 1, p. 146; for more on this group, refer to Neary, "Burakumin." Note that although "Burakumin" is still often used in the English literature, it is now a term of discrimination in Japanese. In Japanese probably the least offensive term is "*Dōwa chiku ni sumu hito*" or the like, meaning "people who live in Dōwa districts." "Dōwa" literally means "harmony" or "conciliation" and refers to the government's anti-discrimination policies.

6. Numbers from Asahi Shimbun, *Asahi Shimbun Japan Almanac 2002*, p. 63. On "old-comers" versus "newcomers," see Tanaka, *Shinpan zainichi gaikokujin.*

7. Asahi Shimbun, *Asahi Shimbun Japan Almanac 2002*, p. 63.

8. The best work on this general topic is probably Oguma, *"Nihonjin" no kyōkai.* Oguma's theme is how national "identity" was defined by Japanese authorities in these areas through the application of policies of assimilation and/or exclusion.

9. Walker, *Conquest of Ainu Lands*, pp. 181–182. This topic will be covered in more detail in Chapter 10.

10. Population figure from Kodansha, *Japan*, vol. 1, p. 21. Also note that many Ainu today live outside Hokkaido, particularly in and around Tokyo. On the current situation of the Ainu, see Siddle, "Ainu: Japan's Indigenous People," as well as the various essays in Fitzhugh and Dubreuil, *Ainu.* This book, which represents the current "state of the art" in Ainu studies, was published in conjunction with a major exhibition mounted by the Arctic Studies Center of the Smithsonian Institution's National Museum of Natural History in 1999. For a highly readable "insider's account" of growing up Ainu, see Kayano, *Our Land Was a Forest.*

11. This is the theme of Siddle, *Race, Resistance and the Ainu*, as well as of his two articles, "Ainu: Japan's Indigenous People" and "From Assimilation to Indigenous Rights."

12. Tsunemoto, "The Ainu Shinpo"; Sasamura, "Beyond the Ainu Shinpo."

13. Probably the best overview in English is Ishiwatari, "Northern Territories."

14. On colonial identity in Sakhalin, see Morris-Suzuki, "Northern Lights."

15. See sources cited in note 92, Chapter 1, as well as Taira, "Troubled National Identity," and Arasaki, *Gendai Nihon to Okinawa.*

16. Needless to say, there is a huge literature on Japanese imperialism and colonialism. For an overview, see Peattie, "Japanese Colonial Empire"; Hata, "Continental Expansion"; and Beasley, *Japanese Imperialism.*

17. Okabe, *Umi o watatta Nihonjin.*

18. Asahi Shimbun, *Asahi Shimbun Japan Almanac 2002*, p. 63.

19. This theme is developed at length in Morris-Suzuki, *Re-inventing Japan.*

20. Regarding this, see Morris-Suzuki, *Re-inventing Japan;* Tanaka, *Japan's Orient;* and Oguma, *Tan'itsu minzoku shinwa no kigen.*

21. Lamarre, *Uncovering Heian Japan*, describes how our views of Heian Japan have been systematically distorted by the "national imagination."

22. Giddens, *Sociology*, p. 246. For discussion of this point by one of the world's leading geneticists, see Cavalli-Sforza et al., *History and Geography of Human Genes*, pp. 16–20. (Cavalli-Sforza provides a popular account in the more recent *Genes, Peoples, and Languages*, pp. 3–32.)

23. Giddens, *Sociology*, p. 246 (emphasis in original).

24. Fairbank et al., *East Asia*, pp. 326–327.

25. Hanihara, "Emishi, Ezo, and Ainu." For more up-to-date genetic information, see Hudson, *Ruins of Identity*, pp. 69–74.

26. During the 1980s and 1990s, much older dates—in some cases going back 700,000 years—were cited for the first appearance of humans in Japan. Many of these early dates have now been shown to be frauds perpetrated by (former) archaeologist Fujimura Shin'ichi. For copies of news reports related to the scandal, see <http://www.asahi.com/paper/special/sekki/>. For a list of fraud-related links, see <http://www.jomongaku.net/note/netsuzo-link.html>.

27. Hanihara, "Dual Structure Model." Also see Hudson, *Ruins of Identity*, pp. 59–81; Katayama, "The Japanese"; and Ishida, "Ancient People." In Japanese, good overviews are provided by Hanihara, "Nihonjin no keisei" and *Nihonjin no tanjō;* the latter is a highly readable, semipopular work.

28. Hanihara, "Dual Structure Model," pp. 15–16.

29. Cavalli-Sforza, *Genes, Peoples, and Languages*, p. 23.

30. Ibid., pp. 26–27.

31. Yamaguchi, "Kojinkotsu," pp. 114–118; Kumata, "Iteki, shoban to tennō," p. 170.

32. Hongō, *Kumaso, Hayato no genshō*, pp. 220–222. For pictures and brief descriptions of different skull types from southern Kyushu, see Kamimura, *Hayato no kōkogaku*, pp. 4–7.

33. Hatch, "Culture." Also see Morris-Suzuki, *Re-inventing Japan*, pp. 60–65.

34. Hatch, "Culture," p. 178.

35. Rosaldo, *Culture and Truth*, p. 169.

36. Kuper, *Culture*, p. 231.

37. Ibid., pp. 229–230.

38. Huntington, *Clash of Civilizations*, pp. 40–48.

39. Lewis and Wigen, *Myth of Continents*, pp. 142–150.

40. Toynbee, *Study of History;* Quigley, *Evolution of Civilizations;* Eisenstadt, *Japanese Civilization.*

41. Lewis and Wigen, *Myth of Continents*, p. 145 (Map 5) and p. 186 (Map 10).

42. For a nuanced argument supporting the cultural unity of East Asia, see Lee Sungsi, *Ajia bunka ken no keisei.*

43. Barnard, "Culture Area," p. 180.

44. Barnard, "Culture Area"; Ehrich and Henderson, "Culture Area."

45. Ōbayashi, *Higashi to nishi*, pp. 14–15.

46. Ibid., p. 12.

47. Ibid., pp. 18–20.

48. Ibid., pp. 36–52.

49. Ibid., pp. 20–35.

50. Ibid., p. 18.

51. Ōbayashi, "Kodai ni okeru mittsu no ryōiki."

52. Ōbayashi, *Higashi to nishi*, pp. 27–28.

53. Amino, *Higashi to nishi.*

54. Ōbayashi, "Kodai ni okeru mittsu no ryōiki," p. 102.

55. Gellner, *Nationalism*, p. 20.

56. Childe, quoted in Dark, *Theoretical Archaeology*, p. 89.

57. Ibid., pp. 1–11.

58. Fujimoto, *Mō futatsu no Nihon bunka.*

59. Readers wishing more detailed descriptions of these various cultures are referred to Barnes, *China Korea and Japan;* Imamura, *Prehistoric Japan;* Kidder, "Earliest Societies in Japan"; and Pearson, *Ancient Japan.*

60. Epi-Jōmon culture: Fujimoto, *Mō futatsu no Nihon bunka*, pp. 27–35, 59–64; Imamura, *Prehistoric Japan*, pp. 199–200; Yamaura and Ushiro, "Prehistoric Hokkaido and Ainu Origins," pp. 42–43; Kikuchi, "Ainu Ties," pp. 49–50.

61. Satsumon culture: Fujimoto, *Mō futatsu no Nihon bunka*, pp. 35–43, 64–67; Imamura, *Prehistoric Japan*, pp. 200–202; Yamaura and Ushiro, "Prehistoric Hokkaido and Ainu Origins," pp. 44–45.

62. Okhotsk culture: Fujimoto, *Mō futatsu no Nihon bunka*, pp. 43–51, 64–67; Imamura, *Prehistoric Japan*, pp. 68–70; Yamaura and Ushiro, "Prehistoric Hokkaido and Ainu Origins," pp. 43–44; Kikuchi, "Ainu Ties," p. 50.

63. Ainu culture: Fujimoto, *Mō futatsu no Nihon bunka*, pp. 51–58, 64–67; Imamura, *Prehistoric Japan*, pp. 70–73; Hudson, *Ruins of Identity*, 208–217. On the importance of ritual sites, see Utagawa, "Archaeology of *Iyomante.*"

64. On the terms "Emishi" and "Ezo," see Kaiho, *Ezo no rekishi*, pp. 28–72.

65. Basic information on climatic differences within the Japanese archipelago is provided by Fujimoto, *Mō futatsu no Nihon bunka*, pp. 14–19.

66. Hudson, *Ruins of Identity*, pp. 82–102.

67. It must be noted that not all authors agree with this scenario. John C. Maher, for example, has argued that Japanese is a "creole" language that developed as the result of interactions between Jōmon indigenes and Yayoi immigrants in North Kyushu and then spread throughout the islands: Maher, "North Kyushu Creole." For Hudson's critique of this model, see *Ruins of Identity*, pp. 89–90.

68. Renfrew, *Archaeology and Language.*

69. Hudson, *Ruins of Identity*, pp. 97–99. For a good description of the Ainu language, see Tamura, "Ainu Language."

70. Quoted in Cavalli-Sforza, *Genes, Peoples, and Languages*, p. 167.

71. Ibid., pp. 133–172. For more detail, refer to Cavalli-Sforza et al., *History and Geography of Human Genes*, pp. 96–105.

72. Imaizumi, "Ritsuryō kokka to Emishi," p. 169.

73. Yagi, "Emishi shakai no chiiki sei to jiritsusei," pp. 250–254, 262.

74. See Yamada, "Ainu gozoku no kyojū han'i"; Sasaki, "Tōhoku chihō ni nokoru Ainu go chimei."

75. Hudson, *Ruins of Identity*, p, 199; Imaizumi, "Ritsuryō kokka to Emishi," pp. 165–167; Komatsu, "Gangyō no ran," pp. 286–288.

76. Fujimoto, *Mō futatsu no Nihon bunka*, p. 112.

77. Available in English translation as Matsuo Bashō, *The Narrow Road to the Deep North and Other Travel Sketches.*

78. The latter position is argued—unpersuasively, I believe—by Kadowaki, "Nihonjin no keisei," pp. 12–19.

79. On *kofun* in the Tōhoku, see Tsuji, "Kofun no hensen to kakki."

80. On *jōsaku*, see Kudō, *Jōsaku to Emishi;* Kuwabara, "Jōsaku o chūshin to suru kodai kanga"; Imaizumi, "Tōhoku no jōsaku"; and Itō, "Kodai kokka no Emishi shihai."

81. On which, see Yiengpruksawan, *Hiraizumi.*

Chapter 3. Ethnicity

1. For background, see Tanaka, *Japan's Orient;* Oguma, *Tan'itsu minzoku shinwa no kigen;* and Morris-Suzuki, *Re-inventing Japan*, pp. 79–109.

2. Hudson, *Ruins of Identity.* Hudson's definition of "ethnicity" is much broader than the one adopted in the present study. Specifically, he includes objective, or "etic," elements as well as subjective, or "emic," ones, on grounds that the former serve as essential building blocks for the latter. Although I agree with this point, I think it makes more sense analytically to distinguish between the objective and subjective elements, reserving the term "ethnicity" for the latter. For a more detailed explanation, see my review of Hudson's book in *Monumenta Nipponica* 55.2 (2000): 283–285.

3. For example, Smith, *Ethnic Origins of Nations* and *National Identity.*

4. Smith, *National Identity*, pp. 20–21.

5. Ibid., p. 21.

6. Ibid., p. 26.

7. Ibid. Needless to say, other authors offer different definitions. Craig Calhoun (*Nationalism*, pp. 4–5), after a judicious survey of the literature, gives the following list of characteristics:

1. Boundaries, of territory, population, or both.
2. Indivisibility—the notion that the nation is an integral unit.
3. Sovereignty, or at least the aspiration to sovereignty, and thus formal equality with other nations, usually as an autonomous and putative self-sufficient state.
4. An "ascending" notion of legitimacy—i.e. the idea that government is just only when supported by popular will or at least when it serves the interests of "the people" or "the nation."
5. Popular participation in collective affairs—a population mobilized on the basis of national membership (whether for war or civic activities).
6. Direct membership, in which each individual is understood to be immediately a part of the nation and in that respect categorically equivalent to other members.
7. Culture, including some combination of language, shared beliefs and values, habitual practices.
8. Temporal depth—a notion of the nation as such existing through time, including past and future generations, and having a history.
9. Common descent or racial characteristics.
10. Special historical or even sacred relations to a certain territory.

8. For the minority view stressing the antiquity of the nation, see Armstrong, *Nations before Nationalism.*

9. Anderson, *Imagined Communities.*

10. For a solid application of this framework to the development of society in Japan, see Pearson, *Ancient Japan*, pp. 26–30.

11. For the reasons behind this, see the "iterative" model of social evolution presented by Chase-Dunn and Hall in *Rise and Demise*, pp. 99–117. Their model is basically a feedback system consisting of eight variables: population growth, environmental degradation, population pressure, emigration, "circumscription," conflict, hierarchy formation, and technological "intensification."

12. See, for example, Hobsbawn and Ranger, *Invention of Tradition.* For a balanced assessment of these two views, see Calhoun, *Nationalism*, pp. 51–57.

13. The best-documented example of such symbiosis is probably the relationship between the agricultural Chinese and the nomadic societies to the north. For an anthropological analysis, see Barfield, *Perilous Frontier.* A less sophisticated but similar analysis is presented in Jagchid and Symons, *Peace, War, and Trade.*

14. Anderson, *Imagined Communities*, p. 6.

15. Tsunoda et al., *Sources of Japanese Tradition*, vol. 1, p. 4 (original: Ishihara, *Shintei Gishi Washinden hoka sanpen*, p. 39).

16. Ōbayashi, "Ethnological Study," p. 18.

17. Quotation from Aston, trans., *Nihongi*, vol. 1, p. 203. Original in *Nihon shoki*, Keikō 40/7/16 (vol. 1, p. 300). As the annotators to the Japanese edition make clear, the passage is a Japanese adaptation of descriptions of barbarians in Chinese sources (*Nihon shoki*, p. 302, n. 4).

18. Piggott, *Emergence of Japanese Kingship*, pp. 233–234.

19. Smith, *National Identity*, p. 53.

20. Ibid.

21. Ishigami, "Kodai kokka to taigai kankei"; Murai, "Ōdo ōmin shisō."

22. Murai, "Ōdo ōmin shisō," pp. 35–36.

23. Batten, *Kokkyō no tanjō*, pp. 166–203.

24. Borgen, "Japanese Nationalism."

25. Murai, "Ōdo ōmin shisō"; Kimura, *"Kokufū bunka" no jidai*, pp. 118–130.

26. On the role of the invasions in promoting Japanese "identity," see Segal, "Mōko shūrai to chūsei teki aidentitii."

27. All quoted in Cooper, *They Came to Japan*, pp. 41–42.

28. Regarding the effect of the encounter with Europe on Japanese identity, see the following works by Toby: "Contesting the Centre," "And the Twain Did Meet," "The 'Indianness' of Iberia," "Imagining and Imaging 'Anthropos,'" and "Kinsei shoki no aidentitii kiki." Also relevant is Massarella, "Some Reflections on Identity Formation."

29. On *Rangaku* there are many fine treatments; one of the best remains Keene, *Japanese Discovery of Europe*. More recently, see the following three essays in Blussé et al., *Bridging the Divide:* Yoshida, "'Dutch Studies'"; Beukers, "Introduction of Western Medicine"; and Torii, "'Dutch Studies.'"

30. There is a huge literature in English alone on Edo-period philosophical discourse. A good overview is provided by the two relevant chapters in vol. 4 of *The Cambridge History of Japan:* Bitō, "Thought and Religion," and Najita, "History and Nature." More detail is provided by the following monographs: Wakabayashi, *Anti-Foreignism and Western Learning;* Koschmann, *The Mito Ideology;* Harootunian, *Things Seen and Unseen;* and Nosco, *Remembering Paradise.* Also valuable as an introduction to recent trends in scholarship is Yamashita, "Reading the New Tokugawa Intellectual Histories."

31. Hanley, *Everyday Things in Premodern Japan*, pp. 189–190; Totman, *History of Japan*, p. 298.

32. Regarding the importance of the domain, in particular, see Roberts, *Mercantilism*, and Ravina, *Land and Lordship.*

33. Totman, *Collapse of the Tokugawa Bakufu;* Beasley, "Foreign Threat"; Jansen, "Meiji Restoration."

34. Gluck, *Japan's Modern Myths*, p. 18.

35. On cultural diversity (but also integration) in the Edo period, see the perceptive work by Berry, "Was Early Modern Japan Culturally Integrated?"

36. On these developments, see the relevant chapters in vol. 5 of *The Cambridge History of Japan*, especially Hirakawa, "Japan's Turn to the West"; Rozman, "Social Change"; Crawcour, "Economic Change"; and Jansen, "Meiji Political Institutions."

37. On *tennōsei*, or the imperial ideology, see Gluck, *Japan's Modern Myths.*

38. Fujitani, *Splendid Monarchy.*

39. Pyle, *New Generation in Meiji Japan;* Huffman, *Creating a Public.*

40. Anderson, *Imagined Communities.*

41. For details, see Gluck, *Japan's Modern Myths.*

42. Mouer and Sugimoto, *Images of Japanese Society;* Yoshino, "Culturalism, Racialism, and Internationalism" and *Cultural Nationalism;* Befu, "Nationalism."

43. Chappell, "Ethnogenesis and Frontiers," p. 268.

44. Fried, *Evolution of Political Society*, pp. 240–242.

45. Hudson, *Ruins of Identity*, p. 193.

46. Ibid., pp. 203–223; quotation from p. 219.

47. Fried, *Evolution of Political Society*, pp. 170–173, and *Notion of Tribe;* Wolf, *Europe and the People without History.*

48. Ferguson and Whitehead, "Violent Edge," p. 3.

49. Kaiho, *Ezo no rekishi*, pp. 29–30.

50. Ibid., pp. 31–40.

51. Ibid., pp. 40–48.

52. Ibid., pp. 44–47.

53. Itō, "Kodai ōken to iminzoku," pp. 9–10.

54. Kikuchi, "Emishi (kai) setsu saikō." Also see Walker, *Conquest of Ainu Lands*, pp. 241–242, n. 11.

55. Kikuchi, "Emishi (kai) setsu saikō," p. 103. Also see Tamura, "Ainu Language," p. 60.

56. Itō, "Emishi to Hayato wa doko ga chigau ka," p. 60.

57. The *Nihon shoki* refers in several places to a group called the "Michihase," whose identity and place of residence are unclear. Some authors believe that "Michihase" refers to Tungus tribes on the Asian continent. *Nihon shoki*, Saimei 4[658], entry for "this year" (vol. 2, p. 336; translation in Aston, vol. 2, p. 257); Saimei 6[660]/3 (vol. 2, p. 342; translation in Aston, vol. 2, p. 263).

58. Kudō, *Jōsaku to Emishi*, pp. 137–143.

59. Regarding these incidents, see Friday, "Pushing Beyond the Pale," and Kudō, *Jōsaku to Emishi*, pp. 70–120.

60. The Michishima family were local aristocrats apparently of "Japanese" origin; for details, see Kumagai, "Kodai Tōhoku no gōzoku," pp. 263–273.

61. On which, see Imaizumi, "Emishi no chōkō to kyōkyū" and "Ritsuryō kokka to Emishi," pp. 191–195; and Itō, "Emishi to Hayato wa doko ga chigau ka," pp. 70–72, and "Kodai kokka no Emishi shihai," pp. 202–209.

62. *Nihon shoki*, Saimei 5[659]/7/3 (vol. 2, pp. 339–340; translation in Aston, vol. 2, pp. 261–262).

63. For example, *Nihon shoki*, Saimei 4[658]/4 (vol. 2, p. 331; translation in Aston, vol. 2, p. 252) and *Nihon shoki*, Saimei 6[660]/3 (vol. 2, p. 342; translation in Aston, vol. 2, pp. 263–264). For a discussion, see Walker, *Conquest of Ainu Lands*, pp. 21–22.

64. Kudō, *Jōsaku to Emishi*, pp. 84–85.

65. Kikuchi, *Ainu minzoku to Nihonjin*, p. 39. According to Yiengpruksawan, *Hiraizumi*, northern Tōhoku (more specifically the Kitakami River Basin) was the site of a "*fushū* nation" (p. 147) in the late Heian period. In the terminology of the present work, of course, it is highly improbable—to say the least—that a "nation" existed in northern Tōhoku (or, indeed, anywhere in the world) in this period of history. As it turns out, however, Yiengpruksawan is not making such a radical claim: "*fushū* nation" is simply a mistranslation of Takahashi Tomio's term "*fushū kokka*" or "*fushū* state." Translation issues aside, however, even the idea of an independent "state" in the northeast is a tremendous exaggeration. Society in the northeast meets none of the criteria of statehood as normally defined; the northern Fujiwara may have exercised a fair degree of autonomy from the Japanese court, but even if they had been totally independent (they were not), sociopolitical organization in Tōhoku was by no means at the state level. This, not "resistance to multiculturalism," as Yiengpruksawan claims (ibid., p. 48) accounts for the failure of most Japanese historians to accept Takahashi's ideas.

66. Kaiho, *Ezo no rekishi*, pp. 53–54.

67. Ibid.

68. *Suwa daimyōjin ekotoba*, p. 511. For a discussion of this text (which is actually part of a picture scroll, as the name implies), see Sasaki, "*Ainu-e*," pp. 80–81.

69. Kaiho, *Chūsei no Ezochi*, pp. 150–172. Also see Hudson, *Ruins of Identity*, pp. 223–224, 231.

70. *Suwa daimyōjin ekotoba*, p. 511.

71. Siddle, "Ainu History," p. 69. Also see Hudson, *Ruins of Identity*, p. 208.

72. Kikuchi, *Ainu minzoku to Nihonjin*, pp. 60–63.

73. Walker, *Conquest of Ainu Lands*, pp. 48–72.

74. Ibid., pp. 204–226; Howell, "Ainu Ethnicity."

75. See Fitzhugh, "Ainu Ethnicity," pp. 10–11.

76. Ölschleger, "Technology, Settlement, and Hunting Ritual," p. 218. For more on *kotan*, see Watanabe, "Ainu Ecosystem."

77. Ölschleger, "Technology, Settlement, and Hunting Ritual, pp. 219–221; Fujimura, "*Kamuy*"; Walker, *Conquest of Ainu Lands*, pp. 74–82. The term "covenant" is Walker's.

78. Howell, *Capitalism from Within*, p. 40.

79. Siddle, *Race, Resistance and the Ainu*, pp. 3–4.

80. Ibid., passim; idem, "Ainu: Japan's Indigenous People"; "Ainu History," pp. 72–73; and "From Assimilation to Indigenous Rights."

81. Nielsson, "States and 'Nation-Groups,'" p. 28.

82. Again, for a general model of the evolution of social systems, see Chase-Dunn and Hall, *Rise and Demise*, pp. 99–117.

83. Renfrew and Bahn, *Archaeology*, p. 181.

84. Chinese residents in Hakata are discussed in Batten, *Kokkyō no tanjō*, pp. 221–228; the bibliography to that work contains a list of many more detailed references.

85. See Murai, "Wakō no taminzokusei o megutte." Also see idem, *Chūsei Wajin den; Umi kara mita Sengoku Nihon;* and *Chūsei Nihon no uchi to soto.*

86. The idea of the "matrix" comes from Lewis and Wigen, *The Myth of Continents*, pp. 153–154. Regarding identity positions, see Morris-Suzuki, *Re-inventing Japan*, pp. 195–200.

87. Howell, "Ainu Ethnicity," pp. 79–80, provides a particularly striking example, albeit one resulting from political manipulation rather than free choice. For another example from modern Japan, this time relating to Okinawan identity, see Smits, *Visions of Ryukyu*, p. 5.

88. Some of these are described in my *Kokkyō no tanjō*, pp. 166–203.

89. Barth, "Introduction," p. 14.

90. Hegmon, "Technology, Style, and Social Practices," pp. 274–275.

91. Ibid., p. 277.

92. On this topic, in general, see Ohnuki-Tierney, *Rice as Self.*

93. On state rituals in the Nara period, see Piggott, *Emergence of Japanese Kingship*, pp. 208–215; on the *daijōsai*, an old but still useful work is Ellwood, *Feast of Kingship;* on the evolution of Shinto in general (including state rituals as well as the various myths in the *Nihon shoki* and *Kojiki*), see Matsumae, "Early Kami Worship." The story of Susano-o appears in Philippi, trans., *Kojiki*, pp. 79–86.

94. "Rice monoculture": Amino, *Nihonron no shiza*, pp. 44–58, and "Deconstructing 'Japan,'" p. 132. Other recent works stressing the importance of nonagriculturists in Japanese society are idem, *Nihon shakai saikō*, pp. 6–56; *Zoku Nihon no rekishi o yominaosu*, pp. 8–47; "Emperor, Rice, and Commoners"; and *"Nihon" to wa nani ka*, pp. 238–330.

95. Howell, "Ainu Ethnicity," p. 69.

96. Ibid., p. 71.

Chapter 4. Premodern Japan in World-Systems Theory

1. Regarding this distinction, see Chase-Dunn and Hall, *Rise and Demise*, pp. 16–19; and Wigen, "Culture, Power, and Place," pp. 1184–1185.

2. Perhaps the best-known example of this approach in East Asian studies is G. William Skinner's work on economic "macroregions" in China: Skinner, ed., *The City in Late Imperial China.*

3. Some authors prefer to omit the hyphen and put "system" in the singular. The seemingly petty debate over terms reflects a more fundamental difference of opinion over whether there has been just one "world system" or several (see below). Regarding terminology, see Wallerstein, "World System versus World-Systems."

4. Wallerstein, *The Modern World-System*, vols. 1–3.

5. Taylor, *Political Geography*, pp. 10–11.

6. Ibid., p. 10.

7. Ibid., p. 19.

8. Ibid., p. 21.

9. Ibid., p. 18.

10. See Blaut, *Colonizer's Model of the World;* and Diamond, *Guns, Germs, and Steel.*

11. On the relationship between economic and politico-military power, see Kennedy, *Rise and Fall.*

12. Hall, "World-Systems and Evolution," p. 13.

13. Taylor, *Political Geography*, pp. 13–16.

14. Ibid.

15. Ibid., pp. 16–17.

16. Wallerstein, "World System versus World-Systems" and "Hold the Tiller Firm"; Amin, "Ancient World-Systems."

17. Bergesen, "Pre- vs. Post-1500ers."

18. Chase-Dunn and Hall, *Rise and Demise*, p. 11.

19. Frank and Gills, *World System.*

20. Regarding these points, see the three essays by these authors in *World System:* Frank and Gills, "The 5,000-Year World System," and Gills and Frank, "Cumulation of Accumulation" and "World System Cycles, Crises, and Hegemonic Shifts."

21. Abu-Lughod, "Discontinuities and Persistence," p. 279 (emphasis in original removed).

22. Ibid., p. 288.

23. Abu-Lughod, *Before European Hegemony*, p. 284.

24. Ibid., p. 366.

25. Ibid.

26. Chase-Dunn and Hall, *Rise and Demise.*

27. Ibid., p. 28.

28. Ibid., p. 52.

29. Ibid., p. 53.

30. Ibid.

31. Ibid.

32. Wilkinson, "Central Civilization," pp. 47–48 (emphasis in original removed).

33. Bentley, *Old World Encounters.*

34. Chase-Dunn and Hall, *Rise and Demise*, p. 150.

35. Ibid., *Rise and Demise*, pp. 168–170; Bentley, *Old World Encounters*, pp. 67–69.

36. Chase-Dunn and Hall, *Rise and Demise*, pp. 200–229.

37. Ibid., p. 204 (emphasis in original removed).

38. Ibid., p. 206.

39. Ibid., p. 210 (emphasis in original removed).

40. Note that this idea has found support in other, more recent, studies of premodern world-systems—for example, Kardulias, *World-Systems Theory*.

41. So and Chiu, *East Asia*.

42. Sanderson, *Social Transformations*, pp. 134–180.

43. Hudson, *Ruins of Identity*.

44. Tanaka, "Sekai shisutemu ron," p. 239.

45. Murai, *Umi kara mita Sengoku Nihon*, pp. 16–17.

Chapter 5. Political and Military Interactions

1. Wilkinson, "Civilizations, Cores"; "Central Civilization"; and "Civilizations *Are* World Systems!"

2. Wilkinson, "Central Civilization," p. 47 (Table 2.1).

3. Chase-Dunn and Hall, *Rise and Demise*, p. 28.

4. A. Lee, *Information and Frontiers*, p. 151. Lee cites the classic study by Mayhew and Levinger, "Size and Density of Interaction."

5. For a formula and an explanation, see Norton, *Human Geography*, pp. 292–293.

6. Kamada, "Nihon kodai no jinkō," p. 270; Hayami, "Jinkōshi," p. 125.

7. For a more detailed discussion of these points, see my *Kokkyō no tanjō*, pp. 102–132.

8. On which, see Nishijima, *Nihon rekishi no kokusai kankyō* and *Kodai Higashi Ajia sekai to Nihon*.

9. For general background, see Barnes, *China Korea and Japan*, pp. 218–220 and 244–245; Piggott, *Emergence of Japanese Kingship*, pp. 15–65; and Farris, *Sacred Texts*, pp. 9–54. The sources in question are translated in Tsunoda et al., *Sources of Japanese Tradition*, vol. 1, pp. 4–9. For the original sources, see Ishihara, *Shintei Gishi Washinden hoka sanpen*, pp. 39–54 *(Wei History)*, 55–59 *(History of the Later Han)*, and 60–64 *(Song History)*.

10. See the works cited in note 35 to Chapter 1, above.

11. These events are described in detail in Batten, *Kokkyō no tanjō*, pp. 59–80, and "Foreign Threat and Domestic Reform." Also see Inoue with Brown, "Century of Reform," pp. 184–188, 201–210.

12. For background on relations with Silla and Parhae in the Nara–early Heian period, see the works cited in note 31 to Chapter 1.

13. Batten, *Kokkyō no tanjō*.

14. On Japan's relations with Tang, see the various works cited in note 30 of Chapter 1. The two books by Reischauer are specifically on Ennin (one is a translation of the diary).

15. On tenth-century "isolationism," the classic study is Ishigami, "Nihon kodai 10 seiki no gaikō." In English, McCullough, "Heian Court," pp. 80–96, provides a good general introduction to Heian-period foreign relations.

16. Batten, *Kokkyō no tanjō*, pp. 210–212; McCullough, "Heian Court," p. 95.

17. Hori, "Economic and Political Effects"; Ishii, "Decline of the Kamakura Bakufu," pp. 131–148; Kawazoe, "Japan and East Asia," pp. 411–423; Conlan, *In Little Need.* Recent works in Japanese include Kaizu, *Mōko shūrai;* Seki, *Kamikaze to bushi zō;* Murai, *Chūsei Nihon no uchi to soto*, pp. 97–123, and *Hōjō Tokimune to Mōko shūrai.*

18. On the Wakō, see the works cited in note 64 of Chapter 1.

19. On these "missions to Ming" *(kenminshi)*, otherwise known as the "tally trade" *(kangō bōeki)*, see Tanaka with Sakai, "Japan's Relations with Overseas Countries," pp. 163–171, and Kawazoe, "Japan and East Asia," pp. 432–440.

20. See sources cited in note 76, Chapter 1.

21. On Westerners and the Wakō, see Murai, *Umi kara mita sengoku Nihon*, pp. 105–143.

22. For details, see Lach, *Asia in the Making of Europe*, vol. 1, bk. 2, pp. 688–706.

23. For translations of the relevant decrees, see Lu, *Japan*, pp. 221–223.

24. Itō, "Emishi to Hayato wa doko ga chigau ka," p. 71.

25. For specific information on individual diplomatic missions and other events, refer to the following exhaustive chronologies of foreign relations: Tajima, "Nihon, Chūgoku, Chōsen taigai kōryū shi nenpyō" (covering the Nara-Heian periods), and Taigai kankei shi sōgō nenpyō henshū iinkai, *Taigai kankei shi sōgō nenpyō* (covering all periods).

26. Dates from chronologies in Shimojō et al., *Shinpan kodai no Nihon 3 Kyushu, Okinawa*, pp. 584–585, and Sudō et al., *Shinpan kodai no Nihon 9 Tōhoku, Hokkaidō*, pp. 576–577.

27. The concept of "secondary state formation" is also invoked in this context by Barnes, *China Korea and Japan*, pp. 241–243, and Piggott, *Emergence of Japanese Kingship*, pp. 10 (Figure 1), 11.

28. Turner, *Frontier in American History*, p. 1.

29. On Turner and his legacy, see Klein, *Frontiers of Historical Imagination.* As noted in the Introduction to the present work, much of the New Western History can be read as a reaction to Turner; Limerick, *Legacy of Conquest*, is a case in point. For an example of comparative history using the "Turner Hypothesis," see Drummond and Nelson, *Western Frontiers of Imperial Rome.*

30. Takahashi, *Henkyō*, p. 18.

31. In earlier times (i.e., the Japanese Yayoi and Kofun periods), however, there was a clear disparity between the two regions. Korean society was much

more "advanced," and the flow of technologies, ideas, and political influence was virtually one-way from the peninsula to the islands.

32. Unification wars: Batten, "Foreign Threat and Domestic Reform"; Mori, *"Hakusukinoe" igo.* Pirate attacks: Ishigami, "Nihon kodai 10 seiki no gaikō," pp. 100–109, and "Kodai kokka to taigai kankei," pp. 253–263, 277–283; Murai, "Ōdo ōmin shisō to 9 seiki no tenkan," pp. 30–37; Batten, *Kokkyō no tanjō*, pp. 165–203.

33. Note that this view is not original with me. For earlier applications of the "peer-polity" concept to the Korean Peninsula and Japan, see Barnes, "Jiehao, Tonghao," and Piggott, *Emergence of Japanese Kingship*, pp. 22–23.

34. Renfrew and Bahn, *Archaeology*, pp. 364–366.

Chapter 6. Bulk Goods

1. However, it can be argued that in premodern times "money" in the form of coins or bullion was traded just like other goods and thus served a fundamentally different purpose from that of money today. See, for example, Pomeranz, *Great Divergence*, pp. 160–161.

2. Heijō-kyō: Tsuboi and Tanaka, *Historic City of Nara*, pp. 126–130; Heian-kyō: McCullough, "The Capital," pp. 121–123; Edo: Totman, *Early Modern Japan*, p. 153; Hanley, *Everyday Things in Premodern Japan*, p. 105.

3. Eighth century: Kamada, "Nihon kodai no jinkō," p. 270; Eighteenth century: Hayami, "Jinkōshi," p. 125.

4. *Ritsuryō* refers to the Chinese-style penal *(ritsu)* and administrative *(ryō)* law codes, which formed the basis of government in this period. On the *ritsuryō* system, see Inoue, "The *Ritsuryō* System"; Kiley, "*Ritsuryō* System"; Steenstrup, *History of Law*, pp. 30–70; Naoki, "The Nara State," pp. 231–241; Torao, "Nara Economic and Social Institutions"; Ishigami, "State and Society"; and Piggott, *Emergence of Japanese Kingship*, pp. 167–235.

5. This is the date the code was implemented; it was drafted much earlier, in 718. The Yōrō Code is the only surviving Japanese *ritsuryō* code; it was preceded by the Ōmi Code of 668, the Asuka Kiyomihara Code of 689, and the Taihō Code of 701. The Ōmi and Asuka Kiyomihara codes are thought to have lacked the penal regulations *(ritsu)* found in later codes. For details, see Miller, *Japan's First Bureaucracy*, pp. 22–44; Inoue with Brown, "Century of Reform," pp. 214–216; Naoki, "The Nara State," p. 231; Ishigami, "State and Society," pp. 23–24 (Figure 2); and Piggott, *Emergence of Japanese Kingship*, pp. 118, 135–139, 167–170.

6. For a discussion of this point, see Batten, "Provincial Administration," pp. 111–114.

7. For an excellent discussion of the various types of historical and archaeological sources available for the Nara period, see Piggott, *Emergence of Japanese Kingship*, pp. 287–303.

8. Provincial and district headquarters: Tanaka, "Early Historical Periods," pp. 82–86; Kinoshita, *Kokufu*, pp. 30–86; Yamanaka, *Kodai chihō kanga*

iseki no kenkyū; Satō, "Kyūto, kokufu, gūke"; Roads: Kinoshita, *Kodai o kangaeru: Kodai dōro;* Motogi, *Kodai no dōro jijō;* Nakamura, *Nihon no kodai dōro o sagasu.*

9. On *mokkan,* see Tanaka, "Early Historical Periods," pp. 76–82; Piggott, "*Mokkan*"; Tsuboi and Tanaka, *Historic City of Nara,* pp. 76–83; and Farris, *Sacred Texts,* pp. 201–232. In Japanese, good surveys of the topic are Kitō, *Mokkan;* and Tōno, *Mokkan ga kataru.*

10. On *nie:* Tsuboi and Tanaka, *Historic City of Nara,* pp. 78–79; Ishigami, "State and Society," p. 30; Farris, *Sacred Texts,* pp. 217–219.

11. Information on tax items in this and the following paragraphs is from the map in Satō, "Chihō shihai," pp. 126–127. Also see map in Sasayama et al., *Yamakawa Nihonshi sōgō zuroku (zōhoban),* p. 24, and discussion of tax items in Watanabe, "Nifuda mokkan."

12. For a discussion of this point for a slightly later period, see Koyama, "Kodai makki no Tōgoku to Saigoku," p. 257.

13. Here and elsewhere I rely heavily on Yamamoto, *Waei taishō Nihon kōkogaku yōgo jiten/Dictionary of Japanese Archaeological Terms,* for English equivalents to Japanese zoological and botanical terms.

14. Regarding the breakdown of the tax system, see Morris, "Land and Society," pp. 199–215.

15. Regarding provincial administration in the Heian period, see Batten, "Provincial Administration," and Kiley, "Provincial Administration."

16. *Shinsarugakuki* (Shirō no kimi jō), pp. 238–239.

17. The literature on *shōen* is, of course, vast, but some of the more important works in English are Nagahara, "Landownership"; Kiley, "Estate and Property" and "Provincial Administration," esp. pp. 283–326; Sato, "Early Development of the *Shōen,*" "Ōyama Estate," and "*Shōen*"; Kudō, "*Shōen*"; Keirstead, *Geography of Power;* Ōyama, "Medieval *Shōen*"; and Morris, "Land and Society," pp. 224–235.

18. Koyama, "Kodai makki no Tōgoku to Saigoku," pp. 256–257.

19. Ibid., pp. 257–258.

20. On the Nara period, see Farris, "Trade, Money, and Merchants." On the Heian period, see Yamamura, "Growth of Commerce," pp. 344–360. Regarding medieval commerce, see Yamamura, op cit.; Toyoda et al., "Growth of Commerce"; Wakita, "Toward a Wider Perspective" and "Cities in Medieval Japan"; Miura, "Villages and Trade"; and Souyri, *World Turned Upside Down,* pp. 153–160.

21. *Shinsarugakuki* (Hachirō no mahito jō), p. 280.

22. Yoshioka, "Tōjiki no michi o saguru."

23. Wakita, "Chūsei doki no ryūtsū."

24. Yamamura, "Growth of Commerce," pp. 364–366, 381–383; Kodama, *Nihon kōtsūshi,* pp. 81–86, 93–95.

25. Reproduced in Hayashiya, *Hyōgo kitaseki irifune nōchō.*

26. Kodama, *Nihon kōtsūshi,* pp. 111–117.

27. Makabe, "Bōeki taikei no hen'yō," pp. 137–138.

28. Sasaki with Hauser, "Sengoku Daimyo."

29. On transportation and travel in the Edo period, the definitive work in English is Vaporis, *Breaking Barriers.* On economic growth, see Wakita, "Social and Economic Consequences," and Nakai and McClain, "Commercial Changes." Regarding the city of Edo itself, a good overview can be found in Jinnai, "Spatial Structure of Edo."

30. On *sankin kōtai,* see Totman, *Early Modern Japan,* pp. 108–110. There is also a book-length study by Tsukahira, *Feudal Control.*

31. Kodama and Sugiyama, *Tōkyo to no rekishi,* pp. 176–184. For background information on mercantile activity and consumption patterns, see Nakai and McClain, "Commercial Changes," and Moriya, "Urban Networks."

32. For historical information on consumption patterns, not just in Edo but countrywide, the best sources in English are Hanley, "Tokugawa Society" and *Everyday Things in Premodern Japan.*

33. Most of the information in this paragraph comes from Vaporis, "Digging for Edo," pp. 83–93. (I have revised the translations of some botanical/zoological terms for the sake of consistency.) On this topic in Japanese, see Koizumi, *Edo no kōkogaku,* and Edo iseki kenkyūkai, *Edo bunka no kōkogaku.*

34. Moriya, "Urban Networks," pp. 99–101.

35. On the question of capitalism, see Sanderson, *Social Transformations,* pp. 134–180, and Howell, *Capitalism from Within,* esp. pp. 2–16.

36. These rights were confirmed in "black-seal" orders issued by Ieyasu and his successors to the lords of Matsumae. For details and a translation of the first order, dating from 1603, see Walker, *Conquest of Ainu Lands,* pp. 36–37.

37. Ibid., pp. 204–226; Howell, "Ainu Ethnicity."

38. Walker, *Conquest of Ainu Lands,* pp. 87–88. Also see Kikuchi, *Ainu minzoku to Nihonjin,* pp. 79–82.

39. Walker, *Conquest of Ainu Lands,* pp. 87–98.

40. Howell, *Capitalism from Within,* pp. 24–49. Also see Kikuchi, *Ainu minzoku to Nihonjin,* pp. 111–121, and the various essays in Hokkaidō, Tōhoku shi kenkyūkai, *Basho ukeoi sei to Ainu.*

41. See Walker, *Conquest of Ainu Lands,* pp. 91–94.

42. Kikuchi, *Ainu minzoku to Nihonjin,* p. 169.

43. For more on herring, see Howell, *Capitalism from Within.*

44. Kikuchi, *Ainu minzoku to Nihonjin,* pp. 181–184; Walker, *Conquest of Ainu Lands,* pp. 91–94.

45. Fujimoto, *Mō futatsu no Nihon bunka,* pp. 56–58.

46. Ibid., pp. 86–92.

47. Arano et al., "Jiki kubunron," pp. 46–47.

48. Kikuchi, *Ainu minzoku to Nihonjin,* p. 186; Walker, *Conquest of Ainu Lands,* pp. 94–97.

Chapter 7. Prestige Goods

1. Peregrine, "Legitimation Crises."

2. Hamashita is a prolific author. Probably his best-known work is a 1990 monograph, *Kindai Chūgoku no kokusaiteki keiki.* (Most of the important ideas in this book can be found in more condensed form in a 1989 article, "Higashi Ajia kokusai taikei.") Hamashita has also served as coeditor of various books and series, among them Mizoguchi et al., eds., *Ajia kara kangaeru* (7 vols.), and Hamashita and Karashima, eds., *Chiiki no sekai shi 1.* Hamashita also has several articles in English, including "The Tribute Trade System and Modern Asia," "Contemporary China and the Study of Modern History," and "The Intra-Regional System in East Asia in Modern Times."

3. Nishijima, *Nihon rekishi no kokusai kankyō* and *Kodai Higashi Ajia sekai to Nihon.*

4. Hamashita, *Kindai Chūgoku no kokusaiteki keiki,* p. 33.

5. Hamashita, "Jo," pp. 7–8. Hamashita also discusses "maritime regions" in a recent popular work, *Okinawa nyūmon.*

6. Abu-Lughod, *Before European Hegemony,* pp. 251–260.

7. Hamashita, "Jo," p. 4.

8. Arano et al., "Jiki kubunron," p. 6.

9. Ibid., p. 40.

10. Although I will not be citing it for each specific point, one very important work on this general topic is von Verschuer, *Le commerce extérieur du Japon.*

11. The (imputed) motivations of Japanese leaders in establishing diplomatic relations with foreign states are discussed in more detail in my book, *Kokkyō no tanjō,* pp. 116–120. For an excellent discussion in English of how and why political leaders in the islands sought to obtain prestige goods through investiture, see Hudson, *Ruins of Identity,* pp. 182–193.

12. On Pimiko, see the sources cited in note 9 of Chapter 5. The mirrors are discussed in Farris, *Sacred Texts,* pp. 42–46, and Edwards, "Mirrors on Ancient Yamato." Also note that although the seal presented to Pimiko is not extant, another gold seal, sent (according to the inscription) by the Han court to the "King of Na in Wa," was discovered in 1784 by a farmer in Shikanoshima, located on the east side of Hakata Bay in what is now Fukuoka prefecture. See Barnes, *China Korea and Japan,* p. 218.

13. See sources cited in note 33 to Chapter 5.

14. This topic is discussed in detail by Farris, *Sacred Texts,* pp. 70–83. For a book-length study of the diffusion of iron tools and iron-making technology in early Japan, see Murakami, *Wajin to tetsu no kōkogaku.*

15. Farris, *Sacred Texts,* p. 82.

16. This point is also made by Hudson, *Ruins of Identity,* p. 188. Note also Hudson's refreshingly honest assessment that "[t]he reasons Yamato became the dominant polity in protohistoric Japan are still poorly understood" (ibid.). This is a fundamental question that has yet to be properly addressed in the

literature, most of which seems to assume that Yamato was simply destined to come out ahead.

17. On Iwai, see Oda, *Kodai o kangaeru: Iwai no ran*, and Yamao, *Tsukushi no kimi Iwai no sensō.*

18. Tōno, *Kentōshi to Shōsōin*, pp. 117–213, and *Kentōshi sen*, pp. 132–146; Lee Sungsi, *Higashi Ajia no ōken to kōeki.*

19. On foreign commerce in the Heian period, see Mori, "Beginning of Overseas Advance" and *Shintei Nissō bōeki no kenkyū;* Ishii, "10 seiki no kokusai hendō to Nissō bōeki"; Kamei, "Kōrokan bōeki" and "Nissō bōeki kankei no tenkai"; Tsuchibashi, "Nissō bōeki no shosō"; and Batten, *Kokkyō no tanjō*, pp. 126–228.

20. On the Chinatown, and Hakata generally, see Saeki, "Hakata." The view that trade was conducted at coastal *shōen* is disputed by Yamauchi Shinji, who argues that the government maintained strong control over trade through the end of the Heian period. This view strikes me as extreme, although I do not have the space to refute it here. (A few details are provided in *Kokkyō no tanjō*, pp. 236–238.) Yamauchi has a number of articles, but the first and most influential is "Nissō no shōen nai mitsu bōeki setsu."

21. This can be established on archaeological grounds, at least for one important category of imports—porcelain. See Kamei, *Nihon bōeki tōjishi no kenkyū*, pp. 115–137.

22. Kodama, *Nihon kōtsūshi*, p. 80; Kawazoe, "Japan and East Asia," pp. 408–411.

23. Mori, "Beginning of Overseas Advance" and *Shintei Nissō bōeki no kenkyū;* Tsuchibashi, "Nissō bōeki no shosō," pp. 62–63.

24. Enomoto, "Sōdai no 'Nihon shōnin' no saikentō."

25. On Japanese ships in Southeast Asia (the "vermilion-seal ships," or *shuinsen*), see Iwao, "Japanese Foreign Trade," pp. 8–10, and Innes, "The Door Ajar," pp. 51–66.

26. Needless to say, a great deal of scholarly ink has been spilled on the topic of Europeans in sixteenth-century Japan. Among good recent works are Massarella, *A World Elsewhere*, and Elisonias, "Christianity and the Daimyo."

27. On which, see Kawazoe, "Japan and East Asia," pp. 432–440.

28. For background information on the changing context of foreign trade during this sixteenth and seventeenth centuries, see Innes, "The Door Ajar," pp. 21–243. Other important sources include Iwao, "Japanese Foreign Trade," and other articles in the same issue of *Acta Asiatica:* Takase, "Unauthorized Commercial Activities"; Katō, "The Japan-Dutch Trade"; Tashiro, "Tsushima-han's Korean Trade"; and Yamawaki, "Great Trading Merchants."

29. At Nagasaki, according to Englebert Kaempfer, Japanese smugglers sometimes followed departing Chinese junks in order to buy their unsold goods. When caught, they were generally executed. Kaempfer, *Kaempfer's Japan*, pp. 221–222.

30. On which, again, see the works by Tōno listed in note 18, above.

31. The comprehensive chronology of foreign relations compiled by Tajima, "Nihon, Chūgoku, Chōsen taigai kōryū shi nenpyō," has a column listing all imports and exports (including gifts carried by embassies) given in the original source materials.

32. *Shinsarugakuki* (Hachirō no mahito jō), pp. 280–281.

33. For descriptions of these and similar items, see the fascinating work by Schafer, *Golden Peaches of Samarkand.*

34. Abu-Lughod, *Before European Hegemony.*

35. Wang, *The Nanhai Trade;* Reischauer, "Notes."

36. Reid, *Southeast Asia.*

37. Seki, "Kōryō no michi to Nihon, Chōsen."

38. There are many published works on the Sinan vessel, but a convenient summary of the finds can be found in Yamamoto, "Shin'an kaitei ibutsu."

39. Tsuchibashi, "Nissō bōeki no shosō," p. 73 (Table 2).

40. Ibid. The first good analysis of the regional distribution of porcelain finds, now somewhat out of date, was by Kamei, *Nihon bōeki tōjishi no kenkyū,* pp. 115–137.

41. For general information on imported coins, see Tōno, *Kahei no Nihonshi,* pp. 67–84.

42. Suzuki, "Shutsudo senka," p. 127 (Table 1).

43. See, for example, Hashiguchi, "'Mainōsen' no juryoku" and "Zeni o umeru koto."

44. On imported coins and monetization, see Yamamura, "Growth of Commerce," pp. 366–368. Amino, *Nihon no rekishi o yominaosu,* pp. 43–77, also provides a good introduction to this topic. Amino sees the fourteenth century, in particular, as a turning point in the development of a monetized, commercial economy.

45. Minegishi, "Chūsei no 'maizōsen' ni tsuite no oboegaki."

46. Suzuki, "Shutsudo senka," p. 128.

47. Morita, "Shinori no 40 man mai no kosen."

48. Commerce in the Edo period is covered in Nakai and McClain, "Commercial Changes." On the minting of coins, see Totman, *Early Modern Japan,* pp. 70–71.

49. Kaempfer, *Kaempfer's Japan,* p. 209.

50. Ibid. The various works cited in note 28, above, also contain helpful information on imports during the early modern period.

51. Hagiwara, "Nagasaki Dejima to Hirado no Oranda shōkan."

52. For more on Dutch goods in Japan, see Oka, "Exotic 'Holland'"; Tanaka-van Daalen, "Popular Use of Imported Materials"; Keene, *Japanese Discovery of Europe,* p. 19.

53. Totman, *Early Modern Japan,* p. 148.

54. J. Lee, "Trade and Economy," p. 8.

55. See Innes, "The Door Ajar," pp. 474–523, and Jansen, *China in the Tokugawa World,* pp. 35–41.

56. Tsuchibashi, "Nissō bōeki no shosō," pp. 63–64.

57. See sources cited in note 11 to Chapter 6.

58. Kikuchi, *Ainu minzoku to Nihonjin*, p. 154. Walker, *Conquest of Ainu Lands*, pp. 75–76 and elsewhere (see index to his book), discusses Ainu hunting of Stellar's sea eagles for their feathers.

59. Katō, "The Japan-Dutch Trade," p. 42. On lacquer exports, see Viallé, "Japanse *[sic]* Export Lacquer."

60. Lach, *Asia in the Making of Europe*, vol. 1, bk. 2, pp. 693, 694, 697.

61. Morris-Suzuki, *Technological Transformation*, p. 30; Iwao, "Japanese Foreign Trade," pp. 16–17.

62. For more on sulfur, see the fascinating commentary in Kaempfer, *Kaempfer's Japan*, pp. 57–58.

63. Lach, *Asia in the Making of Europe*, vol. 1, bk. 1, p. 37.

64. Chūsonji: Yiengpruksawan, *Hiraizumi*. Porcelain: Tsuchibashi, "Nissō bōeki no shosō," pp. 71–72.

65. See Kaempfer, *Kaempfer's Japan*, p. 59.

66. Innes, "The Door Ajar," pp. 524–527; Iwao, "Japanese Foreign Trade," pp. 16–17; Nagazumi, "Decline of Trade," pp. 57, 59.

67. Murai, *Umi kara mita Sengoku Nihon*, pp. 145–183. On mines and mining technology (not just for silver but also gold and copper), see Innes, "The Door Ajar," pp. 524–618, as well as Morris-Suzuki, *Technological Transformation*, pp. 43–49. Silver exports are covered in Innes, "The Door Ajar," pp. 524–526 (among many other places in the text); for additional details, see Katō, "The Japan-Dutch Trade," pp. 41–44.

68. Copper and copper exports: Innes, "The Door Ajar," pp. 526–530; Iwao, "Japanese Foreign Trade," p. 16; Kaempfer, *Kaempfer's Japan*, p. 60; Nagazumi, "Decline of Trade," pp. 59, 61; Suzuki, "Production and Export of Japanese Copper."

69. For other examples of Japanese goods imported to Europe in the Edo period, see Forrer, "Nineteenth Century Japanese Collections."

70. The best source on all of these is Yamazato, *Kodai Nihon to Nantō no kōryū*, pp. 149–186.

71. On which, see Walker, *Conquest of Ainu Lands*, p. 196.

72. Ibid., pp. 109–117.

73. See Sasaki, *Hoppō kara kita kōekimin;* Sasaki, "Trading Brokers and Partners"; and Walker, *Conquest of Ainu Lands*, pp. 128–154.

74. Hanley, *Everyday Things in Premodern Japan*, pp. 80–81, 161.

Chapter 8. Information

1. *The Random House Dictionary of the English Language*, 2d ed. unabridged, s.v. "information."

2. There are a few exceptions, notably Moriya, "Urban Networks and Information Networks," which (among other things) describes the domestic communications system in early modern times. In Japanese there are a

number of studies with "*jōhō*" in the title, many of them relating to premodern relations with China. Examples include Tanaka, "Sōgo ninshiki to jōhō," and von Verschuer, "9 seiki Nihon no jōhō yu'nyū taisei."

3. A. D. Lee, *Information and Frontiers*, p. 139.

4. Ibid., p. 154.

5. Ibid., p. 183.

6. Ibid., pp. 183–184.

7. Ferguson and Whitehead, *War in the Tribal Zone;* see also pp. 102 and 240–241 of the present study.

8. Lee, *Information and Frontiers*, p. 6.

9. See discussion in ibid., pp. 166–184.

10. For background information on diplomatic protocol see (for the ancient period) Wang, "Sino-Japanese Relations"; Tajima, "Nihon no ritsuryō kokka no 'hinrai'"; and (for early modern times) Toby, *State and Diplomacy*, pp. 168–230.

11. See Tajima, "Kentōshi wa naze haken sareta ka," and other sources cited in note 30, Chapter 1.

12. Smits, *Visions of Ryukyu*, pp. 20–23.

13. Batten, "State and Frontier in Early Japan," p. 151; Yamazato, *Kodai Nihon to Nantō no kōryū*, pp. 67–85.

14. For more information, see Keene, *Japanese Discovery of Europe*, pp. 123–155, and Unno, "Cartography in Japan," pp. 443–453.

15. Lee, *Information and Frontiers*, p. 162.

16. Translated into English by Reischauer as *Ennin's Diary*. (The original title is *Nittō guhō junrei kōki* [Record of a pilgrimage to Tang in search of the law].) Also see the companion study by Reischauer, *Ennin's Travels.*

17. Again, one of the most convenient references is Elisonias, "Christianity and the Daimyo." An older but still immensely useful source of information is Lach, *Asia in the Making of Europe*, vol. 1, bk. 2, pp. 651–729. Some of the writings of the various missionaries are collected in Cooper, *They Came to Japan.*

18. See Curtin, *Cross-Cultural Trade.*

19. See Murai, *Umi kara mita Sengoku Nihon*, pp. 127–133.

20. On Korean piracy in the ninth century, see Batten, *Kokkyō no tanjō*, pp. 177–179, 188–94.

21. On immigrants, see Hirano, *Kikajin to kodai kokka;* Batten, "Dazaifu no kokkyō kinō," pp. 397–402.

22. Keene, *Japanese Discovery of Europe*, pp. 46–58.

23. I discuss this topic in more detail in *Kokkyō no tanjō*, pp. 110–114.

24. See note 57 to Chapter 3 for sources.

25. For more details, see Walker, *Conquest of Ainu Lands*, pp. 32–33.

26. Information summarized from Sugimoto and Swain, *Science and Culture*, Appendix, Table A.2 (no pages given). On what Sugimoto and Swain call "Chinese Wave II," another fundamental reference in English is Jansen, *China in the Tokugawa World.*

27. On Jōjin, see Borgen, "*San Tendai Godai sanki*"; "Through Several Glasses Brightly"; "Case of the Plagiaristic Journal"; and "Japanese Nationalism." On cross-border travel by Zen monks, see Collcutt, "Zen and the *Gozan*," or, for more detail, Collcutt, *Five Mountains.*

28. Tōno, *Kentōshi sen*, pp. 158–164.

29. See the sources cited in notes 16 (Toi) and 17 (Mongols) to Chapter 5.

30. For a detailed analysis of intelligence-gathering activities by the Edo shogunate, see Toby, *State and Diplomacy*, pp. 110–167.

31. Toby, "Imagining and Imaging 'Anthropos,'" p. 19.

32. See idem, "The 'Indianness' of Iberia," p. 328. On the eighth-century monk Bodai Senna, also see pp. 152–153 of the present work.

33. On Prince Takaoka, see Tajima, "Shinnyo (Takaoka) Shinnō ikkō no 'nittō' no tabi."

34. Again, this summary of research by Sugimoto and Swain is based on *Science and Culture in Traditional Japan*, Appendix, Table A.2. Another indispensable source on Western technology in the Edo period is Morris-Suzuki, *Technological Transformation of Japan*, pp. 13–54. On *Rangaku*, see the sources cited in note 29, Chapter Three.

35. For details, see Toby, "Imagining and Imaging 'Anthropos.'" On cartography per se, see Unno, "Cartography in Japan." Another relevant article is Yonemoto, "Maps and Metaphors."

36. Again, for details see Toby, *State and Diplomacy*, pp. 110–167.

37. Tsunoda et al., *Sources of Japanese Tradition*, vol. 1, pp. 3–12; Ishihara, *Shintei Gishi Washinden hoka sanpen.*

38. Lach, *Asia in the Making of Europe*, vol. 1, bk. 2, pp. 652–654.

39. Ibid., pp. 709–710, 729.

40. Ibid., p. 705.

41. Kaempfer, *Kaempfer's Japan*, p. 27.

42. Ibid.

43. For details, see Keene, *Japanese Discovery of Europe*, pp. 147–154.

44. Ichimura and Ōishi, *Sakoku.*

Chapter 9. Japan, East Asia, and the World

1. This is also the position taken by Murai in *Umi kara mita Sengoku Nihon.* (See discussion on pp. 141–142, above.)

2. So and Chiu, *East Asia*, p. 32.

3. Ibid., p. 31.

4. Taylor, *Political Geography*, p. 14.

5. Frank and Gills, *World System.*

6. Taylor, *Political Geography*, p. 16.

7. For example, see Atwell, "Some Observations" and "Seventeenth-Century 'General Crisis'"; also see Frank, *ReOrient*, pp. 226–257.

8. The term "stasis" is borrowed from Totman, *Early Modern Japan.* In general, older works describe the second half of the Edo period in terms

of economic "stagnation" or "decline," whereas newer studies emphasize continued (albeit less rapid) growth. For a good discussion, see Hanley, *Everyday Things in Premodern Japan*, esp. pp. 14–24.

9. Metzler, "Capitalist Boom," p. 105.

10. Ibid., p. 106.

11. Another measure of economic isolation is the difference in conversion rates from gold to silver. As Susan Hanley notes, Japan's economy was "so closed that by the mid-nineteenth century the ratio of silver to gold was 5 or 6:1, compared with a 12 to 15:1 ratio in the West." Hanley, *Everyday Things in Premodern Japan*, p. 7.

Chapter 10. Social Power: Causes and Consequences

1. Guy and Sheridan, "On Frontiers," p. 10.

2. Mann, *Sources of Social Power*, p. 6.

3. Ibid., p. 2 (emphasis in original removed).

4. Diamond, *Guns, Germs, and Steel.*

5. This scheme is based partly on Diamond's work and partly on the discussion in Ferguson and Whitehead, "Violent Edge," pp. 8–12.

6. The goals and strategies of "state actors" in the "tribal zone" are discussed by Ferguson and Whitehead, "Violent Edge," p. 7. Doyle, *Empires*, analyzes the various strategies employed by "metropolitan" (i.e., imperial) and "peripheral" actors in the context of imperial expansion.

7. See Thompson and Lamar, "Comparative Frontier History," p. 9.

8. Ferguson and Whitehead, "Violent Edge," pp. 13–14.

9. White, *Middle Ground.* For applications of this concept to Japanese-Ainu relations, see Howell, "Kinsei Hokkaidō," and Walker, *Conquest of Ainu Lands*, esp. pp. 8–12 and 204–226.

10. Scott, *Weapons of the Weak.*

11. Piggott, *Emergence of Japanese Kingship*, pp. 8, 234.

12. Kudō, *Jōsaku to Emishi*, pp. 137–143.

13. Friday, "Pushing beyond the Pale," pp. 14–16. It is difficult to resist drawing the obvious parallels with the U.S. experience in Vietnam or the Soviet experience in Afghanistan.

14. Regarding the organizational disadvantages of tribal societies in the face of imperial expansion, see Doyle, *Empires*, pp. 131–133.

15. *Random House Dictionary of the English Language*, 2d ed. unabridged, s.v. "technology."

16. Fujimoto, *Mō futatsu no Nihon bunka*, p. 43.

17. Matsuzaki, "Dōnan no Wajin to tachi," p. 122.

18. Fujimoto, *Mō futatsu no Nihon bunka*, pp. 56–57; Utagawa, "Ainu bunka no kōkogaku," pp. 173–174.

19. Fukuda, "Tetsu o chūshin ni mita hōppo kōeki," pp. 160–162.

20. Fukasawa, "Ainu minzoku o tōshite miru Nihon kōkogaku," pp. 225–237.

21. Regarding iron production in Japan, see Murakami, *Wajin to tetsu no kōkogaku.*

22. Livi-Bacci, *Concise History*, pp. 26–27.

23. Hayami, "Jinkōshi," pp. 120–127. For more on Japanese demography, see Hayami, *Historical Demography.*

24. For an up-to-date discussion, see Hanley, *Everyday Things in Premodern Japan*, pp. 129–154. For a review of the English literature to 1986, see Totman, "Tokugawa Peasants."

25. Walker, *Conquest of Ainu Lands*, pp. 181–182.

26. McNeill, *Plagues and Peoples.*

27. Ibid., p. 67.

28. Regarding population loss in the Americas, also see Livi-Bacci, *Concise History*, pp. 55–61, and Diamond, *Guns, Germs, and Steel*, pp. 210–212.

29. Crosby, *Columbian Exchange* and *Ecological Imperialism.*

30. Crosby, *Ecological Imperialism*, p. 293.

31. Diamond, *Guns, Germs, and Steel.*

32. McNeill, *Plagues and Peoples*, p. 124.

33. Ibid.

34. Farris, *Population, Disease, and Land*, p. 142.

35. Ibid., p. 73.

36. Jannetta, *Epidemics.*

37. Ibid., pp. 197–198.

38. Ibid., p. 200.

39. Walker, *Conquest of Ainu Lands*, p. 182.

40. Ibid., pp. 188–189.

41. Ibid., p. 193.

42. Ibid., p. 188. For more on the history of syphilis, see Suzuki, *Hone kara mita Nihonjin*, pp. 184–207. According to Suzuki, analysis of skeletal material from archaeological sites in Japan yields no evidence of syphilis-caused bone pathologies prior to 1500. Incidentally, he also calculates (again, on the basis of excavated bones) that fully half of the adult residents of Edo were infected with syphilis in early modern times!

43. Walker, *Conquest of Ainu Lands*, pp. 182–187, gives a concrete discussion of these points with respect to the Shizunai-Mitsuishi smallpox epidemic of 1845.

44. Good recent books on this topic include Zeigler, *Black Death;* Gottfried, *Black Death;* and Herlihy, *Black Death.*

45. Walker, *Conquest of Ainu Lands*, pp. 180–181.

46. Ibid., p. 180; also see Walker, "Matsumae Domain," pp. 246–247.

47. An alternative (and probably more likely) scenario is that the Hayato were simply assimilated within the Japanese population.

48. See the sources cited in note 54 to Chapter 1 and Murai, "Ōdo ōmin shisō," pp. 35–36.

49. See Ponting, *Green History*, for a good general treatment of this topic.

50. On deforestation, see Totman, *Green Archipelago*, pp. 9–33.

Works Cited

All Japanese-language works were published in Tokyo unless otherwise stated.

Abu-Lughod, Janet L. *Before European Hegemony: The World System A.D. 1250–1350.* New York: Oxford University Press, 1989.

———. "Discontinuities and Persistence: One World System or a Succession of Systems?" In *The World System: Five Hundred Years or Five Thousand?*, ed. Andre Gunder Frank and Barry K. Gills, pp. 278–291. London: Routledge, 1993.

Amin, Samir. "The Ancient World-Systems versus the Modern Capitalist World-System." In *The World System: Five Hundred Years or Five Thousand?*, ed. Andre Gunder Frank and Barry K. Gills, pp. 247–277. London: Routledge, 1993.

Amino Yoshihiko. "Deconstructing 'Japan.'" *East Asian History* 3 (1992): 121–142.

———. "Emperor, Rice, and Commoners." In *Multicultural Japan: Palaeolithic to Postmodern*, ed. Donald Denoon, Mark Hudson, Gavan McCormack, and Tessa Morris-Suzuki, pp. 235–244. Cambridge: Cambridge University Press, 1996.

———. *Higashi to nishi ga kataru Nihon no rekishi.* Soshiete bunko 7. Soshiete, 1982.

———. *Nihon no rekishi o yominaosu.* Chikuma purimaa bukkusu 50. Chikuma shobō, 1991.

———. *Nihonron no shiza: Rettō no shakai to kokka.* Shōgakukan, 1990.

———. *Nihon shakai saikō: Kaimin to rettō bunka.* Shōgakukan, 1994.

———. *"Nihon" to wa nani ka.* Nihon no rekishi 00. Kōdansha, 2000.

———. *Zoku Nihon no rekishi o yominaosu.* Chikuma purimaa bukkusu 96. Chikuma shobō, 1996.

Anderson, Benedict. *Imagined Communities: Reflections on the Origin and Spread of Nationalism.* Rev. ed. London: Verso, 1991.

Anderson, Malcolm. *Frontiers: Territory and State Formation in the Modern World.* Cambridge: Polity Press, 1996.
Arano Yasunori. "The Entrenchment of the Concept of 'National Seclusion.'" *Acta Asiatica* 67 (1994): 83–103.
———. "Kaikin to sakoku," In *Ajia no naka no Nihonshi 2 Gaikō to sensō,* ed. Arano Yasunori, Ishii Masatoshi, and Murai Shōsuke, pp. 191–222. Tōkyō daigaku shuppankai, 1992.
———. *Kinsei Nihon to Higashi Ajia.* Tōkyō daigaku shuppankai, 1988.
———. "Kinsei no taigai kan." In *Iwanami kōza Nihon tsūshi 13 Kinsei 3,* pp. 211–249. Iwanami shoten, 1994.
Arano Yasunori, Ishii Masatoshi, and Murai Shōsuke. "Jiki kubunron." In *Ajia no naka no Nihonshi 1 Ajia to Nihon,* ed. Arano Yasunori, Ishii Masatoshi, and Murai Shōsuke, pp. 1–57. Tōkyō daigaku shuppankai, 1992.
Arasaki Moriteru. *Gendai Nihon to Okinawa.* Nihonshi riburetto 66. Yamakawa shuppansha, 2001.
Armstrong, John A. *Nations before Nationalism.* Chapel Hill: University of North Carolina Press, 1982.
Asahi Shimbun, ed. *The Asahi Shimbun Japan Almanac 2002.* Tokyo: Asahi Shimbun, 2001.
Asao Naohiro. "The Sixteenth-Century Unification." In *The Cambridge History of Japan,* vol. 4: *Early Modern Japan,* ed. John Whitney Hall, pp. 40–95. Cambridge: Cambridge University Press, 1991.
Asao Naohiro, Uno Shun'ichi, and Tanaka Migaku, eds. *Kadokawa shinpan Nihonshi jiten.* Kadokawa shoten, 1996.
Aston, W. G., trans. *Nihongi: Chronicles of Japan from the Earliest Times to A.D. 697.* 2 vols. in 1. Rutland, Vt.: Tuttle, 1972.
Atwell, William S. "A Seventeenth-Century 'General Crisis' in East Asia?" *Modern Asian Studies* 24.4 (1990): 661–682.
———. "Some Observations on the 'Seventeenth-Century Crisis' in China and Japan." *Journal of Asian Studies* 45 (1986): 223–244.
Azuma Ushio. "Chōsen sankoku to Wakoku." In *Kōkogaku ni yoru Nihon rekishi 6 Sensō,* ed. Ōtsuka Hatsushige, Shiraishi Taichirō, Nishitani Tadashi, and Machida Akira, pp. 37–51. Yūzankaku, 2000.
Barfield, Thomas J. *The Perilous Frontier: Nomadic Empires and China, 221 B.C. to A.D. 1757.* Cambridge, Mass.: Blackwell, 1989.
Barnard, Alan. "Culture Area." In *The Social Science Encyclopedia,* ed. Adam Kuper and Jessica Kuper, pp. 180–181. London: Routledge, 1985.
Barnes, Gina L. *China Korea and Japan: The Rise of Civilization in East Asia.* London: Thames and Hudson, 1993.
———. "Jiehao, Tonghao: Peer Relations in East Asia." In *Peer Polity Interaction and Socio-Political Change,* ed. C. Renfrew and J. Cherry, pp. 79–92. Cambridge: Cambridge University Press, 1986.
———. *Protohistoric Yamato: Archaeology of the First Japanese State.* Michigan

Papers in Japanese Studies, no. 17. Ann Arbor: Center for Japanese Studies, University of Michigan, 1988.

Barth, Fredrik. "Introduction." In *Ethnic Groups and Boundaries*, ed. Fredrik Barth, pp. 9–38. London: George Allen and Unwin, 1969.

Bartlett, Robert, and Angus MacKay, eds. *Medieval Frontier Societies.* Oxford: Clarendon Press, 1992.

Batten, Bruce. "Dazaifu no kokkyō kinō." In *Kodai ōken to kōryū 8 Saikai to Nantō no seikatsu, bunka*, ed. Shinkawa Tokio, pp. 381–419. Meicho shuppan, 1995.

———. "Foreign Threat and Domestic Reform: The Emergence of the *Ritsuryō* State." *Monumenta Nipponica* 41.2 (1986): 199–219.

———. "Frontiers and Boundaries of Pre-modern Japan." *Journal of Historical Geography* 25.2 (1999): 166–182.

———. "Kodai Nihon no kokkyō to Dazaifu." In *Ikoku to Kyūshū: Rekishi ni okeru kosusai kōryū to chiiki keisei*, ed. Chihōshi kenkyū kyōgikai, pp. 51–73. Yūzankaku, 1992.

———. *Kokkyō no tanjō: Dazaifu kara mita Nihon no genkei.* NHK bukkusu 922. Nihon hōsō shuppan kyōkai, 2001.

———. *Nihon no "kyōkai": Zenkindai no kokka, minzoku, bunka.* Aoki shoten, 2000.

———. "Provincial Administration in Early Japan: From *Ritsuryō kokka* to *Ōchō kokka*." *Harvard Journal of Asiatic Studies* 53.1 (1993): 103–134.

———. Review of Mark L. Hudson, *Ruins of Identity: Ethnogenesis in the Japanese Islands. Monumenta Nipponica* 55.2 (2000): 283–285.

———. "State and Frontier in Early Japan: The Imperial Court and Northern Kyushu, 645–1185." Ph.D. dissertation, Stanford University, Stanford, Calif., 1989.

Beasley, W. G. "The Foreign Threat and the Opening of the Ports." In *The Cambridge History of Japan*, vol. 5: *The Nineteenth Century*, ed. Marius B. Jansen, pp. 259–307. Cambridge: Cambridge University Press, 1989.

———. *The Japanese Experience: A Short History of Japan.* Berkeley and Los Angeles: University of California Press, 1999.

———. *Japanese Imperialism, 1894–1945.* Oxford: Oxford University Press, 1987.

Befu, Harumi. "Nationalism and *Nihonjinron*." In *Cultural Nationalism in East Asia: Representation and Identity*, ed. Harumi Befu, pp. 107–135. Berkeley and Los Angeles: University of California Press, 1993.

Bentley, Jerry H. *Old World Encounters: Cross-Cultural Contacts and Exchanges in Pre-Modern Times.* Oxford: Oxford University Press, 1993.

Bergesen, Albert. "Pre- vs. Post-1500ers." *Comparative Civilizations Review* 30 (1994): 81–90.

Berry, Mary Elizabeth. *Hideyoshi.* Harvard East Asian Series 97. Cambridge: Harvard University Press, 1982.

———. "Was Early Modern Japan Culturally Integrated?" *Modern Asian Studies* 31.3 (1997): 547–581.

Beukers, Harmen. "The Introduction of Western Medicine in Japan." In *Bridging the Divide: Four Hundred Years The Netherlands–Japan*, ed. Leonard Blussé, Willem Remmelink, and Ivo Smits, pp. 105–114. The Netherlands/Japan: Teleac/NOT and Hotei Publishing, 2000.

Birt, Michael P. "Samurai in Passage: The Transformation of the Sixteenth-Century Kanto." *Journal of Japanese Studies* 11.2 (1985): 369–399.

Bitō Masahide. "Thought and Religion: 1550–1700." In *The Cambridge History of Japan*, vol. 4: *Early Modern Japan*, ed. John Whitney Hall, pp. 373–424. Cambridge: Cambridge University Press, 1991.

Blaut, J. M. *The Colonizer's Model of the World: Geographical Diffusionism and Eurocentric History.* New York: Guilford Press, 1993.

Blunden, Caroline, and Mark Elvin. *Cultural Atlas of China.* New York: Facts on File, 1983.

Blussé, Leonard, Willem Remmelink, and Ivo Smits, eds. *Bridging the Divide: Four Hundred Years The Netherlands–Japan.* The Netherlands/Japan: Teleac/NOT and Hotei Publishing, 2000.

Boggs, S. Whittemore. *International Boundaries: A Study of Boundary Functions and Problems.* New York: Columbia University Press, 1940.

Bolitho, Harold. *Treasures among Men: The Fudai Daimyo in Tokugawa Japan.* New Haven, Conn.: Yale University Press, 1974.

Borgen, Robert. "The Case of the Plagiaristic Journal: A Curious Passage from Jōjin's Diary." In *New Leaves: Studies and Translations of Japanese Literature in Honor of Edward Seidensticker*, ed. Aileen Gatten and Anthony Hood Chambers, pp. 63–74. Ann Arbor: Center for Japanese Studies, University of Michigan, 1993.

———. "The Japanese Mission to China, 801–806." *Monumenta Nipponica* 37.1 (1982): 1–25.

———. "Japanese Nationalism: Ancient and Modern." *Meiji gakuin daigaku kokusai gakubu fuzoku kenkyūjo kenkyūjo nenpō* 1 (1998): 49–59.

———. "*San Tendai Godai sanki* as a Source for the Study of Sung History." *Bulletin of Sung Yuan Studies* 19 (1987): 1–16.

———. "Through Several Glasses Brightly: A Japanese Copy of a Chinese Account of Japan." *Sino-Japanese Studies* 2.2 (1990): 5–19.

Bowman, Alan K. *Life and Letters on the Roman Frontier.* New York: Routledge, 1994.

Brauer, R. W. *Boundaries and Frontiers in Medieval Muslim Geography. Transactions of the American Philosophical Society*, vol. 85, part 6. Philadelphia: American Philosophical Society, 1995.

Brown, Philip C. *Central Authority and Local Autonomy in the Formation of Early Modern Japan.* Stanford, Calif.: Stanford University Press, 1993.

Calhoun, Craig. *Nationalism.* Concepts in Social Thought. Minneapolis: University of Minnesota Press, 1997.

Cavalli-Sforza, L. Luca. *Genes, Peoples, and Languages.* Trans. Mark Seielstad. New York: North Point Press, 2000.

Cavalli-Sforza, L. Luca, Paolo Menozzi, and Alberto Piazza. *The History and Geography of Human Genes.* Princeton, N.J.: Princeton University Press, 1994.

Chappell, David A. "Ethnogenesis and Frontiers." *Journal of World History* 4.2 (1993): 267–275.

Chase-Dunn, Christopher, and Thomas D. Hall. *Rise and Demise: Comparing World Systems.* Boulder, Colo.: Westview Press, 1997.

Collcutt, Martin. *Five Mountains: The Rinzai Zen Monastic Institution in Medieval Japan.* Harvard East Asian Monographs 85. Cambridge: Council on East Asian Studies, Harvard University, 1981.

———. "Zen and the *Gozan.*" In *The Cambridge History of Japan*, vol. 3: *Medieval Japan*, ed. Kozo Yamamura, pp. 583–652. Cambridge: Cambridge University Press, 1990.

Collcutt, Martin, Marius Jansen, and Isao Kumakura, eds. *Cultural Atlas of Japan.* New York: Facts on File, 1988.

Conlan, Thomas D., trans. *In Little Need of Divine Intervention: Takezaki Suenaga's Scrolls of the Mongol Invasions of Japan.* Cornell East Asian Series, no. 113. Ithaca, N.Y.: Cornell University East Asia Program, 2001.

Cooper, Michael, ed. *They Came to Japan: An Anthology of European Reports on Japan, 1543–1640.* Michigan Classics in Japanese Studies, no. 15. Ann Arbor: Center for Japanese Studies, University of Michigan, 1995 [1965].

Crawcour, E. Sydney. "Economic Change in the Nineteenth Century." In *The Cambridge History of Japan*, vol. 5: *The Nineteenth Century*, ed. Marius B. Jansen, pp. 569–617. Cambridge: Cambridge University Press, 1989.

Cronon, William. *Changes in the Land: Indians, Colonists, and the Ecology of New England.* New York: Hill and Wang, 1983.

Cronon, William, ed. *Uncommon Ground: Toward Reinventing Nature.* New York: W. W. Norton, 1995.

Cronon, William, George Miles, and Jay Gitlin, eds. *Under an Open Sky: Rethinking America's Western Past.* New York: W. W. Norton, 1992.

Crosby, Alfred W. *The Columbian Exchange: Biological and Cultural Consequences of 1492.* Westport, Conn.: Greenwood Press, 1972.

———. *Ecological Imperialism: The Biological Expansion of Europe, 900–1900.* Cambridge: Cambridge University Press, 1986.

Curtin, Philip D. *Cross-Cultural Trade in World History.* Cambridge: Cambridge University Press, 1984.

Dark, K. R. *Theoretical Archaeology.* Ithaca, N.Y.: Cornell University Press, 1995.

Davis, S. L., and J.R.V. Prescott. *Aboriginal Frontiers and Boundaries in Australia.* Carlton, Victoria, Australia: Melbourne University Press, 1992.

Diamond, Jared. *Guns, Germs, and Steel: The Fates of Human Societies.* New York: W. W. Norton and Co., 1997.

Donnan, Hastings, and Thomas M. Wilson. *Borders: Frontiers of Identity, Nation, and State.* Oxford: Berg (Oxford International Publishers), 1999.

Doyle, Michael W. *Empires.* Ithaca, N.Y.: Cornell University Press, 1986.

Drummond, Steven K., and Lynn H. Nelson. *The Western Frontiers of Imperial Rome.* Armonk, N.Y.: M. E. Sharpe, 1994.

Edmonds, Richard Louis. *Northern Frontiers of Qing China and Tokugawa Japan.* Research Paper no. 213. Chicago: Department of Geography, University of Chicago, 1985.

Edo iseki kenkyūkai, ed. *Edo bunka no kōkogaku.* Yoshikawa kōbunkan, 2000.

Edwards, Walter. "Mirrors on Ancient Yamato: The Kurozuka Kofun Discovery and the Question of Yamatai." *Monumenta Nipponica* 54.1 (1999): 75–110.

Ehrich, Robert W., and Gerald M. Henderson. "Culture Area." In *International Encyclopedia of the Social Sciences,* vol. 3, pp. 563–568. New York: Crowell Collier and Macmillan, 1968.

Eisenstadt, S. N. *Japanese Civilization: A Comparative View.* Chicago: University of Chicago Press, 1996.

Elisonas, Jurgis. "Christianity and the Daimyo." In *The Cambridge History of Japan,* vol. 4: *Early Modern Japan,* ed. John Whitney Hall, pp. 301–372. Cambridge: Cambridge University Press, 1991.

———. "The Inseparable Trinity: Japan's Relations with China and Korea." In *The Cambridge History of Japan,* vol. 4: *Early Modern Japan,* ed. John Whitney Hall, pp. 235–300. Cambridge: Cambridge University Press, 1991.

Ellwood, Robert S. *The Feast of Kingship: Accession Ceremonies in Ancient Japan.* Monumenta Nipponica Monograph. Tokyo: Sophia University Press, 1973.

Elton, Hugh. *Frontiers of the Roman Empire.* Bloomington: Indiana University Press, 1996.

Elvin, Mark. *The Pattern of the Chinese Past.* Stanford, Calif.: Stanford University Press, 1973.

Engishiki. In *Shintei zōho kokushi taikei,* vol. 26, ed. Kuroita Katsumi and Kokushi taikei henshūkai. Yoshikawa kōbunkan, 1973.

Enomoto Wataru. "Sōdai no 'Nihon shōnin' no saikentō." *Shigaku zasshi* 110.2 (2001): 37–60.

Fairbank, John K., ed. *The Chinese World Order.* Cambridge: Harvard University Press, 1968.

Fairbank, John K., Edwin O. Reischauer, and Albert M. Craig. *East Asia: Tradition and Transformation.* Boston: Houghton Mifflin, 1973.

Farris, William Wayne. *Population, Disease, and Land in Early Japan, 645–900.*

Harvard-Yenching Institute Monograph Series 24. Cambridge: Council on East Asian Studies, Harvard University, 1985.

———. *Sacred Texts and Buried Treasures: Issues in the Historical Archaeology of Ancient Japan.* Honolulu: University of Hawai'i Press, 1998.

———. "Trade, Money, and Merchants in Nara Japan." *Monumenta Nipponica* 53.3 (1998): 303–334.

Ferguson, R. Brian, and Neil L. Whitehead. "The Violent Edge of Empire." In *War in the Tribal Zone: Expanding States and Indigenous Warfare*, ed. R. Brian Ferguson and Neil L. Whitehead, pp. 1–30. Santa Fe, N.Mex.: School of American Research Press, 1992.

———, eds. *War in the Tribal Zone: Expanding States and Indigenous Warfare.* Advanced Seminar Series. Santa Fe, N.Mex: School of American Research Press, 1992.

Fitzhugh, William W. "Ainu Ethnicity: A History." In *Ainu: Spirit of a Northern People*, ed. William W. Fitzhugh and Chisato O. Dubreuil, pp. 9–26. Washington, D.C.: Arctic Studies Center, National Museum of Natural History, Smithsonian Institution, in association with University of Washington Press, 1999.

Fitzhugh, William W., and Chisato O. Dubreuil, eds. *Ainu: Spirit of a Northern People.* Washington, D.C.: Arctic Studies Center, National Museum of Natural History, Smithsonian Institution, in association with University of Washington Press, 1999.

Forrer, Matthi. "Nineteenth Century Japanese Collections in the Netherlands." In *Bridging the Divide: Four Hundred Years The Netherlands–Japan*, ed. Leonard Blussé, Willem Remmelink and Ivo Smits, pp. 159–171. The Netherlands/Japan: Teleac/NOT and Hotei Publishing, 2000.

Frank, Andre Gunder. *ReOrient: Global Economy in the Asian Age.* Berkeley and Los Angeles: University of California Press, 1998.

Frank, Andre Gunder, and Barry K. Gills. "The 5,000–Year World System: An Interdisciplinary Introduction." In *The World System: Five Hundred Years or Five Thousand?*, ed. Andre Gunder Frank and Barry K. Gills, pp. 3–55. London: Routledge, 1993.

———, eds. *The World System: Five Hundred Years or Five Thousand?* London: Routledge, 1993.

Friday, Karl. "Pushing beyond the Pale: The Yamato Conquest of the *Emishi* and Northern Japan." *Journal of Japanese Studies* 23.1 (1997): 1–24.

Fried, Morton H. *The Evolution of Political Society: An Essay in Political Anthropology.* New York: Random House, 1967.

———. *The Notion of Tribe.* Menlo Park, Calif.: Cummings Publishing, 1970.

Fujimoto Tsuyoshi. *Mō futatsu no Nihon bunka: Hokkaidō to Nantō no bunka.* UP kōkogaku sensho 2. Tōkyō daigaku shuppankai, 1988.

Fujimura, Hisakazu. "*Kamuy:* Gods You Can Argue With." In *Ainu: Spirit of a Northern People*, ed. William W. Fitzhugh and Chisato O. Dubreuil, pp. 193–197. Washington, D.C.: Arctic Studies Center, National Museum

of Natural History, Smithsonian Institution, in association with University of Washington Press, 1999.
Fujitani, T. *Splendid Monarchy: Power and Pageantry in Modern Japan.* Berkeley and Los Angeles: University of California Press, 1996.
Fukasawa Yuriko. "Ainu minzoku o tōshite miru Nihon kōkogaku." In *Hajimete deau Nihon kōkogaku,* ed. Yasuda Yoshinori, pp. 191–238. Yūhikaku aruma, 1999.
Fukuda Toyohiko. "Tetsu o chūshin ni mita hōppo kōeki." In *Chūsei no fūkei o yomu 1 Ezo no sekai to hoppō kōeki,* ed. Amino Yoshihiko and Ishii Susumu, pp. 153–198. Shinjinbutsu ōraisha, 1995.
Gaubatz, Piper Rae. *Beyond the Great Wall: Urban Form and Transformation on the Chinese Frontiers.* Stanford, Calif.: Stanford University Press, 1996.
Gellner, Ernest. *Nationalism.* Washington Square, N.Y.: New York University Press, 1997.
Giddens, Anthony. *The Nation-State and Violence.* Berkeley and Los Angeles: University of California Press, 1985.
———. *Sociology.* Cambridge: Polity Press, 1989.
Gills, Barry K., and Andre Gunder Frank. "The Cumulation of Accumulation." In *The World System: Five Hundred Years or Five Thousand?,* ed. Andre Gunder Frank and Barry K. Gills, pp. 81–114. London: Routledge, 1993.
———. "World System Cycles, Crises, and Hegemonic Shifts, 1700 B.C. to 1700 A.D." In *The World System: Five Hundred Years or Five Thousand?,* ed. Andre Gunder Frank and Barry K. Gills, pp. 143–199. London: Routledge, 1993.
Gilpin, Robert. *War and Change in World Politics.* Cambridge: Cambridge University Press, 1981.
Gluck, Carol. *Japan's Modern Myths: Ideology in the Late Meiji Period.* Princeton, N.J.: Princeton University Press, 1985.
Gottfried, Robert S. *The Black Death: Natural and Human Disaster in Medieval Europe.* New York: Free Press, 1983.
Green, Stanton W., and Stephen M. Perlman, eds. *The Archaeology of Frontiers and Boundaries.* Studies in Archaeology. San Diego: Academic Press, 1985.
Guy, Donna J., and Thomas E. Sheridan. "On Frontiers: The Northern and Southern Edges of the Spanish Empire in the Americas." In *Contested Ground: Comparative Frontiers on the Northern and Southern Edges of the Spanish Empire,* ed. Donna J. Guy and Thomas E. Sheridan, pp. 3–15. Tucson: University of Arizona Press, 1998.
———, eds. *Contested Ground: Comparative Frontiers on the Northern and Southern Edges of the Spanish Empire.* Tucson: University of Arizona Press, 1998.
Hagiwara Hirobumi. "Nagasaki Dejima to Hirado no Oranda shōkan." In *Kōkogaku ni yoru Nihon rekishi 10 Taigai kōshō,* ed. Ōtsuka Hatsushige,

Shiraishi Taichirō, Nishitani Tadashi, and Machida Akira, pp. 170–178. Yūzankaku, 1997.

Hall, John Whitney. "The *Bakuhan* System." In *The Cambridge History of Japan,* vol. 4: *Early Modern Japan,* ed. John Whitney Hall, pp. 128–182. Cambridge: Cambridge University Press, 1991.

———. *Japan from Prehistory to Modern Times.* Delacorte World History. New York: Dell, 1970.

Hall, John Whitney, Keiji Nagahara, and Kozo Yamakura, eds. *Japan before Tokugawa: Political Consolidation and Economic Growth, 1500 to 1650.* Princeton, N.J.: Princeton University Press, 1981.

Hall, Thomas D. "World-Systems and Evolution: An Appraisal." In *World-Systems Theory in Practice,* ed. P. Nick Kardulias, pp. 1–23. Lanham, Md.: Rowman and Littlefield, 1999.

Hamashita Takeshi. "Contemporary China and the Study of Modern History: Towards an Understanding of Chinese Society." *Acta Asiatica* 62 (1992): 23–43.

———. "Higashi Ajia kokusai taikei." In *Kōza kokusai seiji 1 Kokusai seiji no riron,* pp. 51–80. Tōkyō daigaku shuppankai, 1989.

———. "Jo: Chiiki kenkyū to Ajia." In *Ajia kara kangaeru 2 Chiiki shisutemu,* ed. Mizoguchi Yūzō, Hamashita Takeshi, Hirashi Naoaki, and Miyajima Hiroshi, pp. 1–12. Tōkyō daigaku shuppankai, 1993.

———. *Kindai Chūgoku no kokusaiteki keiki: Chōkō bōeki shisutemu to kindai Ajia.* Tōkyō daigaku shuppankai, 1990.

———. *Okinawa nyūmon: Ajia o tsunagu kaiiki kōzō.* Chikuma shinsho 249. Chikuma shobō, 2000.

Hamashita, Takeshi. "The Intra-Regional System in East Asia in Modern Times." In *Network Power: Japan and Asia,* ed. Peter J. Katzenstein and Takashi Shiraishi, pp. 113–135. Ithaca, N.Y.: Cornell University Press, 1997.

———. "The Tribute Trade System and Modern Asia." *Memoirs of the Research Department of the Toyo Bunko* 46 (1988): 7–25.

Hamashita Takeshi and Karashima Noboru, eds. *Chiiki no sekai shi 1: Chiiki shi to wa nani ka.* Yamakawa shuppansha, 1997.

Hanihara Kazuro. "Dual Structure Model for the Population History of the Japanese." *Japan Review* 2 (1991): 1–33.

———. "Emishi, Ezo, and Ainu: An Anthropological Perspective." *Japan Review* 1 (1990): 35–48.

Hanihara Kazurō. "Nihonjin no keisei." In *Iwanami kōza Nihon tsūshi 1 Nihon rettō to jinrui shakai,* pp. 83–114. Iwanami shoten, 1993.

———. *Nihonjin no tanjō: jinrui wa haruka naru tabi.* Rekishi bunka raiburarii 1. Yoshikawa kōbunkan, 1996.

Hanley, Susan B. *Everyday Things in Premodern Japan: The Forgotten Legacy.* Berkeley and Los Angeles: University of California Press, 1997.

———. "Tokugawa Society: Material Culture, Standard of Living, and Life-

Styles." In *The Cambridge History of Japan*, vol. 4: *Early Modern Japan*, ed. John Whitney Hall, pp. 660–705. Cambridge: Cambridge University Press, 1991.

Harootunian, Harry D. *Things Seen and Unseen: Discourse and Ideology in Tokugawa Nativism.* Chicago: University of Chicago Press, 1988.

Hashiguchi Sadashi. "'Mainōsen' no juryoku." In *Shinshiten Nihon no rekishi 4 Chūsei hen*, ed. Minegishi Sumio and Ikegami Hiroko, pp. 250–259. Shinjinbutsu ōraisha, 1993.

———. "Zeni o umeru koto: Mainōsen o meguru shomondai." In *Ekkyō suru kahei*, ed. Rekishigaku kenkyūkai, pp. 211–245. Aoki shoten, 1999.

Hashimoto Yū. Review of Bruce Batten, *Nihon no "kyōkai": Zenkindai no kokka, minzoku, bunka. Rekishigaku kenkyū* 760 (2002): 52–55.

Hata, Ikuhiko. "Continental Expansion, 1905–1941." In *The Cambridge History of Japan*, vol. 6: *The Twentieth Century*, ed. Peter Duus, pp. 271–314. Cambridge: Cambridge University Press, 1988.

Hatch, Elvin. "Culture." In *The Social Science Encyclopedia*, ed. Adam Kuper and Jessica Kuper, pp. 178–179. London: Routledge, 1985.

Hay, John, ed. *Boundaries in China.* London: Reaktion Books, 1994.

Hayami Akira. "Jinkōshi (Demography)." In *Iwanami kōza Nihon tsūshi 1 Nihon rettō to jinrui shakai*, pp. 115–147. Iwanami shoten, 1993.

Hayami, Akira. *The Historical Demography of Pre-Modern Japan.* Tokyo: University of Tokyo Press, 2001.

Hayashiya Tatsusaburō, ed. *Hyōgo kitaseki irifune nōchō.* Chūō kōron bijutsu shuppan, 1981.

Hegmon, Michelle. "Technology, Style, and Social Practices: Archaeological Approaches." In *The Archaeology of Social Boundaries*, ed. Miriam T. Stark, pp. 264–279. Washington, D.C.: Smithsonian Institution Press, 1998.

Herlihy, David. *The Black Death and the Transformation of the West.* Cambridge: Harvard University Press, 1997.

Hershatter, Gail, Emily Honig, Jonathon N. Lipman, and Randall Stross, eds. *Remapping China: Fissures in Historical Terrain.* Stanford, Calif.: Stanford University Press, 1996.

Hirakawa Sukehiro. "Japan's Turn to the West." In *The Cambridge History of Japan*, vol. 5: *The Nineteenth Century*, ed. Marius B. Jansen, pp. 432–498. Cambridge: Cambridge University Press, 1989.

Hirano Kunio. *Kikajin to kodai kokka.* Yoshikawa kōbunkan, 1993.

———. "The Yamato State and Korea in the Fourth and Fifth Centuries." *Acta Asiatica* 31 (1977): 51–82.

Hobsbawn, Eric, and Terence Ranger, eds. *The Invention of Tradition.* Cambridge: Cambridge University Press, 1983.

Hokkaidō, Tōhoku shi kenkyūkai, ed. *Basho ukeoi sei to Ainu: Kinsei Ezochishi no kōchiku o mezashite.* Sapporo: Hokkaidō shuppan kikaku sentaa, 1998.

Hongō Hiromichi. *Kumaso, Hayato no genshō: Kodai Hyūga no in'ei.* Yoshikawa kōbunkan, 1994.

Hori, Kyotsu. "The Economic and Political Effects of the Mongol Wars." In *Medieval Japan*, ed. John W. Hall and Jeffrey P. Mass, pp. 184–198. New Haven, Conn.: Yale University Press, 1974.

Howell, David L. "The Ainu and the Early Modern Japanese State, 1600–1868." In *Ainu: Spirit of a Northern People*, ed. William W. Fitzhugh and Chisato O. Dubreuil, pp. 96–101. Washington, D.C.: Arctic Studies Center, National Museum of Natural History, Smithsonian Institution, in association with University of Washington Press, 1999.

———. "Ainu Ethnicity and the Boundaries of the Early Modern Japanese State." *Past and Present* 142 (1994): 69–93.

———. *Capitalism from Within: Economy, Society, and the State in a Japanese Fishery*. Berkeley and Los Angeles: University of California Press, 1995.

———. "Ethnicity and Culture in Contemporary Japan." *Journal of Contemporary History* 31 (1996): 171–190.

———. "Kinsei Hokkaidō ni okeru midoru gurando no kanōsei." In *Basho ukeoi sei to Ainu: Kinsei Ezochishi no kōchiku o mezashite*, ed. Hokkaidō, Tōhoku shi kenkyūkai, pp. 415–420. Sapporo: Hokkaidō shuppan kikaku sentaa, 1998.

———. "The Meiji State and the Logic of Ainu Protection." In *New Directions in the Study of Meiji Japan*, ed. Helen Hardacre and Adam L. Kern, pp. 815–847. Leiden: E. J. Brill, 1997.

———. "The Prehistory of the Japanese Nation-State: Status, Ethnicity, and Boundaries." *Early Modern Japan* 5.2 (1995): 19–24.

———. "Territoriality and Collective Identity in Tokugawa Japan." *Daedalus* 127.3 (1998): 105–132.

Hudson, Mark J. *Ruins of Identity: Ethnogenesis in the Japanese Islands*. Honolulu: University of Hawai'i Press, 1999.

Huffman, James L. *Creating a Public: People and Press in Meiji Japan*. Honolulu: University of Hawai'i Press, 1997.

Huntington, Samuel P. *The Clash of Civilizations and the Remaking of World Order*. New York: Simon and Schuster, 1996.

Ichimura Yūichi and Ōishi Shinzaburō. *Sakoku: Yuruyaka na jōhō kakumei*. Kōdansha gendai shinsho 1260 Shinsho Edo jidai 4. Kōdansha, 1995.

Ikeda On, ed. *Kodai o kangaeru: Tō to Nihon*. Yoshikawa kōbunkan, 1992.

Imaizumi Takao. "Emishi no chōkō to kyōkyū." In *Tōhoku kodaishi no kenkyū*, ed. Takahashi Tomio, pp. 105–155. Yoshikawa kōbunkan, 1986.

———. "Ritsuryō kokka to Emishi." In *Shinpan kodai no Nihon 9 Tōhoku, Hokkaidō*, ed. Sudō Takashi, Imaizumi Takao, and Tsuboi Kiyotari, pp. 163–198. Kadokawa shoten, 1992.

———. "Tōhoku no jōsaku wa naze mōkerareta ka." In *Shinshiten Nihon no rekishi 3 Kodai hen 2*, ed. Yoshimura Takehiko and Yoshioka Masayuki, pp. 258–265. Shinjinbutsu ōraisha, 1993.

Imamura, Keiji. *Prehistoric Japan: New Perspectives on Insular East Asia*. Honolulu: University of Hawai'i Press, 1996.

Innes, Robert Leroy. "The Door Ajar: Japan's Foreign Trade in the Seventeenth Century." Ph.D. dissertation, University of Michigan, Ann Arbor, 1980.

Inoue Mitsusada. "The *Ritsuryō* System in Japan." *Acta Asiatica* 31 (1977): 83–112.

Inoue Mitsusada with Delmer M. Brown. "The Century of Reform." In *The Cambridge History of Japan*, vol. 1: *Ancient Japan*, ed. Delmer M. Brown, pp. 163–220. Cambridge: Cambridge University Press, 1993.

Isaac, Benjamin. *The Limits of Empire: The Roman Army in the East.* Rev. ed. Oxford: Clarendon Press, 1992 [1990].

Ishida, Hajime. "Ancient People of the North Pacific Rim: Ainu Biological Relationships with Their Neighbors." In *Ainu: Spirit of a Northern People*, ed. William W. Fitzhugh and Chisato O. Dubreuil, pp. 53–56. Washington, D.C.: Arctic Studies Center, National Museum of Natural History, Smithsonian Institution, in association with University of Washington Press, 1999.

Ishigami Eiichi. "Kodai Higashi Ajia chiiki to Nihon." In *Nihon no shakaishi 1 Rettō naigai no kōtsū to kokka*, pp. 55–96. Iwanami shoten, 1987.

———. "Kodai kokka to taigai kankei." In *Kōza Nihon rekishi 2 Kodai 2*, ed. Rekishigaku kenkyūkai and Nihonshi kenkyūkai, pp. 247–286. Tōkyō daigaku shuppankai, 1984.

———. "Nihon kodai 10 seiki no gaikō." In *Higashi Ajia sekai ni okeru Nihon kodaishi kōza 7 Higashi Ajia no henbō to Nihon ritsuryō kokka*, pp. 97–143. Gakuseisha, 1982.

———. "State and Society in Ancient Japan." *Acta Asiatica* 69 (1995): 14–38.

Ishihara Hiromichi, ed. *Shintei Gishi Washinden hoka sanpen.* Chūgoku seishi Nihonden (1), Iwanami bunko 33–401–1. Iwanami shoten, 1985.

Ishii Masatoshi. *Nihon Bokkai kankei shi no kenkyū.* Yoshikawa kōbunkan, 2001.

———. "10 seiki no kokusai hendō to Nissō bōeki." In *Shinpan Nihon no kodai 2 Ajia kara mita Nihon*, ed. Tamura Kōichi and Suzuki Yasutami, pp. 339–362. Kadokawa shoten, 1992.

Ishii Susumi. "The Decline of the Kamakura Bakufu." In *The Cambridge History of Japan*, vol. 3: *Medieval Japan*, ed. Kozo Yamamura, pp. 128–174. Cambridge: Cambridge University Press, 1990.

Ishimoda Shō. *Nihon kodai kokkaron*, pt. 1. Iwanami shoten, 1973.

Ishiwatari, Toshiyasu. "The Northern Territories." In *Contested Territory: Border Disputes at the Edge of the Former Soviet Union*, ed. Tuomas Forsberg, pp. 224–254. Aldershot, England: Edward Elgar, 1995.

Itō Jun. "Emishi to Hayato wa doko ga chigau ka." In *Sōten Nihon no rekishi 3 Kodai hen 2*, ed. Yoshimura Takehiko and Yoshioka Masayuki, pp. 59–74. Shinjinbutsu ōraisha, 1991.

———. "Kodai kokka no Emishi shihai." In *Kodai ōken to kōryū 1 Kodai Emishi no sekai to kōryū*, ed. Suzuki Yasutami, pp. 169–214. Meicho shuppan, 1996.

———. "Kodai kokka no ryōdo, ryōiki." In *Chizu de tadoru Nihonshi*, ed. Satō

Kazuhiko, Sasaki Ken'ichi, and Sakamoto Noboru, pp. 13–17. Tōkyōdō shuppan, 1995.

———. "Kodai ōken to iminzoku." *Rekishigaku kenkyū* 665 (1994): 2–13.

Iwao Seiichi. "Japanese Foreign Trade in the Sixteenth and Seventeenth Centuries." *Acta Asiatica* 30 (1976): 1–18.

Jagchid, Sechin, and Van Jay Symons. *Peace, War, and Trade along the Great Wall: Nomadic-Chinese Interactions through Two Millennia.* Bloomington: Indiana University Press, 1989.

Jannetta, Anne Bowman. *Epidemics and Mortality in Early Modern Japan.* Princeton, N.J.: Princeton University Press, 1987.

Jansen, Marius B. *China in the Tokugawa World.* Cambridge: Harvard University Press, 1992.

———. "Meiji Political Institutions." In *The Cambridge History of Japan*, vol. 5: *The Nineteenth Century*, ed. Marius B. Jansen, pp. 618–673. Cambridge: Cambridge University Press, 1989.

———. "The Meiji Restoration." In *The Cambridge History of Japan*, vol. 5: *The Nineteenth Century*, ed. Marius B. Jansen, pp. 308–366. Cambridge: Cambridge University Press, 1989.

Jinnai, Hidenobu. "The Spatial Structure of Edo." In *Tokugawa Japan: The Social and Economic Antecedents of Modern Japan*, ed. Chie Nakane and Shinzaburō Ōishi, pp. 124–146. Tokyo: University of Tokyo Press, 1990.

Jones, Stephen B. "Boundary Concepts in the Setting of Place and Time." *Annals of the Association of American Geographers* 49 (1959): 241–255.

Kadowaki Teiji. "Nihonjin no keisei." In *Ajia no naka no Nihonshi 4 Chiiki to etonosu*, ed. Arano Yasunori, Ishii Masatoshi, and Murai Shōsuke, pp. 1–28. Tōkyō daigaku shuppankai, 1992.

Kaempfer, Englebert. *Kaempfer's Japan: Tokugawa Culture Observed.* Trans., ed., and annotated by Beatrice M. Bodart-Bailey. Honolulu: University of Hawai'i Press, 1999.

Kaiho Mineo. *Chūsei no Ezochi.* Yoshikawa kōbunkan, 1987.

———. *Ezo no rekishi: Kita no hitibito to "Nihon."* Kōdansha sensho mechie 69. Kōdansha, 1996.

Kaizu Ichirō. *Mōko shūrai: Taigai sensō no shakaishi.* Rekishi bunka raiburarii 32. Yoshikawa kōbunkan, 1998.

Kamada Motokazu. "Nihon kodai no jinkō." In *Nihon no kodai bekkan Nihonjin to wa nani ka*, ed. Kishi Toshio, Mori Kōichi, and Ōbayashi Taryō, pp. 245–272. Chūō kōronsha, 1988.

Kamei Meitoku. "Kōrokan bōeki." In *Shinpan kodai no Nihon 3 Kyūshū, Okinawa hen*, ed. Shimojō Nobuyuki, Hirano Hiyoruki, Chinen Isamu, and Takara Kurayoshi, pp. 345–356. Kadokawa shoten, 1991.

———. *Nihon bōeki tōjishi no kenkyū.* Dōhōsha shuppan, 1986.

———. "Nissō bōeki kankei no tenkai." In *Iwanami kōza Nihon tsūshi 6 Kodai 5*, pp. 107–140. Iwanami shoten, 1995.

Kamimura Toshio. *Hayato no kōkogaku.* Kōkogaku raiburarii 30. Nyūsaiensusha, 1984.

Kamiya Nobuyuki. "Japanese Control of Ezochi and the Role of Northern Koryŏ." *Acta Asiatica* 67 (1994): 49–68.

Kang, Etsuko Hae-Jin. *Diplomacy and Ideology in Japanese-Korean Relations: From the Fifteenth to the Eighteenth Century.* New York: St. Martin's Press, 1997.

Kardulias, P. Nick, ed. *World-Systems Theory in Practice.* Lanham, Md.: Rowman and Littlefield, 1999.

Katayama Kazumichi. "The Japanese as an Asia-Pacific Population." In *Multicultural Japan: Palaeolithic to Postmodern*, ed. Donald Denoon, Mark Hudson, Gavan McCormack, and Tessa Morris-Suzuki, pp. 19–30. Cambridge: Cambridge University Press, 1996.

Katō Eiichi. "The Japan-Dutch Trade in the Formative Period of the Seclusion Policy—Particularly on the Raw Silk Trade by the Dutch Factory at Hirado, 1620–1640." *Acta Asiatica* 30 (1976): 34–84.

———. "Research Trends in the Study of the History of Japanese Foreign Relations at the Start of the Early Modern Period: On the Reexamination of 'National Seclusion'—From the 1970's to 1990's." *Acta Asiatica* 67 (1994): 1–29.

Katsumata Shizuo. "15–16 seiki no Nihon: Sengoku no sōran." In *Iwanami kōza Nihon tsūshi 10 Chūsei 4*, pp. 1–57. Iwanami shoten, 1994.

Kawazoe Shōji. "Japan and East Asia." In *The Cambridge History of Japan*, vol. 3: *Medieval Japan*, ed. Kozo Yamamura, pp. 396–446. Cambridge: Cambridge University Press, 1990.

Kayano Shigeru. *Our Land Was a Forest: An Ainu Memoir.* Trans. Kyoko Selden and Lili Welden. Transitions: Asia and Asian America. Boulder, Colo.: Westview Press, 1994.

Keene, Donald. *The Japanese Discovery of Europe, 1720–1830.* Stanford, Calif.: Stanford University Press, 1969 [1952].

Keirstead, Thomas. *The Geography of Power in Medieval Japan.* Princeton, N.J.: Princeton University Press, 1992.

Kennedy, Paul. *The Rise and Fall of the Great Powers.* New York: Random House, 1987.

Kidder, J. Edward, Jr. "The Earliest Societies in Japan." In *The Cambridge History of Japan*, vol. 1: *Ancient Japan*, ed. Delmer M. Brown, pp. 48–107. Cambridge: Cambridge University Press, 1993.

Kikuchi Isao. *Ainu minzoku to Nihonjin: Higashi Ajia no naka no Ezochi.* Asahi sensho 510. Asashi shinbunsha, 1994.

Kikuchi Tetsuo. "Emishi (kai) setsu saikō." *Shikan* 120 (1989): 100–114.

Kikuchi Tetsuo and Fukuda Toyohiko, eds. *Yomigaeru chūsei 4 Kita no chūsei: Tsugaru, Hokkaidō.* Heibonsha, 1989.

Kikuchi, Toshihiko. "Ainu Ties with Ancient Cultures of Northeast Asia." In *Ainu: Spirit of a Northern People*, ed. William W. Fitzhugh and Chisato O.

Dubreuil, pp. 47–51. Washington, D.C.: Arctic Studies Center, National Museum of Natural History, Smithsonian Institution, in association with University of Washington Press, 1999.

Kiley, Cornelius J. "Estate and Property in the Late Heian Period." In *Medieval Japan: Essays in Institutional History*, ed. John Whitney Hall and Jeffrey P. Mass, pp. 109–124. New Haven, Conn.: Yale University Press, 1974.

———. "Provincial Administration and Land Tenure in Early Heian." In *The Cambridge History of Japan*, vol. 2: *Heian Japan*, ed. Donald H. Shively and William H. McCullough, pp. 236–340. Cambridge: Cambridge University Press, 1999.

———. "*Ritsuryō* System." In *Kodansha Encyclopedia of Japan*, vol. 6, pp. 322–332. Tokyo: Kodansha, 1983.

———. "State and Dynasty in Archaic Yamato." *Journal of Asian Studies* 33.1 (1977): 25–49.

Kimura Hiroshi. *Nichiro kokkyō kōshōshi.* Chūkō shinsho 1147. Chūō kōronsha, 1993.

Kimura Shigemitsu. *"Kokufū bunka" no jidai.* Aoki Library Nihon no rekishi. Aoki shoten, 1997.

Kinoshita Ryō. *Kokufu: Sono hensen o omo ni shite.* Kyōikusha rekishi shinsho (Nihon) 44. Kyōikusha, 1988.

———, ed. *Kodai o kangaeru: Kodai dōro.* Yoshikawa kōbunkan, 1996.

Kitō Kiyoaki. *Mokkan.* Kōkogaku raiburarii 57. Nyūsaiensusha, 1990.

Klein, Kerwin Lee. *Frontiers of Historical Imagination: Narrating the European Conquest of Native America, 1890–1990.* Berkeley and Los Angeles: University of California Press, 1999.

———. "Reclaiming the 'F' Word, or Being and Becoming Postwestern." *Pacific Historical Review* 65.2 (1996): 179–215.

Kodama Kōta, ed. *Nihon kōtsūshi.* Yoshikawa kōbunkan, 1992.

Kodama Kōta and Sugiyama Hiroshi. *Tōkyo to no rekishi.* Kenshi shiriizu 13. Yamakawa shuppansha, 1969.

Kodansha, ed. *Japan, an Illustrated Encyclopedia.* 2 vols. Tokyo: Kodansha, 1993.

Koizumi Hiroshi. *Edo no kōkogaku.* Kōkogaku raiburarii 48. Nyūsaiensusha, 1987.

Komatsu Masao. "Gangyō no ran ki ni okeru Dewa no kuni no Emishi shakai." In *Kodai ōken to kōryū 1 Kodai Emishi no sekai to kōryū*, ed. Suzuki Yasutami, pp. 281–318. Meicho shuppan, 1996.

Koschmann, J. Victor. *The Mito Ideology: Discourse, Reform, and Insurrection in Late Tokugawa Japan, 1790–1864.* Berkeley and Los Angeles: University of California Press, 1987.

Koyama Yasunori. "Kodai makki no Tōgoku to Saigoku." In *Iwanami kōza Nihon rekishi 4 Kodai 4*, pp. 231–269. Iwanami shoten, 1976.

Kristof, Ladis K. D. "The Nature of Frontiers and Boundaries." *Annals of the Association of American Geographers* 49 (1959): 269–282.

Kudō Keiichi. "*Shōen.*" *Acta Asiatica* 44 (1983): 1–27.
Kudō Masaki. *Emishi no kodaishi.* Heibonsha shinsho 071. Heibonsha, 2001.
———. *Jōsaku to Emishi.* Kōkogaku raiburarii 51. Nyūsaiensusha, 1989.
———. *Kodai no Emishi.* Kawade shobō shinsha, 1992.
Kuhn, Thomas S. *The Structure of Scientific Revolutions.* 2d ed. Chicago: University of Chicago Press, 1970 [1962].
Kumagai Kimio. "Kodai Tōhoku no gōzoku." In *Shinpan kodai no Nihon 9 Tōhoku, Hokkaidō,* ed. Sudō Takashi, Imaizumi Takao, and Tsuboi Kiyotari, pp. 261–288. Kadokawa shoten, 1992.
Kumata Ryōsuke. "Iteki, shoban to tennō." In *Kodai tennōsei o kangaeru,* ed. Ōtsu Tōru, Ōsumi Kiyoharu, Seki Kazuhiko, Kumata Ryōsuke, Maruyama Yumiko, Uejima Susumu, and Yonetani Masafumi, pp. 129–178. Nihon no rekishi 08. Kōdansha, 2001.
———. "Kodai kokka to Emishi, Hayato." In *Iwanami kōza Nihon tsūshi 4 Kodai 3,* pp. 187–224. Iwanami shoten, 1994.
Kuper, Adam. *Culture: The Anthropologists' Account.* Cambridge: Harvard University Press, 1999.
Kuwabara Shigeo. "Jōsaku o chūshin to suru kodai kanga." In *Shinpan kodai no Nihon 9 Tōhoku, Hokkaidō,* ed. Sudō Takashi, Imaizumi Takao, and Tsuboi Kiyotari, pp. 201–230. Kadokawa shoten, 1992.
Lach, Donald F. *Asia in the Making of Europe,* vol. 1: *The Century of Discovery,* bks. 1 and 2. Chicago: University of Chicago Press, 1965.
Lamarre, Thomas. *Uncovering Heian Japan: An Archaeology of Sensation and Inscription.* Asia-Pacific Culture, Politics, and Society. Durham, N.C.: Duke University Press, 2000.
Lattimore, Owen. *Inner Asian Frontiers of China.* Boston: Beacon Press, 1962.
———. *Studies in Frontier History: Collected Papers, 1928–1958.* London: Oxford University Press, 1962.
Lee, A. D. *Information and Frontiers: Roman Foreign Relations in Late Antiquity.* Cambridge: Cambridge University Press, 1993.
Lee, John. "Trade and Economy in Preindustrial East Asia, c. 1500–c. 1800: East Asia in the Age of Global Integration." *Journal of Asian Studies* 58.1 (1999): 2–26.
Lee Sungsi (Ri Sonshi). *Ajia bunka ken no keisei.* Sekaishi riburetto 7. Yamakawa shuppansha, 2000.
———. *Higashi Ajia no ōken to kōeki.* Aoki Library Nihon no rekishi. Aoki shoten, 1997.
Lewis, Martin W., and Kären E. Wigen. *The Myth of Continents: A Critique of Metageography.* Berkeley and Los Angeles: University of California Press, 1997.
Li Takanori. *Hyōshō kūkan no kindai: Meiji "Nihon" no media hensei.* Shin'yōsha, 1996.
Limerick, Patricia Nelson. *The Legacy of Conquest: The Unbroken Past of the American West.* New York: W. W. Norton and Co., 1987.

———. *Something in the Soil: Legacies and Reckonings in the New West.* New York: W. W. Norton and Co., 2000.

Livi-Bacci, Massimo. *A Concise History of World Population.* Trans. Carl Ipsen. 2d ed. Oxford: Blackwell, 1997 [1992].

Lu, David J., ed. *Japan: A Documentary History.* Armonk, N.Y.: M. E. Sharpe, 1997.

Luttwak, Edward N. *The Grand Strategy of the Roman Empire: From the First Century A.D. to the Third.* Baltimore: Johns Hopkins University Press, 1976.

Machida shishi hensan iinkai, ed. *Machida shishi,* vol. 1. Machida: Machida shi, 1974.

Maher, John C. "North Kyushu Creole: A Language-Contact Model for the Origins of Japanese." In *Multicultural Japan: Palaeolithic to Postmodern,* ed. Donald Denoon, Mark Hudson, Gavan McCormack, and Tessa Morris-Suzuki, pp. 31–45. Cambridge: Cambridge University Press, 1996.

Makabe Tadahiko. "Bōeki taikei no hen'yō." In *Kōkogaku ni yoru Nihon rekishi 9 Kōeki to kōtsū,* ed. Ōtsuka Hatsushige, Shiraishi Taichirō, Nishitani Tadashi, and Machida Akira, pp. 137–151. Yūzankaku, 1997.

Mann, Michael. *The Sources of Social Power,* vol. 1: *A History of Power from the Beginning to A.D. 1760.* Cambridge: Cambridge University Press, 1986.

Massarella, Derek. "Some Reflections on Identity Formation in East Asia in the Sixteenth and Seventeenth Centuries." In *Multicultural Japan: Palaeolithic to Postmodern,* ed. Donald Denoon, Mark Hudson, Gavan McCormack, and Tessa Morris-Suzuki, pp. 135–152. Cambridge: Cambridge University Press, 1996.

———. *A World Elsewhere: Europe's Encounter with Japan in the Sixteenth and Seventeenth Centuries.* New Haven, Conn.: Yale University Press, 1990.

Matsumae Takeshi. "Early Kami Worship." In *The Cambridge History of Japan,* vol. 1: *Ancient Japan,* ed. Delmer M. Brown, pp. 317–358. Cambridge: Cambridge University Press, 1993.

Matsuo Bashō. *The Narrow Road to the Deep North and Other Travel Sketches.* Trans. Nobuyuki Yuasa. London: Penguin Books, 1966.

Matsuzaki Mizuho. "Dōnan no Wajin to tachi." In *Yomigaeru chūsei 4 Kita no chūsei: Tsugaru Hokkaidō,* ed. Kikuchi Tetsuo and Fukuda Toyohiko, pp. 100–124. Heibonsha, 1989.

Mayhew, Bruce H., and Roger L. Levinger. "Size and Density of Interaction in Human Aggregates." *American Journal of Sociology* 82.1 (1977): 86–110.

McCormack, Gavan. "Introduction." In *Multicultural Japan: Palaeolithic to Postmodern,* ed. Donald Denoon, Mark Hudson, Gavan McCormack, and Tessa Morris-Suzuki, pp. 1–15. Cambridge: Cambridge University Press, 1996.

McCullough, William H. "The Capital and Its Society." In *The Cambridge History of Japan,* vol. 2: *Heian Japan,* ed. Donald H. Shively and William H. McCullough, pp. 97–182. Cambridge: Cambridge University Press, 1999.

———. "The Heian Court, 794–1070." In *The Cambridge History of Japan,* vol. 2: *Heian Japan*, ed. Donald H. Shively and William H. McCullough, pp. 20–96. Cambridge: Cambridge University Press, 1999.

McNeill, William H. *Plagues and Peoples.* Garden City, N.Y.: Anchor Press, 1976.

Metzler, Mark. "Capitalist Boom, Feudal Bust: Long Waves in Economics and Politics in Pre-Industrial Japan." *Review* 17 (1994): 57–119.

Miller, Richard J. *Japan's First Bureaucracy: A Study of Eighth-Century Government.* Cornell University East Asia Papers, no. 19. Ithaca, N.Y.: Cornell University China-Japan Program, 1979.

Minegishi Sumio. "Chūsei no 'maizōsen' ni tsuite no oboegaki: Zaisan no kiki kanri no shiten kara." In *Ekkyō suru kahei*, ed. Rekishigaku kenkyūkai, pp. 247–266. Aoki shoten, 1999.

Miura Keiichi. "Villages and Trade in Medieval Japan." *Acta Asiatica* 44 (1983): 53–76.

Mizoguchi Yūzō, Hamashita Takeshi, Hirashi Naoaki, and Miyajima Hiroshi, eds. *Ajia kara kangaeru.* 7 vols. Tōkyō daigaku shuppankai, 1993–1994.

Mori Katsumi. "The Beginning of Overseas Advance of Japanese Merchant Ships." *Acta Asiatica* 23 (1972): 1–24.

———. *Kentōshi.* Shibundō, 1966.

———. *Shintei Nissō bōeki no kenkyū.* Mori Katsumi chosakushū, vol. 1. Kokusho kankōkai, 1975.

Mori Kimiyuki. *"Hakusukinoe" igo: Kokka kiki to Higashi Ajia gaikō.* Kōdansha sensho mechie 132. Kōdansha, 1998.

———. *Kodai Nihon no taigai ninshiki to kōtsū.* Yoshikawa kōbunkan, 1998.

Morita Tomotada. "Shinori no 40 man mai no kosen." In *Yomigaeru chūsei 4 Kita no chūsei Tsugaru Hokkaidō*, ed. Kikuchi Tetsuo and Fukuda Toyohiko, pp. 125–131. Heibonsha, 1989.

Moriya, Katsuhisa. "Urban Networks and Information Networks." In *Tokugawa Japan: The Social and Economic Antecedents of Modern Japan*, ed. Chie Nakane and Shinzaburō Ōishi, pp. 97–123. Tokyo: University of Tokyo Press, 1990.

Morris, Dana. "Land and Society." In *The Cambridge History of Japan*, vol. 2: *Heian Japan*, ed. Donald H. Shively and William H. McCullough, pp. 183–235. Cambridge: Cambridge University Press, 1999.

Morris-Suzuki, Tessa. "Creating the Frontier: Border, Identity, and History in Japan's Far North." *East Asian History* 7 (1994): 1–24.

———. "A Descent into the Past: The Frontier in the Construction of Japanese Identity." In *Multicultural Japan: Palaeolithic to Postmodern*, ed. Donald Denoon, Mark Hudson, Gavan McCormack, and Tessa Morris-Suzuki, pp. 81–94. Cambridge: Cambridge University Press, 1996.

———. *Henkyō kara nagameru: Ainu ga keiken suru kindai.* Misuzu shobō, 2000.

———. "Northern Lights: The Making and Unmaking of Karafuto Identity." *Journal of Asian Studies* 60.3 (2001): 645–671.

———. *Re-inventing Japan: Time, Space, Nation. Japan in the Modern World.* New York: M. E. Sharpe, 1998.
———. *The Technological Transformation of Japan: From the Seventeenth to the Twenty-First Century.* Cambridge: Cambridge University Press, 1994.
Motogi Masayasu. *Kodai no dōro jijō*, Rekishi bunka raiburarii 108. Yoshikawa kōbunkan, 2000.
Mouer, Ross, and Yoshio Sugimoto. *Images of Japanese Society: A Study in the Social Construction of Reality.* London: Kegan Paul International, 1990.
Mozai Torao, Nishijima Sadao, Tanaka Takeo, and Ishii Masatoshi, eds. *Kentōshi kenkyū to shiryō.* Tōkai daigaku shuppankai, 1987.
Murai Shōsuke. *Ajia no naka no chūsei Nihon.* Azekura shobō, 1988.
———. "The Boundaries of Medieval Japan." *Acta Asiatica* 81 (2001): 72–91.
———. *Chūsei Nihon no uchi to soto.* Chikuma purimaa bukkusu 128. Chikuma shobō, 1999.
———. *Chūsei Wajin den.* Iwanami shinsho 274. Iwanami shoten, 1993.
———. *Hōjō Tokimune to Mōko shūrai: Jidai, sekai, kojin o yomu.* NHK bukkusu 902. Nihon hōsō shuppan kyōkai, 2001.
———. "Kikaigashima kō: Chūsei kokka no seikyō." *Beppu daigaku Ajia rekishi bunka kenkyūjo hō* 17 (1999): 1–14.
———. *Kokkyō o koete: Higashi Ajia kaiiki sekai no chūsei.* Azekura shobō, 1998.
———. "Ōdo ōmin shisō to 9 seiki no tenkan." *Shisō* 847 (1995): 23–45.
———. *Umi kara mita Sengoku Nihon: Rettōshi kara sekaishi e.* Chikuma shinsho 127. Chikuma shobō, 1997.
———. "Wakō no taminzokusei o megutte." In *Chūsei kōki ni okeru Higashi Ajia no kokusai kankei*, ed. Ōsumi Kazuo and Murai Shōsuke, pp. 27–66. Yamakawa shuppansha, 1997.
Murakami Yasuyuki. *Wajin to tetsu no kōkogaku.* Shiriizu: Nihonshi no naka no kōkogaku. Aoki shoten, 1999.
Nagahara Keiji. "Landownership under the *Shōen-Kokugaryō* System." *Journal of Japanese Studies* 1.2 (1975): 269–296.
———. "The Lord-Vassal System and Public Authority *(Kōgi):* The Case of the *Sengoku Daimyō.*" *Acta Asiatica* 49 (1985): 34–45.
Nagayama Shūichi. "Hayato to ritsuryō sei." In *Shinpan kodai no Nihon 3 Kyūshū, Okinawa hen*, ed. Shimojō Nobuyuki, Hirano Hiyoruki, Chinen Isamu, and Takara Kurayoshi, pp. 163–177. Kadokawa shoten, 1991.
Nagazumi Yōko. "The Decline of Trade and Russian Expansion in East Asia." In *Bridging the Divide: Four Hundred Years The Netherlands–Japan*, ed. Leonard Blussé, Willem Remmelink, and Ivo Smits, pp. 57–72. The Netherlands/Japan: Teleac/NOT and Hotei Publishing, 2000.
———, ed. *"Sakoku" o minaosu.* Shiriizu kokusai kōryū 1. Yamakawa shuppansha, 1999.
Najita, Tetsuo. "History and Nature in Eighteenth-Century Tokugawa Thought." In *The Cambridge History of Japan*, vol. 4: *Early Modern Japan*,

ed. John Whitney Hall, pp. 596–659. Cambridge: Cambridge University Press, 1991.

Nakai Nobuhiko and James L. McClain. "Commercial Changes and Urban Growth in Early Modern Japan. In *The Cambridge History of Japan*, vol. 4: *Early Modern Japan*, ed. John Whitney Hall, pp. 519–595. Cambridge: Cambridge University Press, 1991.

Nakamura Akizō. *Hayato no kodaishi.* Heibonsha shinsho 119. Heibonsha, 2001.

———. *Hayato to ritsuryō kokka.* Meicho shuppan, 1993.

———. *Kodai Hayato shakai no kōzō to tenkai.* Iwata shoin, 1988.

———. *Kumaso, Hayato no shakaishiteki kenkyū.* Meicho shuppan, 1986.

———. *Shintei Hayato no kenkyū.* Maruyama gakugei tosho, 1993.

Nakamura Taichi. *Nihon no kodai dōro o sagasu: Ritsuryō kokka no autobaan.* Heibonsha shinsho 045. Heibonsha, 2000.

Naoki Kōjirō. "The Nara State." In *The Cambridge History of Japan*, vol. 1: *Ancient Japan*, ed. Delmer M. Brown, pp. 221–267. Cambridge: Cambridge University Press, 1993.

Neary, Ian. "Burakumin in Contemporary Japan." In *Japan's Minorities: The Illusion of Homogeneity*, ed. Michael Weiner, pp. 50–78. Sheffield Centre for Japanese Studies/Routledge Series. London: Routledge, 1997.

Nielsson, G. P. "States and 'Nation-Groups': A Global Taxonomy." In *New Nationalism of the Developed West*, ed. Edward A. Tiryakian and Ronald Rogowski, pp. 27–56. London: George Allen and Unwin, 1985.

Nihon shoki. 2 vols. In *Nihon koten bungaku taikei*, vols. 67–68, ed. Sakamoto Tarō, Ienaga Saburō, Inoue Mitsusada, and Ōno Susumu. Iwanami shoten, 1965–1967.

Nishijima Sadao. *Kodai Higashi Ajia sekai to Nihon.* Iwanami gendai bunko gakujutsu 25. Iwanami shoten, 2000.

———. *Nihon rekishi no kokusai kankyō.* UP sensho. Tōkyō daigaku shuppankai, 1985.

Norton, William. *Human Geography.* 2d ed. Oxford: Oxford University Press, 1995.

Nosco, Peter. *Remembering Paradise: Nativism and Nostalgia in Eighteenth-Century Japan.* Harvard-Yenching Institute Monograph Series 31. Cambridge: Council on East Asian Studies, Harvard University, 1990.

Ōbayashi Taryō. "The Ethnological Study of Japan's Ethnic Culture." *Acta Asiatica* 61 (1991): 1–23.

———. *Higashi to nishi, umi to yama.* Shōgakukan, 1990.

———. "Kodai ni okeru mittsu no ryōiki." In *Nihon no kodai 2 Rettō no chiiki bunka*, ed. Mori Kōichi, pp. 73–104. Chūō kōronsha, 1986.

Oda Fujio, ed. *Kodai o kangaeru: Iwai no ran.* Yoshikawa kōbunkan, 1991.

———. *Kodai o kangaeru: Okinoshima to kodai saishi.* Yoshikawa kōbunkan, 1988.

Oguma Eiji. *"Nihonjin" no kyōkai.* Shin'yōsha, 1998.

———. *Tan'itsu minzoku shinwa no kigen: "Nihonjin" no jigazō no keifu.* Shin'yōsha, 1995.

Ohnuki-Tierney, Emiko. *Rice as Self: Japanese Identities through Time.* Princeton, N.J.: Princeton University Press, 1993.

Ōishi Naomasa. "Sotogahama, Ezo kō." In *Nihon kodaishi kenkyū*, ed. Seki Akira sensei kanreki kinenkai, pp. 565–598. Yoshikawa kōbunkan, 1980.

Ōishi, Shinzaburō. "The Bakuhan System." In *Tokugawa Japan: The Social and Economic Antecedents of Modern Japan*, ed. Chie Nakane and Shinzaburō Ōishi, pp. 11–36. Tokyo: University of Tokyo Press, 1990.

Oka Yasumasa. "Exotic 'Holland' in Japanese Art." In *Bridging the Divide: Four Hundred Years The Netherlands–Japan*, ed. Leonard Blussé, Willem Remmelink, and Ivo Smits, pp. 141–154. The Netherlands/Japan: Teleac/NOT and Hotei Publishing, 2000.

Okazaki Takashi. "Japan and the Continent." In *The Cambridge History of Japan*, vol. 1: *Ancient Japan*, ed. Delmer M. Brown, pp. 268–316. Cambridge: Cambridge University Press, 1993.

Ölschleger, Hans Dieter. "Technology, Settlement, and Hunting Ritual." In *Ainu: Spirit of a Northern People*, ed. William W. Fitzhugh and Chisato O. Dubreuil, pp. 208–221. Washington, D.C.: Arctic Studies Center, National Museum of Natural History, Smithsonian Institution, in association with University of Washington Press, 1999.

Osa Setsuko. "Ezogachishima ō Kasha no Chōsen kenshi o megutte (1)." *Kyūshū sangyō daigaku kokusai bunka gakubu kiyō* 1 (1994): 33–47.

———. "Ezogachishima ō Kasha no Chōsen kenshi o megutte (2)." *Kyūshū sangyō daigaku kokusai bunka gakubu kiyō* 2 (1994): 35–54.

Ōyama Kyōhei. "Medieval *Shōen*." In *The Cambridge History of Japan*, vol. 3: *Medieval Japan*, ed. Kozo Yamamura, pp. 89–127. Cambridge: Cambridge University Press, 1990.

Palmer, E. "Beyond Geography: The Geography of the Beyond in Ancient Japan." *GeoJournal* 33 (1994): 479–485.

Pearson, Richard, ed. *Ancient Japan.* New York: George Braziller, 1992.

Peattie, Mark R. "The Japanese Colonial Empire, 1895–1945." In *The Cambridge History of Japan*, vol. 6: *The Twentieth Century*, ed. Peter Duus, pp. 217–270. Cambridge: Cambridge University Press, 1988.

Pelletier, Philippe. *La Japonésie: Géopolitique et géographie historique de la suinsularité au Japon.* Paris: CNRS Editions, 1997.

Peregrine, Peter N. "Legitimation Crises in Prehistoric Worlds." In *World-Systems Theory in Practice*, ed. P. Nick Kardulias, pp. 37–52. Lanham, Md.: Rowman and Littlefield, 1999.

Philippi, Donald, trans. *Kojiki.* Tokyo: University of Tokyo Press, 1969.

Piggott, Joan R. *The Emergence of Japanese Kingship.* Stanford, Calif.: Stanford University Press, 1997.

———. "*Mokkan:* Wooden Documents from the Nara Period." *Monumenta Nipponica* 45.4 (1990): 449–470.

Pomeranz, Kenneth. *The Great Divergence: China, Europe, and the Making of the Modern World Economy.* Princeton, N.J.: Princeton University Press, 2000.

Ponting, Clive. *A Green History of the World.* London: Penguin Books, 1992.
Prescott, J.R.V. *The Maritime Political Boundaries of the World.* London: Methuen, 1985.
———. *Political Frontiers and Boundaries.* London: Unwin Hyman, 1987.
Pyle, Kenneth B. *The New Generation in Meiji Japan: Problems in Cultural Identity, 1885–1895.* Stanford, Calif.: Stanford University Press, 1969.
Quigley, Carroll. *The Evolution of Civilizations: An Introduction to Historical Analysis.* 2d ed. Indianapolis: Liberty Press, 1979 [1961].
Ravina, Mark. *Land and Lordship in Early Modern Japan.* Stanford, Calif.: Stanford University Press, 1999.
Reid, Anthony. *Southeast Asia in the Age of Commerce 1450–1680,* vol. 2: *Expansion and Crisis.* New Haven, Conn.: Yale University Press, 1993.
Reischauer, Edwin O. *Ennin's Travels in T'ang China.* New York: Ronald Press, 1955.
———. *The Japanese Today: Change and Continuity.* Cambridge: Belknap Press of Harvard University Press, 1980.
———. *My Life between Japan and America.* New York: Harper and Row, 1986.
———. "Notes on T'ang Dynasty Sea Routes." *Harvard Journal of Asiatic Studies* 5 (1940–1941): 142–164.
———, trans. *Ennin's Diary.* New York: Ronald Press, 1955.
Renfrew, Colin. *Archaeology and Language: The Puzzle of Indo-European Origins.* London: Penguin Books, 1989.
Renfrew, Colin, and Paul Bahn. *Archaeology: Theories, Methods, and Practice.* 2d ed. New York: Thames and Hudson, 1996 [1991].
Reynolds, Henry. *Frontier: Aborigines, Settlers, and Land.* St. Leonards, NSW, Australia: George Allen and Unwin, 1987.
Roberts, Luke S. *Mercantilism in a Japanese Domain: The Merchant Origins of Economic Nationalism in Eighteenth-Century Tosa.* Cambridge: Cambridge University Press, 1998.
Robinson, Kenneth R. "Centering the King of Chosŏn: Aspects of Korean Maritime Diplomacy, 1392–1592." *Journal of Asian Studies* 59.1 (2000): 109–125.
———. "The Imposter Branch of the Hatakeyama Family and Japanese-Chosŏn Relations, 1455–1580s." *Ajia bunka kenkyū/Asian Cultural Studies (Kokusai kirisutokyō daigaku gakuhō 3–A)* 25 (1999): 67–87.
———. "The Jiubian and Ezogachishima Embassies to Chosŏn, 1478–1482." *Chōsenshi kenkyūkai ronbunshū* 35 (1997): 56–86.
———. "The Tsushima Governor and Regulation of Japanese Access to Chosŏn in the Fifteenth and Sixteenth Centuries." *Korean Studies* 20 (1996): 23–50.
Rosaldo, Renato. *Culture and Truth: The Remaking of Social Analysis.* Boston: Beacon Press, 1989.
Rozman, Gilbert. "Social Change." In *The Cambridge History of Japan,* vol. 5: *The Nineteenth Century,* ed. Marius B. Jansen, pp. 499–568. Cambridge: Cambridge University Press, 1989.

Saeki Arikiyo. *Saigo no kentōshi.* Kōdansha gendai shinsho 520. Kōdansha, 1982.

Saeki Kōji. "Hakata." In *Iwanami kōza Nihon tsūshi 10 Chūsei 4*, pp. 283–300. Iwanami shoten, 1994.

Sahlins, Peter. *Boundaries: The Making of France and Spain in the Pyrenees.* Berkeley and Los Angeles: University of California Press, 1989.

Sakayori Masashi. *Bokkai to kodai no Nihon.* Azekura shobō, 2001.

Sanderson, Stephen K. *Social Transformations: A General Theory of Historical Development.* Expanded ed. Lanham, Md.: Rowman and Littlefield, 1999 [1995].

Sasaki Gin'ya with William B. Hauser. "Sengoku Daimyo Rule and Commerce." In *Japan before Tokugawa: Political Consolidation and Economic Growth, 1500 to 1650*, ed. John Whitney Hall, Keiji Nagahara, and Kozo Yamakura, pp. 125–148. Princeton, N.J.: Princeton University Press, 1981.

Sasaki Shirō. *Hoppō kara kita kōekimin: Kinu to kegawa to Santanjin.* NHK bukkusu 772. Nihon hōsō shuppan kyōkai, 1996.

Sasaki, Shiro. "Trading Brokers and Partners with China, Russia, and Japan." In *Ainu: Spirit of a Northern People*, ed. William W. Fitzhugh and Chisato O. Dubreuil, pp. 86–91. Washington, D.C.: Arctic Studies Center, National Museum of Natural History, Smithsonian Institution, in association with University of Washington Press, 1999.

Sasaki Toshikazu. "Tōhoku chihō ni nokoru Ainu go chimei." In *Kodai no Emishi*, by Kudō Masaki, pp. 92–100. Kawade shobō shinsha, 1992.

Sasaki, Toshikazu. "*Ainu-e:* A Historical Review." In *Ainu: Spirit of a Northern People*, ed. William W. Fitzhugh and Chisato O. Dubreuil, pp. 79–85. Washington, D.C.: Arctic Studies Center, National Museum of Natural History, Smithsonian Institution, in association with University of Washington Press, 1999.

Sasamura, Jiro. "Beyond the Ainu Shinpo: An Ainu View." In *Ainu: Spirit of a Northern People*, ed. William W. Fitzhugh and Chisato O. Dubreuil, pp. 369–370. Washington, D.C.: Arctic Studies Center, National Museum of Natural History, Smithsonian Institution, in association with University of Washington Press, 1999.

Sasayama Haruo, Yoshie Akio, Ishii Susumu, Takagi Shōsaku, Ōguchi Yūjirō, Itō Takashi, and Takamura Naosuke, eds. *Yamakawa Nihonshi sōgō zuroku (zōhoban).* Yamakawa shuppansha, 1996.

Sato, Elizabeth S. "The Early Development of the *Shōen.*" In *Medieval Japan: Essays in Institutional History*, ed. John Whitney Hall and Jeffrey P. Mass, pp. 91–108. New Haven, Conn.: Yale University Press, 1974.

———. "Ōyama Estate and *Insei* Land Policies." *Monumenta Nipponica* 34.1 (1979): 73–100.

———. "*Shōen.*" In *Kodansha Encyclopedia of Japan*, vol. 7, pp. 155–158. Tokyo: Kodansha, 1983.

Satō Makoto. "Kyūto, kokufu, gūke." In *Iwanami kōza Nihon tsūshi 4 Kodai 3*, pp. 113–145. Iwanami shoten, 1994.
Satō Sōjun. "Chihō shihai: gūke to kokufu." In *Shūkan Asahi hyakka Nihon no rekishi 48 Kodai 4 Heijō sento to ritsuryō*, ed. Asahi shinbunsha, pp. 124–128. Asahi shinbunsha, 1988.
Schafer, Edward H. *The Golden Peaches of Samarkand: A Study of T'ang Exotics.* Berkeley and Los Angeles: University of California Press, 1963.
Scott, James C. *Weapons of the Weak: Everyday Forms of Peasant Resistance.* New Haven, Conn.: Yale University Press, 1985.
Segal, Ethan. "Mōko shūrai to chūsei teki aidentitii." *Shiyū* 33 (2001): 9–18.
Seki Shūichi. "Kōryō no michi to Nihon, Chōsen." In *Ajia no naka no Nihonshi 3 Kaijō no michi*, ed. Arano Yasunori, Ishii Masatoshi, and Murai Shōsuke, pp. 265–280. Tōkyō daigaku shuppankai, 1992.
Seki Yukihiko. *Kamikaze to bushi zō: Mōko gassen no shinjitsu.* Rekishi bunka raiburarii 120. Yoshikawa kōbunkan, 2001.
Serida Kentarō. "Kokusai hō." In *Imidas 1994*, pp. 461–474. Shūeisha, 1993.
Shils, Edward A. *Center and Periphery: Essays in Macrosociology.* Chicago: University of Chicago Press, 1975.
Shimojō Nobuyuki, Hirano Hiyoruki, Chinen Isamu, and Takara Kurayoshi, eds. *Shinpan kodai no Nihon 3 Kyushu, Okinawa.* Kadokawa shoten, 1991.
Shinsarugakuki. In *Tōyō bunko 424*, ed. Kawaguchi Hisao. Heibonsha, 1983.
Siddle, Richard. "The Ainu and the Discourse of 'Race.'" In *The Construction of Racial Identities in China and Japan*, ed. Frank Dikötter, pp. 136–157. Honolulu: University of Hawai'i Press, 1997.
———. "Ainu History: An Overview." In *Ainu: Spirit of a Northern People*, ed. William W. Fitzhugh and Chisato O. Dubreuil, pp. 67–73. Washington, D.C.: Arctic Studies Center, National Museum of Natural History, Smithsonian Institution, in association with University of Washington Press, 1999.
———. "Ainu: Japan's Indigenous People." In *Japan's Minorities: The Illusion of Homogeneity*, ed. Michael Weiner, pp. 17–49. London: Routledge, 1997.
———. "From Assimilation to Indigenous Rights: Ainu Resistance since 1869." In *Ainu: Spirit of a Northern People*, ed. William W. Fitzhugh and Chisato O. Dubreuil, pp. 108–115. Washington, D.C.: Arctic Studies Center, National Museum of Natural History, Smithsonian Institution, in association with University of Washington Press, 1999.
———. *Race, Resistance and the Ainu of Japan.* Sheffield Centre for Japanese Studies/Routledge Series. London: Routledge, 1996.
Skinner, G. William, ed. *The City in Late Imperial China.* Stanford, Calif.: Stanford University Press, 1977.
Smith, Anthony D. *The Ethnic Origins of Nations.* Oxford: Blackwell, 1986.
———. *National Identity.* London: Penguin Books, 1991.

Smits, Gregory. "Ambiguous Boundaries: Redefining Royal Authority in the Kingdom of Ryukyu." *Harvard Journal of Asiatic Studies* 60.1 (2000): 89–123.

———. *Visions of Ryukyu: Identity and Ideology in Early-Modern Thought and Politics.* Honolulu: University of Hawai'i Press, 1999.

So, Alvin Y., and Stephen W. K. Chiu. *East Asia and the World Economy.* Thousand Oaks, Calif.: Sage, 1995.

So, Kwan-wai. *Japanese Piracy in Ming China during the Sixteenth Century.* Michigan State University Press, 1975.

Souyri, Pierre François. *The World Turned Upside Down: Medieval Japanese Society.* Trans. Käthe Roth. New York: Columbia University Press, 2001.

Stark, Miriam T., ed. *The Archaeology of Social Boundaries.* Smithsonian Series in Archaeological Inquiry. Washington, D.C.: Smithsonian Institution Press, 1998.

Steenstrup, Carl. *A History of Law in Japan until 1868.* Leiden: E. J. Brill, 1991.

Stephan, John J. *The Kuril Islands: Russo-Japanese Frontier in the Pacific.* Oxford: Clarendon Press, 1974.

Strassoldo, Raimondo. "The Study of Boundaries: A Systems-Oriented, Multi-Disciplinary, Bibliographical Essay." *Jerusalem Journal of International Relations* 2.3 (1977): 81–107.

Sudō Takashi, Imaizumi Takao, and Tsuboi Kiyotari, eds. *Shinpan kodai no Nihon 9 Tōhoku, Hokkaidō.* Kadokawa shoten, 1992.

Suganuma, Unryu. *Sovereign Rights and Territorial Space in Sino-Japanese Relations: Irredentism and the Diaoyu/Senkaku Islands.* Asian Interactions and Comparisons. Honolulu: Association for Asian Studies and University of Hawai'i Press, 2000.

Sugimoto, Masayoshi, and David L. Swain. *Science and Culture in Traditional Japan.* MIT East Asian Science Series 6. Rutland, Vt.: Charles E. Tuttle, 1989.

Suwa daimyōjin ekotoba. In *Zoku gunsho ruijū, Jingibu (maki 73)*, vol. 3, pt. 2, pp. 494–539. Zoku gunsho ruijū kanseikai, 1973.

Suzuki Hideo. *Kodai no Wakoku to Chōsen shokoku.* Aoki shoten, 1996.

Suzuki Kimio. "Shutsudo senka kara chūsei no zeni no shiyō o fukugen suru." In *Shinshiten Nihon no rekishi 4 Chūsei hen*, ed. Minegishi Sumio and Ikegami Hiroko, pp. 126–131. Shinjinbutsu ōraisha, 1993.

Suzuki Takao. *Hone kara mita Nihonjin: Kobyōrigaku ga kataru rekishi.* Kōdansha sensho mechie 142. Kōdansha, 1998.

Suzuki Yasuko. "The Production and Export of Japanese Copper." In *Bridging the Divide: Four Hundred Years The Netherlands–Japan*, ed. Leonard Blussé, Willem Remmelink, and Ivo Smits, p. 62. The Netherlands/Japan: Teleac/NOT and Hotei Publishing, 2000.

Suzuki Yasutami. *Kodai taigai kankei shi no kenkyū.* Yoshikawa kōbunkan, 1985.

Taigai kankei shi sōgō nenpyō henshū iinkai, ed. *Taigai kankei shi sōgō nenpyō*. Yoshikawa kōbunkan, 1999.

Taira, Koji. "Troubled National Identity: The Ryukyuans/Okinawans." In *Japan's Minorities: The Illusion of Homogeneity*, ed. Michael Weiner, pp. 140–177. London: Routledge, 1997.

Tajima Isao. "Kentōshi wa naze haken sareta ka." In *Sōten Nihon no rekishi 3 Kodai hen 2*, ed. Yoshimura Takehiko and Yoshioka Masayuki, pp. 313–333. Shinjinbutsu ōraisha, 1991.

———. "Nihon, Chūgoku, Chōsen taigai kōryū shi nenpyō: Taihō gannen–Bunji gannen." In *Bōeki tōji: Nara Heian no Chūgoku tōji*, ed. Nara kenritsu Kashihara kōkogaku kenkyūjo fuzoku hakubutsukan. Kyoto: Rinsen shoten, 1993.

———. "Nihon no ritsuryō kokka no 'hinrai': gaikō girei yori mita tennō to daijōkan." *Shirin* 68.3 (1985): 35–86.

———. "Shinnyo (Takaoka) Shinnō ikkō no 'nittō' no tabi." *Rekishi to chiri* 502 (1997): 37–54.

Takahashi Tomio. *Henkyō: Mō hitotsu no Nihonshi*. Kyōikusha rekishi shinsho (Nihonshi) 13. Kyōikusha, 1979.

Takara Kurayoshi. *Ajia no naka no Ryūkyū ōkoku*. Rekishi bunka raiburarii 47. Yoshikawa kōbunkan, 1998.

Takase Kōichirō. "Unauthorized Commercial Activities by Jesuit Missionaries in Japan." *Acta Asiatica* 30 (1976): 19–33.

Tamura, Suzuko. "Ainu Language: Features and Relationships." In *Ainu: Spirit of a Northern People*, ed. William W. Fitzhugh and Chisato O. Dubreuil, pp. 57–65. Washington, D.C.: Arctic Studies Center, National Museum of Natural History, Smithsonian Institution, in association with University of Washington Press, 1999.

Tanaka Akihiko. "Sekai shisutemu ron." In *Kōza kokusai seiji 1 Kokusai seiji no riron*, pp. 237–265. Tōkyō daigaku shuppankai, 1989.

Tanaka Hiroshi. *Shinpan zainichi gaikokujin*. Iwanami shinsho 370. Iwanami shoten, 1995.

Tanaka Migaku. "The Early Historical Periods." In *Recent Archaeological Discoveries in Japan*, ed. Tsuboi Kiyotari, pp. 72–91. Tokyo: Centre for East Asian Cultural Studies, 1987.

Tanaka, Stefan. *Japan's Orient: Rendering Pasts into History*. Berkeley and Los Angeles: University of California Press, 1993.

Tanaka Takeo. "Sōgo ninshiki to jōhō." In *Ajia no naka no Nihonshi 5 Jiishiki to sōgo rikai*, ed. Arano Yasunori, Ishii Masatoshi, and Murai Shōsuke, pp. 205–242. Tōkyō daigaku shuppankai, 1993.

Tanaka Takeo with Robert Sakai. "Japan's Relations with Overseas Countries." In *Japan in the Muromachi Age*, ed. John W. Hall and Toyoda Takeshi, pp. 159–178. Berkeley and Los Angeles: University of California Press, 1976.

Tanaka-van Daalen, Isabel. "Popular Use of Imported Materials in Japan." In *Bridging the Divide: Four Hundred Years The Netherlands–Japan*, ed. Leonard Blussé, Willem Remmelink, and Ivo Smits, p. 150. The Netherlands/Japan: Teleac/NOT and Hotei Publishing, 2000.

Tashiro Kazui. "Tsushima-han's Korean Trade, 1684–1710." *Acta Asiatica* 30 (1976): 85–105.

Taylor, Peter J. *Political Geography: World-Economy, Nation-State, and Locality.* 3d ed. Essex: Longman Scientific and Technical, 1993 [1985].

Thompson, Leonard, and Howard Lamar. "Comparative Frontier History." In *The Frontier in History: North America and South Africa Compared*, ed. Howard Lamar and Leonard Thompson, pp. 3–13. New Haven, Conn.: Yale University Press, 1981.

Thongchai Winichakul. *Siam Mapped: A History of the Geo-Body of a Nation.* Honolulu: University of Hawai'i Press, 1994.

Toby, Ronald P. "And the Twain Did Meet: East-West Encounters in the 'Age of Discovery.'" *Update* 56 (1992): 9–12.

———. "Contesting the Centre: International Sources of Japanese National Identity." *International History Review* 7.3 (1985): 347–363.

———. "Imagining and Imaging 'Anthropos' in Early-Modern Japan." *Visual Anthropology Review* 14.1 (1998): 19–44.

———. "The 'Indianness' of Iberia and Changing Japanese Iconographies of Other." In *Implicit Understandings: Observing, Reporting, and Reflecting on the Encounters between Europeans and Other Peoples in the Early Modern Era*, ed. Stuart B. Schwartz, pp. 323–351. Cambridge: Cambridge University Press, 1994.

———. "Kinsei shoki no aidentitii kiki: Sankoku/bankoku to 'Nihon.'" *Shiyū* 33 (2001): 19–26.

———. "Leaving the Closed Country: New Models for Early-Modern Japan." *Transactions of the International Conference of Orientalists in Japan* 35 (1990): 213–221.

———. "Rescuing the Nation from History: The State of the State in Early Modern Japan." *Monumenta Nipponica* 56.2 (2001): 197–237.

———. *State and Diplomacy in Early Modern Japan: Asia in the Development of the Tokugawa Bakufu.* Reprint ed. Stanford, Calif.: Stanford University Press, 1992 [1984].

———. "Tō no kanata yori: Tenjikujin, Nanbanjin to chū, kinsei ikōki no hen'yō." In *Kindai Nihon ni okeru Higashi Ajia mondai*, ed. Furuya Tetsuo and Yamamuro Shin'ichi, pp. 16–41. Yoshikawa kōbunkan, 2001.

Tōno Haruyuki. "Japanese Embassies to T'ang China and Their Ships." *Acta Asiatica* 69 (1995): 39–62.

———. *Kahei no Nihonshi.* Asahi sensho 574. Asahi shinbunsha, 1999.

———. *Kentōshi sen: Higashi Ajia no naka de.* Asahi sensho 634. Asahi shinbunsha, 1999.

———. *Kentōshi to Shōsōin.* Iwanami shoten, 1992.

———. *Mokkan ga kataru Nihon no kodai.* Dōjidai raiburarii 319. Iwanami shoten, 1997.

Torao Toshiya. "Nara Economic and Social Institutions." In *The Cambridge History of Japan*, vol. 1: *Ancient Japan*, ed. Delmer M. Brown, pp. 415–452. Cambridge: Cambridge University Press, 1993.

Torii Yumiko. "'Dutch Studies': Interpreters, Language, Geography, and World History." In *Bridging the Divide: Four Hundred Years The Netherlands–Japan*, ed. Leonard Blussé, Willem Remmelink, and Ivo Smits, pp. 117–137. The Netherlands/Japan: Teleac/NOT and Hotei Publishing, 2000.

Totman, Conrad. *The Collapse of the Tokugawa Bakufu, 1862–1868*. Berkeley and Los Angeles: University of California Press, 1980.

———. *Early Modern Japan*. Berkeley and Los Angeles: University of California Press, 1993.

———. *The Green Archipelago: Forestry in Preindustrial Japan*. Berkeley and Los Angeles: University of California Press, 1989.

———. *A History of Japan*. Blackwell History of the World. Oxford: Blackwell, 2000.

———. "Tokugawa Peasants: Win, Lose, or Draw?" *Monumenta Nipponica* 41.4 (1986): 457–476.

Toynbee, A. *A Study of History (Somervell Abridgement)*. Oxford: Oxford University Press, 1946.

Toyoda Takeshi, Sugiyama Hiroshi, and V. Dixon Morris. "The Growth of Commerce and the Trades." In *Japan in the Muromachi Age*, ed. John W. Hall and Toyoda Takeshi, pp. 129–144. Berkeley and Los Angeles: University of California Press, 1976.

Tsuboi Kiyotari and Tanaka Migaku. *The Historic City of Nara: An Archaeological Approach*. Tokyo: Centre for East Asian Cultural Studies, 1991.

Tsuchibashi Riko. "Nissō bōeki no shosō." In *Kōkogaku ni yoru Nihon rekishi 10 Taigai kōshō*, ed. Ōtsuka Hatsushige, Shiraishi Taichirō, Nishitani Tadashi, and Machida Akira, pp. 61–76. Yūzankaku, 1997.

Tsude Hiroshi. "The Kofun Period and State Formation." *Acta Asiatica* 63 (1992): 64–86.

Tsuji Hideto. "Kofun no hensen to kakki." In *Shinpan kodai no Nihon 9 Tōhoku, Hokkaidō*, ed. Sudō Takashi, Imaizumi Takao, and Tsuboi Kiyotari, pp. 107–133. Kadokawa shoten, 1992.

Tsukahira, Toshio G. *Feudal Control in Tokugawa Japan: The Sankin Kōtai System*. Harvard East Asian Monographs 20. Cambridge: Harvard East Asia Research Center, 1966.

Tsunemoto, Teruki. "The Ainu Shinpo: A New Beginning." In *Ainu: Spirit of a Northern People*, ed. William W. Fitzhugh and Chisato O. Dubreuil, pp. 366–368. Washington, D.C.: Arctic Studies Center, National Museum of Natural History, Smithsonian Institution, in association with University of Washington Press, 1999.

Tsunoda, Ryusaku, Wm. Theodore de Bary, and Donald Keene, eds. *Sources of Japanese Tradition*, vol. 1. New York: Columbia University Press, 1958.

Tsuruta Kei. "The Establishment and Characteristics of the 'Tsushima Gate.'" *Acta Asiatica* 67 (1994): 30–48.

———. "Kinsei Nihon no yottsu no 'kuchi.'" In *Ajia no naka no Nihonshi 2 Gaikō to sensō*, ed. Arano Yasunori, Ishii Masatoshi, and Murai Shōsuke, pp. 297–316. Tōkyō daigaku shuppankai, 1992.

Turner, Frederick Jackson. *The Frontier in American History*. New York: Holt, Rinehart and Winston, 1920.

Unno, Kazutaka. "Cartography in Japan." In *The History of Cartography*, vol. 2, bk. 2: *Cartography in the Traditional East and Southeast Asian Societies*, ed. J. B. Harley and David Woodward, pp. 346–477. Chicago: University of Chicago Press, 1994.

Utagawa Hiroshi. "Ainu bunka no kōkogaku." In *Yomigaeru chūsei 4 Kita no chūsei Tsugaru Hokkaidō*, ed. Kikuchi Tetsuo and Fukuda Toyohiko, pp. 166–180. Heibonsha, 1989.

Utagawa, Hiroshi. "The Archaeology of *Iyomante*." In *Ainu: Spirit of a Northern People*, ed. William W. Fitzhugh and Chisato O. Dubreuil, pp. 256–260. Washington, D.C.: Arctic Studies Center, National Museum of Natural History, Smithsonian Institution, in association with University of Washington Press, 1999.

Vaporis, Constantine N. *Breaking Barriers: Travel and the State in Early Modern Japan*. Harvard East Asian Monographs 163. Cambridge: Council on East Asian Studies, Harvard University, 1994.

———. "Digging for Edo: Archaeology and Japan's Premodern Urban Past." *Monumenta Nipponica* 53.1 (1998): 73–102.

Viallé, Cynthia. "Japanse *[sic]* Export Lacquer." In *Bridging the Divide: Four Hundred Years The Netherlands–Japan*, ed. Leonard Blussé, Willem Remmelink, and Ivo Smits, p. 162. The Netherlands/Japan: Teleac/NOT and Hotei Publishing, 2000.

von Verschuer, Charlotte. "9 seiki Nihon no jōhō yu'nyū taisei." *Ajia yūgaku* 26 (2001): 50–66.

———. *Le commerce extérieur du Japon: Des origenes au XVIe siècle*. Paris: Maisonneuve and Larose, 1988.

———. *Les relations officielles du Japon avec la Chine aux VIIIe et IXe siècles*. Geneva, Switzerland: Droz, 1985.

———. "Looking from Within and Without: Ancient and Medieval External Relations." *Monumenta Nipponica* 55.4 (2000): 537–566.

Wakabayashi, Bob Tadashi. *Anti-Foreignism and Western Learning in Early-Modern Japan: The New Theses of 1825*. Harvard East Asian Monographs 126. Cambridge: Council on East Asian Studies, Harvard University, 1986.

Wakita Haruko, "Chūsei doki no ryūtsū." In *Iwanami kōza Nihon tsūshi 9 Chūsei 3*, pp. 295–317. Iwanami shoten, 1994.

———. "Cities in Medieval Japan." *Acta Asiatica* 44 (1983): 28–52.

———. "Toward a Wider Perspective on Medieval Commerce." *Journal of Japanese Studies* 1.2 (1975): 321–345.

Wakita Osamu. "The Social and Economic Consequences of Unification." In *The Cambridge History of Japan*, vol. 4: *Early Modern Japan*, ed. John Whitney Hall, pp. 96–127. Cambridge: Cambridge University Press, 1991.

Waldron, Arthur. *The Great Wall of China: From History to Myth.* Cambridge: Cambridge University Press, 1990.

Walker, Brett L. *The Conquest of Ainu Lands: Ecology and Culture in Japanese Expansion, 1590–1800.* Berkeley and Los Angeles: University of California Press, 2001.

———. "The Early Modern Japanese State and Ainu Vaccinations: Redefining the Body Politic 1799–1868." *Past and Present* 163 (1999): 121–160.

———. "Foreign Contagions, Ainu Medical Culture, and Conquest." In *Ainu: Spirit of a Northern People*, ed. William W. Fitzhugh and Chisato O. Dubreuil, pp. 102–107. Washington, D.C.: Arctic Studies Center, National Museum of Natural History, Smithsonian Institution, in association with University of Washington Press, 1999.

———. "Matsumae Domain and the Conquest of Ainu Lands: Ecology and Culture in Tokugawa Expansionism, 1593–1799." Ph.D. dissertation, University of Oregon, Eugene, 1997.

———. "Reappraising the Sakoku Paradigm: The Ezo Trade and the Extension of Tokugawa Political Space into Hokkaido." *Journal of Asian History* 30.2 (1996): 169–192.

Wallerstein, Immanuel. "Hold the Tiller Firm: On Method and the Unit of Analysis." In *Civilizations and World Systems: Studying World-Historical Change*, ed. Stephen K. Sanderson, pp. 239–247. Walnut Creek, Calif.: AltaMira Press, 1995.

———. *The Modern World-System*, vol. 1. New York: Academic Press, 1974.

———. *The Modern World-System*, vol. 2. New York: Academic Press, 1980.

———. *The Modern World-System*, vol. 3. New York: Academic Press, 1988.

———. "World System versus World-Systems: A Critique." In *The World System: Five Hundred Years or Five Thousand?*, ed. Andre Gunder Frank and Barry K. Gills, pp. 292–296. London: Routledge, 1993.

Wang Gungwu. *The Nanhai Trade: The Early History of Chinese Trade in the South China Sea.* Reprint ed. Singapore: Times Academic Press, 1998 [1958].

Wang, Zhen-ping. "Sino-Japanese Relations before the Eleventh Century: Modes of Diplomatic Communication Reexamined in Terms of the Concept of Reciprocity." Ph.D. dissertation, Princeton University, Princeton, N.J., 1989.

Watanabe Akihiro. "Nifuda mokkan kara mita Nara jidai no kakuchi no tokusanbutsu." In *Kōkogaku ni yoru Nihon rekishi 2 Sangyō 1 Shuryō, gyogyō, nōgyō*, ed. Ōtsuka Hatsushige, Shiraishi Taichirō, Nishitani Tadashi, and Machida Akira, pp. 67–70. Yūzankaku, 1996.

Watanabe, Hiroshi. "The Ainu Ecosystem." In *Ainu: Spirit of a Northern People*, ed. William W. Fitzhugh and Chisato O. Dubreuil, pp. 198–201. Washington, D.C.: Arctic Studies Center, National Museum of Natural History, Smithsonian Institution, in association with University of Washington Press, 1999.

White, James W. *Ikki: Social Conflict and Political Protest in Early Modern Japan.* Ithaca, N.Y.: Cornell University Press, 1995.

White, Richard. *"It's Your Misfortune and None of My Own": A New History of the American West.* Norman, Okla.: University of Oklahoma Press, 1991.

———. *The Middle Ground: Indians, Empires, and Republics in the Great Lakes Region, 1650–1815.* Cambridge: Cambridge University Press, 1991.

Whittaker, C. R. *Frontiers of the Roman Empire: A Social and Economic Study.* Baltimore: Johns Hopkins University Press, 1994.

Wigen, Kären. "Culture, Power, and Place: The New Landscapes of East Asian Regionalism." *American Historical Review* 104.4 (1999): 1183–1201.

———. "The Geographic Imagination in Early Modern Japanese History: Retrospect and Prospect." *Journal of Asian Studies* 51.1 (1992): 3–29.

Wilkinson, David. "Central Civilization." In *Civilizations and World Systems: Studying World-Historical Change*, ed. Stephen K. Sanderson, pp. 46–74. Walnut Creek, Calif.: AltaMira Press, 1995.

———. "Civilizations *Are* World Systems!" In *Civilizations and World Systems: Studying World-Historical Change*, ed. Stephen K. Sanderson, pp. 249–260. Walnut Creek, Calif.: AltaMira Press, 1995.

———. "Civilizations, Cores, World-Economies, and Oikumenes." In *The World System: Five Hundred Years or Five Thousand?*, ed. Andre Gunder Frank and Barry K. Gills, pp. 221–246. London: Routledge, 1993.

Wolf, Eric R. *Europe and the People without History.* Berkeley and Los Angeles: University of California Press, 1982.

Worster, Donald. *Under Western Skies: Nature and History in the American West.* Oxford: Oxford University Press, 1992.

Yagi Mitsunori. "Emishi shakai no chiiki sei to jiritsusei: Mutsu o chūshin to shite." In *Kodai ōken to kōryū 1 Kodai Emishi no sekai to kōryū*, ed. Suzuki Yasutami, pp. 249–280. Meicho shuppan, 1996.

Yamada Hidezō. "Ainu gozoku no kyojū han'i." In *Hoppō no kodai bunka*, ed. Niino Naoyoshi and Yamada Hidezō, pp. 73–117. Mainichi shinbunsha, 1974.

Yamaguchi Bin. "Kojinkotsu ni miru hokubu Nihonjin no keisei." In *Kita Nihon no kōkogaku: Minami to kita no chiikisei*, ed. Nihon kōkogaku kyōkai, pp. 100–123. Yoshikawa kōbunkan, 1994.

Yamamoto Nobuo. "Shin'an kaitei ibutsu." In *Kōkogaku ni yoru Nihon rekishi 10 Taigai kōshō*, ed. Ōtsuka Hatsushige, Shiraishi Taichirō, Nishitani Tadashi, and Machida Akira, pp. 151–169. Yūzankaku, 1997.

Yamamoto Tadanao. *Waei taishō Nihon kōkogaku yōgo jiten/Dictionary of Japanese Archaeological Terms.* Tōkyō bijutsu, 2001.

Yamamura, Kozo. "The Growth of Commerce in Medieval Japan." In *The Cambridge History of Japan*, vol. 3: *Medieval Japan*, ed. Kozo Yamamura, pp. 344–395. Cambridge: Cambridge University Press, 1990.

Yamanaka Toshiji. *Kodai chihō kanga iseki no kenkyū.* Hanawa shobō, 1994.

Yamao Yuhikisa. *Kodai no Nitchō kankei.* Hanawa sensho 93. Hanawa shobō, 1989.

———. *Tsukushi no kimi Iwai no sensō: Higashi Ajia no naka no kodai kokka.* Shin Nihon shuppansha, 1999.

Yamashita, Samuel Hideo. "Reading the New Tokugawa Intellectual Histories." *Journal of Japanese Studies* 22.1 (1996): 1–48.

Yamauchi Shinji. "Nissō no shōen nai mitsu bōeki setsu ni kansuru gimon." *Rekishi kagaku* 117 (1989): 11–24.

Yamaura, Kiyoshi, and Hiroshi Ushiro. "Prehistoric Hokkaido and Ainu Origins." In *Ainu: Spirit of a Northern People*, ed. William W. Fitzhugh and Chisato O. Dubreuil, pp. 39–46. Washington, D.C.: Arctic Studies Center, National Museum of Natural History, Smithsonian Institution, in association with University of Washington Press, 1999.

Yamawaki Teijirō. "The Great Trading Merchants, Cocksinja and His Son." *Acta Asiatica* 30 (1976): 106–116.

Yamazato Jun'ichi. *Kodai Nihon to Nantō no kōryū.* Yoshikawa kōbunkan, 1999.

Yiengpruksawan, Mimi Hall. *Hiraizumi: Buddhist Art and Regional Politics in Twelfth-Century Japan.* Cambridge: Harvard University Asia Center, 1998.

Yonemoto, Marcia. "Maps and Metaphors of the 'Small Eastern Sea' in Tokugawa Japan (1603–1868)." *Geographical Review* 89.2 (1999): 169–187.

Yoshida, T. "'Dutch Studies' and Natural Sciences." In *Bridging the Divide: Four Hundred Years The Netherlands–Japan*, ed. Leonard Blussé, Willem Remmelink, and Ivo Smits, 91–101. The Netherlands/Japan: Teleac/NOT and Hotei Publishing, 2000.

Yoshimura Takehiko. "Wa no goō to wa dare ka." In *Sōten Nihon no rekishi 2 Kodai hen 1*, ed. Shiraishi Taichirō and Yoshimura Takehiko, pp. 62–73. Shinjinbutsu ōraisha, 1990.

Yoshino, Kosaku. "Culturalism, Racialism, and Internationalism in the Discourse on Japanese Identity." In *Making Majorities: Constituting the Nation in Japan, Korea, China, Malaysia, Fiji, Turkey, and the United States*, ed. Dru C. Gladney, pp. 13–30. Stanford, Calif.: Stanford University Press, 1998.

———. *Cultural Nationalism in Contemporary Japan.* London: Routledge, 1992.

Yoshioka Yasunobu. "Tōjiki no michi o saguru." In *Shinshiten Nihon no rekishi 4 Chūsei hen*, ed. Minegishi Sumio and Ikegami Hiroko, pp. 140–147. Shinjinbutsu ōraisha, 1993.

Zeigler, Philip. *The Black Death.* London: Penguin Books, 1982.

Index

Italic numbers refer to maps and figures.

About the Author

Bruce L. Batten was educated at the University of Oregon and at Stanford University, from which he received his doctorate in 1989. He has lived in Japan since the mid-1980s and is currently professor of Japanese history and director of the Center for International Studies at Obirin University in Tokyo. Professor Batten has published two previous books in Japanese and is also known for his educational and cultural commentary on NHK, Japan's public television network.